M

Ing

Hispanos

English Idioms for Spanish Speakers

Second Edition

By

Eugene Savaiano, Ph.D.
Professor Emeritus of Spanish
Wichita State University, Wichita, Kansas

and

Lynn W. Winget, Ph.D.
Professor Emeritus of Spanish
Wichita State University, Wichita, Kansas

BARRON'S

All inquiries should be addressed to:
Barron's Educational Series, Inc.
250 Wireless Boulevard
Hauppauge, New York 11788
www.barronseduc.com

ISBN-13: 978-0-7641-3752-5
ISBN-10: 0-7641-3752-2

Library of Congress Catalog Card Number 2007014508

Library of Congress Cataloging-in-Publication Data
Savaiano, Eugene.
[2001 Spanish and English idioms. Part 2]
Modismos ingleses para hispanos = English idioms for Spanish speakers / Eugene Savaiano, Lynn W. Winget. — 2nd ed.
p. cm.
"Also published as Part II of 2001 Spanish and English idioms"—T.p. verso.
ISBN-13: 978-0-7641-3752-5 (alk. paper)
ISBN-10: 0-7641-3752-2 (alk. paper)
1. English language—Conversation and phrase books—Spanish. 2. English language—Idioms—Dictionaries—Spanish. I. Winget, Lynn W. II. Barron's Educational Series, Inc. III. Title. IV. Title: English idioms for Spanish speakers.
PE1129.S8S33 2008
463′. 21.—dc22 2007014508

PRINTED IN CHINA

9 8 7 6 5 4 3 2 1

Contents

Prólogo v

Modismos Ingleses (English Idioms) 1

Modismos Españoles Corrientes 333

Indice 352

Prólogo

Esta edición de bolsillo está destinada principalmente a españoles y latinoamericanos que tienen interés en el idioma inglés para los propósitos de estudio o de viajes por países de habla inglesa. Esta obra será también útil para anglohablantes que desean aprender modismos españoles mediante la localización de modismos ingleses y subsecuente estudio de su traducción al español. El núcleo de la obra consta de aproximadamente 2.500 modismos ingleses, ordenados alfabéticamente bajo su respectiva palabra clave. Se presentan los modismos, en su mayoría, acompañados de oraciones ilustrativas breves pero completas. Esperamos que este procedimiento ayude a eliminar las frustraciones que a veces experimentan los que consultan diccionarios en que se compilan modismos aislados y sin contexto alguno.

Para los fines de esta edición de bolsillo, se entiende que un modismo puede ser casi cualquier expresión que (1) conste de por lo menos dos palabras en una o ambas de las lenguas en cuestión y (2) se exprese de modo diferente en las dos lenguas ('to be cold' = 'tener frío', o 'to pull one's leg' = 'tomarle el pelo'). Hemos incluido también un número de expresiones que son iguales en las dos lenguas, basándonos en la teoría de que el estudiante querrá tener la seguridad de que efectivamente esto es así. Nos referimos al "buen" estudiante, quien ha aprendido que 'to take place' no es 'tomar lugar' y que 'to have a good time' no es 'tener un buen tiempo' y quien probablemente se resistirá a dar por sentado que 'to take part in' se traduce 'tomar parte en' y bien podrá sentirse agradecido cuando le aseguremos explícitamente que dicha traducción es correcta.

La mayoría de los modismos se hallan en la lengua moderna hablada y el inglés es principalmente el que se habla en los Estados Unidos más bien que el de la Gran Bretaña. Hemos recogido materia tanto de una variedad de fuentes peninsulares e hispanoamericanas con ejemplos del lenguaje coloquial como de diccionarios clásicos, libros de texto y listas de modismos.

Los paréntesis indican la materia que es optativa o bien alternativa. Por ejemplo, 'al (buen) tuntún' implica que la expresión puede ser o 'al tuntún' o 'al buen tuntún', pero 'a (en) nombre de' significa que la expresión puede ser o 'a nombre de' o 'en nombre de', y de ninguna manera podrá interpretarse como 'a en nombre de'.

Para que el diccionario resulte más práctico, hemos incluido un índice inglés-español, listas de abreviaturas, tablas de pesos y medidas y una lista de modismos españoles comunes, con la palabra inglesa entre paréntesis.

En conclusión, queremos expresar nuestros sinceros agradecimientos a todas las personas que de una manera u otra nos han ayudado en la preparación de esta edición de bolsillo, y en especial a nuestros colegas Kenneth Pettersen y John Koppenhaver.

Modismos Ingleses
(English Idioms)

A

a — *uno*

. . . a . . . — *por (a) . . .*

He eats five days a week. *Come cinco días por (a la) semana.*

about — *acerca de*

to be about — *tratar de.*

The novel is about the gaucho. *La novela trata del gaucho.*

to be about to — *estar a punto de; estar para.*

He is about to get married. *Está a punto de (para) casarse.*

accident — *el accidente*

by accident — *por casualidad.*

We met by accident. *Nos conocimos por casualidad.*

accord — *el acuerdo*

of one's own accord — *por propia voluntad.*

He sent it to us of his own accord. *Nos lo mandó por propia voluntad.*

according — *conforme*

according to — *a medida de.*

They paid me according to the work I did. *Me pagaron a medida de mi trabajo.*

according to — *de acuerdo con; según, con arreglo a.*

He built it according to my plans. *Lo construyó de acuerdo con (según; con arreglo a) mis planes.*

account — *la cuenta*

not on any account — *bajo ningún pretexto.*

I'll not accept on any account. *Bajo ningún pretexto aceptaré.*

on account of — *a causa de; por motivo de.*
We went on account of the wedding. *Fuimos a causa de (por motivo de) la boda.*

to balance the account — *echar la cuenta.*
I balanced the account. *Eché la cuenta.*

to be of no account — *no tener importancia.*
It's of no account. *No tiene importancia.*

to give an account of — *dar cuenta de.*
He gave a good account of himself. *Dio buena cuenta de sí.*

to keep an account — *llevar una cuenta.*
He keeps an account of all that he spends. *Lleva una cuenta de todo lo que gasta.*

to take into account — *tener en cuenta.*
Take into account that prices have gone up. *Tenga en cuenta que los precios han subido.*

---

to account — *echar la cuenta*

to account for — *ser el motivo de.*
That accounts for his attitude. *Es el motivo de su actitud.*

---

across — *a través*

across from — *frente a.*
Across from the church there is a university. *Frente a la iglesia hay una universidad.*

---

to acknowledge — *reconocer, confesar*

to acknowledge . . . to be right (to agree with) — *dar la razón a.*
He finally had to acknowledge that I was right (had to agree with me). *Por fin tuvo que darme la razón.*

---

acre — *el acre*

God's acre — *el cementerio.*
Last year poor Lynn ended up in God's acre. *El año pasado la pobre Lynn terminó en el cementerio.*

act — *el acto*

balancing act — *un acto de malabarismo.*

To get both parties to agree was quite a balancing act. *Lograr que los dos partidos se pusieran de acuerdo fue un gran acto de malabarismo.*

in the act — *en flagrante; con las manos en la masa.*

The policeman caught the thief in the act. *El policía cogió al ladrón en flagrante (con las manos en la masa).*

to be an act of God — *ser un caso de fuerza mayor.*

It was an act of God. *Fue un caso de fuerza mayor.*

to put on an act — *hacer comedia.*

He put on an act when the police stopped him. *Hizo comedia cuando lo detuvo la policía.*

to read someone the riot act — *llamar a la obediencia.*

If they don't get to bed in five minutes, I'll read them the riot act. *Si no se acuestan en cinco minutos, me van a escuchar.*

---

to act — *actuar*

to act as — *hacer las veces de.*

She acts as secretary. *Hace las veces de secretaria.*

to act up — *no funcionar bien.*

My car has been acting up lately. *Últimamente mi coche no está funcionando bien.*

to act up — *comportarse mal.*

They asked him to leave the party because he was acting up. *Le pidieron que se fuera de la fiesta porque se estaba comportando mal.*

---

action — *la acción*

course of action — *la forma de proceder.*

The best course of action is to talk to them. *La mejor forma de proceder es hablar con ellos.*

to suit the action to the word — *unir la acción a la palabra.*

He suits the action to the word. *Une la acción a la palabra.*

to take action against — *proceder en contra de.*

The district attorney took action against the criminals. *El fiscal procedió en contra de los criminales.*

where the action is — *un lugar animado y activo.*
The South Side is where the action is. *En el Barrio Sur es donde se arma la grande.*

addition — *la adición*
in addition to — *además de.*
In addition to being handsome, he's intelligent. *Además de ser guapo, es inteligente.*

to address — *dirigirse a*
to address as — *tratar de.*
He addressed me as "Miss." *Me trató de señorita.*

ado — *la bulla*
Much ado about nothing. — *Mucho ruido para nada; Mucho ruido y pocas nueces.*

without further ado — *sin más ni más.*
Without further ado, we left. *Sin más ni más, salimos.*

advance — *el avance*
in advance — *de antemano.*
It's necessary to reserve a room in advance. *Hay que reservar un cuarto de antemano.*

advantage — *la ventaja*
to be to one's advantage — *convenirle.*
It's to your advantage to arrive on time. *Le conviene llegar a tiempo.*

to have an advantage over — *llevar una ventaja.*
She had an advantage over him. *Le llevaba una ventaja.*

to take advantage of — *abusar de.*
He took advantage of my generosity. *Abusó de mi generosidad.*

to take advantage of — *aprovechar; aprovecharse de.*
They took advantage of the opportunity. *(Se) Aprovecharon (de) la oportunidad.*

to advise — *aconsejar*

to be advised — *ser aconsejado.*

They were advised to sell their shares. *Se les aconsejó vender sus acciones.*

to keep advised — *tener al corriente.*

Please keep me advised on this matter. *Por favor manténgame al corriente sobre este asunto.*

advocate — *el abogado*

devil's advocate — *el abogado del diablo.*

Why do you always play the devil's advocate and defend that good-for-nothing? *¿Por qué siempre haces de abogado del diablo y defiendes a ese inútil?*

affair — *el asunto*

to be one's affair — *corresponderle.*

It's not his affair. *No le corresponde.*

state of affairs — *la situación imperante.*

The state of affairs in Bolivia is tense. *La situación en Bolivia es tensa.*

against — *contra; contra de; en frente a*

to be up against — *enfrentar.*

He is up against a very difficult decision. *Debe enfrentar una decisión muy difícil.*

age — *la edad*

dark ages — *el oscurantismo medioeval.*

A lobotomy? That's from the dark ages! *¿Una lobotomía? ¡Eso es de los tiempos bárbaros!*

to act one's age — *comportarse de acuerdo con su edad.*

He doesn't act his age. *No se comporta de acuerdo con su edad.*

to be of age — *ser mayor de edad.*

He's not of age. *No es mayor de edad.*

to come of age — *llegar a la mayoría de edad.*

She came of age. *Llegó a la mayoría de edad.*

to agree — *convenir*

not to agree (to disagree) with someone — *hacerle daño.*

He ate something that didn't agree (that disagreed) with him. *Comió algo que le hizo daño.*

ahead — *delante*

to be ahead of — *llevar la delantera (llevar ventaja).*

As far as rockets are concerned, nobody is ahead of us. *En cuanto a cohetes, nadie nos lleva la delantera (lleva ventaja).*

to go ahead with — *llevar adelante.*

We're going ahead with our plans. *Llevamos adelante nuestros planes.*

to aim — *apuntar*

to aim to — *tener la intención de.*

He aims to graduate in June. *Tiene la intención de recibirse en junio.*

to be aiming at (to have designs on) — *tener la mira puesta en.*

That senator is aiming at (has designs on) the presidency. *Ese senador tiene la mira puesta en la presidencia.*

air — *el aire*

by air — *por avión; en avión.*

He went to France by air. *Fue a Francia en avión.*

hot air — *la palabrería; las promesas falsas.*

His arguments were full of hot air. *Sus argumentos eran casi pura palabrería.*

in the air — *en vilo.*

It is suspended in the air. *Está colgado en vilo.*

out in the open (air) — *al aire libre.*

They spent the night out in the open (air). *Pasaron la noche al aire libre.*

to get a breath of fresh air — *tomar el fresco.*

We're getting a breath of fresh air. *Estamos tomando el fresco.*

to give someone the air — *darle calabazas.*

She gave him the air. *Le dio calabazas.*

to put on airs — *darse tono.*

She puts on airs. *Se da tono.*

to vanish into thin air — *desaparecer (repentinamente).*

Once the game was over, the spectators vanished into thin air. *Terminado el partido, los espectadores desaparecieron.*

to walk on air — *rebosar de felicidad.*

When she became his girlfriend, he was walking on air. *Cuando ella se convirtió en su novia, él no cabía en su pellejo.*

---

to align — *alinear; alinearse; unirse a otros*

non-aligned — *neutralista.*

The non-aligned countries have a hard time maneuvering at the UN. *Los países neutralistas tienen dificultades para maniobrar en la ONU.*

---

alive — *vivo*

alive and kicking — *vivito y coleando.*

He's still alive and kicking. *Está todavía vivito y coleando.*

---

all — *todo*

above all — *ante todo; sobre todo.*

Above all one must be honest. *Ante todo (Sobre todo) hay que ser honrado.*

after all — *al fin y al cabo.*

It didn't snow after all. *Al fin y al cabo no nevó.*

after all — *en (al) fin de cuentas; después de todo.*

After all, it's my money. *En (Al) fin de cuentas (Después de todo) es mi dinero.*

all along — *desde el principio.*

We knew all along that she wouldn't go. *Desde el principio sabíamos que ella no iría.*

all at once (all of a sudden) — *de repente; de pronto.*

All at once (All of a sudden) a dog entered. *De repente (De pronto) entró un perro.*

all but — *casi; casi por completo.*

All the complaints have all but disappeared. *Ya casi han desaparecido las quejas.*

all day long — *todo el día.*

They traveled all day long. *Viajaron todo el día.*

all in all — *en definitiva.*

All in all it was a good game. *En definitiva fue un buen partido.*

all of them — *unos y otros.*

All of them walked away. *Unos y otros se alejaron.*

all out — *a todo lo que da; a toda marcha; a todo vapor.*

This engine has been working all out for a week. *Este motor ha funcionado al máximo por una semana.*

all over — *por (en) todas partes.*

It's the same all over. *Es igual por (en) todas partes.*

(to be) all right — *(estar) bien (bueno).*

Everything is all right. *Todo está bien (bueno).*

all the better — *tanto mejor; mejor que mejor.*

all the same — *a pesar de todo; no obstante.*

All the same, I think you should stay. *A pesar de todo (No obstante), creo que debe quedarse.*

all the same — *de todos modos.*

He came all the same. *Vino de todos modos.*

all the worse — *tanto peor; peor que peor.*

an all-time high — *sin precedentes.*

Our attendance reached an all-time high. *Tuvimos una asistencia sin precedentes.*

all told — *en total.*

All told there are ten of us. *En total somos diez.*

for all I know — *que sepa yo.*

For all I know he's not at home yet. *Que sepa yo todavía no está en casa.*

it's all in... — *todo depende de...*

It's all in the way she behaves tomorrow. *Todo depende de la manera en que se comporte mañana.*

It's all over. — *Ya ha terminado (ya se acabó).*

It's all the same. — *Lo mismo da; Es igual.*

not at all — *en absoluto.*

Do you mind if I smoke? Not at all. *¿Le molesta si fumo? En absoluto.*

not . . . at all — *nada (en absoluto).*
He doesn't speak it at all. *No lo habla nada (en absoluto).*

to be all for — *ser buen partidario de.*
I'm all for liberty. *Soy buen partidario de la libertad.*

to be all in — *estar rendido.*
I'm all in. *Estoy rendido.*

to be all set — *estar listo; estar dispuesto.*
Everything is all set. *Todo está listo (dispuesto).*

to be all the rage — *estar muy de moda.*
It's all the rage. *Está muy de moda.*

warts and all — *tanto lo bueno como lo malo.*
You must tell me the truth, warts and all. *Debes decirme la verdad, lo bueno junto con lo malo.*

---

alley — *el callejón*

a blind alley — *un callejón sin salida.*
We entered a blind alley. *Nos metimos en un callejón sin salida.*

---

to allow — *dejar*

to allow (to make allowance) for — *tener en cuenta.*
We allowed (made allowance) for his age. *Tuvimos en cuenta su edad.*

---

alone — *solo*

all alone — *a solas.*
She was left all alone. *Se quedó a solas.*

to go it alone — *actuar sin ayuda de nadie.*
Being unable to find partners, he decided to go it alone with the business. *Incapaz de encontrar socios, decidió emprender el negocio por su cuenta.*

to let (leave) alone — *dejar en paz.*
Let (Leave) me alone. *Déjeme en paz.*

---

along — *a lo largo*

all along — *desde un (el) principio.*
He had it all along. *Lo tenía desde un (el) principio.*

to amount — *importar, ascender*

to amount to — *ascender, subir a.*

The bill amounts to ninety dollars. *La cuenta asciende (sube) a noventa dólares.*

to amount to — *reducirse a.*

What it amounts to is that we cannot buy the house. *Se reduce al hecho de que no podemos comprar la casa.*

to amount to — *valer.*

That guy doesn't amount to much. *Ese tipo no vale mucho.*

---

to answer — *contestar*

to answer one's purpose — *ser adecuado.*

It didn't answer our purpose. *No nos fue adecuado.*

---

any — *alguno*

any minute (time) now — *de un momento a otro; de hoy a mañana.*

They'll get here any minute (time) now. *Llegarán de un momento a otro (de hoy a mañana).*

if any — *si hubiera uno; si los hubiera.*

You will take care of the sick, if any. *Usted se encargará de los enfermos, si los hubiera.*

---

anyone — *alguno; alguna; alguien; cualquiera*

anyone for . . . ? — *¿Desea alguien . . . ?*

Anyone for a drink? *¿Alguien quiere un trago?*

---

anything — *algo*

not to be able to do anything with — *no poder con.*

He can't do anything with his boss. *No puede con su jefe.*

not to be able to make anything out of — *no conseguir comprender.*

I can't make anything out of this letter. *No consigo comprender esta carta.*

---

to appear — *aparecer*

to appear at (in) — *asomarse a.*

She appeared at (in) the window. *Se asomó a la ventana.*

appearance — *la apariencia*

to put in an appearance — *hacer acto de presencia.*

They put in an appearance. *Hicieron acto de presencia.*

appetite — *el apetito*

to give one an appetite — *abrirle el apetito.*

The exercise gave me an appetite. *El ejercicio me abrió el apetito.*

apple — *la manzana*

the apple of one's eye — *la niña de sus ojos.*

She's the apple of his eye. *Es la niña de sus ojos.*

to polish the apple — *hacerle la barba al profesor.*

He polishes the apple. *Le hace la barba al profesor.*

to apply — *aplicar; aplicarse a; dedicarse*

to apply for — *solicitar.*

I want to apply for that job. *Quiero solicitar ese puesto.*

area — *la zona; el área*

disaster area — *la zona de desastre.*

After the hurricane, the county was declared a disaster area. *Después del huracán, el condado fue declarado zona de desastre.*

argument — *la discusión, la disputa*

to get into arguments — *entrar en disputas.*

He never gets into arguments. *Nunca entra en disputas.*

to arise — *levantarse*

to arise from — *obedecer a.*

It arises from a lack of respect. *Obedece a una falta de respeto.*

arm — *el brazo*

a shot in the arm — *un nuevo estímulo; un nuevo refuerzo.*

My dad's unexpected help was a shot in the arm. *La inesperada ayuda de mi padre me dio renovadas energías.*

arm in arm — *cogidos del brazo.*

They were walking arm in arm. *Andaban cogidos del brazo.*

at arm's length — *a distancia.*
He kept her at arm's length. *La mantuvo a distancia.*

the long arm of the law — *el peso de la ley; la justicia; la policía.*
He ran for two years, but the long arm of the law caught him at the end. *Estaba huyendo por dos años, pero la justicia lo atrapó al final.*

to pay an arm and a leg — *pagar en exceso.*
He had to pay an arm and a leg to get these seats. *Tuvo que pagar un ojo de la cara por estos puestos.*

to rise up in arms — *alzarse en armas.*
They rose up in arms. *Se alzaron en armas.*

to twist a person's arm — *obligar, forzar a alguien.*
You've got to twist his arm if you hope to get any money from him. *Si esperas recibir dinero de él, debes forzarlo.*

army — *el ejército*

to join the army — *incorporarse a filas.*
He'll join the army. *Se incorporará a filas.*

around — *alrededor*

to be around . . . — *rondar ya . . .*
He's around thirty. *Ronda ya los treinta años.*

arrangement — *el arreglo*

to make arrangements — *tomar las medidas necesarias.*
I made arrangements to see her. *Tomé las medidas necesarias para verla.*

as — *como*

as a child — *de niño.*
As a child he cried a lot. *De niño lloraba mucho.*

as for — *lo que es; en cuanto a.*
As for my father, he agrees. *Lo que es (En cuanto a) mi padre, está de acuerdo.*

as yet — *hasta ahora.*
As yet they haven't arrived. *Hasta ahora no han llegado.*

ashamed — *avergonzado*

to be ashamed — *tener vergüenza; darle vergüenza.*

I'm ashamed. *Tengo vergüenza (Me da vergüenza).*

---

aside — *aparte, al lado*

aside from — *aparte de.*

Aside from boxing he doesn't like sports. *Aparte del boxeo no le gustan los deportes.*

---

to ask — *pedir; preguntar*

to ask for it — *buscárselas.*

He was a bad driver and then started drinking: he was asking for it. *Era un mal conductor y luego se puso a beber: estaba buscándoselas.*

---

asleep — *dormido*

to fall asleep — *conciliar el sueño.*

I couldn't fall asleep. *No pude conciliar el sueño.*

---

astonished — *asombrado*

to be astonished at — *asombrarse de (con).*

They were astonished at his ideas. *Se asombraron de (con) sus ideas.*

---

assassination — *el asesinato*

character assassination — *la difamación.*

The yellow press specializes in character assassination of celebrities. *La prensa amarilla se especializa en difamación de celebridades.*

---

astray — *extraviado*

to lead astray — *llevar por mal camino.*

His friends led him astray. *Sus amigos le llevaron por mal camino.*

---

at — *en, a*

at about . . . — *a eso de la(s) . . .*

They are coming at about four. *Vienen a eso de las cuatro.*

at (for) less than — *en menos de.*

You get them at (for) less than three pesos. *Se consiguen en menos de tres pesos.*

at that — *por demás; por cierto.*

She's not very bright and her ideas are very outdated at that. *No es muy inteligente y, por cierto, sus ideas son muy anticuadas.*

to live at — *vivir en.*

He lives at the Smiths'. *Vive en casa de los Smith.*

to attend — *atender, asistir*

to attend to — *ocuparse de.*

Isn't there anyone to attend to that matter? *¿No hay quien se ocupe de ese asunto?*

attention — *la atención*

to attract one's attention — *llamarle la atención.*

It attracted my attention. *Me llamó la atención.*

to call one's attention to — *llamarle la atención sobre.*

He called our attention to the mistake. *Nos llamó la atención sobre el error.*

to pay attention — *prestar (poner) atención; hacer caso.*

He never pays attention. *Nunca presta (pone) atención (Nunca hace caso).*

to stand at attention — *cuadrarse.*

As soon as the captain arrived we stood at attention. *Nos cuadramos tan pronto llegó el capitán.*

avail — *el provecho*

to avail oneself of — *valerse de.*

You must avail yourself of all the resources you can. *Debes valerte de todos los recursos que puedes.*

to be of no avail — *ser inútil.*

It was of no avail. *Fue inútil.*

available — *disponible*

to make available to someone — *facilitarle.*

He made his car available to me. *Me facilitó su coche.*

average — *el promedio*

on the average — *por término medio.*

It rains once a month, on the average. *Llueve una vez al mes, por término medio.*

awake — *despierto*

to be wide awake — *estar completamente despierto.*

I'm wide awake. *Estoy completamente despierto.*

aware — *enterado*

to be aware of — *estar al tanto de.*

I'm aware of the problems. *Estoy al tanto de los problemas.*

axe — *el hacha (f)*

to have an axe to grind — *tener algún fin interesado.*

He always has an axe to grind. *Siempre tiene algún fin interesado.*

B

back — *la espalda*

on one's back — *a cuestas.*

I was carrying it on my back. *Lo llevaba a cuestas.*

to be back — *estar de vuelta.*

She's back. *Está de vuelta.*

to break one's back — *partirse el espinazo.*

They break their backs digging. *Se parten el espinazo cavando.*

to have one's back to the wall — *encontrarse entre la espada y la pared.*

We had our backs to the wall. *Nos encontramos entre la espada y la pared.*

to have one's back turned — *estar dando la espalda.*

She had her back (turned) to me. *Me estaba dando la espalda.*

to turn one's back — *volver (dar) la espalda.*

I turned my back on her. *Le volví (di) la espalda.*

to back — *moverse hacia atrás, respaldar*

to back down — *volverse atrás.*
He backed down. *Se volvió atrás.*

to back out — *retirarse; romper su compromiso, echarse atrás.*
He was going with us but backed out. *Iba con nosotros pero se retiró (rompió su compromiso; se echó atrás).*

to back someone up — *apoyar.*
His family backed him up. *Su familia lo apoyó.*

to back up — *marchar atrás.*
He didn't know how to back up. *No sabía hacer marchar atrás el coche.*

---

bacon — *el tocino*

to bring home the bacon — *tener éxito.*
They brought home the bacon. *Tuvieron éxito.*

---

bad — *malo*

from bad to worse — *de mal en peor.*
His luck is going from bad to worse. *Su suerte va de mal en peor.*

it's too bad — *es una lástima.*
Tomorrow is the parade; it's too bad that you broke your leg. *Mañana es el desfile; es una lástima que te hubieras roto la pierna.*

---

bag — *la bolsa*

to be in the bag — *ser cosa hecha.*
It's in the bag. *Es cosa hecha.*

to leave holding the bag — *dejar con la carga en las costillas.*
She left me holding the bag. *Me dejó con la carga en las costillas.*

to let the cat out of the bag — *escapársele el secreto.*
He let the cat out of the bag. *Se le escapó el secreto.*

---

ball — *la pelota*

That's the way the ball bounces. *Así es la vida.*

to be on the ball — *estar informado.*
He's been at it for a long time, so he's really on the ball. *Ha estado en eso por largo tiempo, así que está muy bien informado.*

to get behind the eight ball — *encontrarse en situación difícil.*
I haven't worked on the project for a week and now I'm behind the eight ball. *No he trabajado en este proyecto por una semana y ahora me encuentro en apuros.*

to have a lot on the ball — *tener capacidad.*
He's got a lot on the ball. *Tiene gran capacidad.*

to get all balled up — *hacerse bolas; estar hecho un lío.*
He got all balled up. *Se hizo bolas (Está hecho un lío).*

to get the ball rolling — *empezar.*
They'll get the ball rolling tomorrow. *Empezarán mañana.*

to have a ball — *divertirse mucho; pasarlo en grande.*
We had a ball. *Nos divertimos mucho (Lo pasamos en grande).*

to keep the ball rolling — *mantener el interés.*
He did it to keep the ball rolling. *Lo hizo para mantener el interés.*

to play ball with — *obrar en armonía con.*
He had to play ball with his boss in order to succeed. *Tuvo que obrar en armonía con su jefe para tener éxito.*

---

bandwagon — *el carro de banda de música*

to get on the bandwagon — *unirse a la mayoría.*
It's best to get on the bandwagon. *Es mejor unirse a la mayoría.*

---

bang — *el estrépito*

to go over with a bang — *ser un éxito tremendo.*
It went over with a bang. *Fue un éxito tremendo.*

---

to bank — *depositar (dinero)*

to bank on — *contar con.*
You can't bank on his help. *No puedes contar con su ayuda.*

---

to bar — *trancar; obstruir; impedir*

to bar from — *excluir de.*
He was barred from the church. *Él fue excluido de la iglesia.*

to bar in — *encerrar en.*
She was barred in the dungeon. *Ella fue confinada a un calabozo.*

bare — *desnudo*

bare-assed (vulg.) — *en cueros; desnudo.*

There we saw him, running bare-assed in the park! *¡Allí lo vimos! ¡Corriendo en cueros por el parque!*

to lay bare — *poner al descubierto.*

And the mystery was laid bare at last! *¡Y el misterio quedó finalmente al descubierto!*

---

bargain — *la ganga*

to strike a bargain — *cerrar un trato (llegar a un acuerdo).*

After arguing for an hour, they struck a bargain. *Después de una hora de discusión, cerraron un trato (llegaron a un acuerdo).*

---

barrel — *el barril*

to get to the bottom of the barrel — *haber agotado todos los recursos.*

After paying the taxes we got to the bottom of the barrel and had to get a loan. *Después de pagar los impuestos quedamos sin recursos y debimos pedir un préstamo.*

to have over a barrel — *tener agarrado de las greñas.*

I couldn't help it. He had me over a barrel. *No pude más. Me tenía agarrado de las greñas.*

---

base — *la base*

not to get to first base — *no conseguir nada; fracasar desde el comienzo.*

You won't get to first base with her if you don't do something about your breath. *Si no haces algo con tu aliento, no llegarás a ninguna parte con ella.*

to get to first base — *vencer el primer obstáculo.*

With that resume, I'll get to first base at once. *Con ese curriculum, venceré el primer obstáculo de inmediato.*

---

to base — *basar, fundar*

to base oneself (one's opinion) on — *fundarse en.*

I'm basing myself (my opinion) on what he said last week. *Me fundo en lo que dijo la semana pasada.*

---

basis — *la base*

to be on a first-name basis — *tutearse.*

They're on a first-name basis. *Se tutean.*

bat — *el murciélago*

as blind as a bat — *más ciego que un topo.*

She's blind as a bat, but she refuses to wear glasses. *Es más ciega que un topo, pero rehusa usar anteojos.*

like a bat out of hell — *como alma que lleva el diablo.*

He took off like a bat out of hell. *Salió como alma que lleva el diablo.*

to bat — *golpear*

to go to bat for — *defender.*

He went to bat for his employees. *Defendió a sus empleados.*

to bawl — *vocear*

to bawl out — *regañar.*

The teacher bawled out the kid who broke the window. *El maestro regañó al chico que rompió la ventana.*

bay — *la bahía*

to hold at bay — *tener a raya.*

They held us at bay. *Nos tuvieron a raya.*

to be — *ser, estar*

as it were — *por decirlo así.*

He's the father, as it were, of the modern novel. *Es el padre, por decirlo así, de la novela moderna.*

however it may be — *sea como fuere.*

However it may be, their marriage ended in divorce. *Sea como fuere, su matrimonio terminó en divorcio.*

. . . -to-be — *futuro . . . .*

She's his wife-to-be. *Es su futura esposa.*

to be at it again — *estar otra vez con las mismas.*

Are you at it again? *¿Ya estás con las mismas de nuevo?*

to be becoming — *quedarle (irle) muy bien.*

Her skirt is becoming to her. *La falda le queda (va) muy bien.*

to be onto someone — *conocerle el juego.*

Since we're already onto him, he can't fool us. *Como ya le conocemos el juego, no nos puede engañar.*

to be willing to — *estar dispuesto a.*

They are willing to attack. *Están dispuestos a atacar.*

would-be — *el aspirante.*

All the would-be artists met at the corner bar. *Todos los aspirantes a artista se reunían en el bar de la esquina.*

would that it were so — *ojalá que así fuera.*

They say that genetic engineering will cure a lot of illnesses; would that it were so. *Dicen que la ingeniería genética curará muchas enfermedades; ojalá que así fuera.*

bean — *el frijol, la judía*

full of beans — *vigoroso; enérgico.*

Despite his age, he's still full of beans. *Pese a su edad, continúa lleno de energía.*

to spill the beans — *descubrirlo todo.*

He spilled the beans. *Lo descubrió todo.*

to bear — *cargar*

to bear with someone — *ser paciente.*

Please bear with us a little longer. *Haga el favor de ser paciente un poco más.*

what the traffic will bear — *todo lo que se pueda; aprovechar al máximo.*

We will charge what the traffic will bear for these suits. *Cobraremos todo lo que podamos por estos trajes.*

bearing — *la orientación; el rumbo*

to lose one's bearings — *desorientarse; aturdirse.*

The market was so crowded that he soon lost his bearings. *Había tanta gente en el mercado que pronto se desorientó.*

to beat — *batir*

it beats me — *no tengo ni idea.*

It beats me why he does that. *No tengo ni idea por qué hace eso.*

to beat against — *estrellarse contra.*

The moth was beating against the light bulb. *La polilla se estrellaba contra la bombilla.*

to beat back — *repeler; hacer retroceder.*

Our army beat back the enemy. *Nuestro ejército repelió al enemigo.*

to beat down — *superar; vencer.*

Slowly but surely, we beat them down. *Lento pero seguro, los fuimos superando.*

to beat it — *largarse.*

Beat it! *¡Lárgate!*

to beat one to it — *cogerle (tomarle) la delantera.*

I tried to get there first but Mario beat me to it. *Quise llegar primero pero Mario me cogió (tomó) la delantera.*

to beat someone up — *apalear a alguien.*

They beat him up until he was unconscious. *Lo apalearon hasta que quedó inconsciente.*

to beat up — *batir.*

You beat up the eggs for three minutes. *Bates los huevos por tres minutos.*

beauty — *la belleza*

Beauty is but skin deep. — *Las apariencias engañan.*

Beauty is in the eye of the beholder. — *Sobre gustos no hay nada escrito.*

because — *porque*

because of — *a (por) causa de.*

We're staying because of our parents. *Nos quedamos a (por) causa de nuestros padres.*

just because — *porque sí; porque no.*

I did it just because. *Lo hice porque sí.*

I didn't do it just because. *Lo hice porque no.*

to become — *hacerse, llegar a ser*

what has become of — *qué ha sido de, qué se ha hecho.*

What has become of the maid? *¿Qué ha sido de la criada? (¿Qué se ha hecho la criada?)*

becoming — *conveniente*

to be becoming to — *sentarle bien.*

That dress is very becoming to her. *Ese vestido le sienta muy bien.*

bed — *la cama*

to go to bed with the chickens — *acostarse con las gallinas.*

They go to bed with the chickens. *Se acuestan con las gallinas.*

to put to bed — *reducir a cama.*

The cold put me to bed. *El resfriado me redujo a cama.*

to stay in bed — *guardar cama.*

He stayed in bed two days. *Guardó cama dos días.*

bedfellow — *el compañero de cama; el aliado; el asociado*

strange bedfellows — *alianza de personas incompatibles.*

German Catholics and communists are strange bedfellows, but they fought the Nazis together. *Los católicos y los comunistas de Alemania pueden haber sido incompatibles, pero lucharon juntos contra los nazis.*

bee — *la abeja*

a bee in one's bonnet — *una idea fija en la mente.*

She's got a bee in her bonnet. *Tiene una idea fija en la mente.*

beeline — *la línea recta*

to make a beeline for — *salir disparado hacia.*

We made a beeline for the dining room. *Salimos disparados hacia el comedor.*

behalf — *el favor*

on behalf of — *en nombre de.*

He welcomed them on behalf of the president. *Les dio la bienvenida en nombre del presidente.*

on one's behalf — *a su favor.*
He wrote on my behalf. *Escribió a mi favor.*

behind — *detrás*
from behind — *de espaldas.*
She was attacked from behind. *Fue atacada de espaldas.*

to believe — *creer*
believe it or not — *aunque parezca mentira.*
Believe it or not, it's true. *Aunque parezca mentira, es la verdad.*
to make believe — *hacer como.*
He made believe he didn't know. *Hizo como si no lo supiera.*
you'd better believe it — *así es; claro.*
Lincoln's depressions? You'd better believe it — it is very well documented. *¿Las depresiones de Lincoln? Claro, eso está muy bien documentado.*

bell — *la campana*
to ring a bell — *sonarle (a algo conocido).*
That name rings a bell. *Ese nombre me suena (a algo conocido).*

to belong — *pertenecer*
where one belongs — *donde le llaman.*
I don't go where I don't belong. *No voy a donde no me llaman.*

beneath — *abajo*
to feel it beneath one — *tener a menos.*
She doesn't feel it beneath her to cook. *No tiene a menos cocinar.*

benefit — *el beneficio*
the benefit of the doubt — *un margen de confianza.*
They gave us the benefit of the doubt. *Nos concedieron un margen de confianza.*
to be of benefit — *ser útil.*
It will be of benefit to us. *Nos será útil.*

bent — *encorvado, inclinado*

to be bent on — *empeñarse en.*

He's bent on proving me wrong. *Se empeña en probar que yo estoy equivocado.*

berth — *el sitio; el puesto*

to give somebody a wide berth — *evitar; esquivar.*

There goes your ex . . . let's give her a wide berth. *Allí va tu ex-esposa . . . mejor esquivémosla.*

beside — *cerca de, junto a*

to be beside oneself — *estar fuera de sí.*

She's beside herself. *Está fuera de sí.*

besides — *además*

besides — *además de; a más de.*

Besides being too small, she can't sing. *Además de (A más de) ser muy pequeña, no sabe cantar.*

best — *mejor*

at best — *en el mejor de los casos.*

We'll win five games at best. *Ganaremos cinco partidos en el mejor de los casos.*

at one's best — *en uno de sus mejores momentos.*

He wasn't at his best. *No estaba en uno de sus mejores momentos.*

second best — *el segundo; el mejor después del primero.*

Their team ended second best in the championship. *Su equipo terminó segundo en el campeonato.*

to do one's best — *hacer lo posible.*

He does his best. *Hace lo posible.*

to know best — *ser el mejor juez; saber más que nadie.*

Mother knows best. *La mamá sabe más que nadie.*

to make the best of — *sacar el mejor partido posible de.*

He made the best of the situation. *Sacó el mejor partido posible de la situación.*

with the best of them — *como el más pintado.*

He can dance the tango with the best of them. *Sabe bailar el tango como el más pintado.*

to bet — *apostar*

I'll bet — *a que.*

I'll bet that it will rain. *A que llueve.*

You bet! — *¡Ya lo creo!*

better — *mejor*

Better late than never. — *Más vale tarde que nunca.*

for better or for worse — *para bien o para mal.*

She got married, for better or for worse. *Se casó para bien o para mal.*

one's better half — *su cara mitad; su media naranja.*

My better half will accompany me. *Mi cara mitad (media naranja) me acompañará.*

to be better off — *estar mejor.*

He's better off here. *Está mejor aquí.*

to do better than that — *mejorar algo.*

Seventy-eight points? Surely you can do better than that! *¿Setenta y ocho puntos? ¡Seguro que lo puedes hacer mejor!*

to get better — *mejorarse.*

She's getting better. *Se está mejorando.*

to get the better of — *poder más que.*

He got the better of me. *Pudo más que yo.*

to know better — *conocer la falsedad de algo.*

He tells me that I'm the only woman he ever loved, but I know better. *Me asegura que soy la única mujer que ha amado, pero yo bien sé la verdad.*

to think better of it — *cambiar de opinión.*

I was about to go but I thought better of it. *Estaba para ir pero cambié de opinión.*

big — *grande*

The bigger they come, the harder they fall. *De gran subida, gran caída.*

bill — *la cuenta*

to foot the bill — *pagar la cuenta.*

My father didn't want to foot the bill. *Mi padre no quiso pagar la cuenta.*

bind — *el apuro*

to get in a bind — *meterse en un apuro.*

By trying to help them, I got in a bind. *Tratando de ayudarlos, me metí en un apuro.*

binge — *la juerga*

to go on a binge — *ir de juerga.*

They are going on a binge. *Van de juerga.*

bird — *pájaro*

A bird in the hand is worth two in the bush. — *Vale más pájaro en mano que ciento volando.*

birds of a feather — *de la misma calaña.*

They're birds of a feather. *Son de la misma calaña.*

Birds of a feather flock together — *Dios los cría y ellos se juntan.*

for the birds — *para los tontos.*

Easy-listening music is for the birds. *La música azucarada es para los simplones.*

naked as a jay bird (as the day he was born) — *en cueros.*

He went out on the street naked as a jay bird (as the day he was born). *Salió a la calle en cueros.*

The early bird gets the worm. — *Al que madruga, Dios le ayuda.*

to kill two birds with one stone — *matar dos pájaros de (en) un tiro.*

birth — *el nacimiento*

to give birth to — *dar a luz a.*

She gave birth to a son. *Dio a luz a un hijo.*

bit — *pedacito; el freno, el bocado; moneda antigua*

a good bit — *una buena cantidad.*

He left a good bit in the basket. *Dejó una buena cantidad en la canasta.*

every bit — *todo.*

I understood every bit of it. *Lo entendí todo.*

not a bit — *ni pizca.*

He doesn't eat a bit of meat. *No come ni pizca de carne.*

quite a bit — *bastante.*

He dances quite a bit. *Baila bastante.*

to do one's bit — *apartar su granito de arena.*

He always does his bit. *Siempre aparta su granito de arena.*

two-bit — *de poco valor.*

He's a two-bit artist. *Es un artista de poco valor.*

---

to bite — *morder*

to bite off more than one can chew — *medir mal sus propias fuerzas.*

He bit off more than he can chew. *Midió mal sus propias fuerzas.*

---

black — *negro*

in black and white — *por escrito.*

I want to see it in black and white. *Lo quiero ver por escrito.*

in the black — *con superávit.*

The company is operating in the black. *La compañía funciona con superávit.*

---

blame — *la culpa*

to be to blame — *tener la culpa.*

We're not to blame for her death. *No tenemos la culpa de su muerte.*

to put (lay) the blame on — *echarle la culpa a.*

First he put (laid) the blame on Philip and then shifted the blame on to us. *Primero le echó la culpa a Felipe y luego nos la echó a nosotros.*

---

blank — *blanco*

to be blank — *estar en blanco.*

This page is blank. *Esta página está en blanco.*

to draw a blank — *no conseguirlo.*

I tried to find him but I drew a blank. *Quise encontrarlo pero no lo conseguí.*

blanket — *la manta*

a wet blanket — *un aguafiestas.*

He's a wet blanket. *Es un aguafiestas.*

to blast — *detonar*

to blast off — *despegar.*

The rocket will blast off tomorrow. *El cohete despegará mañana.*

to bleed — *sangrar*

to bleed white (dry) — *sangrar de las venas.*

His relatives are bleeding him white (dry). *Sus parientes lo están sangrando de las venas.*

blessing — *la bendición*

mixed blessing — *dudoso bien o dudosa ventaja.*

An inexpensive but dangerous nuclear power plant is a mixed blessing. *Una central nuclear barata pero peligrosa en un bien muy dudoso.*

to count one's blessings — *considerarse afortunado.*

With so much unemployment, count your blessings that you have a part-time job. *Con tanto desempleo, considérate afortunado de tener un trabajo de media jornada.*

blind — *ciego*

blind date — *la cita romántica de dos desconocidos.*

Blind dates are full of surprises. *Las citas con desconocidos resultan en muchas sorpresas.*

to blindfold — *vendar los ojos*

to be able to do it blindfolded — *saber hacerlo a ojos cerrados.*

He can do that blindfolded. *Sabe hacer eso a ojos cerrados.*

block — *el bloque*

stumbling block — *el obstáculo; el tropiezo.*

Math is his stumbling block in school. *Las matemáticas son su obstáculo en la escuela.*

to knock someone's block off — *romperle la cabeza.*
He threatened to knock his block off. *Amenazó (con) romperle la cabeza.*

blood — *la sangre*

in cold blood — *a sangre fría.*
They killed him in cold blood. *Lo mataron a sangre fría.*

You can't get blood out of a turnip. *Nadie puede dar lo que no tiene.*

blow — *el golpe*

to come to blows — *llegar a las manos; liarse a mamporros.*
They came to blows. *Llegaron a las manos (Se liaron a mamporros).*

to blow — *soplar*

to blow down — *echar al suelo.*
The wind blew down the sign. *El viento echó al suelo el letrero.*

to blow hot and cold — *pasar de un extremo a otro.*
The team blows hot and cold. *El equipo pasa de un extremo a otro.*

to blow out — *reventarse.*
His tire blew out (on him). *Se le reventó la llanta.*

to blow over — *pasar (olvidarse).*
They are angry now, but don't worry, it will blow over soon. *Están enojados ahora, pero no te preocupes, pronto pasará (se olvidará).*

to blow up — *explotar; volar.*
The engineer blew up the bridge. *El ingeniero explotó (voló) el puente.*

blue — *azul*

out of the blue — *como caído de las nubes.*
He appeared out of the blue. *Apareció como caído de las nubes.*

to have the blues — *sentir tristeza.*
He's got the blues. *Siente tristeza.*

board — *la tabla*

across-the-board — *general.*
They gave everyone an across-the-board raise. *Dieron a todos un aumento general de sueldo.*

to boast — *jactarse*

to boast of — *echárselas de.*

He boasts of being smart. *Se las echa de listo.*

boat — *el bote*

to be in the same boat — *estar en la misma situación.*

We lost our jobs and our health insurances; we're in the same boat. *Perdimos nuestros trabajos y nuestros seguros de salud; estamos en las mismas.*

body — *el cuerpo*

in a body — *en comitiva.*

They came in a body to complain. *Vinieron en comitiva para quejarse.*

over one's dead body — *pasando por encima de su cadáver.*

You'll take it over my dead body. *Se lo llevará pasando por encima de mi cadáver.*

bogey-man — *el Cuco; el Coco.*

If you don't close your eyes and sleep, the bogey-man will come and get you. *Si no cierras los ojos y te duermes, el Cuco vendrá a buscarte.*

to boil — *hervir*

to boil down to — *reducirse a.*

All this complicated theory boils down to a simple formula. *Toda esta complicada teoría se reduce a una sencilla fórmula.*

bone — *el hueso*

a bone of contention — *la manzana de la discordia.*

It's a bone of contention with him. *Es la manzana de la discordia con él.*

to have a bone to pick — *tener que habérselas.*

I've got a bone to pick with you. *Tengo que habérmelas con usted.*

to make no bones about it — *no andar con rodeos en decirlo.*

He didn't like it and made no bones about it. *No le gustó y no anduvo con rodeos en decirlo.*

boner — *el error*

to pull a boner — *meter la pata.*

He pulled a boner. *Metió la pata.*

book — *el libro*

in my book — *en mi concepto.*

In my book, Madrid is a beautiful city. *En mi concepto, Madrid es una ciudad hermosa.*

the good book — *la Biblia.*

It is found in the good book. *Se encuentra en la Biblia.*

to be in one's good (bad) book — *gozar del favor (o padecer el desagrado) de alguien.*

He sold ten cars, so he's in the boss's good book. *Vendió diez carros, así que goza del favor de su jefe.*

to crack a book — *abrir un libro (para estudiarlo).*

Even though he never cracks a book, he always gets good grades. *Aunque nunca abre un libro, siempre saca buenas notas.*

to go by the book — *seguir algo al pie de la letra.*

That guy will never show any flexibility — he always does things by the book. *Ese tipo nunca mostrará flexibilidad alguna — todo lo hace al pie de la letra.*

to keep books — *llevar libros.*

He keeps books for a publishing house. *Lleva libros para una casa editorial.*

to know like a book — *conocer a fondo.*

I know him like a book. *Lo conozco a fondo.*

to throw the book at — *castigar con todo rigor.*

The army threw the book at him. *El ejército lo castigó con todo rigor.*

boot — *la bota*

to die with one's boots on — *morir al pie del cañón; morir vestido.*

They died with their boots on. *Murieron al pie del cañón (Murieron vestidos).*

to bore — *aburrir, fastidiar*

to bore to death (bore stiff) — *matar de aburrimiento.*

My brother is bored to death (bored stiff) by that professor's lectures. *A mi hermano le matan de aburrimiento las conferencias de ese profesor.*

born — *nacido*

to be born lucky — *nacer de pie(s).*

Everybody in that family is born lucky. *Todos los de esa familia nacen de pie(s).*

to be born yesterday — *ser niño.*

I wasn't born yesterday. *No soy niño.*

both — *ambos*

both . . . and . . . — *tanto . . . como . . .; lo mismo . . . que . . .*

Both the heat and the cold bother her. *Tanto el calor como el frío (Lo mismo el calor que el frío) la molestan.*

to bother — *molestar*

don't bother — *no se moleste.*

Don't bother to get up. *No se moleste en levantarse.*

bottom — *el fondo*

at the bottom of the ladder — *sin nada.*

He began at the bottom of the ladder. *Empezó sin nada.*

at the bottom of the page — *al pie (al final) de la página.*

It's at the bottom of the page. *Está al pie (final) de la página.*

Bottoms up! — *¡Salud! (dicho al brindar).*

to get to the bottom — *aclarar.*

We got to the bottom of the mystery. *Aclaramos el misterio.*

to knock the bottom out of — *echar abajo.*

It knocked the bottom out of his project. *Echó abajo su proyecto.*

bound — *obligado*

to be bound for — *ir rumbo a; ir con destino a.*

I'm bound for home. *Voy rumbo a (con destino a) mi casa.*

to be bound to — *tener que; estar destinado a.*

It's bound to rain. *Tiene que (Está destinado a) llover.*

to bow — *inclinarse*

to bow out — *dejar de participar.*

He bowed out. *Dejó de participar.*

Boxing Day — *el día que sigue a la Navidad.*

Tips are given to servants, mail carriers, and concierges on Boxing Day. *El día después de Navidad está indicado para dar propinas a sirvientes, carteros y conserjes.*

boy — *el muchacho*

boys will be boys — *cosa de niños.*

Another streetlight broken? Boys will be boys, but there is a limit. *¿Otro farol roto? Será cosa de niños, pero todo tiene su límite.*

to be someone's fair-haired boy — *ser pu preferido (predilecto).*

He was the professor's fair-haired boy. *Era el preferido (predilecto) del profesor.*

brain — *el cerebro*

to rack one's brains (to beat one's brains out) — *calentarse (romper; devanarse) la cabeza.*

He racked his brains (beat his brains out). *Se calentó (Rompió) (Se devanó) la cabeza.*

brand — *la marca*

brand new — *flamante.*

He was sporting a brand new wristwatch. *Lucía un flamante reloj de pulsera.*

bread — *el pan*

to know which side one's bread is buttered on — *arrimarse al sol que más calienta (saber lo que le conviene).*

I know which side my bread is buttered on. *Me arrimo al sol que más calienta (sé lo que me conviene).*

to put on bread and water — *poner a pan y agua.*
They put him on bread and water. *Lo pusieron a pan y agua.*

break — *la oportunidad; la interrupción*

to give someone a break — *echarle una mano; darle una oportunidad.*
She gave me a break. *Me echó una mano (Me dio una oportunidad).*

to have a good break — *tener buena suerte.*
He had a good break. *Tuvo buena suerte.*

to take a break — *tomarse un descanso.*
They took a break every day at ten. *Se tomaban un descanso todos los días a las diez.*

to break — *romper*

to be broke — *estar sin blanca.*
I'm broke. *Estoy sin blanca.*

to break down — *romperse.*
The washing machine broke down. *La lavadora se rompió.*

to break even — *cubrir gastos.*
We can't break even. *No podemos cubrir gastos.*

to break into — *entrar (por fuerza) en.*
A thief broke into my office. *Un ladrón entró (por fuerza) en mi oficina.*

to break loose — *escaparse.*
He broke loose from his cell. *Se escapó de su celda.*

to break off — *romper; terminar.*
They broke off their friendship. *Rompieron (Terminaron) su amistad.*

to break one's spirit — *doblegarle el ánimo.*
They broke his spirit. *Le doblegaron el ánimo.*

to break out — *estallar.*
War broke out. *Estalló la guerra.*

to break out in tears — *deshacerse en lágrimas.*
She breaks out in tears easily. *Se deshace en lágrimas fácilmente.*

breakdown — *la avería*

a nervous breakdown — *un colapso nervioso; una crisis nerviosa.*

She suffered a nervous breakdown. *Sufrió un colapso nervioso (una crisis nerviosa).*

breast — *el pecho*

to make a clean breast of it — *confesarlo todo.*

He made a clean breast of it. *Lo confesó todo.*

breath — *el aliento*

all in one breath — *todo de un aliento.*

He said it all in one breath. *Lo dijo todo de un aliento.*

in the same breath — *casi al mismo tiempo.*

She consented to come and in the same breath said that she couldn't. *Consintió en venir y casi al mismo tiempo dijo que no podía.*

to be out of breath — *estar sin aliento.*

I'm out of breath. *Estoy sin aliento.*

to catch one's breath (i.e., to gasp) — *tomar aliento.*

We caught our breath. *Tomamos aliento.*

to take one's breath away — *dejarle boquiabierto; asombrarle.*

Her intelligence took my breath away. *Su inteligencia me dejó boquiabierto (me asombró).*

to waste one's breath — *perder el tiempo.*

I wasted my breath teaching him to speak Spanish. *Perdí el tiempo enseñándole a hablar español.*

under one's breath — *en voz baja.*

He said it under his breath. *Lo dijo en voz baja.*

breeze — *la brisa*

to breeze through — *pasar algo con facilidad.*

She breezed through that exam in twenty minutes. *En veinte minutos terminó fácilmente ese examen.*

to shoot the breeze — *conversar tranquilamente.*

We were drinking beer and shooting the breeze the whole afternoon. *Estuvimos tomando cerveza y conversando toda la tarde.*

bride — *la novia*

to give the bride away — *llevar a la novia al altar.*

The father gave the bride away and sighed. *El padre llevó a la novia al altar y suspiró.*

bridge — *el puente*

to burn one's bridges behind one — *quemar sus naves.*

He burned his bridges behind him. *Quemó sus naves.*

to bring — *traer*

to bring about — *causar.*

The flood was brought about by the rains. *La inundación fue causada por las lluvias.*

to bring back — *devolver.*

He brought back my book. *Me devolvió el libro.*

to bring closer — *acercar.*

Classical music brought them closer. *La música clásica los acercó.*

to bring down the house — *hacer venirse abajo el teatro.*

Her song brought down the house. *Su canción hizo venirse abajo el teatro.*

to bring it on oneself — *buscárselas.*

Being lazy and shameless, he brought it on himself. *Se las buscó con su pereza y su falta de vergüenza.*

to bring out — *presentar.*

The factory brought out a new model of the airplane. *La fábrica presentó un nuevo modelo de avión.*

to bring out — *sacar.*

She brought out her best dishes. *Sacó su mejor vajilla.*

to bring someone to (around) — *reanimar.*

We brought him to (around) with artificial respiration. *Lo reanimamos con respiración artificial.*

to bring (pull) up — *arrimar.*

Bring (Pull) up a chair. *Arrime una silla.*

to bring up — *criar; educar.*

Since she was an orphan, her grandparents brought her up. *Como era huérfana, la criaron (educaron) sus abuelos.*

to bring up — *sacar a relucir.*

He brought up all my shortcomings. *Sacó a relucir todos mis defectos.*

brow — *la frente*

to knit one's brow — *fruncir el ceño.*

She knitted her brow when she saw me. *Frunció el ceño cuando me vio.*

brunt — *la fuerza*

to bear the brunt — *llevar el peso.*

I bore the brunt of the responsibility. *Llevé el peso de la responsabilidad.*

brush — *el cepillo; la escobilla*

tarred with the same brush — *ser lobos de una misma camada.*

Those little thieves may look different, but they are tarred with the same brush. *Esos ladroncitos pueden verse distintos, pero son cortados del mismo patrón.*

to brush — *cepillar*

to brush up on — *repasar.*

They're brushing up on their English. *Están repasando su inglés.*

buck — *el dólar*

to make a fast buck — *hacer dinero rápidamente.*

He got a tip, tried to make a fast buck, and lost everything. *Le dieron un soplo, él trató de amasar un montón de dinero con rapidez, pero lo perdió todo.*

buck — *la ficha*

to pass the buck — *echar la carga.*

He passed the buck to me. *Me echó la carga a mí.*

to buck — *encorvarse*

Buck up! — *¡Anímese!*

bucket — *el balde*

to kick the bucket — *estirar la pata; morir.*

He got very sick and then he kicked the bucket. *Se enfermó de gravedad y luego estiró la pata.*

bud — *el pimpollo*

to nip in the bud — *cortar de raíz.*

Our plan was nipped in the bud. *Nuestro plan fue cortado de raíz.*

to bug — *molestar*

What's bugging her? — *¿Qué mosca la ha picado?*

to build — *construir*

to build up — *amasar.*

We have built up a large fortune. *Hemos amasado una gran fortuna.*

to build up — *aumentar.*

We built up our stock. *Aumentamos nuestras existencias.*

bull — *el toro*

to take the bull by the horns — *agarrar al toro por los cuernos.*

They took the bull by the horns and made the decision. *Agarraron al toro por los cuernos y tomaron la decisión.*

to bump — *topar*

to bump into — *darse de cara con.*

We bumped into him at the university. *Nos dimos de cara con él en la universidad.*

to bump off — *matar, despachar.*

The gangster bumped off his rival. *El gangster mató (despachó) a su rival.*

to burst — *estallar*

to burst out laughing (crying) — *romper (echarse) a reír (llorar)* .

He burst out laughing (crying). *Rompió (Se echó) a reír (llorar).*

bush — *el arbusto*

to beat around the bush — *andar por las ramas; andar con rodeos.*

She always beats around the bush. *Siempre anda por las ramas (con rodeos).*

business — *el negocio*

It's his (her, etc.) business. — *Allá él (ella, etc.).*

It's my business. — *Es cosa mía.*

it's none of . . . 's business — *no es cuenta de. . . .*

It's none of John's business. *No es cuenta de Juan.*

monkey business — *el truco; la treta; la jugarreta.*

I want reliable information, not that monkey business of theirs! *¡Quiero información digna de confianza y no esos inventos de ellos!*

show business — *los asuntos y negocios del mundo de los espectáculos.*

Some singers stay in show business into their sixties. *Algunos cantantes continúan sus carreras artísticas pasados los sesenta.*

that business about — *lo (eso) de.*

That business about the murder grieves me. *Lo (Eso) del asesinato me da pena.*

to be sick of the whole business — *estar harto de todo el asunto.*

Strange documents, high taxes, nasty lawyers . . . I'm sick of the whole business. *Documentos raros, impuestos altos, abogados antipáticos . . . estoy harto de todo ese asunto.*

to get down to business — *ponerse a la obra.*

We're wasting time. Let's get down to business. *Estamos perdiendo tiempo. Pongámonos a la obra.*

to give him the business — *darle una paliza; matarlo.*

Johnny and I gave him the business in a dark place. *Yo y Juan le dimos una paliza en un lugar bien oscuro.*

to mean business — *hablar en serio.*

I mean business. *Hablo en serio.*

to mind one's own business — *no meterse en lo que no le toca.*

He told her to mind her own business. *Le dijo que no se metiera en lo que no le tocaba.*

but — *pero*

No buts about it! — *¡No hay pero que valga!*

to butter — *untar con mantequilla*

to butter up — *chuparle las medias.*

That student likes to butter up the professor. *A ese alumno le gusta chuparle las medias al profesor.*

to buy — *comprar*

to buy out — *comprar.*

I bought out his business. *Compré su negocio.*

to buy up — *adquirir; acaparar.*

I bought up all the land I could. *Adquirí (Acaparé) todo el terreno que pude.*

bygone — *lo pasado; lo antiguo*

let bygones be bygones — *lo pasado, olvidado.*

Must you keep reminding me of this? Let bygones be bygones! *¿Debes continuamente recordarme eso? ¡Olvidemos eso de una vez!*

C

Cain — *Caín*

to raise Cain — *armar un alboroto.*

When he sees it, he'll raise Cain. *Cuando lo vea, armará un alboroto.*

cake — *el pastel*

That takes the cake! — *¡Eso sí que es el colmo!*

to sell like hot cakes — *venderse como pan caliente.*

The new rock group's CDs are selling like hot cakes. *Los CD del nuevo grupo de rock están vendiéndose como si fueran indulgencias plenarias.*

to take the cake (i.e., to take the prize) — *llevarse la palma.*

Her dance took the cake. *Su baile se llevó la palma.*

call — *la llamada*

to have a close call — *salvarse por los pelos.*

We had a close call. *Nos salvamos por los pelos.*

within call — *al alcance de la voz.*

Stay within call. *Quédese al alcance de mi voz.*

to call — *llamar*

social call — *la visita de cortesía.*

Officially it was just a social call, but he had a business proposal as well. *Oficialmente era sólo una visita de cortesía, pero también tenía una oferta comercial.*

to call down (i.e., to chide) — *regañar.*

Her teacher called her down. *Su maestra la regañó.*

to call for — *requerir.*

That calls for a lot of patience. *Requiere mucha paciencia.*

to call for — *venir a buscar.*

He called for me at ten. *Vino a buscarme a las diez.*

to call on — *visitar a.*

We called on Mrs. López. *Visitamos a la señora de López.*

to call up — *llamar por teléfono.*

He called me up. *Me llamó por teléfono.*

candle — *la vela*

not to hold a candle to — *no poder compararse con.*

He can't hold a candle to his sister. *No puede compararse con su hermana.*

to burn the candle at both ends — *gastar locamente las fuerzas.*

He burns the candle at both ends. *Está gastando locamente sus fuerzas.*

canoe — *la canoa*

to paddle one's own canoe — *bastarse a sí mismo.*

From the time he was a child, he was used to paddling his own canoe. *Desde niño estaba acostumbrado a bastarse a sí mismo.*

cap — *la gorra; el gorro*

to put on one's thinking cap — *avivar uno el seso.*

To find that, I must put on my thinking cap. *Para poder encontrar eso, debo ponerme a pensar.*

capacity — *la capacidad*

in the capacity of — *en calidad de.*

He's here in the capacity of program director. *Está aquí en calidad de director del programa.*

to capitalize — *capitalizar*

to capitalize on — *aprovechar.*

If he had capitalized on all the courses he took, he would be a CEO by now. *Si él hubiera aprovechado todos los cursos que tomó, sería un director ejecutivo ahora.*

card — *la carta*

house of cards — *un castillo de naipes.*

His business collapsed like a house of cards. *Su empresa se fue abajo como un castillo de naipes.*

to put one's cards on the table — *poner las cartas boca arriba; poner las cartas sobre la mesa.*

When we put our cards on the table we understood each other. *Al poner las cartas boca arriba (sobre la mesa) nos entendimos.*

care — *el cuidado*

in care of — *al cuidado de.*

I left it in care of the manager. *Lo dejé al cuidado del gerente.*

That takes care of that (So much for that). — *Asunto terminado.*

to take care of — *ocuparse (encargarse) de.*

He took care of the matter. *Se ocupó (Se encargó) del asunto.*

to care — *cuidar*

not to be able to care less — *no importarle lo más mínimo.*

He couldn't care less. *No le importaba lo más mínimo.*

careful — *cuidadoso*

Be careful! — *¡Tenga cuidado!*

be careful not to . . . — *cuidado con. . . .*

Be careful not to fall! *¡Cuidado con caerse!*

to carry — *llevar*

to carry out — *llevar a cabo; efectuar*

He carried out the plan. *Llevó a cabo (Efectuó) el proyecto.*

to carry the ball — *encargarse de todo; tener toda la responsabilidad.*

He carries the ball. *Se encarga de todo (Tiene toda la responsabilidad).*

cart — *la carreta*

to put the cart before the horse — *tomar el rábano por las hojas; empezar la casa por el tejado.*

That's putting the cart before the horse. *Eso es tomar el rábano por las hojas (empezar la casa por el tejado).*

to upset the apple cart — *echar todo a perder.*

He upset the apple cart with his comments. *Echó todo a perder con sus comentarios.*

case — *el caso*

an open-and-shut case — *algo muy simple y obvio.*

We got him with the stolen wallet in his pocket, so it was an open-and-shut case. *Lo agarramos con la billetera robada en su bolsillo, así que fue un caso sencillísimo.*

as the case may be — *según el caso.*

They come in the morning or in the afternoon, as the case may be. *Vienen por la mañana o por la tarde según el caso.*

in any case — *de todas formas.*

In any case, I'll accept. *De todas formas, aceptaré.*

in case — *en caso de.*

In case you know, call us. *En caso de saber, llámenos.*

just in case — *por si acaso; por si las moscas.*

Take two more, just in case. *Llévese dos más, por si acaso (por si las moscas).*

to have a case — *tener un argumento convincente.*

They don't have a case. *No tienen un argumento convincente.*

cash — *el dinero contante*

cash on the barrel head — *en dinero contante y sonante.*

He wanted me to pay him cash on the barrel head. *Quería que yo le pagara en dinero contante y sonante.*

to pay (spot) cash — *pagar al contado; pagar con dinero contante.*

He pays (spot) cash. *Paga al contado (con dinero contante).*

---

to cast — *echar*

to cast responsibilities on one — *echarle encima responsabilidades.*

They cast many responsibilities on him. *Le echaron encima muchas responsabilidades.*

---

cat — *el gato*

copycat — *un imitador.*

He's a copycat. *Es un imitador.*

There are more ways than one to skin a cat. — *Hay muchos modos de matar pulgas.*

to let the cat out of the bag — *descubrirlo todo; revelar el secreto.*

He let the cat out of the bag. *Lo descubrió todo (Reveló el secreto).*

to rain cats and dogs (pitchforks) — *llover a cántaros (llover chuzos).*

It's raining cats and dogs (pitchforks). *Está lloviendo a cántaros (Llueve chuzos).*

---

catch — *la presa, el botín*

to be a good catch — *ser un buen partido.*

That girl is a good catch. *Esa chica es un buen partido.*

---

to catch — *coger, asir*

to catch hold of — *agarrar.*

I caught hold of it. *Lo agarré.*

to catch on — *tener eco.*

It's a good idea, but I doubt that it will catch on. *Es una buena idea, pero dudo que tenga eco.*

to catch on to — *entender.*

He didn't catch on to the plan. *No entendió el plan.*

to catch up with — *alcanzar; dar alcance.*

He caught up with us. *Nos alcanzó (dio alcance).*

to cave — *cavar*

to cave in — *ceder.*

His wife kept on nagging until he caved in. *Su esposa lo jorobó sin parar hasta que cedió.*

ceiling — *el cielo raso, el techo (interior)*

to hit the ceiling — *ponerse como una fiera; poner el grito en cielo.*

She hit the ceiling when she found out what her sister had done. *Se puso como una fiera (Puso el grito en el cielo) al saber lo que había hecho su hermana.*

certain — *cierto*

a certain — *un tal.*

A certain Mr. Pérez told me. *Me lo dijo un tal señor Pérez.*

for certain — *a ciencia cierta.*

I know it for certain. *Lo sé a ciencia cierta.*

on a certain — *uno de tantos.*

On a certain Monday, they went away. *Uno de tantos lunes se marcharon.*

chance — *la ocasión, la oportunidad; el azar*

by chance — *por casualidad.*

Do you by chance have my book? *¿Tiene por casualidad mi libro?*

chances are that — *posiblemente.*

It's snowing; chances are that they will not come. *Está nevando; probablemente no vendrán.*

to let the chance slip by — *perder la ocasión.*

We let the chance slip by. *Perdimos la ocasión.*

to stand a chance — *tener la posibilidad (probabilidad).*

He doesn't stand a chance of winning. *No tiene ninguna posibilidad (probabilidad) de ganar.*

to take a chance — *aventurarse.*

I don't want to take a chance. *No quiero aventurarme.*

change — *el cambio*

winds of change — *los aires renovadores.*

Winds of change are blowing through the halls of the old university. *Aires renovadores soplan por los corredores de la vieja universidad.*

channel — *el canal; el conducto*

through channels — *por conducto reglamentario.*

You cannot send this document any way you want to; it has to go through channels. *Usted no puede mandar este documento de cualquier manera; debe hacerlo por conducto reglamentario.*

character — *el carácter*

to be quite a character — *ser un tipo original.*

He's quite a character. *Es un tipo original.*

charge — *el cargo*

reversed charge — *el cobro revertido.*

Getting a reversed charge from my son means he's in some trouble. *Una llamada de cobro revertido de mi hijo significa que se ha metido en algún lío.*

to be in charge — *estar a cargo; estar al frente.*

He's in charge of the group. *Está a cargo (al frente) del grupo.*

to take charge — *hacerse cargo; encargarse de.*

He took charge of the clerks. *Se hizo cargo (Se encargó) de los dependientes.*

charity — *la caridad*

Charity begins at home. — *La caridad bien entendida empieza por uno mismo.*

chase — *la caza*

a wild-goose chase — *una empresa hecha sin provecho.*

It turned out to be a wild-goose chase. *Resultó ser una empresa hecha sin provecho.*

check — *el cheque.*

rain check — *billete dado para asistir a un espectáculo o comprar un producto en una ocasión futura; promesa de alguna acción futura.*

We ran out of Heineken at $0.99, but I'll give you a rain check. *Se nos agotó la Heineken que ofrecíamos a $0,99 pero le daré un billete para compra futura.*

to check — *verificar; detener, refrenar*

to check against — *comparar.*

We checked the first edition against the second and found very little difference. *Comparamos la primera edición con la segunda y vimos muy poca diferencia.*

to check in (out) — *registrarse (marcharse).*

He checked in on Monday and checked out on Wednesday. *Se registró en el hotel el lunes y se marchó el miércoles.*

to check oneself — *refrenarse.*

He was about to say it but he checked himself. *Estaba a punto de decirlo pero se refrenó.*

to check through — *hacer pasar por control.*

You must check the jewels through customs. *Debe hacer pasar las joyas por control de aduana.*

to check up on — *hacer indagaciones sobre.*

He checked up on his students. *Hizo indagaciones sobre sus alumnos.*

to check with — *consultar.*

Check with me before you leave. *Consúlteme antes de salir.*

to keep in check — *tener a raya.*

Penicillin kept the infection in check. *La penicilina mantuvo la infección a raya.*

check-up — *el reconocimiento*

to give a check-up — *hacer un reconocimiento general.*

The doctor gave me a check-up. *El médico me hizo un reconocimiento general.*

to cheer — *animar*

to cheer up — *animarse.*

I cheered up when I saw her. *Me animé cuando la vi.*

cherry — *la cereza*

bowl of cherries — *el paraíso.*

Life has been a bowl of cherries for her since she won the lottery. *La vida ha sido un paraíso para ella desde que ganó la lotería.*

chest — *el pecho*

to throw out one's chest — *sacar el pecho.*

He threw out his chest. *Sacó el pecho.*

chestnut — *la castaña*

to pull someone's chestnuts out of the fire — *sacarle las castañas del fuego.*

We were always pulling his chestnuts out of the fire. *Siempre le sacábamos las castañas del fuego.*

chicken — *la gallina, el pollo*

to be chicken — *ser gallina.*

Come on, try it, don't be chicken. *Anda, pruébalo, no seas gallina.*

Don't count your chickens before they are hatched. — *No venda la piel del oso antes de haberlo cazado.*

chin — *la barba, el mentón*

to keep one's chin up — *no desanimarse.*

Keep your chin up. *No se desanime.*

chip — *la astilla*

the chips are down — *la suerte está echada.*

When the chips are down, there's no turning back. *Cuando la suerte está echada, no se puede volver atrás.*

to be a chip off the old block. — *De tal palo, tal astilla.*

to have a chip on one's shoulder — *ser muy provocador; ser un resentido.*

He always has a chip on his shoulder. *Es muy provocador (un resentido).*

to let the chips fall where they may — *pase lo que pase.*

I know there are reputations at stake, but we'll let the chips fall where they may and we'll establish the truth. *Yo sé que hay reputaciones en juego, pero pase lo que pase llegaremos a la verdad.*

circle — *el círculo*

a vicious circle — *un círculo vicioso.*

Life is a vicious circle. *La vida es un círculo vicioso.*

to come full circle — *volver al punto de partida.*

First he wanted to study medicine, then poetry, and then he came full circle, back to medicine. *Primero quiso estudiar medicina, luego poesía, y finalmente volvió al punto de partida con medicina.*

to go around in circles — *dar vueltas.*

Why don't we drop this? We're just going around in circles and not getting anywhere. *¿Por qué no dejamos esto? Estamos dando vueltas sin llegar a ninguna parte.*

circumstance — *la circunstancia*

under no circumstances (not under any circumstances) — *de ningún modo; en ningún caso.*

Under no circumstances am I going to do that (I'm not going to do that under any circumstances). *De ningún modo (En ningún caso) voy a hacer eso.*

under the circumstances — *dadas las circunstancias; en estas circunstancias.*

Under the circumstances it's the only thing we can do. *Dadas las circunstancias (En estas circunstancias) es lo único que podemos hacer.*

citizen — *el ciudadano*

senior citizen — *la persona de la tercera edad.*

Senior citizens get a discount in this store. *En esta tienda se dan descuentos a las personas de la tercera edad.*

clean — *limpio*

to come clean — *confesarlo todo.*

He came clean. *Lo confesó todo.*

to clean — *limpiar*

to clean out — *dejar sin nada.*

They cleaned us out. *Nos dejaron sin nada.*

cleaners — *la tintorería*

to take to the cleaners — *dejar en la calle.*

Don't play poker with them. They'll take you to the cleaners. *No juegues al póker con ellos. Te dejarán en la calle.*

clear — *claro*

clear-cut — *bien delimitado.*

It's a clear-cut plan. *Es un plan bien delimitado.*

to be in the clear — *estar libre de culpa.*

He's in the clear. *Está libre de culpa.*

to make clear — *dar a entender; sacar en claro.*

She made it clear that she wasn't interested. *Dio a entender (Sacó en claro) que no tenía interés.*

to clear — *aclarar*

to clear up — *clarificar; poner en claro.*

He cleared up the matter with his explanation. *Clarificó (Puso en claro) el asunto con su explicación.*

to clear up — *despejarse; aclararse.*

By eleven it had cleared up. *Para las once se había despejado (aclarado).*

climber — *el trepador; el escalador*

social climber — *el advenedizo; la persona con ambiciones sociales.*

He appears at all social events and always says the right things, but one can see that he's just a social climber. *Se aparece en todos los festejos sociales y siempre dice lo que hay que decir, pero una puede ver que no es más que un advenedizo.*

clock — *el reloj*

around the clock — *día y noche.*

We worked around the clock. *Trabajamos día y noche.*

close — *el fin*

to draw to a close — *tocar a su fin; estar para terminar.*

The year is drawing to a close. *El año está tocando a su fin (está para terminar).*

close — *cerca*

to get close to . . . — *frisar en los . . . años.*

He's getting close to 75. *Frisa en los setenta y cinco años.*

to close — *recorrer; cubrir*

to close down — *clausurar.*

They finally closed down that illegal bar. *Por fin clausuraron ese bar ilegal.*

to close in — *acercarse rodeando.*

The FBI is closing in on the hijackers. *El FBI está estrechando el cerco a los secuestradores.*

closet — *gabinete; alacena*

skeleton in the closet — *un secreto familiar vergonzoso.*

Infidelities and offspring out of wedlock were the most common skeletons in the closet. *Las infidelidades y los hijos naturales eran los secretos vergonzosos más frecuentes en las familias.*

cloth — *el vestido clerical*

man of the cloth — *el sacerdote; el ministro.*

I trust his word; after all, he's a man of the cloth. *Yo confío en su palabra; después de todo es un sacerdote.*

cloud — *la nube*

cloud nine — *el séptimo cielo.*

He's on cloud nine. *Está en el séptimo cielo.*

Every cloud has a silver lining. — *No hay mal que por bien no venga.*

to be under a cloud — *estar bajo sospecha.*

It cannot be proven that she was unfaithful, but she is under a cloud. *No puede probarse que fue infiel, pero se sospecha de ella.*

to be (up) in the clouds — *estar en las nubes.*

It is useless to ask him for advice; he's always up in the clouds. *Es inútil pedirle consejos; siempre está en las nubes.*

coast — *la costa*

The coast is clear. — *Ya no hay moros en la costa.*

cock — *el gallo*

the cock of the walk — *el gallito del lugar.*

He always wanted to be the cock of the walk. *Siempre quería ser el gallito del lugar.*

cocktail — *el cóctel*

to mix (up) a cocktail — *preparar un cóctel.*

He mixed us (up) a cocktail. *Nos preparó un cóctel.*

coincidence — *la coincidencia*

by coincidence — *por casualidad.*

He found out by mere coincidence. *Lo supo por pura casualidad.*

cold — *el frío; el resfriado, el catarro*

to bring in from (out of) the cold — *sacar del aislamiento.*

His friendly personality brought him out of the cold among the workers. *Su amistosa personalidad lo sacó del aislamiento entre los trabajadores.*

to catch cold — *coger catarro.*

He caught cold in the rain. *Cogió catarro en la lluvia.*

to leave out in the cold — *dejar colgado.*

We were left out in the cold. *Nos dejaron colgados.*

cold — *frío*

to be cold (the weather) — *hacer frío.*

It's cold today. *Hace frío hoy.*

to be cold (a person) — *tener frío.*

I'm cold. *Tengo frío.*

collar — *el cuello*

to get hot under the collar — *enojarse, enfadarse.*

He got hot under the collar when he heard the news. *Se enojó (se enfadó) al oír la noticia.*

white collar — *de oficina.*

He was looking for a white-collar job. *Buscaba un empleo de oficina.*

color — *el color*

off-color — *impropio; atrevido.*

His off-color jokes were annoying to some. *Sus atrevidos chistes molestaban a algunas personas.*

to call to the colors — *llamar a filas.*

He was called to the colors. *Lo llamaron a filas.*

to lend color — *dar color.*

The presence of the gypsies lent color to the scene. *La presencia de los gitanos le daba color a la escena.*

with flying colors — *con completo éxito; quedar lucido.*

I passed the interview with flying colors. *Pasé la entrevista con gran éxito.*

to come — *venir*

as they come — *como nadie, como el que más.*

Gloomy and cold, they are as Nordic as they come. *Melancólicos y fríos, son tan nórdicos como el que más.*

Come and get it! — *¡A comer!*

Come on! — *¡Vamos!*

come to think of it — *ahora caigo en que.*

Come to think of it, he sent me one. *Ahora caigo en que me mandó uno.*

Come what may (Come hell or high water) — *contra viento y marea.*

She's going to marry him come what may (come hell or high water). *Va a casarse con él contra viento y marea.*

How come? — *¿Cómo se explica?*

I'm coming! — *¡Allá voy!*

to come about — *suceder.*

How did it come about? *¿Cómo sucedió?*

to come across — *encontrarse con.*

I came across an old photo. *Me encontré con una vieja foto.*

to come along — *acompañar.*
She asked me to come along. *Me pidió que la acompañara.*

to come along — *andar.*
How's your aunt coming along? *¿Cómo anda su tía?*

to come back — *regresar.*
Come straight back. *Regrese en seguida (sin detenerse).*

to come down to — *reducirse a.*
What it comes down to is that they didn't want to go. *A lo que se reduce es que no querían ir.*

to come from — *ser de.*
He comes from Malta. *Es de Malta.*

to come in handy — *servir bien.*
The tool came in handy. *La herrarmienta me sirvió bien.*

to come off — *caérsele.*
A button came off. *Se me cayó un botón.*

to come out ahead — *salir ganando.*
If they listen to my advice they'll come out ahead. *Si escuchan mis consejos saldrán ganando.*

to come out well (badly) — *salir bien (mal).*
He came out well (badly) in his exam. *Salió bien (mal) en su examen.*

to come to — *volver en sí.*
He seemed dazed when he came to. *Parecía ofuscado cuando volvió en sí.*

to come to pass — *cumplirse.*
If it comes to pass, we'll be without funds. *Si se cumple, estaremos sin fondos.*

to come true — *realizarse.*
His dream came true. *Su sueño se realizó.*

to have it coming — *esperar algo malo.*
We have it coming, boys . . . the enemy will attack at dawn. *Nos espera una grande muchachos . . . el enemigo atacará en la madrugada.*

comfort — *el consuelo*
creature comforts — *la comodidad material.*

Nobody can be happy without some creature comforts. *Nadie puede ser feliz sin algo de comodidad material.*

to be cold comfort — *ser un pobre consuelo.*
What he said was cold comfort. *Lo que dijo fue un pobre consuelo.*

command — *el dominio*
to have a good command — *dominar bien.*
He has a good command of Spanish. *Domina bien el español.*

commotion — *la conmoción*
to cause a commotion — *armar un alboroto.*
He caused a commotion. *Armó un alboroto.*

company — *la compañía*
to keep company with — *cortejar a.*
He keeps company with his secretary. *Corteja a su secretaria.*

to keep someone company — *hacerle compañía.*
She's keeping him company. *Le hace compañía.*

to part company — *tomar rumbos distintos.*
They were good friends for several years but they finally parted company. *Fueron buenos amigos por varios años pero al fin tomaron rumbos distintos.*

to compel — *compeler*
to be compelled to — *verse forzado (obligado) a.*
He's compelled to leave the city. *Se ve forzado (obligado) a marcharse de la ciudad.*

to con — *estafar; timar*
to con into — *persuadir engañosamente.*
He was conned into buying those worthless shares. *Fue persuadido tramposamente a comprar esas acciones sin valor.*

to concern — *concernir, interesar*
as far as I'm concerned — *por lo que a mí se refiere; por lo que a mí me toca.*

As far as I'm concerned, take it. *Por lo que a mí se refiere (me toca) lléveselo.*

To whom it may concern. — *A quien le corresponda; a quien pueda interesar.*

conclusion — *la conclusión*

to jump to conclusions — *juzgar a la ligera.*

She likes to jump to conclusions. *Le gusta juzgar a la ligera.*

condition — *la condición; el estado*

in mint condition — *como nuevo.*

That used car is in mint condition. *Ese carro usado está como nuevo.*

to confide — *confiar*

to confide in — *hacer una confidencia.*

He confided in us. *Nos hizo una confidencia.*

conformity — *la conformidad*

to be in conformity with — *estar de conformidad con.*

It's in conformity with our laws. *Está de conformidad con nuestras leyes.*

consideration — *la consideración*

out of consideration for — *por consideración a.*

She rests out of consideration for her health. *Descansa por consideración a su salud.*

conspicuous — *conspicuo*

to be conspicuous by one's absence — *brillar por su ausencia.*

She's conspicuous by her absence. *Brilla por su ausencia.*

to make oneself conspicuous — *llamar la atención.*

He always makes himself conspicuous. *Siempre llama la atención.*

construction — *la construcción*

under construction — *en obras.*

There is a dam under construction. *Hay una presa en obras.*

to contain — *contener; abarcar; incluir*

self-contained — *completo; autónomo; independiente.*

In the present world, no country can have a self-contained economy. *En el mundo actual, ningún país puede tener un sistema económico autónomo.*

contempt — *el desprecio*

Familiarity breeds contempt. — *La confianza hace perder el respeto.*

contrary — *contrario*

on the contrary — *al contrario.*

She's not ugly. On the contrary, she's very pretty. *No es fea. Al contrario, es muy bonita.*

control — *el control*

to be under control — *andar perfectamente.*

Everything is under control. *Todo anda perfectamente.*

convenience — *la comodidad*

at one's earliest convenience — *a la primera oportunidad.*

Answer at your earliest convenience. *Conteste a la primera oportunidad.*

conversation — *la conversación*

to strike up a conversation — *entablar una conversación.*

He likes to strike up a conversation with strangers. *Le gusta entablar una conversación con desconocidos.*

to convince — *convencer*

to be convinced — *estar persuadido de.*

I'm convinced that it's correct. *Estoy persuadido de que es correcto.*

to cook — *cocinar*

to cook one's goose — *firmar su sentencia de muerte; perderlo todo.*

Now he's cooked his goose! *Ya ha firmado su sentencia de muerte (lo ha perdido todo).*

cookie — *la galleta (dulce)*

That's the way the cookie crumbles. — *Así es la vida.*

---

cool — *fresco; sereno*

to keep cool — *conservar la serenidad.*

He kept cool. *Conservó la serenidad.*

to lose one's cool — *perder la cabeza.*

When he heard the accusation, he lost his cool. *Al oír la acusación perdió la cabeza.*

---

to cool — *serenarse; refrescarse*

Cool off! — *¡Serénese!*

to cool off — *enfriarse.*

My tea cooled off. *Mi té se enfrió.*

---

core — *el corazón, el centro*

hard core — *el núcleo duro.*

The hard core of the Liberal Party voted against. *El núcleo duro del Partido Liberal votó en contra.*

hard-core — *escandaloso.*

Hard-core pornography is appreciated in Singapore. *En Singapur aprecian la pornografía más indecente.*

to the core — *hasta la médula; de pies a cabeza.*

He's stingy to the core. *Es tacaño hasta la médula (de pies a cabeza).*

---

corner — *el rincón*

to cut corners — *economizar.*

Having lost her job, she had to cut corners. *Habiendo perdido su empleo, debió hacer economías.*

to look out of the corner of one's eye — *mirar de reojo.*

She's looking at us out of the corner of her eye. *Nos está mirando de reojo.*

to round a corner — *superar una etapa.*

We disagreed a lot about our children's education, but we have rounded that corner already. *Estábamos muy en desacuerdo sobre la educación de nuestros hijos, pero ya hemos superado esa etapa.*

cost — *la costa*

at all cost — *a todo trance; a toda costa; cueste lo que cueste.*

She'll do it at all cost. *Lo hará a todo trance (a toda costa; cueste lo que cueste).*

to count — *contar*

to count — *entrar en la cuenta.*

It doesn't count. *No entra en la cuenta.*

to count on — *contar con.*

He's counting on us. *Cuenta con nosotros.*

to count out — *no contar con.*

I'm counting you out. *No cuento con usted.*

counter — *el mostrador*

over the counter — *libremente.*

Liquor is not sold over the counter here. *No se venden licores libremente aquí.*

under the counter (table) — *en secreto.*

He buys his gold under the counter (table). *Compra el oro en secreto.*

courage — *el ánimo*

to pluck up one's courage — *recobrar ánimo.*

I plucked up my courage and entered. *Recobré ánimo y entré.*

course — *el curso*

in due course — *a su debido tiempo.*

You'll know in due course. *Sabrá a su debido tiempo.*

in the course of time — *con el transcurso del tiempo.*

In the course of time the Moors left Spain. *Con el transcurso del tiempo, los moros salieron de España.*

of course — *claro; desde luego; por supuesto.*

Of course, it's not true. *Claro (Desde luego; Por supuesto) que no es verdad.*

of course — *cómo no.*

You have it? Of course! *¿Lo tiene? ¡Cómo no!*

to be on a collision course — *estar dos vehículos a punto de chocar.*

The two aircraft were on a collision course. *Los dos aviones estaban por chocar uno contra otro.*

to hold one's course — *mantener el rumbo.*

Despite all difficulties, he held his course. *Pese a las dificultades, él mantuvo su rumbo.*

to take its course — *seguir su curso.*

Let's allow this matter to take its course. *Dejemos que este asunto siga su curso.*

court — *la corte*

a friend at court — *un amigo influyente.*

You could have that law changed if you had a friend at court. *Podrías lograr que cambien esa ley si tuvieras un amigo influyente.*

a ward of the court — *un menor o un huérfano bajo tutela judicial.*

His parents died in an accident, so John became a ward of the court. *Como sus padres murieron en un accidente, John quedó bajo tutela judicial.*

courtesy — *la cortesía*

out of courtesy — *por cortesía.*

I invited her out of courtesy. *La invité por cortesía.*

crack — *la grieta; el instante; la prueba*

at the crack of dawn — *al romper el alba.*

We left at the crack of dawn. *Salimos al romper el alba.*

to make cracks about — *burlarse de.*

He makes cracks about her. *Se burla de ella.*

to take a crack at — *probar.*

I took a crack at tennis when I was 15. *Probé el tenis cuando tenía 15 años.*

to crawl — *arrastrarse*

to crawl in — *entrar a gatas.*

He crawled in. *Entró a gatas.*

crazy — *loco*

to drive one crazy (mad) — *volverle loco; sacarle de las casillas.*

She's driving me crazy (mad). *Me vuelve loco (Me saca de mis casillas).*

to go crazy — *volverse loco.*
He went crazy. *Se volvió loco.*

cream — *la crema*
to skim the cream — *escoger lo mejor.*
That research company skimmed the cream of the applicants. *Esa empresa de investigación escogía a los mejores candidatos.*

credit — *el crédito*
on credit — *a crédito; al fiado.*
We buy on credit. *Compramos a crédito (al fiado).*

to deserve credit for something — *tener que reconocer algo a alguien.*
He lost, but he deserves credit for his enormous dedication. *Perdió, pero hay que reconocerle su enorme dedicación.*

to do credit — *hacerle quedar bien; honrarle a uno.*
His generosity does him credit. *Su generosidad lo honra.*

to give credit — *dar mérito.*
You've got to give him a lot of credit. *Hay que darle mucho mérito.*

creeps — *el hormigueo*
to give one the creeps — *darle escalofríos.*
It gives me the creeps. *Me da escalofríos.*

crime — *el crimen*
Crime doesn't pay. — *No hay crimen sin castigo.*

crop — *la cosecha; la siega*
the pick of the crop — *lo mejor de lo mejor.*
Only the pick of the crop is accepted in the Special Forces. *Las Fuerzas Especiales sólo aceptan lo mejor de lo mejor.*

to cross — *cruzar*
to cross out — *tachar.*
He crossed out the last line. *Tachó la última línea.*

cross-country — *a campo traviesa*

to go cross-country — *ir (a) campo traviesa.*

They're going cross-country. *Van (a) campo traviesa.*

crow — *el cuervo*

as the crow flies — *a vuelo de pájaro.*

It's ten miles as the crow flies. *Está a diez millas a vuelo de pájaro.*

to make someone eat crow — *hacerle tragar saliva; hacerle sufrir la humillación.*

They made him eat crow. *Le hicieron tragar saliva (sufrir la humillación).*

to crow — *cacarear*

to crow over (or about) — *exultar; jactarse.*

Don't crow over yet — things may change. *No te jactes todavía: las cosas pueden cambiar.*

crush — *el aplastamiento*

to have a crush on — *estar encaprichado con; estar perdido por.*

She has a crush on her boss. *Está encaprichada con (Está perdida por) su jefe.*

to crush — *aplastar*

to be crushed by — *quedarse abrumado con.*

We were crushed by his death. *Nos quedamos abrumados con su muerte.*

crust — *la corteza*

the upper crust — *la alta sociedad.*

He likes to mix with the upper crust. *Le gusta mezclarse con la alta sociedad.*

cry — *el grito*

to be a far cry from — *distar mucho de ser.*

This is a far cry from what I expected. *Esto dista mucho de ser lo que esperaba.*

to cry — *gritar; llorar*

to cry out — *lanzar un grito.*

I cried out. *Lancé un grito.*

cucumber — *el pepino*

cool as a cucumber — *como si nada.*

He listened to the bad news cool as a cucumber. *Escuchó la mala noticia como si nada.*

cuff — *el puño*

to speak off the cuff — *hablar improvisado.*

She spoke off the cuff. *Habló improvisado.*

cup — *la taza*

not to be one's cup of tea — *no ser de su gusto.*

Baseball is not my cup of tea. *El béisbol no es de mi gusto.*

to cure — *curar*

What can't be cured must be endured. — *A lo hecho, pecho.*

custom — *la costumbre*

time-honored custom — *una costumbre consagrada por el tiempo; una costumbre venerable.*

Birthdays are a time-honored custom. *Los cumpleaños son una costumbre tradicional.*

to cut — *cortar*

cut and dried — *decidido de antemano.*

It was all cut and dried. *Todo fue decidido de antemano.*

to be cut out for — *tener talento para.*

He's not cut out to be an artist. *No tiene talento para ser artista.*

to cut away — *recortar.*

She cut the drawing away. *Recortó el dibujo.*

to cut class — *faltar a clase.*

He cut class. *Faltó a clase.*

to cut down — *reducir.*

We must cut expenses down. *Debemos reducir los gastos.*

to cut in — *interrumpir.*

She cut in on our conversation. *Interrumpió nuestra conversación.*

to cut off — *cortar.*

They cut off the end. *Cortaron el extremo.*

to cut off — *no dejar continuar.*

He was trying to tell a joke, but his wife cut him off. *Trataba de contar un chiste, pero su mujer no lo dejó continuar.*

to cut out — *dejar de.*

He cut out smoking. *Dejó de fumar.*

to cut (clip) out — *recortar.*

She cut out my picture from the newspaper. *Recortó mi retrato del periódico.*

to cut short — *interrumpir.*

He cut short his visit. *Interrumpió su visita.*

to cut through — *atajar por.*

Let's cut through this park. *Hagamos un atajo por el parque.*

to cut up — *cortar en pedazos.*

He cut up the melon. *Cortó en pedazos el melón.*

D

daisy — *la margarita*

to be pushing daisies — *estar muerto.*

He continued smoking and now he's pushing daisies. *Continuó fumando y ahora está muerto.*

dark — *oscuro*

to get dark — *hacerse de noche.*

I want to get there before it gets dark. *Quiero llegar antes que se haga de noche.*

to keep in the dark — *tener a obscuras.*

He kept her in the dark. *La tenía a obscuras.*

darling — *el predilecto*

to be . . . 's darling — *ser el ojo derecho de. . . .*

She's her father's darling. *Es el ojo derecho de su padre.*

date — *la fecha*

at an early date — *en fecha próxima.*

We'll decide at an early date. *Decidiremos en fecha próxima.*

double date — *la salida de a dos parejas.*

We went on a double date, but we all got bored. *Salimos de a dos parejas, pero nos aburrimos.*

out of date — *anticuado; pasado de moda.*

The book is out of date. *El libro es anticuado (pasado de moda)*

target date — *fecha fijada.*

The target date to finish the bridge is April 10. *La fecha fijada para terminar el puente es el 10 de abril.*

to be up to date — *estar al corriente; estar al tanto.*

He's up to date on everything. *Está al corriente (al tanto) de todo.*

to bring up to date (on) — *poner al corriente (al día) de.*

He brought us up to date on the issue. *Nos puso al corriente (al día) del problema.*

to date — *hasta la fecha.*

To date it hasn't been seen. *Hasta la fecha no se ha visto.*

---

to date — *datar*

to date — *salir con.*

He dates my sister. *Sale con mi hermana.*

to date back to — *remontar a; datar de.*

It dates back to the Middle Ages. *Remonta a (Data de) la Edad Media.*

---

dawn — *el alba*

at (the break of) dawn — *al rayar (romper) el alba (al amanecer).*

He got up at (the break of) dawn. *Se levantó al rayar (romper) el alba (al amanecer).*

to dawn on — *occurrírsele.*

Suddenly it dawned on me that she was lying. *De repente me di cuenta de que estaba mintiendo.*

day — *el día*

as plain as day — *tan claro como el agua.*

It's as plain as day. *Está tan claro como el agua.*

by the day — *día por día.*

He gets fatter by the day. *Se va engordando día por día.*

day in and day out — *día tras día.*

He swims day in and day out. *Nada día tras día.*

day-to-day — *cotidiano.*

His day-to-day activities are interesting. *Sus actividades cotidianas son interesantes.*

dog days — *la canícula.*

Dog-day nights in New York are unbearable. *En Nueva York las noches de verano más calientes son insoportables.*

for one's days to be numbered — *tener los días contados.*

His days are numbered. *Tiene los días contados.*

from day to day — *de día en día.*

We live from day to day. *Vivimos de día en día.*

if he (she) is a day — *por lo menos.*

She is forty-five, if she is a day. *Tiene cuarenta y cinco como mínimo.*

the good old days — *los buenos tiempos pasados.*

Cheap houses and obedient kids — those were the good old days. *Casas baratas y niños obedientes — esos eran los buenos tiempos pasados.*

this very day — *hoy mismo.*

I need it this very day. *Lo necesito hoy mismo.*

Those were the days! — *¡Qué tiempos aquellos!*

to call it a day — *dar el día por terminado.*

At 8:30 p.m. they called it a day. *A las ocho y media de la noche dieron el día por terminado.*

to carry the day — *triunfar; ganar.*

The Conservative Party carried the day in the election. *El Partido Conservador triunfó en la última elección.*

to have a day off — *tener un día libre.*

I've got a day off. *Tengo un día libre.*

to have a field day — *pasarlo bien.*

When the boss left, the workers had a field day. *Cuando el jefe se fue, los obreros lo pasaron en grande.*

to make one's day — *halagar.*

His good report about my performance made my day. *Su buen informe sobre mi desempeño me halagó muchísimo.*

to save for a rainy day — *guardar para un caso de emergencia.*

They are saving it for a rainy day. *Lo guardan para un caso de emergencia.*

to scare the daylights out of someone — *aterrorizar, aterrar a alguien.*

She scared the daylights out of her father when she jumped from a window. *Dio a su padre un susto de muerte cuando saltó desde una ventana.*

daylight — *la luz del día*

in broad daylight — *en pleno día.*

It happened in broad daylight. *Pasó en pleno día.*

dead — *muerto*

dead tired — *muerto de cansancio.*

He came home dead tired. *Llegó a casa muerto de cansancio.*

in the dead of winter — *en lo más frío del invierno.*

Even in the dead of winter he took a walk every day. *Hasta en lo más frío del invierno daba un paseo todos los días.*

to be dead set against — *oponerse decididamente.*

I'm dead set against it. *Me opongo decididamente.*

to be dead to the world — *estar profundamente dormido.*

He's dead to the world. *Está profundamente dormido.*

to play dead (to play possum) — *hacer(se) el muerto.*

He played dead (played possum). *(Se) hizo el muerto.*

deaf — *sordo*

to be stone deaf — *estar sordo como una tapia.*

He's stone deaf. *Está sordo como una tapia.*

deal — *el negocio*

a square deal — *trato equitativo.*

The Indian hasn't always had a square deal. *El indio no siempre ha tenido trato equitativo.*

big deal — *un asunto importante.*

This promotion is a big deal for me. *Este ascenso es algo muy importante para mí.*

Big deal! — *¡Tremenda cosa!*

by a good deal — *ni con mucho.*

He didn't achieve his goal by a good deal. *No realizó su fin, ni con mucho.*

It's a deal. — *Trato hecho.*

to get a raw deal — *jugarle una mala pasada.*

He got a raw deal. *Le jugaron una mala pasada.*

death — *la muerte*

a struggle to the death — *una lucha a muerte.*

It's a struggle to the death. *Es una lucha a muerte.*

to be at death's door — *estar en las últimas.*

They say that his father is at death's door. *Se dice que su padre está en las últimas.*

to beat to death — *matar a palos.*

They beat him to death. *Lo mataron a palos.*

to death — *sumamente; en extremo.*

I am tired to death. *Estoy muerto de cansancio.*

to put to death — *dar muerte.*

He was put to death by order of the king. *Fue ejecutado por orden del rey.*

wouldn't be caught dead — *ni aunque me (lo) maten.*

I wouldn't be caught dead in the Museum of Modern Art. *Yo no iría al Museo de Arte Moderno ni aunque me maten.*

decision — *la decisión*

to make a decision — *tomar una determinación (decisión).*

We must make a decision. *Tenemos que tomar una determinación (decisión).*

deck — *la cubierta*

to hit the deck — *levantarse (y ponerse a trabajar).*

When I worked for my uncle, I had to hit the deck at six every morning. *Cuando trabajaba para mi tío, tenía que levantarme a las seis todas las mañanas.*

degree — *el grado; el rango; la categoría*

by degrees — *paso a paso; gradualmente.*

Our love cooled off by degrees. *Nuestro amor fue enfriándose paso a paso.*

to a degree — *hasta cierto punto.*

Yes, I owe him my present position to a degree, but don't forget my significant academic background. *Sí, hasta cierto punto le debo mi presente cargo, pero no olvides mis considerables antecedentes académicos.*

delivery — *la entrega*

general delivery — *la lista de correos.*

His address is unknown; his parcels are sent to general delivery. *Su dirección se desconoce; sus encomiendas se envían a la lista de correos.*

home delivery — *servicio a domicilio.*

No home delivery. *No hacemos servicio a domicilio.*

to depend — *depender*

That depends. — *Según y conforme.*

to depend on — *depender de.*

It depends on you. *Depende de usted.*

depth — *la profundidad*

in depth — *a fondo.*

This contract must be studied in depth. *Este contrato debe estudiarse a fondo.*

description — *la descripción*

a blow-by-blow description — *una descripción con pelos y señales.*

He gave us a blow-by-blow description. *Nos dio una descripción con pelos y señales.*

desert — *el merecido*

to give someone his just deserts — *darle lo suyo.*

He gives each one his just deserts. *Da a cada cual lo suyo.*

despair — *la desesperación*

to sink into despair — *echarse a la desesperación.*

He sank into despair. *Se echó a la desesperación.*

detour — *el desvío*

to make a detour — *dar un rodeo.*

I made a detour. *Di un rodeo.*

devil — *el diablo*

between the devil and the deep blue sea — *entre la espada y la pared.*

I found myself between the devil and the deep blue sea. *Me encontré entre la espada y la pared.*

Speak of the devil. — *Hablando del ruin de Roma, luego asoma.*

there will be the devil to pay — *ahí será el diablo.*

If you do that there will be the devil to pay. *Si hace eso ahí será el diablo.*

to give the devil his due — *ser justo, hasta con el diablo.*

You've got to give the devil his due. *Hay que ser justo, hasta con el diablo.*

to raise the devil — *armar un alboroto.*

They went out and raised the devil. *Salieron y armaron un alboroto.*

to die — *morir*

to be dying to — *reventar de ganas de.*

He was dying to see that film. *Reventaba de ganas de ver esa película.*

to die away (down) — *desaparecer; cesar.*

The noise died away (down). *El ruido desapareció (cesó).*

to die out — *acabarse; apagarse.*

The fire died out. *El fuego se acabó (se apagó).*

die-hard — *intransigente*

die-hard — *empedernido.*

He's a die-hard Republican. *Es un republicano empedernido.*

difference — *la diferencia*

It makes no difference. — *Es igual; Lo mismo da.*

What difference does it make? — *¿Qué más da?*

difficulty — *la dificultad*

with utmost difficulty — *a duras penas.*

He reached it with utmost difficulty. *Lo alcanzó a duras penas.*

dig — *el codazo*

to take a dig at — *lanzar una sátira contra.*

He took a dig at the editor. *Lanzó una sátira contra el redactor.*

to dig — *cavar*

to dig in — *poner manos a la obra.*

We all had to dig in in order to finish it. *Todos tuvimos que poner manos a la obra para terminarlo.*

to dig up — *desenterrar.*

They dug up an old scandal. *Desenterraron un viejo escándalo.*

dime — *moneda de diez centavos*

to be a dime a dozen — *abundar como la mala hierba.*

These days English teachers are a dime a dozen. *Hoy en día los profesores de inglés abundan como la mala hierba.*

dint — *la fuerza*

by dint of — *a (en) fuerza de; a costa de.*

He learned it all by dint of studying. *Lo aprendió todo a (en) fuerza (a costa) de estudiar.*

dirt — *el polvo; la tierra*

pay dirt — *éxito; hallazgo.*

With that new line of products we finally hit pay dirt. *Con esa nueva línea de productos finalmente tuvimos éxito.*

discouraged — *desalentado*

to get discouraged — *caérsele las alas (del corazón).*

He got discouraged. *Se le cayeron las alas (del corazón).*

disguise — *el disfraz*

blessing in disguise — *algo inesperadamente positivo.*

Missing the plane was a blessing in disguise, because it crashed during takeoff. *Perder ese avión fue una bendición pues éste se estrelló al despegar.*

dish — *el plato*

to do the dishes — *lavar los platos.*

She does the dishes. *Lava los platos.*

dispense — *dispensar*

to dispense with — *prescindir de.*

Please, let's dispense with formalities. *Por favor, omitamos las formalidades.*

disposal — *la disposición*

to put at one's disposal — *poner a su disposición.*

I put myself at his disposal. *Me puse a su disposición.*

distance — *la distancia*

in the distance — *a lo lejos.*

They could be seen in the distance. *Se veían a lo lejos.*

district — *el distrito.*

red-light district — *barrio destinado a la prostitución.*

She wondered why her neighborhood was so noisy; then she found out it was the red-light district. *Se preguntaba por qué su barrio era tan vocinglero y luego se enteró que estaba en una zona de tolerancia.*

ditch — *la zanja*

to the last ditch — *hasta quemar el último cartucho.*

He'll fight to the last ditch. *Luchará hasta quemar el último cartucho.*

to do — *hacer*

and be done with it — *de una vez.*

Buy it and be done with it. *Cómprelo de una vez.*

easy does it — *con calma.*

Don't rush it, follow the instructions, easy does it. *No te apresures, sigue las instrucciones, hazlo con calma.*

How are you doing? — *¿Cómo le va?*

How do you do? — *Mucho gusto en conocerle.*

in doing so — *en consecuencia; debido a lo cual; por eso.*
He dove, and in doing so hit his head and nearly drowned. *Se zambulló, y como resultado se golpeó la cabeza y casi se ahoga.*

nothing doing — *de ninguna manera; ni soñarlo.*
You want to borrow this book? Nothing doing — you didn't return the last one. *¿Quieres tomar prestado ese libro? Ni pensarlo, pues no me has devuelto el último que te presté.*

That does it! — *¡No faltaba más!*
That does it! I'll never speak to her again. *¡No faltaba más! ¡Nunca volveré a hablarle!*

to do away with — *deshacerse de.*
They did away with the evidence. *Se deshicieron de la prueba.*

to do over — *volver a hacer.*
He did his work over. *Volvió a hacer su trabajo.*

to do well — *quedar bien; irle bien.*
How did you do? — I did very well. *¿Cómo te fue? — Me fue muy bien.*

to do with — *hacer de.*
What have you done with my sword? *¿Qué ha hecho de mi espada?*

to do without — *pasar(se) sin; prescindir de.*
He can't do without his coffee. *No puede pasar(se) sin (prescindir de) su café.*

dog — *perro*

Every dog has his day. — *A cada santo le llega su fiesta.*

Let sleeping dogs lie. — *Deje las cosas como son.*

to be the dog in the manger — *ser como el perro del hortelano.*
Give it to me if you don't want it. Don't be the dog in the manger. *Dámelo a mí si tú no lo quieres. No seas como el perro del hortelano.*

to go to the dogs — *echarse a perder.*
He's going to the dogs. *Se está echando a perder.*

to put on the dog — *darse tono (aires).*
He likes to put on the dog. *Le gusta darse tono (aires).*

top dog — *el gallito del lugar.*

Mr. Jiménez is (the) top dog around here. *El señor Jiménez es el gallito del lugar por aquí.*

You can't teach an old dog new tricks. — *No se puede conseguir que un viejo cambie de ideas.*

doghouse — *la perrera*

to be in the doghouse — *estar en desgracia.*

He came home drunk and now he's in the doghouse. *Llegó a casa borracho y ahora se ha desgraciado con su mujer.*

to doll — *engalanar*

to doll up — *engalanarse.*

She got all dolled up to go to the party. *Se engalanó para ir a la fiesta.*

domain — *el dominio; el campo de acción*

public domain — *la propiedad pública.*

That song is no longer copyrighted; it is in the public domain. *Esa canción ya no está protegida por los derechos de autor y es ahora propiedad pública.*

door — *la puerta*

next door — *al lado.*

Next door there's a doctor. *Al lado hay un médico.*

to darken one's door — *poner los pies en la casa.*

He never darkened my door again. *No volvió a poner los pies en mi casa.*

to show to the door (i.e., show out) — *despedir en la puerta.*

With his usual politeness, he showed me to the door. *Con la cortesía de siempre, me despidió en la puerta.*

to show to the door (i.e., throw out) — *pedir que salga.*

Offended by my actions, he showed me to the door. *Ofendido por mis acciones, me pidío que saliera.*

to slam the door — *dar un portazo.*

She slammed the door. *Dio un portazo.*

to slam the door in someone's face — *cerrarle (darle con) la puerta en las narices.*

She slammed the door in my face. *Me cerró (Me dio con) la puerta en las narices.*

doorstep — *el escalón de la puerta*

at one's doorstep — *a la puerta de la casa.*

He's very old, and Death is already at his doorstep. — *Está muy viejo y la Muerte ya espera a la puerta de su casa.*

dot — *el punto*

on the dot — *en punto.*

They left at six on the dot. *Salieron a las seis en punto.*

double — *el doble*

on the double — *inmediatamente.*

I want that report on the double! *¡Quiero ese informe de inmediato!*

to double back — *volver atrás.*

After getting to the city, we doubled back to the farm. *Después de llegar a la ciudad, volvimos a la granja.*

doubt — *la duda*

beyond the shadow of a doubt — *sin sombra de duda.*

He is the guilty one beyond the shadow of a doubt. *El es el culpable sin sombra de duda.*

no doubt — *sin duda.*

He's no doubt right. *Sin duda tiene razón.*

to be in doubt — *estar en duda.*

The outcome is in doubt. *El resultado está en duda.*

to cast doubt on — *poner en duda.*

They cast doubt on her conduct. *Pusieron en duda su conducta.*

down — *abajo*

deep down — *en el fondo.*

Deep down, we all fear health examinations. *En el fondo, todos tememos a los exámenes de salud.*

to be down and out — *no tener donde caerse muerto.*

She's down and out. *No tiene donde caerse muerta.*

to get down to work — *ponerse a trabajar; aplicarse al trabajo.*
He got down to work. *Se puso a trabajar (Se aplicó al trabajo).*

when it comes right down to it — *a la hora de la verdad.*
When it came right down to it, he refused to accept. *A la hora de la verdad no quiso aceptar.*

downcast — *abatido; deprimido*

to be downcast — *estar abatido.*
He's been downcast since she left him. *Ha estado abatido desde que ella lo dejó.*

downhill — *cuesta abajo*

to be downhill all the way — *ser cosa de coser y cantar (ser cuesta abajo).*
Our work will be downhill all the way. *Nuestro trabajo será cosa de coser y cantar (será cuesta abajo).*

to go downhill — *ir de capa caída.*
She's been going downhill lately. *Va de capa caída últimamente.*

to drag — *arrastrar*

to drag off — *llevarse a rastras.*
They dragged her off. *Se la llevaron a rastras.*

drain — *el desaguadero*

brain drain — *la pérdida de profesionales debido a su emigración.*
The brain drain from undeveloped nations is terrible. *La pérdida de profesionales por emigración es grave en los países subdesarrollados.*

to go down the drain — *no servir de nada.*
All our efforts have gone down the drain. *Todos nuestros esfuerzos no han servido de nada.*

to draw — *extraer; tirar; dibujar*

to draw someone out — *sonsacarle.*
They couldn't draw him out. *No pudieron sonsacarle.*

to draw up — *preparar.*
I drew up a plan. *Preparé un plan.*

to dress — *vestirse*

to dress down — *echar un rapapolvo.*

He dressed me down for arriving late. *Me echó un rapapolvo por haber llegado tarde.*

to dress in — *vestirse de.*

She dresses in velvet. *Se viste de terciopelo.*

drib — *corrupción de* **drip:** la gota

dribs and drabs — *en cantidades pequeñas.*

A freelancer's income comes in dribs and drabs. *El ingreso de un trabajador independiente llega en pequeñas cantidades.*

drink — *la bebida; el trago*

soft drink — *el refresco; la bebida no alcohólica.*

Water is healthier than all those soft drinks. *El agua es más saludable que todos esos refrescos.*

to drink — *beber*

to drink to something — *estar de acuerdo con alguien.*

So you think that our government is lying? I'll drink to that. *¿Así que opina que nuestro gobierno está mintiendo? Estoy totalmente de acuerdo.*

to drive — *conducir, manejar*

drive-in — *con servicio para automovilistas.*

Here's a drive-in restaurant. *Aquí hay un restaurante con servicio en coche.*

to drive at — *querer decir.*

We didn't know what he was driving at. *No sabíamos lo que quería decir.*

to drive away — *irse, partir en coche.*

She drove away in her blue car and we never saw her again. *Se fue en su coche azul y nunca la volvimos a ver.*

to drive back — *hacer retroceder; rechazar.*

We drove the enemy back six miles. *Hicimos retroceder seis millas al enemigo.*

to drive by — *pasar por en coche.*

They drove by our neighborhood. *Pasaron por nuestro barrio en auto.*

to drive from — *echar.*

The Germans were driven from France. *Los alemanes fueron rechazados de Francia.*

to drive on — *seguir avanzando.*

Despite the rain, he drove on. *Pese a la lluvia, siguió manejando.*

to drive (one) crazy — *sacar(le) de sus casillas.*

Her way of talking drives me crazy. *Su manera de hablar me saca de mis casillas.*

to drive through — *atravesar.*

We drove through a beautiful forest. *Atravesamos un hermoso bosque en el auto.*

driver — *el conductor*

a hit-and-run driver — *un automovilista que se da a la fuga.*

He was run over by a hit-and-run driver. *Fue atropellado por un automovilista que se dio a la fuga.*

to drop — *dejar caer*

name-dropper — *persona que desea impresionar mencionando nombres de personas famosas.*

That name-dropper boasts of having known six presidents. *Esa trata de impresionar alardeando que conoció a seis presidentes.*

to drop a line — *poner unas líneas.*

We dropped him a line. *Le pusimos unas líneas.*

to drop in on — *visitar inesperadamente.*

The neighbors dropped in on us last night. *Los vecinos nos visitaron inesperadamente anoche.*

to drop out — *dejar de asistir.*

He dropped out of my class. *Dejó de asistir a mi clase.*

drunk — *borracho*

to get dead drunk — *emborracharse a muerte.*

We got dead drunk. *Nos emborrachamos a muerte.*

to dry — *secar*

to dry out — *secarse.*

This shirt will never dry out. *Esta camisa no se secará nunca.*

to dry up — *secarse.*

The field dried up. *El campo se secó.*

duck — *el pato*

lame duck — *político que no ha sido reelegido y que está por terminar su período.*

Pedrero is a lame duck, so to ask him to fight for that proposal is a waste of time. *Pedrero no ha sido reelegido y pronto se irá, así que pedirle que luche por esa proposición es una pérdida de tiempo.*

to be a dead duck — *estar listo (quedar frito).*

I'm a dead duck if my brother finds out about it. *Estoy listo (Quedo frito) si lo llega a saber mi hermano.*

dumbfounded — *atónito, pasmado*

to be dumbfounded — *perder el habla.*

When we saw him dressed as a clown, we were dumbfounded. *Al verle vestido de payaso perdimos el habla.*

dust — *el polvo*

to bite the dust — *morder el polvo.*

He bit the dust. *Mordió el polvo.*

Dutch — *holandés*

to go Dutch — *pagar cada uno lo suyo.*

We went Dutch. *Cada uno pagó lo suyo.*

duty — *el deber*

heavy duty — *de servicio pesado.*

Those are heavy-duty pants! *¡Esos pantalones son de batalla!*

to be on duty — *estar de servicio (de turno).*

She's on duty. *Está de servicio (de turno).*

to report for duty — *acudir al trabajo.*

He reports for duty at eight. *Acude a su trabajo a las ocho.*

to shirk one's duty — *faltar a las obligaciones.*
He shirked his duty. *Faltó a sus obligaciones.*

E

eager — *ansioso*

to be eager to — *tener empeño (interés) en; estar ansioso de.*
He's eager to learn. *Tiene empeño (interés) en (Está ansioso de) aprender.*

earnest — *seriedad; empeño*

in earnest — *en serio; de veras.*
He started studying math in earnest. *Empezó a estudiar matemáticas en serio.*

ear — *el oído, la oreja*

by ear — *al (de) oído.*
She plays by ear. *Toca al (de) oído.*

to be all ears — *ser todo oídos; abrir los oídos.*
It's a good idea to be all ears when they're explaining things like that. *Es conveniente ser todo oídos (abrir los oídos) cuando están explicando cosas así.*

to have someone's ear — *tener influencia con. . .*
I don't have the president's ear. *No tengo influencia con el presidente.*

to play by ear — *tocar de oído.*
He plays the piano by ear. *Toca el piano de oído.*

to prick up one's ears — *aguzar el oído (los oídos).*
When he heard her voice, he pricked up his ears. *Al oír su voz, aguzó el oído (los oídos).*

to talk one's ear off — *hablar hasta por los codos.*
He talks your ear off. *Habla hasta por los codos.*

to turn a deaf ear — *hacerse (el) sordo.*
He turned a deaf ear. *Se hizo (el) sordo.*

up to one's ears — *hasta los ojos.*

I'm up to my ears in work. *Estoy hasta los ojos en trabajo.*

earth — *la tierra*

how on earth — *cómo diablos.*

How on earth did you do it? *¿Cómo diablos lo hizo?*

to come down to earth — *bajar de las nubes.*

He wouldn't come down to earth. *No quería bajar de las nubes.*

ease — *la tranquilidad, la comodidad*

to be (ill) at ease — *estar a (dis)gusto.*

I'm never (ill) at ease in this atmosphere. *Nunca estoy a (dis)gusto en este ambiente.*

easy — *fácil*

Easy come, easy go. — *Lo que el agua trae el agua lleva.*

to make things easy — *dar toda clase de facilidades.*

He made things easy for them. *Les dio toda clase de facilidades.*

to take it easy — *descansar.*

Take it easy for a few days. *Descanse por unos días.*

to eat — *comer*

to eat out — *comer en un restaurante.*

We ate out last night. *Comimos en un restaurante anoche.*

What's eating you? — *¿Qué mosca le ha picado?*

edge — *el borde*

to be on edge — *estar nervioso.*

Everyone is on edge. *Todo el mundo está nervioso.*

to have the edge on someone — *llevarle la ventaja.*

She has the edge on me. *Me lleva la ventaja.*

to set one's teeth on edge — *darle dentera.*

It sets my teeth on edge. *Me da dentera.*

to edge — *avanzar de lado*

to edge in — *abrir paso poco a poco.*

We were able to edge in. *Pudimos abrir paso poco a poco.*

effect — *el efecto*

in effect — *en pie; en vigor.*

It is still in effect. *Sigue en pie (en vigor).*

to go into effect — *entrar en vigor.*

It went into effect yesterday. *Entró en vigor ayer.*

to have a bad effect — *hacer mal efecto.*

It has a bad effect on them. *Les hace mal efecto.*

egg — *el huevo*

a nest egg — *los ahorros.*

He has quite a nest egg in the bank. *Tiene muchos ahorros en el banco.*

to lay an egg — *fracasar completamente.*

He sure laid an egg with that opera. *Por cierto que su ópera fue un fracaso total.*

to put all one's eggs in one basket — *jugarlo todo a una carta.*

He put all his eggs in one basket. *Lo jugó todo a una carta.*

to walk on eggs — *conducirse con extremo cuidado.*

He walked on eggs for several months at his new job. *Por varios meses anduvo con enorme cuidado en su nuevo trabajo.*

elbow — *el codo*

to rub elbows with — *rozarse mucho (tratar) con.*

He rubs elbows with lawyers. *Se roza mucho (trata) con abogados.*

to elbow — *codear*

to elbow one's way through — *abrirse paso a codazos.*

They had to elbow their way through. *Tuvieron que abrirse paso a codazos.*

element — *el elemento*

to be in one's element — *estar en su elemento.*

When it's a question of dancing the tango, they're in their element. *Cuando es cuestión de bailar el tango, están en su elemento.*

elephant — *el elefante*

white elephant — *posesión que trae más problemas que ventajas.*

The Bugatti has style, but it is so expensive and the insurance is so high that it's really a white elephant. *El Bugatti tiene gran estilo, pero es tan caro y el seguro es tan elevado que realmente no vale la pena.*

---

eleventh — *undécimo*

eleventh-hour — *de la última hora.*

It was an eleventh-hour decision. *Fue una decisión de la última hora.*

---

else — *otro; diferente; más*

. . . or else — *. . . o si no ya verás.*

You'll be here at 11 or else. *Estarás aquí a las 11, o si no ya verás.*

---

end — *el fin*

at the end of — *al cabo (fin) de.*

At the end of one hour, it was over. *Al cabo (fin) de una hora, se terminó.*

at the end of nowhere — *en el quinto infierno.*

They live at the end of nowhere. *Viven en el quinto infierno.*

no end of — *un sin fin (la mar) de.*

He has no end of problems. *Tiene un sin fin (la mar) de problemas.*

to be on the receiving end — *ser el blanco de algo.*

She was upset at him for being on the receiving end of all his jokes. *Estaba abochornada por haberse convertido en el blanco de todos sus chistes.*

to bring to an end — *dar fin a.*

The storm brought the outing to an end. *La tormenta dio fin al paseo.*

to come to a bad end — *acabar mal.*

He came to a bad end. *Acabó mal.*

to come to an end — *acabarse.*

The dispute came to an end. *La disputa se acabó.*

to come to an untimely end — *tener un final inesperado.*

His life came to an untimely end. *Su vida tuvo un final inesperado.*

to make (both) ends meet — *pasar con lo que se tiene.*

It's hard to make (both) ends meet. *Es difícil pasar con lo que se tiene.*

to put an end to — *acabar con.*
They put an end to their quarrels. *Acabaron con sus peleas.*

to the bitter end — *hasta la muerte.*
He struggled to the bitter end. *Luchó hasta la muerte.*

to end — *terminar*
to end up by — *acabar (terminar) por.*
They ended up by getting married. *Acabaron (terminaron) por casarse.*

Where will it all end? — *¿Dónde va a parar?*

English — *el inglés*
in plain English — *sin rodeos.*
He told it to her in plain English. *Se lo dijo sin rodeos.*

to enjoy — *gozar*
to enjoy oneself — *pasarlo bien.*
Enjoy yourself. *Que lo pase bien.*

enough — *bastante, suficiente*
Enough is enough! — *¡Basta ya!*

It's enough to make you cry (laugh). — *Es para llorar (reír).*
not to be enough — *no alcanzar.*
There isn't enough money. *No alcanza el dinero.*
to be enough — *bastar.*
Seeing it once is enough for me. *Me basta con verlo una vez.*

to be more than enough — *sobrar.*
There's more than enough water. *Sobra agua.*

envy — *la envidia*
green with envy — *muerto de envidia.*
She was green with envy when she saw my ring. *Quedó muerta de envidia al ver mi anillo.*

equal — *igual*
to be equal to — *estar a la altura de.*
I'm not equal to this task. *No estoy a la altura de esta tarea.*

equally — *igualmente*

to treat equally — *tratar por igual.*

They treat us equally. *Nos tratan por igual.*

errand — *recado, mandado*

to run an errand — *hacer un mandado.*

He's running an errand for his father. *Está haciendo un mandado por su padre.*

to send on an errand — *enviar a un recado.*

She sent me on an errand. *Me envió a un recado.*

estate — *la propiedad; los bienes*

real estate — *bienes raíces o inmuebles.*

He is a real estate agent. *Es un vendedor de bienes raíces.*

eve — *la víspera*

to be on the eve of — *estor en vísperas de.*

He was on the eve of his promotion to colonel. *Estaba en vísperas de su ascenso a coronel.*

even — *aun, hasta; igualmente, con uniformidad*

even so — *con todo (así y todo).*

Even so, we have the best there is. *Con todo (Así y todo) tenemos lo mejor que hay.*

not even — *ni siquiera.*

Not even the water was good. *Ni siquiera el agua era buena.*

to be even — *estar en paz.*

We're even. *Estamos en paz.*

to break even — *ni ganar ni perder.*

They broke even. *Ni ganaron ni perdieron.*

to get even with — *pagársela.*

I'll get even with them. *Me la pagarán.*

event — *el suceso*

in any event — *en todo caso; de todas maneras.*

In any event we'll do everything possible. *En todo caso (De todas maneras) haremos todo lo posible.*

ever — *jamás*

better than ever — *mejor que nunca.*

I feel better than ever. *Me siento mejor que nunca.*

ever since — *desde entonces.*

He's been cold ever since. *Desde entonces ha tenido frío.*

ever since — *desde que.*

Ever since she found out the truth, she refuses to visit us. *Desde que supo la verdad, se niega a visitarnos.*

forever and ever — *para siempre jamás.*

They've left forever and ever. *Se han marchado para siempre jamás.*

if ever — *si alguna vez.*

If ever you come to México, visit us. *Si alguna vez viene a México, visítenos.*

if ever there was one — *nadie como él (ella, ellos, ellas, eso, esos).*

Johnson was a politician, if ever there was one. *Nunca hubo un político del calibre de Johnson.*

What ever do you want? — *¿Qué más quieres?*

every — *cada*

every other . . . — *un . . . sí y otro no.*

We go every other day. *Vamos un día sí y otro no.*

evil — *malo*

evil-minded — *mal pensado.*

He's evil-minded. *Es mal pensado.*

the root of all evil — *la causa de todos los males.*

Some say that the root of all evil is human ambition. *Algunos dicen que la causa de todos los males es la ambición humana.*

examination — *el examen*

competitive examination — *el concurso.*

The competitive examination for that post was hard. *El concurso para obtener ese puesto fue difícil.*

example — *el ejemplo*

to set an example — *servir de (dar) ejemplo.*

She sets an example for her daughters. *Sirve de (Da) ejemplo a sus hijas.*

excess — *el exceso*

to excess — *en demasía.*

He drank to excess. *Tomaba en demasía.*

exchange — *el cambio*

in exchange for — *a cambio de.*

I gave him my watch in exchange for his lighter. *Le di mi reloj a cambio de su encendedor.*

excuse — *la excusa*

to use as an excuse — *tomar de pretexto.*

She used it as an excuse to miss class. *Lo tomó de pretexto para faltar a la clase.*

to excuse — *excusar*

excuse me — *con permiso.*

Excuse me. I have to leave. *Con permiso. Tengo que marcharme.*

excuse me — *perdone.*

Excuse me! I didn't see you. *¡Perdone! No lo vi.*

expected — *esperado*

when least expected — *el día menos pensado; cuando menos se piense.*

It will arrive when least expected. *Llegará el día menos pensado (cuando menos se piense).*

expense — *el gasto*

at the expense of — *a expensas (costa) de.*

He won at the expense of his friends. *Ganó a expensas (costa) de sus compañeros.*

to go to the expense — *meterse en gastos.*

He didn't want to go to the expense. *No quiso meterse en gastos.*

to expose — *exhibir; mostrar*

to be exposed as — *pasar por; quedar como.*

Thanks to that document, he was exposed as a liar. *Gracias a ese documento, quedó como mentiroso.*

extent — *el grado*

to a great extent — *en gran parte.*

To a great extent it is due to his good health. *Se debe en gran parte a su buena salud.*

to some extent — *hasta cierto punto.*

To some extent, that is true. *Hasta cierto punto es verdad.*

to such an extent — *a tal punto.*

It irritated him to such an extent that he refused to go. *Lo molestó a tal punto que se negó a ir.*

eye — *el ojo*

in the public eye — *en la escena (a la luz) pública.*

He is no longer in the public eye. *Ya no está en la escena (a la luz) pública.*

There is more to it than meets the eye. — *La cosa tiene más miga de lo que parece.*

to catch one's eye — *captarle la atención.*

She caught my eye. *Me captó la atención.*

to cry one's eyes out — *llorar a mares.*

She cried her eyes out. *Lloró a mares.*

to have an eye for — *tener mucha vista para.*

She has an eye for beauty. *Tiene mucha vista para la belleza.*

to keep an eye on — *vigilar a.*

Keep an eye on that kid. *Vigile a ese chico.*

to keep one's eyes peeled — *tener los ojos abiertos.*

Keep your eyes peeled. *Tenga los ojos abiertos.*

to lay eyes on — *echar la vista encima.*

He never laid eyes on them again. *Nunca volvió a echarles la vista encima.*

to raise one's eyes — *levantar la vista.*

She didn't raise her eyes. *No levantó la vista.*

to see eye to eye — *estar de acuerdo.*

We don't see eye to eye on anything. *No estamos de acuerdo en nada.*

to turn a blind eye — *hacer la vista gorda.*

I saw it but turned a blind eye. *Lo vi pero hice la vista gorda.*

without batting an eye — *sin pestañear.*

He lied without batting an eye. *Mintió sin pestañear.*

eyeball — *el globo del ojo*

eyeball to eyeball — *cara a cara.*

Kennedy and Khruschev argued that subject eyeball to eyeball. *Kennedy y Jruschov discutieron ese tema cara a cara.*

eyebrow — *la ceja*

to raise eyebrows — *provocar sorpresa.*

His red socks raised eyebrows at the office. *Sus calcetines rojos causaron sorpresa en la oficina.*

eyelid — *el párpado*

not to bat an eyelid — *impasible; sin pestañear.*

He saw the explosion but didn't bat an eyelid. *Vio la explosión y ni siquiera pestañeó.*

F

face — *la cara*

face down — *boca abajo.*

He fell face down. *Se cayó boca abajo.*

face to face — *frente a frente; cara a cara.*

They discussed it face to face. *Lo discutieron frente a frente (cara a cara).*

face up — *boca arriba.*

They found him face up. *Lo encontraron boca arriba.*

in the face — *a la cara.*

They look each other in the face. *Se miran a la cara.*

in the face of . . . — *frente a . . .*
He was brave in the face of death. *Fue valiente frente a la muerte.*

on the face of it — *a juzgar por las apariencias.*
On the face of it, I can't accept it. *A juzgar por las apariencias, no lo puedo aceptar.*

right to one's face — *en la cara.*
I told him right to his face. *Se lo dije en la cara.*

to fall flat on one's face — *caer de bruces.*
I fell flat on my face. *Caí de bruces.*

to get red in the face — *subírsele el pavo; ruborizarse.*
She got red in the face. *Se le subió el pavo (Se ruborizó).*

to keep a straight face — *contener la risa.*
She couldn't keep a straight face. *No pudo contener la risa.*

to lose face — *sufrir una pérdida de prestigio.*
They lost face in that deal. *Sufrieron una pérdida de prestigio en ese negocio.*

to make a face — *hacer una mueca.*
She tasted it and made a face. *Lo probó e hizo una mueca.*

to make an about-face — *cambiar de opinión (decisión).*
He made an about-face. *Cambió de opinión (decisión).*

to save face — *salvar las apariencias.*
He saved face by paying the fine. *Salvó las apariencias pagando la multa.*

to show one's face — *asomar la cara*
She wouldn't show her face. *No quería asomar la cara.*

---

to face — *encararse con*

to face — *dar (frente) a.*
It faces the river. *Da (frente) al río.*

to face (up to) it — *hacer frente a la situación (a las consecuencias).*
There's so much to do I can't face (up to) it. *Hay tanto que hacer que no puedo hacer frente a la situación (a las consecuencias).*

fact — *el hecho*

in fact — *en efecto.*

He'll be here soon. In fact, he's coming tomorrow. *Estará aquí muy pronto. En efecto viene mañana.*

to get down to the facts — *ir al asunto.*

Let's get down to the facts. *Vamos al asunto.*

to know for a fact — *saber a ciencia cierta.*

I know for a fact that he is a spy. *Estoy totalmente seguro de que él es un espía.*

---

fail — *la falta*

fail-safe — *autoprotectivo.*

The power plant has fail-safe systems everywhere. *La central eléctrica está llena de sistemas autoprotectivos.*

without fail — *sin falta.*

Come tomorrow without fail. *Venga mañana sin falta.*

---

to fail — *faltar a; dejar de*

to fail to — *dejar de.*

Don't fail to see it. *No deje de verlo.*

to fail to show up for — *faltar a.*

He failed to show up for the appointment. *Faltó a la cita.*

---

fair — *justo*

fair and square — *con absoluta honradez.*

He treated us fair and square. *Nos trató con absoluta honradez.*

---

faith — *la fe*

in good (bad) faith — *de buena (mala) fe.*

He did it in good (bad) faith. *Lo hizo de buena (mala) fe.*

to pin one's faith on — *tener puesta la esperanza en.*

She had pinned her faith on graduating. *Tenía puesta su esperanza en graduarse.*

to fall — *caer*

to fall apart — *deshacerse.*

The club has fallen apart. *El club se ha deshecho.*

to fall behind — *retrasarse.*

I have fallen behind in my studies. *Me he retrasado en mis estudios.*

to fall flat — *fracasar.*

His report fell flat. *Su informe fracasó.*

to fall for — *prendarse de.*

He fell for her. *Se prendó de ella.*

to fall for — *tragar(se).*

Nobody's going to fall for a lie like that. *Nadie va a tragar(se) una mentira así.*

to fall in love with — *enamorarse de.*

He fell in love with his teacher. *Se enamoró de su maestra.*

to fall off — *caerse de.*

He fell off the ladder. *Se cayó de la escalera.*

to fall off — *disminuir.*

The quality of his work is falling off. *La calidad de su trabajo está disminuyendo.*

to fall short — *no llegar a ser.*

It fell short of being a masterpiece. *No llegó a ser una obra maestra.*

to fall through — *fracasar.*

Our plans fell through. *Nuestros planes fracasaron.*

falling-out — *la riña*

to have a falling-out — *reñirse con.*

I've had a falling-out with her. *Me he reñido con ella.*

fan — *el aficionado*

to be a fan of — *ser aficionado a.*

He's a movie fan. *Es aficionado al cine.*

fancy — *la fantasía*

to strike one's fancy — *encapricharse de.*

The new styles have struck her fancy. *Se ha encaprichado de las nuevas modas.*

to take a fancy to — *prendarse de.*

He took a fancy to his secretary. *Se prendó de su secretaria.*

far — *lejos*

as far as one knows — *que sepa uno.*

As far as we know, it's not true. *Que sepamos nosotros, no es verdad.*

by far — *con mucho.*

It's by far the cheapest. *Es con mucho el más barato.*

far and near — *en (por) todas partes.*

He has traveled far and near. *Ha viajado en (por) todas partes.*

Far from it! — *¡Ni mucho menos! (¡Ni con mucho!).*

far into the night — *hasta las altas horas de la noche.*

We studied far into the night. *Estudiamos hasta las altas horas de la noche.*

far-out — *muy avanzado, novedoso, especial.*

What a far-out outfit! *¡Qué traje tan novedoso!*

so far — *en lo que va de.*

So far this winter it hasn't snowed. *En lo que va de invierno no ha nevado.*

thus far — *hasta ahora; hasta aquí.*

Thus far we haven't seen anybody. *Hasta aquí no hemos visto a nadie.*

to come from far and wide — *venir de todas partes.*

They came from far and wide. *Vinieron de todas partes.*

to come from far away — *venir de lejos.*

They come from far away. *Vienen de lejos.*

to go far — *ir lejos.*

With all that talent, he'll go far. *Con tanto talento irá lejos.*

farther — *más lejos*

farther on — *más allá.*

It's farther on. *Está más allá.*

fashion — *la moda*

after a fashion — *a su modo.*

He described it after a fashion. *Lo describió a su modo.*

to go out of fashion — *pasar de moda.*

They went out of fashion. *Pasaron de moda.*

fashionable — *elegante*

to become fashionable — *ponerse de moda.*

They became fashionable last year. *Se pusieron de moda el año pasado.*

fast — *rápido; firme*

to hold fast — *mantenerse firme.*

He held fast in his decision. *Se mantuvo firme en su decisión.*

to play fast and loose — *proceder sin miramientos.*

They played fast and loose with their business deals and got the attention of the IRS. *No se anduvieron con muchas contemplaciones en sus negocios y se ganaron la atención de Impuestos Internos.*

to pull a fast one — *engañar.*

He pulled a fast one on us. *Nos engañó.*

fat — *la grasa*

The fat is in the fire. — *El mal ya está hecho; La cosa ya no tiene remedio.*

to live off the fat of the land — *nadar en la abundancia.*

They are living off the fat of the land. *Nadan en la abundancia.*

fate — *el hado, la suerte*

to leave to one's fate — *dejar a su suerte.*

I left him to his fate. *Lo dejé a su suerte.*

fault — *la culpa*

to a fault — *excesivamente; exageradamente.*

Bill is punctual to a fault — sometimes he waits outside just to arrive precisely on time. *Bill es excesivamente puntual — a veces espera afuera sólo para llegar justo a tiempo.*

to be at fault — *ser el culpable; tener la culpa.*

He's at fault. *Es el culpable (Tiene la culpa).*

to find fault with — *criticar; encontrar defectos en.*

He finds fault with all I do. *Critica (Encuentra defectos en) todo lo que hago.*

favor — *el favor*

in one's favor — *a su favor.*

It was decided in my favor. *Se decidió a mi favor.*

feather — *la pluma*

It's a feather in his cap. — *Se ha apuntado un tanto; Es un triunfo personal.*

feature — *la característica*

redeeming feature — *la buena cualidad; el punto a su favor.*

He's nasty and boring, but generosity is his redeeming feature. *Es desagradable y aburrido, pero su buena cualidad es que es generoso.*

fed — *alimentado*

to be fed up with — *estar harto de; estar hasta la coronilla de.*

I'm fed up with this. *Estoy harto (hasta la coronilla) de esto.*

feed — *el alimento*

chicken feed — *una insignificancia; dinero menudo.*

All I have left is chicken feed. *Todo lo que me queda es una insignificancia (dinero menudo).*

to feel — *sentir*

to feel bad — *sentirse apenado.*

He feels bad because he failed. *Se siente apenado por haber salido mal.*

to feel for someone — *compadecer a alguien.*

I feel for him — he's very sick. *Lo compadezco — está muy enfermo.*

to feel free — *no vacilar.*

Feel free to let me know if I can help you. *No vacile en avisarme si puedo ayudarlo.*

to feel like — *tener ganas de.*

I feel like sleeping. *Tengo ganas de dormir.*

feelings — *la sensibilidad*

hard feelings — *rencor.*

He left with hard feelings. — *Salió con rencor.*

for one's feelings to be hurt — *estar muy sentido.*
My feelings are hurt. *Estoy muy sentido.*

mixed feelings — *reacciones diversas.*
His talk was received with mixed feelings. *Su charla fue acogida con reacciones diversas.*

to hurt one's feelings — *ofenderle.*
She hurt our feelings. *Nos ofendió.*

---

fence — *la cerca, la valla*

to be on the fence — *estar indeciso; no querer comprometerse.*
I don't know whether they're going to be on our side; they're still on the fence. *No se si van a ponerse de nuestra parte; todavía están indecisos.*

to mend one's fences — *recuperar su prestigio o renombre.*
He made a racist comment and now he's trying to mend his fences with the public. *Hizo un comentario racista y ahora está tratando de recuperar la confianza del público.*

---

fiddle — *el violín*

to be as fit as a fiddle — *estar de buena salud.*
He's as fit as a fiddle. *Está de buena salud.*

to play second fiddle — *hacer el papel de segundón.*
He has to play second fiddle. *Tiene que hacer el papel de segundón.*

---

to fiddle — *tocar el violín*

to fiddle with — *jugar nerviosamente con.*
She was fiddling with her ring. *Jugaba nerviosamente son su anillo.*

---

fifty — *cincuenta*

to go fifty-fifty — *ir a medias.*
Let's go fifty-fifty. *Vamos a medias.*

---

figure — *la figura*

to cut a fine figure — *causar una buena impresión.*
He always cuts a fine figure. *Siempre causa una buena impresión.*

---

to figure — *figurar*

it figures — *se comprende; es de suponer.*

After his behavior last night, it figures that she'll never see him again. *Después de su comportamiento anoche, es de suponer que ella no volverá a verlo.*

to figure on — *contar con.*

Let's figure on going. *Contemos con que vamos.*

to figure out — *entender.*

I can't figure out what he said. *No entiendo lo que dijo.*

to figure up (out) — *calcular.*

Figure up (out) what I owe you. *Calcule cuánto le debo.*

---

file — *la fila*

in single file — *en fila india.*

They advanced in single file. *Avanzaron en fila india.*

on file — *archivado.*

I have it on file. *Lo tengo archivado.*

---

fill — *el hartazgo*

to have one's fill of — *hartarse de.*

I've had my fill of this. *Me he hartado de esto.*

---

to fill — *llenar*

to fill in (out) — *llenar.*

Fill in (out) this form. *Llene este formulario.*

to fill in for — *suplir.*

They filled in for us during the meeting. *Nos suplieron durante la reunión.*

to fill the gap — *llenar un vacío.*

It fills the gap. *Llena un vacío.*

---

to find — *encontrar*

to find out — *saber; enterarse de.*

He found out that she was married. *Supo (Se enteró de) que ella estaba casada.*

finder — *el hallador*

Finders keepers, losers weepers. — *Quien fue a Sevilla perdió su silla.*

fine — *bueno*

fine and dandy — *excelente.*

All this is fine and dandy, but where is the money? *Todo esto está muy bien, ¿pero dónde está el dinero?*

fine — *delgado*

to cut it fine — *no dejar margen de tiempo.*

You cut it too fine with the train departure, and you lost it. *No dejaste ningún margen de tiempo con el tren y lo perdiste.*

finger — *el dedo*

to get one's fingers burnt — *pillarse los dedos.*

He got his fingers burnt. *Se pilló los dedos.*

to lay a finger on — *poner la mano encima.*

Don't lay a finger on my child. *No le ponga la mano encima a mi hijo.*

not to lift a finger — *no querer hacer nada.*

He didn't lift a finger. *No quiso hacer nada.*

to slip through one's fingers — *escapársele de las manos.*

I let it slip through my fingers. *Lo dejé escapárseme de las manos.*

to wrap (twist) . . . around one's little finger — *manejar a . . . a su antojo.*

He wraps (twists) his mother around his little finger. *Maneja a su madre a su antojo.*

fire — *el fuego*

to catch fire — *incendiarse.*

The house caught fire. *La casa se incendió.*

to open fire — *abrir fuego.*

They opened fire. *Abrieron fuego.*

to set fire to — *prender (pegar) fuego a.*

They set fire to the building. *Prendieron (Pegaron) fuego al edificio.*

to fire — *disparar, hacer fuego; despedir*

Fire away! — *¡Dispare!*

first — *primero*

at first — *al (en un) principio.*

At first, I accepted it. *Al (En un) principio lo acepté.*

first and foremost — *ante todo.*

First and foremost, we must try harder. *Ante todo tenemos que esforzarnos más.*

First come, first served. — *Servirán primero a los que lleguen primero.*

to come first — *ser lo primero.*

His work comes first. *Su trabajo es lo primero.*

fish — *el pez*

neither fish nor fowl — *ni lo uno ni lo otro.*

With those Louis XV chairs and Tiffany lamps the room's style is neither fish nor fowl. *Con esas sillas Luis XV y lámparas Tiffany, el estilo del cuarto no es ni chicha ni limonada.*

fit — *el ajuste; el ataque*

by fits and starts — *a rachas; a empujones; sin regularidad.*

He always works by fits and starts. *Siempre trabaja a rachas (a empujones; sin regularidad).*

fit for — *apto para.*

He is fit for duty. *Cumple con los requisitos del ejército.*

to feel fit — *sentirse bien.*

She feels fit again. *Se siente bien otra vez.*

to see fit — *juzgar conveniente; tener a bien.*

They saw fit to sell it. *Juzgaron conveniente (Tuvieron a bien) venderlo.*

to throw (to have) a fit — *poner el grito en el cielo; darle un patatús.*

When she saw it, she threw (had) a fit. *Cuando lo vio, puso el grito en el cielo (le dio un patatús).*

to fit — *ajustar*

to fit in — *estar de acuerdo.*

It doesn't fit in with my ideas. *No está de acuerdo con mis ideas.*

to fit in — *llevarse bien.*

He doesn't fit in with our group. *No se lleva bien con nuestro grupo.*

five — *cinco*

to take five — *tomar cinco minutos de descanso.*

OK men, enough, take five. *Está bueno, basta, descansen cinco minutos.*

flag — *la bandera*

to show the flag — *hacer acto de presencia.*

Let's go to that meeting, just to show the flag. *Vamos a esa reunión, sólo para hacer acto de presencia.*

flame — *la llama*

an old flame — *un viejo amor.*

She met an old flame. *Se encontró con un viejo amor.*

to burst into flames — *inflamarse.*

It burst into flames. *Se inflamó.*

flash — *el relámpago*

a flash in the pan — *humo de pajas.*

The idea was only a flash in the pan. *La idea fue sólo humo de pajas.*

in a flash — *de un salto.*

He was here in a flash. *Estuvo aquí de un salto.*

flat — *plano*

to fall flat — *caer de plano; caer de redondo.*

He fell flat on the floor. *Cayó de plano (redondo) al suelo.*

to leave someone flat — *dejarlo plantado.*

His wife left him flat. *Su esposa lo dejó plantado.*

flat-footed — *de pies achatados*

to catch flat-footed — *coger de sorpresa.*

The decision caught us flat-footed. *La decisión nos cogió de sorpresa.*

flesh — *la carne*

in the flesh — *en persona.*

We were surprised to see the president himself there in the flesh. *Nos sorprendió ver allí al propio presidente en persona.*

to press the flesh — *estrechar manos.*

Politicians press the flesh at all times. *Los políticos se lo pasan estrechando manos.*

flight — *el vuelo*

charter flight — *vuelo especial.*

They went by charter flight. *Fueron por vuelo especial.*

to take flight — *alzar el vuelo.*

After the robbery, the thieves took flight. *Después del robo los ladrones alzaron el vuelo.*

to flip — *echar; lanzar*

to flip over — *dar una voltereta.*

The car crashed and flipped over. *El carro se estrelló y se dio vuelta.*

to flock — *congregarse*

to flock together — *andar juntos.*

The foreigners always flock together. *Los extranjeros siempre andan juntos.*

floor — *el piso*

to ask for (to take) the floor — *pedir (tomar) la palabra.*

He asked for (took) the floor. *Pidió (Tomó) la palabra.*

floor — *el suelo*

to pace the floor (pace up and down) — *pasearse de un lado para (a) otro.*

Waiting for the doctor's decision, he paced the floor (paced up and down). *Esperando la decisión del médico, se paseaba de un lado para (a) otro.*

to fly — *volar*

to fly by — *pasar volando.*

This month has flown by. *Este mes ha pasado volando.*

fly-by-night — *fugaz; engañador.*

That's one of those fly-by-night businesses; they get the money and disappear. *Esa es una de esas empresas que aparecen, sacan plata y desaparecen.*

to fly in — *llegar (en avión).*

He flew in from Manila. *Llegó en avión desde Manila.*

fond — *cariñoso*

to be fond of — *tener afición a.*

We are fond of music. *Tenemos afición a la música.*

food — *la comida*

to give food for thought — *dar que pensar.*

His speech gave us food for thought. *Su discurso nos dio que pensar.*

fool — *el tonto*

to be nobody's fool — *no tener pelo de tonto.*

He's nobody's fool. *No tiene pelo de tonto.*

to make a fool of someone — *ponerle en ridículo.*

He made a fool of her. *La puso en ridículo.*

to make a fool of oneself — *hacer el ridículo.*

He's making a fool of himself. *Está haciendo el ridículo.*

to play (act) the fool — *hacer el tonto.*

He played (acted) the fool. *Hizo el tonto.*

to fool — *tontear, engañar*

to fool around — *perder tiempo; malgastar el tiempo.*

They fired him because he fools around too much. *Lo despidieron porque pierde demasiado tiempo (malgasta el tiempo).*

foolproof — *a prueba de mal trato*

a foolproof method — *un método infalible.*

It's a foolproof method. *Es un método infalible.*

foot — *el pie*

My foot! — *¿Y tú crees eso?*

The President says he'll lower taxes? My foot! *¿El presidente dice que bajará los impuestos? ¿Y tú crees eso?*

on foot — *a pie.*

They're going on foot. *Van a pie.*

to drag one's feet — *tardar en obrar.*
Salaries were not raised because the president dragged his feet. *No se realizó el aumento de los sueldos porque el rector tardó en obrar.*

to get cold feet — *acobardarse.*
They were going to climb the mountain, but then got cold feet. *Iban a escalar la montaña, pero luego se acobardaron.*

to have one's feet on the ground — *estar bien plantado.*
I think you can have confidence in him. He seems to have his feet on the ground. *Creo que puedes confiar en él. Parece estar bien plantado.*

to put one's best foot forward — *esmerarse en hacer lo mejor posible.*
She put her best foot forward in order to impress him. *Se esmeró en hacer lo mejor posible para impresionarlo.*

to put one's foot down —*oponerse enérgicamente.*
Raúl wanted to learn karate, but his father put his foot down. *Raúl quería aprender karate, pero su padre se opuso enérgicamente.*

to put one's foot in one's mouth — *meter la pata.*
He put his foot in his mouth. *Metió la pata.*

to set foot in — *poner los pies en; pisar.*
He refuses to set foot in that house. *Se niega a poner los pies en (pisar) esa casa.*

to sweep off one's feet — *arrebatar a uno; hacer perder la cabeza.*
I was playing hard to get, but he swept me off my feet. *Yo estaba coqueteando, pero él me hizo perder la cabeza.*

---

for — *por, para*

for — *(desde) hace.*
I've been here for an hour. *Estoy aquí (desde) hace una hora.*

to be for — *preferir.*
I'm for going to the beach. *Prefiero ir a la playa.*

---

force — *la fuerza*

by sheer force — *a viva fuerza.*
She succeeded by sheer force. *Lo logró a viva fuerza.*

in force — *en masa.*
His friends visited him in force. *Sus amigos lo visitaron en masa.*

task force — *la agrupación de fuerzas para cierto propósito.*

The task force of experts to preserve the Academy of Arts will meet today. *La comisión de expertos para conservar la Academia de Arte se reunirá hoy.*

to be in force — *estar en vigor.*

The law is no longer in force. *La ley ya no está en vigor.*

forest — *el bosque*

You cannot see the forest for the trees. — *Los árboles no dejan ver el bosque.*

form — *la forma*

for form's sake (as a matter of form) — *por (pura) fórmula.*

For form's sake (As a matter of form), he asked us if we wanted to go along. *Por (pura) fórmula nos preguntó si queríamos acompañarlo.*

frame — *el marco*

to be in a good frame of mind — *estar de buen humor.*

Today he is not in a very good frame of mind. *Hoy no está de muy buen humor.*

free — *libre*

free — *de balde; gratis.*

They sent it to me free. *Me lo mandaron de balde (gratis).*

free-for-all — *la pelotera; la contienda general.*

The fight among those two ended with a free-for-all in the bar. *La pelea entre esos dos terminó con una pelotera general en el bar.*

to go scot free — *salir impune.*

He went scot free. *Salió impune.*

to set free — *poner en libertad.*

They set him free. *Lo pusieron en libertad.*

Friday — *viernes*

man Friday — *el hombre de confianza; la mano derecha.*

John may look like a humble clerk, but he's the man Friday to the president. *Juan puede parecer un humilde funcionario, pero es la mano derecha del presidente.*

friend — *el amigo*

A friend in need is a friend indeed. — *En el peligro se conoce al amigo.*

to make friends with — *hacerse amigos.*

They made friends with us immediately. *Se hicieron amigos nuestros en seguida.*

friendship — *la amistad*

to strike up a friendship — *trabar amistad.*

He struck up a friendship with us. *Trabó amistad con nosotros.*

from — *de*

from . . . to . . . — *de . . . en . . . .*

We went from town to town. *Fuimos de pueblo en pueblo.*

to frown — *fruncir el entrecejo*

to be frowned upon — *recibir la desaprobación de otros.*

To put your feet on the desk is frowned upon. *Poner los pies sobre el escritorio es mal mirado.*

fruit — *la fruta, el fruto*

to bear fruit — *dar frutos.*

It doesn't bear fruit. *No da frutos.*

fry — *pececillos; nidada*

small fry — *los niños pequeños; la gente menuda.*

There goes the small fry from the nursery. *Allí va la parvada del jardín infantil.*

fuel — *el combustible*

to add fuel to the flames — *echar aceite al fuego.*

She always adds fuel to the flames. *Siempre echa aceite al fuego.*

full — *lleno*

full-fledged — *desarrollado; todo.*

She has become a full-fledged dancer. *Se ha convertido en toda una bailarina.*

full-time — *la jornada completa de trabajo.*

Only full-time personnel can get health insurance. *Sólo el personal de jornada completa puede contar con seguro de salud.*

to be full of oneself — *ser presumido.*

She is so full of herself that she doesn't realize nobody likes her. *Es tan presumida que ni se da cuenta de que no la quiere nadie.*

fun — *la diversión*

for fun — *por gusto; por divertirse.*

We did it for fun. *Lo hicimos por gusto (por divertirnos).*

to have fun — *divertirse.*

They had fun. *Se divirtieron.*

to make fun of — *burlarse de.*

She made fun of me. *Se burló de mí.*

funny — *gracioso*

to be funny — *tener gracia; ser gracioso.*

It's funny. *Tiene gracia (Es gracioso).*

to strike one funny — *parecerle raro.*

He strikes me funny. *Me parece raro.*

fur — *la piel*

to make the fur fly — *armar camorra; producir gran revuelo.*

I am sure that the fur will fly during that meeting. *Estoy seguro que en esa reunión se armará la grande.*

fuss — *la alharaca*

It's not worth making such a fuss over. — *No es para tanto.*

to make a fuss over — *hacer muchas alharacas.*

She made a fuss over having to prepare the supper. *Hizo muchas alharacas porque tenía que preparar la cena.*

futility — *la futilidad; la inutilidad*

an exercise in futility — *una labor inútil.*

To try to solve such problems is an exercise in futility. *Es cosa inútil tratar de resolver semejantes problemas.*

G

to gain — *ganar*

to gain on — *ir alcanzando.*

Let's run faster. They're gaining on us. *Corramos más de prisa. Nos van alcanzando.*

game — *el juego, la partida*

a new ball game — *algo completamente nuevo o distinto.*

With Anna it was easy, but getting Mary to agree with you is a whole new ball game. *Con Ana fue fácil, pero lograr que María se ponga de acuerdo contigo es algo totalmente distinto.*

con game — *la estafa.*

That kind of con game is well known. *Ese tipo de estafa es cuento viejo.*

fair game — *el derecho de criticar a alguien impunemente.*

Her private life is fair game for the press. *La prensa comenta sobre su vida privada con toda libertad.*

I'm game. — *de acuerdo; cuenten conmigo.*

To go to the casino? I'm game. *¿Ir al casino? Cuenten conmigo.*

the name of the game — *lo que todos hacen; lo que se estila.*

Aggressive competition is the name of the game in this company. *La competencia agresiva es lo que se estila en esta empresa.*

to play a game — *echar una partida.*

They played a game of cards. *Echaron una partida de naipes.*

to throw a game — *dejarse ganar.*

Pirelli was accused of throwing a game last May. *Acusaron a Pirelli de dejarse ganar durante un partido en mayo.*

gap — *la sima*

credibility gap — *el escepticismo; la desconfianza.*

The credibility gap between the President and the Senate has widened. *Ha aumentado la desconfianza entre el presidente y el senado.*

the generation gap — *el conflicto generacional.*

The generation gap is evident. *El conflicto generacional es evidente.*

---

gas — *el gas, la gasolina*

Step on it (the gas)! — *¡Apresúrese!*

---

gate — *la puerta; la entrada*

gate-crasher — *el intruso; el colado.*

Not even the special guards could stop the gate-crashers. *Ni siquiera los guardias especiales pudieron detener a los colados.*

---

to get — *conseguir*

Get it out of your head! — *¡Quíteselo de la cabeza!*

not to get over — *no acostumbrarse a.*

We can't get over it. *No podemos acostumbrarnos a la idea.*

There's no getting around it — *no hay que darle vueltas.*

There's no getting around it, she made a mistake. *No hay que darle vueltas, ha cometido un error.*

There's no getting away from it. — *La cosa es clara.*

to get ahead — *prosperar.*

It's hard to get ahead in the world. *Es difícil prosperar en el mundo.*

to get along — *irlo pasando.*

Although her husband is dead, she is getting along. *Aunque está muerto su esposo, ella lo va pasando.*

to get along well — *defenderse bien.*

She gets along well in Spanish. *Se defiende bien en español.*

to get along with — *llevarse bien con.*

She gets along with everyone. *Se lleva bien con todos.*

to get along without — *pasarse sin.*

I can't get along without coffee. *No puedo pasarme sin café.*

to get away — *escaparse.*
The thief got away. *El ladrón se escapó.*

to get away with it — *no ser castigado.*
He lied and got away with it. *Mintió y no fue castigado.*

to get back — *volver.*
We got back at ten. *Volvimos a las diez.*

to get back at — *pagar en la misma moneda.*
He played a dirty trick on me, but I'm going to get back at him. *Me jugó una mala pasada, pero le voy a pagar en la misma moneda.*

to get by — *ir tirando.*
We're getting by. *Vamos tirando.*

to get by one — *escapársele a uno.*
The meaning of his speech got by us. *El significado de su discurso se nos escapó.*

to get cheaply — *salirle barato.*
We got it cheaply. *Nos salió barato.*

to get going — *ponerse en marcha.*
We got going at six. *Nos pusimos en marcha a las seis.*

to get involved in — *entregarse a.*
I got involved in Red Cross work. *Me entregué al trabajo de la Cruz Roja.*

to get it — *caer en la cuenta.*
I get it. *Caigo en la cuenta.*

to get off — *bajar (salir; apearse de).*
He got off the train. *Bajó (Salió, Se apeó) del tren.*

to get on — *subir a.*
He got on the bus. *Subió al autobús.*

to get over — *restablecerse (curarse) de.*
She got over the flu. *Se restableció (se curó) de la gripe.*

to get ready — *prepararse.*
They all got ready to leave. *Todos se prepararon para salir.*

to get there — *llegar.*
We got there at one. *Llegamos a la una.*

to get through — *pasar.*
We finally got through. *Por fin pasamos.*

to get through — *terminar.*
We got through working at ten. *Terminamos el trabajo a las diez.*

to get to — *poder.*
I never got to see it. *Nunca pude verlo.*

to get together — *ponerse de acuerdo.*
They finally got together. *Por fin, se pusieron de acuerdo.*

to get together — *reunirse.*
They got together to decide. *Se reunieron para decidir.*

to get up — *levantarse.*
She gets up at six. *Se levanta a las seis.*

to get what is coming to one — *recibir lo merecido.*
It looks as if they have finally gotten what was coming to them. *Parece que por fin han recibido lo merecido.*

What's gotten into him? — *¿Qué mosca le ha picado?*

---

ghost — *el fantasma*

to give up the ghost — *entregar el alma.*
He gave up the ghost. *Entregó el alma.*

---

gift — *el regalo*

to have the gift of gab — *ser de mucha labia.*
He has the gift of gab. *Es un hombre de mucha labia.*

to present with a gift — *hacer un regalo.*
He presented me with a gift. *Me hizo un regalo.*

---

to give — *dar*

give-and-take — *concesiones mutuas.*
After a lot of give-and-take, they reached an agreement. *Después de muchas concesiones mutuas, llegaron a un convenio.*

to give away — *regalar.*
He gives away his old shoes. *Regala sus zapatos viejos.*

to give in — *darse por vencido; doblar la cabeza.*
He gave in. *Se dio por vencido (Dobló la cabeza).*

to give off — *producir.*
It gives off a bad odor. *Produce un mal olor.*

to give out — *acabarse.*

The beer gave out. *Se acabó la cerveza.*

to give out — *repartir.*

He gave out one bottle to each employee. *Repartió una botella a cada empleado.*

to give to understand — *dar a entender.*

He gave me to understand that he was boss. *Me dio a entender que mandaba él.*

to give up — *dejar de.*

He gave up smoking. *Dejó de fumar.*

to give up — *rendirse.*

When they surrounded him he gave up. *Cuando lo rodearon, se rindió.*

glad — *alegre*

How glad we are! — *¡Cuánto nos alegramos!*

to be glad to see someone — *tener mucho gusto en verlo.*

I'm glad to see you. *(Tengo) mucho gusto en verlo.*

glance — *la ojeada*

at first glance — *a primera vista.*

At first glance he doesn't impress me. *A primera vista no me impresiona.*

to glance — *lanzar una mirada*

to glance over — *examinar de paso.*

I glanced over his examination. *Examiné de paso su examen.*

glove — *el guante*

to fit like a glove — *sentarle muy bien.*

His coat fits like a glove. *Su abrigo le sienta muy bien.*

to handle with kid gloves — *tener entre algodones; tratar con sumo cuidado.*

She handles him with kid gloves. *Lo tiene entre algodones (Lo trata con sumo cuidado).*

go — *marcha, movimiento; tentativa*

anything goes — *todo está bien; todo está permitido.*

There aren't any rules in this place; anything goes. *En este lugar no hay reglamento alguno; todo está permitido.*

no-go — *imposible.*

We tried to make it to the top, but it was a no-go. *Tratamos de llegar a la cumbre, pero fue imposible.*

to be on the go — *estar en actividad; no pararse.*

He's always on the go. *Siempre está en actividad (Nunca se para).*

to have a go at it — *probarlo.*

He had a go at it but failed. *Lo probó pero fracasó.*

to have lots of go — *tener mucha energía.*

He has lots of go. *Tiene mucha energía.*

---

to go — *ir*

Go on! — *¡Qué va! (¡Qué tontería!)*

How goes it? (How's it going?) —*¿Qué tal?*

not to be able to go on — *no poder más.*

He can't go on. *No puede más.*

to be enough to go around — *alcanzar.*

There aren't enough chairs to go around. *No alcanzan las sillas.*

to be going on — *estar acercándose a.*

She's going on forty. *Está ya acercándose a los cuarenta.*

to be gone — *haberse agotado o acabado; haberse muerto.*

It's all gone. *Se agotó todo.*

to go — *faltar; quedar.*

There are still two hours to go. *Todavía faltan dos horas.*

to go — *para llevar.*

I want a pizza to go. *Quiero una pizza para llevar.*

to go after — *ir tras de; perseguir.*

The sheriff went after the thief. *El sheriff fue tras el ladrón.*

to go ahead — *seguir adelante.*

They are going ahead with the work. *Siguen adelante con el trabajo.*

to go all out — *echar la casa por la ventana.*
She went all out to celebrate my birthday. *Echó la casa por la ventana para celebrar mi cumpleaños.*

to go all out — *hacer un esfuerzo supremo.*
They went all out. *Hicieron un esfuerzo supremo.*

to go along with — *aceptar; apoyar.*
He won't go along with our plans. *No quiere aceptar (apoyar) nuestros planes.*

to go around — *ir por.*
He goes around the university as if he were lost. *Va por la universidad como si estuviera perdido.*

to go as far as to say — *atreverse a decir.*
I won't go as far as to say that she's smart. *No me atrevo a decir que sea lista.*

to go astray — *extraviarse.*
The book I sent went astray. *El libro que mandé se extravió.*

to go away — *irse; marcharse.*
He went away and left her crying. *Se marchó y la dejó llorando.*

to go back on one's word — *no cumplir su palabra.*
He went back on his word. *No cumplió su palabra.*

to go bad — *echarse a perder.*
The fruit went bad. *La fruta se echó a perder.*

to go better — *subir la apuesta (cartas).*
He saw the ace and went 5 dollars better. *Vio el as y subió la puesta en 5 dólares.*

to go by — *pasar; pasar al lado de.*
She went by his side and lowered her eyes. *Pasó a su lado y bajó los ojos.*

to go by — *guiarse por.*
He goes by the rules established in the state. *Se guía por las leyes establecidas en el estado.*

to go by — *ser conocido por.*
He goes by the name of Jimmy. *Se le conoce con el nombre de Jimmy.*

to go down — *hundirse; descender; caer.*
He went down with his ship. *Se hundió con su barco.*

to go down with — *enfermarse.*
He went down with pneumonia. *Se enfermó de pulmonía.*

to go for — *ser atraído por.*
He goes for tall girls. *Es atraído por las muchachas altas.*

to go for broke — *jugarse el todo por el todo.*
They went for broke and invested every penny they had on that business. *Se jugaron el todo por el todo e invirtieron hasta el último centavo en ese negocio.*

to go get — *ir a buscar.*
Go get me a book. *Vaya a buscarme un libro.*

to go in for — *ser aficionado a.*
We go in for jai alai. *Somos aficionados al jai alai.*

to go off — *explotar.*
The bomb went off. *La bomba explotó.*

to go on — *seguir.*
He goes on day after day. *Sigue día tras día.*
He goes on smoking. *Sigue fumando.*

to go out — *salir.*
He went out alone. *Salió solo.*

to go over — *examinar; estudiar; repasar.*
He went over the records once more. *Repasó los documentos una vez más.*

to go over to — *pasarse; cambiarse al otro lado (partido, religión, ejército).*
The Nationalist went over to the Republicans. *El Nacionalista se pasó al lado de los Republicanos.*

to go past — *pasar; pasar de largo.*
The taxi went past and didn't even slow down. *El taxi pasó de largo sin siquiera detenerse.*

to go smoothly — *ir sobre ruedas.*
Things went smoothly at first. *Al principio todo fue sobre ruedas.*

to go straight — *seguir la vía recta.*
When he got out of jail he went straight. *Al salir de la cárcel siguió la vía recta.*

to go through — *aprobarse.*
My request went through. *Mi petición se aprobó.*

to go through — *pasar.*
It went through the test. *Pasó la prueba.*

to go through — *sufrir.*
She has to go through an operation. *Tiene que sufrir una operación.*

to go under — *hundise; fracasar.*
His business went under and he filed for bankruptcy. *Su negocio fracasó y él se declaró en quiebra.*

to go with — *hacer juego con.*
It doesn't go with this tie. *No hace juego con esta corbata.*

to go wrong — *ir por mal camino.*
Her son went wrong. *Su hijo fue por mal camino.*

to go wrong — *salir mal.*
Everything went wrong today. *Todo me salió mal hoy.*

to have . . . to go — *quedarle. . . .*
You have five minutes to go. *Le quedan cinco minutos.*

to make a go of — *tener (lograr) éxito en.*
He didn't make a go of his business. *No tuvo (logró) éxito en sus negocios.*

God — *Dios*

God willing — *Si Dios quiere (Dios mediante)*
God willing, we'll spend Christmas together. *Pasaremos las pascuas juntos, si Dios quiere (Dios mediante).*

---

gold — *el oro*

to be as good as gold — *ser más bueno que el pan.*
He's as good as gold. *Es más bueno que el pan.*

---

good — *bueno*

for good — *para siempre.*
She left home for good. *Salió de se casa para siempre.*

good and . . . — *bien . . .*
We got home good and tired. *Llegamos a casa bien cansados.*

Good for you! — *¡Bien hecho!*

never to have it so good — *nunca haber estado tan bien.*
Believe me my boy, the lower class never had it so good as now. *Créeme muchacho, la clase baja nunca ha estado tan bien como ahora.*

to be as good as done — *poder darse por hecho.*
It's as good as done. *Puede darse por hecho.*

to be good enough to — *tener la bondad de.*
He was good enough to help me. *Tuvo la bondad de ayudarme.*

to be good for — *servir (ser de provecho) para.*
It's no good for anything. *No sirve (No es de provecho) para nada.*

to be no good — *ser un inútil.*
He's no good for anything. *Es un inútil para lo que sea.*

to be up to no good — *estar tramando algo.*
Don't trust him. He's up to no good. *No te fíes de él. Está tramando algo.*

to do one good (harm) — *venirle bien (mal).*
It has done me good (harm). *Me ha venido bien (mal).*

to make good — *prosperar.*
He's making good in his new job. *Está prosperando en su nuevo puesto.*

to make good — *compensar; indemnizar; pagar.*
I will make good the money my father owes to the bank. *Yo pagaré el dinero que mi padre debe al banco.*

to make good — *demostrar.*
He made good his love for Vivian by marrying her. *Demostró su amor por Vivian casándose con ella.*

what good is it (what's the good of) — *para qué (sirve).*
What good is it to work (What's the good of working) all day? *¿Para qué (sirve) trabajar todo el día?*

when one is good and ready — *cuando le parezca.*
I'll do it when I'm good and ready. *Lo haré cuando me parezca.*

grab — *el agarro; la toma; el asimiento*

to be up for grabs — *estar libre; estar disponible.*
When a war is lost, the commander's post is up for grabs. *Cuando una guerra está perdida, el puesto de comandante está a disposición de cualquiera.*

grade — *el grado; la clase; la categoría*

to make the grade — *tener éxito.*
He made the grade in Accounting, and now he's the CEO. *Tuvo éxito en Contabilidad y ahora es Director Ejecutivo.*

grain — *el grano*

not a grain of truth — *ni pizca de verdad.*

There's not a grain of truth in what he says. *No hay ni pizca de verdad en lo que dice.*

to go against the grain — *repugnarle.*

It went against the grain. *Me repugnó.*

to grant — *conceder*

to take for granted — *dar por sentado (supuesto; hecho).*

I took it for granted. *Lo di por sentado (supuesto; hecho).*

grape — *la uva*

sour-grape — *envidioso.*

Pay no attention to those sour-grape comments. *No prestes atención a esos comentarios envidiosos.*

grapevine — *la parra; el rumor*

through the grapevine — *por rumores; por vía clandestina.*

I heard through the grapevine that Joan is a lesbian. *Escuché rumores de que Joan es una lesbiana.*

to gratify — *satisfacer; agradar*

to be gratified — *estar satisfecho.*

The President is gratified with their work. *El presidente está satisfecho con su labor.*

grease — *la grasa; el lubricante*

elbow grease — *el esfuerzo.*

That contract took a lot of elbow grease. *Ese contrato requirió un gran esfuerzo.*

grief — *la desgracia; el desastre*

to come to grief — *venirse abajo.*

His plans to marry her came to grief when she found another. *Sus planes de casarse con ella se vinieron abajo cuando ella encontró a otro.*

to grin — *sonreírse bonachonamente*

to grin and bear it — *poner a mal tiempo buena cara.*

He'll have to grin and bear it. *Tendrá que poner a mal tiempo buena cara.*

grip — *el asimiento, el agarro*

to come to grips with — *afrontar; enfrentarse con.*

He won't come to grips with his situation. *No quiere afrontar (enfrentarse con) su situación.*

ground — *la tierra*

to be on firm ground — *estar en lo firme.*

When they say it's impossible, they're on firm ground. *Al decir que es imposible están en lo firme.*

to stand one's ground — *mantenerse firme.*

Despite the criticism, he stood his ground. *A pesar de la crítica, se mantuvo firme.*

group — *el grupo*

fact-finding group — *la comisión de estudio.*

A fact-finding group was created to investigate the causes of the disaster. *Se creó una comisión de estudio para investigar las causas del desastre.*

to grow — *crecer, cultivar*

grown-ups — *personas mayores.*

It's for grown-ups. *Es para personas mayores.*

to grow on one — *gustarle más.*

The more I look at it the more it grows on me. *Cuanto más lo miro, (tanto) más me gusta.*

to grow out of it — *quitársele.*

He stutters but he'll grow out of it. *Tartamudea pero se le quitará.*

grudge — *el rencor*

to bear (to hold) a grudge — *guardar rencor.*

He never bears (holds) a grudge. *Nunca guarda rencor.*

guard — *la guardia*

to be on one's guard — *estar sobre aviso.*

He's always on his guard. *Siempre está sobre aviso.*

to catch one off one's guard — *cogerle desprevenido.*

They caught us off our guard. *Nos cogieron desprevenidos.*

to guard against — *guardarse de.*

You ought to guard against eating too much. *Debe guardarse de comer demasiado.*

guess — *la suposición*

Your guess is as good as mine. — *Usted sabe tanto como yo.*

to guess — *suponer, adivinar*

I guess so. — *Creo que sí.*

gun — *el arma de fuego*

to jump the gun — *precipitarse.*

He jumped the gun in making the announcement. *Se precipitó al hacer el anuncio.*

smoking gun — *la prueba irrefutable.*

The smoking gun was the letter she wrote to her lover. *La prueba irrefutable fue la carta que escribió a su amante.*

to stick to one's guns — *no dar el brazo a torcer.*

In spite of all the arguments, he stuck to his guns. *A pesar de todos los argumentos, no dio el brazo a torcer.*

H

habit — *el hábito*

to kick the habit — *dejar de ser adicto a algo, especialmente el tabaco.*

He kicked the habit . . . about fifty times. *Abandonó su adicción . . . unas cincuenta veces ya.*

hair — *el pelo*

to let one's hair down — *sincerarse.*

Finally he let his hair down with me. *Por fin se sinceró conmigo.*

to make one's hair stand on end — *ponerle los pelos de punta.*

Her story made our hair stand on end. *Su historia nos puso los pelos de punta.*

to part one's hair — *peinarse con raya.*

He parts his hair. *Se peina con raya.*

to split hairs — *andar en quisquillas; pararse en pelillos.*

That's splitting hairs. *Eso es andar en quisquillas (pararse en pelillos).*

to turn a hair — *inmutarse.*

He didn't turn a hair when he found it out. *No se inmutó cuando lo supo.*

---

half — *medio*

better half — *la cara mitad.*

I don't think my better half would agree. *No creo que mi cara mitad esté de acuerdo.*

half . . . and half . . . — *entre . . . y. . . .*

He said it half joking and half serious. *Lo dijo entre chistoso y serio.*

half closed — *a medio cerrar.*

We found the door half closed. *Encontramos la puerta a medio cerrar.*

half done — *a medias.*

He leaves things half done. *Deja las cosas a medias.*

half-hearted — *a medias; débil.*

His attempts to regain her love were half-hearted. *Sus intentos de recuperar su amor eran poco decididos.*

to be too clever by half — *pasarse de listo.*

They are too clever by half if they believe they'll get him to sign that document. *Se pasan de listos si imaginan que lograrán que él firme ese documento.*

to cut in half — *partir por la mitad.*

They cut the apple in half. *Partieron la manzana por la mitad.*

---

hand — *la mano*

all hands — *toda la tripulación.*

I want all hands on deck right now. *Quiero a toda la tripulación sobre la cubierta ahora mismo.*

big hand — *la ovación.*

The new artist got a big hand at the club. *El nuevo artista recibió una ovación en el club*

by hand — *a mano.*

They used to write all their letters by hand. *Escribían todas sus cartas a mano.*

Don't bite the hand that feeds you. — *No muerdas la mano que te da de comer.*

hand in hand — *cogidos de la mano.*

They approached hand in hand. *Se acercaron cogidos de la mano.*

hand-me-down — *la ropa de segunda mano.*

They were poor, so being dressed in hand-me-downs was considered normal. *Eran pobres, y por eso recibir ropa de segunda mano era considerado normal.*

hands down — *fácilmente.*

He won hands down. *Ganó fácilmente.*

Hands off! — *¡No tocar!*

on the one hand, . . . ; on the other, . . . — *de (por) un lado, . . . ; de (por) otro, ...*

On the one hand she likes her work; on the other, she gets tired of sitting. *De (por) un lado, le gusta su trabajo; de (por) otro, se cansa de estar sentada.*

on the other hand — *en cambio; al contrario.*

This one, on the other hand, is ours. *Este, en cambio (al contrario), es el nuestro.*

on the other hand — *por otra parte (otro lado).*

On the other hand, we may need more. *Por otra parte (otro lado) puede ser que nos haga falta más.*

to be an old hand — *ser experto.*

He's an old hand at golf. *Es un experto jugador de golf.*

to be hand in glove — *ser uña y carne.*

They're hand in glove. *Son uña y carne.*

to be on hand — *estar disponible.*
He's never on hand when I need him. *Nunca está disponible cuando lo necesito.*

to change hands — *cambiar de dueño.*
The hotel changed hands. *El hotel cambió de dueño.*

to clap one's hands (to applaud) — *aplaudir.*
He clapped his hands (applauded). *Aplaudió.*

to clap one's hands — *dar palmadas.*
He clapped his hands to attract the waiter's attention. *Dio unas palmadas para llamarle la atención al camarero.*

to get out of hand — *desmandarse.*
The situation got out of hand. *La situación se desmandó.*

to give someone a big hand — *darle fuertes aplausos.*
They gave her a big hand. *Le dieron fuertes aplausos.*

to go from hand to hand — *ir de mano en mano.*
It went from hand to hand. *Fue de mano en mano.*

to have a free hand — *tener carta blanca (plena libertad).*
He has a free hand in his job. *Tiene carta blanca (plena libertad) en su trabajo.*

to have at hand — *tener a mano.*
He had it at hand. *Lo tenía a mano.*

to have in one's hands — *tener en su poder.*
I have in my hands your letter. *Tengo en mi poder su grata.*

to have one's hands full — *estar muy ocupado.*
With school, kids and cooking, I have my hands full. *Con la escuela, los niños y la cocina, ando muy ocupada.*

to have the upper hand — *dominar la situación.*
He had the upper hand. *Dominaba la situación.*

to keep one's hand in — *seguir teniendo práctica.*
He's studying Spanish just to keep his hand in. *Estudia español sólo para seguir teniendo práctica.*

to lay one's hands on — *encontrar.*
I can't lay my hands on that report. *No puedo encontrar ese informe.*

to lend (to give) a hand — *dar (echar) una mano.*
He lent (gave) me a hand. *Me dio (echó) una mano.*

to live from hand to mouth — *vivir al día.*
The poor man lives from hand to mouth. *El pobre vive al día.*

to play right into one's hands — *redundar en su beneficio.*
What he did played right into our hands. *Lo que hizo redundó en nuestro beneficio.*

to shake hands with — *dar (estrechar) la mano (a).*
He shook hands with me. *Me dio (estrechó) la mano.*

to wait on hand and foot — *cuidar a cuerpo de rey.*
She waits on her children hand and foot. *Cuida a sus hijos a cuerpo de rey.*

to wash one's hands of — *lavarse las manos de.*
He washed his hands of that enterprise. *Se lavó las manos de esa empresa.*

to win hands down — *ganar sin ninguna dificultad.*
We won hands down. *Ganamos sin ninguna dificultad.*

to work hand in hand — *trabajar en buena armonía.*
They work hand in hand. *Trabajan en buena armonía.*

with a steady hand — *con pulso firme.*
He aims with a steady hand. *Apunta con pulso firme.*

---

to hand — *dar, entregar*

to hand down — *transmitir; comunicar.*
The jury handed down the verdict. *El jurado comunicó el veredicto.*

to hand in — *presentar.*
The executive handed in his resignation. *El ejecutivo presentó su renuncia.*

to hand over — *entregar.*
Harald handed the kingdom over to his son. *Harald entregó el reino a su hijo.*

---

handful — *el puñado*

by the handful — *a manos llenas.*
He wasted money by the handful. *Malgastó dinero a manos llenas.*

to hang — *colgar*

to hang on someone's words — *estar pendiente de sus palabras.*

She hangs on his words. *Está pendiente de sus palabras.*

hard — *duro*

hard and fast — *estricto; rígido.*

The rules in this outfit are hard and fast. *Las reglas en este grupo son estrictas e inflexibles.*

hard-boiled — *hervido por largo tiempo; huevo duro.*

One needs about six minutes to get hard-boiled eggs. *Uno necesita unos seis minutos para hacer huevos duros.*

hard-boiled — *insensible; impasible.*

Those are hard-boiled veterans from the front. *Esos son veteranos endurecidos en el frente.*

to be hard — *costar trabajo.*

It's hard for us to imagine. *Nos cuesta trabajo imaginarlo.*

to be hard to deal with — *ser difícil de tratar.*

If you weren't so hard to deal with, you would have become an executive. *Si no hubieras sido tan difícil de tratar, habrías llegado a ser un ejecutivo.*

to do something the hard way — *hacer algo en forma complicada.*

That's too difficult! Why must you do everything the hard way? *¡Eso es demasiado difícil! ¿Por qué debes hacer todo en forma tan complicada?*

to make it hard for — *hacerle las cosas difíciles a.*

The captain made things hard for the new corporal. *El capitán le hizo las cosas difíciles al nuevo cabo.*

to play hard to get — *hacerse de rogar.*

He likes to play hard to get, but he is desperate to make a deal. *Le gusta hacerse el difícil, pero está desesperado por llevar el negocio a cabo.*

to take something hard — *tomarlo a pecho.*

He took it hard. *Lo tomó a pecho.*

hard-hearted — *duro de corazón*

to be hard-hearted — *tener corazón de piedra.*

He's hard-hearted. *Tiene corazón de piedra.*

haste — *la prisa*

in great haste — *a escape; a toda prisa.*

He took off in great haste. *Se despidió a escape (a toda prisa).*

Haste makes waste. — *Vísteme despacio que tengo prisa.*

hat — *el sombrero*

at the drop of a hat — *por el menor motivo.*

He gets angry at the drop of a hat. *Se enoja por cualquier cosa.*

hat in hand — *con el sombrero en la mano.*

All he could do was to show up hat in hand and ask for a job. *Todo lo que pudo hacer fue presentarse humildemente a pedir trabajo.*

to be old hat — *ser muy anticuado.*

His ideas are old hat. *Sus ideas son muy anticuadas.*

to remove one's hat — *descubrirse.*

They removed their hats reverently. *Se descubrieron con reverencia.*

to take off one's hat to — *descubrirse ante.*

I take off my hat to his courage. *Me descubro ante su valor.*

to talk through one's hat — *decir tonterías (disparates).*

As usual, he's talking through his hat. *Como de costumbre dice tonterías (disparates).*

to wear many hats — *desempeñar muchos cargos al mismo tiempo.*

As president of the university, he wears many hats. *Como rector de la universidad desempeña muchos cargos al mismo tiempo.*

hatchet — *el hacha*

to bury the hatchet — *hacer las paces.*

They buried the hatchet. *Hicieron las paces.*

to dig up the hatchet — *hacer guerra; declarar hostilidades.*

If they do that, we'll dig up the hatchet and go to war again! *¡Si hacen eso, les haremos guerra de nuevo!*

haul — *el tirón*

Over the long haul — *a la larga.*

Over the long haul it will be to our advantage. *A la larga será para nuestro provecho.*

to have — *tener*

a has-been — *una estrella del pasado.*

Many has-beens cannot adjust to a life without applause. *Muchas estrellas son incapaces de adaptarse a una vida sin aplausos.*

and what have you — *todo lo que se te ocurra; un cuanto hay.*

The store has green shoes, red shoes, big shoes, small shoes, and what have you. *En la tienda hay zapatos verdes, rojos, grandes, chicos y para qué sigo.*

had better — *mejor.*

You had better stay. *Mejor sería que se quedara.*

had rather — *preferiría.*

She had rather be unhappy than poor. *Ella preferiría ser infeliz a ser pobre.*

to be had — *ser engañado.*

You've been had. *Fue engañado.*

to have before one — *tener delante sí.*

You have before you the tallest building on earth. *Tienes delante tuyo el edificio más alto del mundo.*

to have had it — *no poder más.*

I've had it! *¡No puedo más!*

to have in hand — *tener entre manos.*

She has her work well in hand. *Tiene su trabajo entre manos.*

to have it in for — *tenérsela jurada.*

He's got it in for us. *Nos la tiene jurada.*

to have it out — *poner las cosas en claro; habérselas.*

He had it out with his wife. *Puso las cosas en claro (Se las ha habido) con su esposa.*

to have on — *tener puesto.*

He has on his new suit. *Tiene puesto su traje nuevo.*

to have to — *tener que.*

He has (He's got) to find a job. *Tiene que encontrar empleo.*

to have to do with — *tener que ver con.*

They have nothing to do with this company. *No tienen nada que ver con esta compañía.*

haven — *abrigo; asilo; refugio*

tax haven — *refugio fiscal.*

The Cayman Islands used to be a tax haven. *Las Islas Caimán fueron en su tiempo un refugio fiscal.*

haves — *los ricos*

the haves and the have-nots — *los ricos y los pobres.*

It's a matter of the haves and the have-nots. *Es cuestión de los ricos y los pobres.*

havoc — *el estrago*

to play havoc with — *destruir.*

The wind played havoc with our kite. *El viento destruyó nuestra cometa.*

hawk — *el halcón*

hawks and doves — *los belicistas y los pacifistas.*

Hawks and doves are insulting each other in Congress. *Los belicistas y los pacifistas están insultándose en el congreso.*

hay — *el heno*

to hit the hay — *irse a la cama.*

Let's hit the hay. *Vámonos a la cama.*

to make hay while the sun shines — *batir el hierro cuando está al rojo.*

It's better to make hay while the sun shines. *Es mejor batir el hierro cuando está al rojo.*

haywire — *el alambre para empacar heno*

to go haywire — *volverse loco; confundirse; estropearse.*

The remote control went haywire and the TV screen froze. *El control remoto se estropeó y la pantalla del televisor quedó paralizada.*

head — *la cabeza*

at the head — *por delante; a la cabeza.*

There's a horseman at the head. *Viene un jinete por delante (a la cabeza).*

head first (on one's head) — *de cabeza.*

They all fell head first (on their heads). *Todos se cayeron de cabeza.*

head on — *de cabeza.*

They met head on. *Se encontraron de cabeza.*

Heads or tails? — *¿Cara o cruz?*

not to be able to make head or tail (out) of something — *no verle ni pies ni cabeza.*

I cannot make head or tail (out) of it. *No le veo ni pies ni cabeza.*

to be head and shoulders above one — *aventajarle en mucho.*

As for singing, he's head and shoulders above me. *En cuanto a cantar, me aventaja en mucho.*

to be head over heels in love — *estar perdidamente enamorado.*

He's head over heels in love. *Está perdidamente enamorado.*

to beat one's head against a wall — *topar con una pared.*

I think you're beating your head against a wall. *Creo que está topando con una pared.*

to bury one's head in the sand — *cerrar los ojos a la realidad.*

She buried her head in the sand. *Cerró los ojos a la realidad.*

to come to a head — *estar que arde.*

Things are coming to a head. *La cosa está que arde.*

to go to one's head — *subírsele a la cabeza.*

His success went to his head. *Su éxito se le subió a la cabeza.*

to keep one's head — *quedarse con calma.*

He kept his head despite the tragedy. *Se quedó con calma a pesar de la tragedia.*

to live over one's head — *vivir más allá de los recursos.*

They live over their heads and don't think about the consequences. *Viven por encima de sus recursos y no piensan en las consecuencias.*

to lose one's head — *perder los estribos (la cabeza).*

She lost her head. *Perdió los estribos (la cabeza).*

to make one's head swim — *aturdirse.*

It made my head swim. *Me aturdió.*

to put heads together — *consultarse mutuamente.*

We put our heads together. *Nos consultamos mutuamente.*

to take into one's head — *metérsele en la cabeza.*

She took it into her head to get married. *Se le metió en la cabeza casarse.*

heart — *el corazón*

after one's own heart — *como le gustan a uno.*

He's a boy after my own heart. *Es un chico como a mí me gustan.*

at heart — *en el fondo.*

At heart, he's generous. *En el fondo es generoso.*

Take heart! — *¡Anímese!; ¡Cobre aliento!*

to bare one's heart — *abrir el pecho.*

Last night my daughter bared her heart to me. *Anoche mi hija me abrió su pecho.*

to carry one's heart on one's sleeve — *tener el corazón en la mano.*

He carries his heart on his sleeve. *Tiene el corazón en la mano.*

to do one's heart good — *alegrarle el corazón.*

It did my heart good. *Me alegró el corazón.*

to eat one's heart out — *consumirse de pena.*

She's eating her heart out over her husband's death. *Se está consumiendo de pena por la muerte de su esposo.*

to get to the heart of the problem — *llegar al fondo del problema.*

We wanted to get to the heart of the problem. *Queríamos llegar al fondo del problema.*

to have one's heart in one's mouth — *tener el corazón en un puño.*

I had my heart in my mouth. *Tenía el corazón en un puño.*

to have one's heart set on — *tener la esperanza puesta en.*

He had his heart set on going to college. *Tenía la esperanza puesta en asistir a una universidad.*

to know by heart — *saber de memoria (al dedillo).*

I know it by heart. *Lo sé de memoria (al dedillo).*

to learn by heart — *aprender de memoria.*

I learned it by heart. *Lo aprendí de memoria.*

to one's heart's content — *a sus anchas; sin restricciones.*

At this all-you-can-eat restaurant you can eat shrimp to your heart's content. *En ese restaurante de porciones ilimitadas puedes comer camarones a tus anchas.*

to take to heart — *tomar a pecho(s).*

He took what I said to heart. *Tomó a pecho(s) lo que dije.*

heaven — *el cielo*

Good heavens! — *¡Dios mío!; ¡Válgame Dios!*

Heaven forbid! — *¡Dios nos (me) libre!*

heed — *la atención*

to take heed — *hacer caso.*

I'm sorry you didn't take heed to what I said. *Siento que no haya hecho caso de lo que dije.*

heel — *el tacón, el talón*

to be hard on one's heels — *pisarle los talones.*

They were hard on his heels. *Le pisaban los talones.*

to be well heeled — *ser muy rico.*

He's well heeled. *Es muy rico.*

to cool one's heels — *hacer antesala.*

They left him cooling his heels. *Lo dejaron haciendo antesala.*

to take to one's heels — *echar a correr; poner pies en polvorosa.*

He took to his heels. *Echó a correr (Puso pies en polvorosa).*

hell — *el infierno*

all hell to break loose — *armarse la grande.*

If he doesn't obey his boss, all hell will break loose. *Si no obedece a su jefe, se armará la grande.*

come hell or high water — *contra viento y marea.*

We'll get to San Francisco come hell or high water. *Llegaremos a San Francisco contra viento y marea.*

until hell freezes over — *hasta el día del juicio.*

He can stay in jail until hell freezes over. *Puede quedarse en la cárcel hasta el día del juicio.*

what the hell — *qué diablos.*

What the hell are you doing here? *¿Qué diablos haces aquí?*

to help — *ayudar*

It can't be helped (It's beyond help). — *No hay (No tiene más) remedio.*

not to be able to help — *no poder menos de.*

He can't help loving her. *No puede menos de amarla.*

to help out — *ayudar.*

He always helps out. *Siempre ayuda.*

to help someone out — *sacarle del apuro.*

He helped us out. *Nos sacó del apuro.*

here — *aquí*

around here — *por aquí.*

He spends a lot of time around here. *Pasa mucho tiempo por aquí.*

here is — *aquí tiene.*

Here is a copy. *Aquí tiene un ejemplar.*

here is — *aquí viene.*

Here's Mary. *Aquí viene María.*

in here — *aquí dentro.*

They're waiting in here. *Están esperando aquí dentro.*

neither here nor there — *no venir al caso.*

Your opinion is neither here nor there. *Su opinión simplemente no viene al caso.*

right here — *aquí mismo.*

It happened right here. *Pasó aquí mismo.*

herring — *el arenque*

red herring — *distracción premeditada.*

Her comment was a red herring to confuse Eric. *Su comentario fue una distracción calculada para despistar a Eric.*

to hide — *esconder; esconderse*

hide-and-seek — *el juego del escondite.*

The children were playing hide-and-seek. *Los niños estaban jugando al escondite.*

high — *alto*

to act high and mighty — *darse mucha importancia.*

He acts high and mighty. *Se da mucha importancia.*

to leave high and dry — *dejar en seco (plantado).*

He left her high and dry. *La dejó en seco (plantada).*

to look high and low — *buscar por todas partes (de arriba abajo).*

I looked high and low for it. *Lo busqué por todas partes (de arriba abajo).*

hint — *la indirecta*

to take the hint — *darse por aludido.*

He took the hint. *Se dio por aludido.*

to throw out a hint — *lanzar una indirecta.*

He threw out a hint. *Lanzó una indirecta.*

hip — *la cadera*

to shoot from the hip — *proceder precipitadamente.*

This presentation requires preparation and cold reasoning; you cannot shoot from the hip. *Esta presentación requiere preparación y frío razonamiento; aquí no puedes actuar impetuosamente.*

hit — *el éxito, el golpe*

hit or miss — *al azar; a la buena de Dios.*

Marriage often is a hit or miss enterprise. *A menudo, el matrimonio es una aventura al azar.*

to make a hit — *caerle en (la) gracia.*

She made a hit with everyone. *Les cayó en (la) gracia a todos.*

to hit — *golpear*

to hit it off well — *entenderse (llevarse) bien.*

They hit it off well. *Se entienden (Se llevan) bien.*

to hit on the idea of — *ocurrírsele.*

He hit on the idea of traveling. *Se le ocurrió viajar.*

hog — *el cerdo; el chancho*

to live high off the hog — *darse la gran vida.*

The old landowners lived high off the hog. *Los viejos terratenientes se daban la gran vida.*

hold — *el agarro*

to take hold of — *agarrar.*

He took hold of the handle. *Agarró el asa.*

to take hold of oneself — *dominarse; controlarse.*

Try to take hold of yourself. *Trate de dominarse (controlarse).*

to hold — *tener (agarrado)*

Hold it! — *¡Un momento!*

to be held — *tener lugar.*

We will hold the meeting (The meeting will be held) in my office. *La reunión tendrá lugar en mi oficina.*

to hold good — *servir.*

This rule doesn't hold good in this situation. *Esta regla no sirve en esta situación.*

to hold on — *esperar.*

Hold on a second. *Espere un segundo.*

to hold on to — *agarrarse bien de.*

Hold on to the saddle. *Agárrese bien de la silla.*

to hold one's own — *mantenerse firme.*

Despite being new, he's holding his own quite well. *Pese a ser nuevo, se las está arreglando lo más bien.*

to hold out — *resistir.*

The enemy held out for two days. *El enemigo resistió dos días.*

to hold out for — *insistir en.*

He held out for ten dollars. *Insistió en diez dólares.*

to hold over — *continuar (representando).*

The play was held over for another week. *Continuaron (representando) la comedia otra semana.*

to hold still — *estarse quieto.*

The baby wouldn't hold still. *El nene no quiso estarse quieto.*

to hold up — *asaltar.*

They held up the bank. *Asaltaron el banco.*

to hold up — *detener.*

They held us up for a week. *Nos detuvieron una semana.*

hole — *el agujero*

to pick holes in — *hallar defectos.*

He picked holes in our proposal. *Halló defectos en nuestra propuesta.*

holiday — *el día feriado; las vacaciones*

tax holiday — *la moratoria fiscal.*

Sometimes tax holidays are granted by the government to disaster areas. *A veces el gobierno otorga una exención en el pago de impuestos a zonas de catástrofe.*

home — *la casa*

Make yourself at home. — *Está usted en su casa.*

to be (at) home — *estar en casa.*

He's not (at) home. *No está en casa.*

to bring home — *hacer comprender.*

It took a hundred years of injustice to bring home the need for reform. *Tomó cien años de injusticia para que se comprendiese la necesidad de hacer reformas.*

to see someone home — *acompañar a casa.*

He'll see the babysitter home. *Acompañará a casa a la niñera.*

to strike home — *dar en lo vivo.*

My ideas struck home. *Mis ideas dieron en lo vivo.*

homesick — *nostálgico.*

to be homesick — *añorar su casa; sentir nostalgia de su casa.*

She's homesick. *Añora su casa (Siente nostalgia de su casa).*

to honor — *honrar*

to honor — *aceptar.*

They won't honor my check here. *No quieren aceptar mi cheque aquí.*

hook — *el gancho*

by hook or by crook — *de una manera u otra.*

We're going to get it by hook or by crook. *Vamos a conseguirlo de una manera u otra.*

to get (someone) off the hook — *sacar (a alguien) del apuro.*

I'll pay you 100,000 to get me off the hook. *Te pagaré 100.000 para que me saques del apuro.*

to swallow hook, line, and sinker — *tragar el anzuelo.*

He swallowed it hook, line, and sinker. *Tragó el anzuelo.*

to hook — *enganchar*

to get hooked on — *aficionarse a.*

He got hooked on classic jazz. *Se aficionó al jazz clásico.*

to hook up — *abrochar; enganchar; unir.*

Hook these two wagons up. *Engancha estos dos vagones.*

hooky

to play hooky — *hacer novillos.*

He was playing hooky. *Estaba haciendo novillos.*

to hop — *brincar, saltar*

to be hopping mad — *echar chispas.*

She's hopping mad. *Está echando chispas.*

hope — *la esperanza*

to pin one's hope on — *cifrar sus esperanzas en.*

He pinned all his hopes on winning the lottery. *Él había puesto todas sus esperanzas en ganar la lotería.*

to hope — *esperar*

I should hope so! — *¡No faltaría más!*

hopeless — *desesperado*

to be hopeless at — *ser una desgracia para.*

I'm hopeless at bridge. *Soy una desgracia para el bridge.*

horn — *el cuerno*

to lock horns — *pelear; disputar.*

We locked horns over the contract's terms. *Empezamos a pelear sobre los términos del contrato.*

horn — *la bocina, el claxon*

to blow one's own horn — *alabarse a sí mismo.*

He always blows his own horn. *Siempre se alaba a sí mismo.*

horse — *el caballo*

dark horse — *un contrincante o ganador desconocido.*

The French team is the dark horse in these games. *El contrincante desconocido en estos juegos es el equipo francés.*

That's a horse of a different (another) color. — *Eso es harina de otro costal.*

to flog a dead horse — *fatigarse en vano.*

If you try to get that money back, you'll be flogging a dead horse. *Si tratas de recuperar ese dinero, estarás fatigándote en vano.*

to get on one's high horse — *ponerse muy arrogante.*

He got on his high horse. *Se puso muy arrogante.*

horseback — *el lomo de caballo*

on horseback — *montado a caballo.*

They came on horseback. *Vinieron montados a caballo.*

host — *el anfitrión; el huésped*

to play host — *atender a los invitados.*

The President played host at the meeting in the White House. *El presidente actuó de anfitrión durante la reunión en la Casa Blanca.*

hot — *caliente*

to be hot (the weather) — *hacer calor.*

It's hot today. *Hace calor hoy.*

to be hot (a person) — *tener calor.*

I'm hot. *Tengo calor.*

to get hot — *entusiasmarse.*

I got hot about buying a new TV. *Me entusiasmé por comprar un televisor nuevo.*

to make it hot — *hacer la vida imposible.*

She makes it hot for everybody. *Hace la vida imposible a (para) todos.*

to sell like hot cakes — *venderse como pan bendito.*

Perfume sells like hot cakes in France. *El perfume se vende como pan bendito en Francia.*

hour — *la hora*

after hours — *después de horas de oficina.*

I don't work after hours. *Yo no trabajo después de horas de oficina.*

at all hours — *a toda hora.*

It's open at all hours. *Está abierto a toda hora.*

rush hour(s) — *las horas de aglomeración.*

We don't leave during rush hour(s). *No salimos durante las horas de aglomeración.*

the wee hours of the morning — *las primeras horas de la mañana.*

He came in at the wee hours of the morning. *Entró en las primeras horas de la mañana.*

to keep late hours — *trasnochar.*

He keeps late hours. *Trasnocha.*

house — *la casa*

to be on the house — *ir por cuenta de la casa.*

The wine is on the house. *El vino va por cuenta de la casa.*

to have (hold) open house — *recibir amistades.*

We're having (holding) open house tomorrow at three. *Mañana recibimos amistades a las tres.*

to keep house — *hacer los quehaceres domésticos.*

She likes to keep house. *Le gusta hacer los quehaceres domésticos.*

to paper the house — *repartir pases.*

Of course the circus is full . . . they papered the house! *Por supuesto que el circo está lleno, ¡si repartieron pases hasta llenarlo!*

how — *cómo*

How about that? — *¿Qué le parece?*

how else — *cómo, si no.*

How else can you do it? *¿Cómo, si no, se puede hacer?*

howl — *el aullido*

to raise a big howl — *poner el grito en el cielo.*

They raised a big howl. *Pusieron el grito en el cielo.*

Hoyle

according to Hoyle — *como Dios manda.*

They insist on having everything done according to Hoyle. *Insisten en que todo se haga como Dios manda.*

to humble — *humillar*

to humble oneself — *rebajarse.*

She humbled herself before him. *Se rebajó ante él.*

hunger — *el hambre (f.)*

to be hungry — *tener hambre.*

He's not hungry. *No tiene hambre.*

hurry — *la prisa*

Hurry back. — *Vuelva en seguida.*

Hurry up. — *Apresúrese; Dese prisa.*

to be in a hurry — *estar de (con) prisa; tener prisa; andar de prisa.*

He's in a hurry. *Está de (Tiene) prisa (Anda de prisa).*

to leave in a hurry — *salir en volandas.*

He left in a hurry. *Salió en volandas.*

to hurt — *lastimar*

to hurt someone — *hacerle daño (mal).*

It hurt him. *Le hizo daño (mal).*

to hush — *callar*

to hush up the scandal — *echar tierra al (acallar el) escándalo.*

We hushed up the scandal. *Echamos tierra al (acallamos el) escándalo.*

I

i — *la i*

to dot every i and cross every t — *poner los puntos sobre las íes.*

He dots every i and crosses every t. *Pone los puntos sobre las íes.*

I — *yo*

I, for one — *personalmente.*

I, for one, don't agree with him. *Personalmente, no estoy de acuerdo con él.*

It is I — *soy yo.*

It is I who will tell them. *Soy yo el que les dirá.*

I say — *oye; escucha.*

I say, did you hear what happened to her? *Oye, ¿escuchaste lo que le pasó a ella?*

I see — *ya veo; entiendo.*

Oh, I see. So what's next? *Oh, ya veo. Entonces, ¿qué va a pasar ahora?*

I take it that — *entiendo que.*

I take it that you prefer to go to Boston. *Entiendo que usted prefiere ir a Boston.*

I would rather — *preferiría.*

I would rather go to New York. *Yo preferiría ir a Nueva York.*

ice — *el hielo*

on ice — *aplazado; postergado.*

Let's keep this project on ice until we get enough financing. *Aplacemos este proyecto hasta obtener el financiamiento necesario.*

to break the ice — *romper el hielo.*

He broke the ice with his joke. *Rompió el hielo con su chiste.*

to cut no ice — *no pintar nada.*

He cuts no ice with the manager. *No pinta nada con el gerente.*

to skate on thin ice — *hallarse en una situación comprometida.*

We're skating on thin ice. *Nos hallamos en una situación comprometida.*

idea — *la idea*

Don't get any ideas . . . — *No te hagas ilusiones de . . .*

Don't get any ideas about marrying my daughter. *No te hagas ilusiones de casarte con mi hija.*

What's the idea? — *¿De qué se trata?; ¿Qué le pasa?*

ill — *enfermo*

to take ill — *caer enfermo; enfermarse.*

She took ill. *Cayó enferma (Se enfermó).*

impression — *la impresión*

to make an impression — *dejar huella.*

He's made an impression. *Ha dejado huella.*

in — *dentro*

the ins and outs — *los recovecos.*

You have to know all the ins and outs to work there. *Hay que conocer todos los recovecos para trabajar allí.*

to be in — *estar de moda.*

White shirts are in again. *Las camisas blancas están de moda de nuevo.*

to be in for — *esperarle.*

We're in for a cold night. *Nos espera una noche fría.*

inch — *la pulgada*

Give him an inch and he'll take a mile. — *Le da la mano y se toma el brazo (pie).*

inch by inch — *palmo a palmo.*

They examined it inch by inch. *Lo examinaron palmo a palmo.*

to inch — *avanzar a poquitos*

to inch along — *avanzar a paso de tortuga.*

The convoy inched along. *El convoy avanzó a paso de tortuga.*

indeed — *de veras*

No indeed. — *Eso sí que no.*

Yes indeed. — *Ya lo creo; Eso sí.*

informed — *informado*

to be informed about — *estar al corriente (al tanto) de*

I'm not informed about politics. *No estoy al corriente (al tanto) de la política.*

to inquire — *averiguar, preguntar*

to inquire about — *preguntar por.*

He inquired about her. *Preguntó por ella.*

insane — *loco*

to go insane — *perder la razón.*

I think that she's going insane. *Creo que va a perder la razón.*

inside — *adentro*

inside and out — *por dentro y por fuera.*

They covered it inside and out with flowers. *Lo cubrieron por dentro y por fuera con flores.*

inside (wrong side) out — *al revés.*

The boy put his jacket on inside (wrong side) out. *El chico se puso la chaqueta al revés.*

installment — *la entrega*

to pay by installments — *pagar a plazos.*

He's paying by installments. *Está pagando a plazos.*

instrumental — *instrumental*

to be instrumental in — *contribuir a.*

He was instrumental in my getting it. *Contribuyó a que lo consiguiera.*

insult — *el insulto*

to add insult to injury — *como si esto fuera poco.*

To add insult to injury, he took two. *Como si esto fuera poco, se llevó dos.*

intent — *la intención*

for all intents and purposes — *prácticamente; en realidad.*

The airlines have many passenger classes, but for all intents and purposes most people fly economy class. *Las aerolíneas tienen muchas clases para pasajeros, pero en realidad la mayoría vuela en clase económica.*

interest — *el interés*

to draw interest — *devengar interés.*

His money is drawing interest. *Su dinero devenga interés.*

to take an interest in — *interesarse por.*

He takes an interest in everything. *Se interesa por todo.*

interval — *el intervalo*

at intervals — *de vez en cuando.*

At intervals she stopped by to see her mother. *De vez en cuando pasaba a ver a su madre.*

to involve — *enredar, enmarañar*

to be involved in — *estar metido en.*

She's involved in so many things that she has no time for her family. *Está metida en tantas cosas que no tiene tiempo para su familia.*

to iron — *planchar*

to iron out one's difficulties — *resolver las dificultades.*

We ironed out our difficulties. *Resolvimos nuestras dificultades.*

J

jack — *el mozo*

Jack of all trades, master of none. — *Aprendiz de todo, oficial de nada.*

to jack — *alzar*

to jack up the prices — *aumentar los precios.*

They jacked up the prices. *Aumentaron los precios.*

jam — *el aprieto*

to be in a jam — *estar en un aprieto.*

He's in a jam. *Está en un aprieto.*

to get out of a jam — *salir de un apuro.*

It's not always easy to get out of a jam. *No siempre es fácil salir de un apuro.*

to get someone out of a jam — *sacar de un apuro.*

I got him out of a jam. *Lo saqué de un apuro.*

jazz — *el jazz*

to jazz up — *avivar; tonificar.*

These crazy paintings will jazz up his room. *Estos cuadros tan locos darán más vida a su cuarto.*

jiffy — *el periquete*

in a jiffy — *en un santiamén; en un dos por tres.*

It will be here in a jiffy. *Llegará en un santiamén (dos por tres).*

job — *el trabajo*

a ticklish job — *algo delicado o difícil.*

To stop seeing her will be a ticklish job. *Dejar de verla será una tarea delicada.*

odd jobs — *trabajos pequeños; empleo ocasional.*

He's always doing odd jobs instead of getting something serious. *Siempre está haciendo trabajitos de poca monta en vez de obtener un trabajo serio.*

to do a halfway job — *hacer un trabajo a medias.*

They fired him because he always did a halfway job. *Lo despidieron porque siempre hacía su trabajo a medias.*

to land a job — *obtener un empleo.*

He lands jobs by way of his connections. *Obtiene empleos a fuerza de contactos.*

to join — *unir*

to join — *acompañar.*

He joined us on our trip. *Nos acompañó en nuestro viaje.*

to join — *venir a sentarse con.*

He joined us at our table. *Vino a sentarse con nosotros en nuestra mesa.*

to join —*hacerse socio de.*

He joined the club. *Se hizo socio del club.*

---

joke — *el chiste, la broma*

as a joke (jokingly) — *en broma.*

Don't get mad; I said it as a joke. *No te enojes, lo dije en broma.*

to crack jokes — *hacer chistes.*

He's always cracking jokes. *Siempre hace chistes.*

to play a (practical) joke — *gastar (hacer) una broma (pesada).*

They played a (practical) joke on him. *Le gastaron (hicieron) una broma (pesada).*

to take a joke — *soportar una broma.*

He can't take a joke. *No sabe soportar una broma.*

John — Juan

Dear John letter — *carta femenina de despedida.*

Many soldiers in the front receive Dear John letters. *Muchos soldados en el frente reciben cartas de despedida de sus mujeres.*

Joneses — *los Jones*

to keep up with the Joneses — *hacer lo que hace el vecino.*

It's useless to try to keep up with the Joneses. *Es inútil tratar de hacer lo que hace el vecino.*

---

to jot — *escribir a prisa*

to jot down — *apuntar (tomar nota de).*

I jotted down the address. *Apunté (tomé nota de) la dirección.*

---

to judge —*juzgar*

judging by — *a juzgar por.*

Judging by what is seen, it's luxurious. *A juzgar por lo que se ve, es de lujo.*

judgment — *el juicio; el criterio; el discernimiento*

against one's better judgment — *contra los deseos de uno.*

I will go to Miami if you insist, but it will be against my better judgment. *Iré a Miami si insiste, pero no comparto su opinión al respecto.*

jugular — *la yugular*

to go for the jugular — *atacar a fondo.*

He goes for the jugular in every business transaction. *En cada negociación, él siempre es el más agresivo.*

juice — *el jugo*

to stew in one's own juice — *freír en su aceite; cocer en su propia salsa.*

We left her to stew in her own juice. *La dejamos freír en su aceite (cocer en su propia salsa).*

jump — *el salto*

to get the jump on someone — *ganarle la acción.*

I got the jump on him. *Le gané la acción.*

to jump — *saltar*

to jump at the opportunity — *apresurarse a aceptar la oportunidad.*

I jumped at the opportunity. *Me apresuré a aceptar la oportunidad.*

just — *justo*

just about — *más o menos.*

It's just about two weeks. *Son más o menos dos semanas.*

just around the corner — *a la vuelta de la esquina.*

They live just around the corner. *Viven a la vuelta de la esquina.*

just as one thought — *tal como pensaba uno.*

She had it, just as I thought. *Lo tenía ella, tal como pensaba yo.*

just like — *lo mismo (igual) que.*

She's blonde, just like her mother. *Es rubia, lo mismo (igual) que su madre.*

to have just — *acabar de.*

He has just left. *Acaba de salir.*

justice — *la justicia*

poetic justice — *la justicia divina.*

The violent death of the tyrant was poetic justice. *La violenta muerte del tirano fue justicia divina.*

K

keel — *la quilla*

on an even keel — *ordenadamente; sin contratiempos.*

Our business moves along on an even keel. *Nuestra empresa sigue adelante sin contratiempo alguno.*

keen — *agudo*

to be keen about — *tener mucho entusiasmo por.*

I'm not keen about the plan. *No tengo mucho entusiasmo por el plan.*

keep — *la manutención*

to earn one's keep — *ganarse la vida.*

He earns his keep. *Se gana la vida.*

to play for keeps — *jugar de veras.*

He is playing for keeps. *Está jugando de veras.*

to keep — *guardar; mantener*

to keep abreast — *estar al corriente.*

It's hard to keep abreast of the war. *Es difícil estar al corriente de la guerra.*

to keep at — *perseverar.*

He always keeps at what he is doing. *Siempre persevera.*

to keep on — *seguir.*

She keeps on driving despite her age. *Sigue manejando (conduciendo) a pesar de su edad.*

to keep out of sight — *mantenerse fuera de vista.*

He kept out of sight. *Se mantuvo fuera de vista.*

to keep to oneself — *quedarse a solas.*

He doesn't have much fun because he always keeps to himself. *Se divierte poco porque siempre se queda a solas.*

to keep . . . to oneself — *no decirle a nadie.*

I want you to keep this to yourself. *No quiero que le digas esto a nadie.*

to keep up with — *mantener el mismo paso que.*

The child can't keep up with his mother. *El niño no puede mantener el mismo paso que su mamá.*

---

kick — *el puntapié, la coz*

for kicks — *por gusto.*

He does it just for kicks. *Lo hace por puro gusto.*

to get a kick out of — *encantarle.*

We get a kick out of traveling. *Nos encanta viajar.*

---

to kick — *dar puntapiés, dar coces, dar patadas*

to kick (to chip) in — *contribuir.*

We all kicked (chipped) in and bought him a book. *Todos contribuimos y le compramos un libro.*

to kick out — *expulsar.*

He got kicked out because of bad grades. *Lo expulsaron por sus malas notas.*

---

to kid — *bromear*

No kidding! — *¡No me digas! ¿En serio?*

She had triplets? No kidding! *¿Tuvo trillizos? ¿En serio?*

---

to kill — *matar*

dressed fit to kill (all dressed up) — *vestido de veinticinco alfileres.*

She came dressed fit to kill (all dressed up). *Vino vestida de veinticinco alfileres.*

---

killing — *la matanza*

to make a killing — *hacer su agosto.*

I made a killing on the stockmarket. *Hice mi agosto en la bolsa.*

kind — *la clase, la especie*

a kind (sort) of (a) . . . — *una especie de.*

He lives in a kind (sort) of (a) hut. *Vive en una especie de choza.*

to be one of a kind — *ser único.*

That table is one of a kind, because the artist handcrafts it from a single log. *Esa mesa es única, porque el artista la labra de un solo leño.*

to be two of a kind — *ser tal para cual.*

They are two of a kind. *Son tal para cual.*

nothing of the kind — *nada de eso.*

I said nothing of the kind. *No dije nada de eso.*

king — *el rey*

fit for a king — *digno de un rey.*

She served us a dinner fit for a king. *Nos sirvió una comida digna de un rey.*

kingdom — *el reino*

to blow to kingdom come — *destruir.*

The new bomb will blow them to kingdom come. *La nueva bomba los destruirá por completo.*

kite — *la cometa*

Go fly a kite. — *Váyase a freír espárragos.*

kitty — *pozo; banco de apuestas*

to sweeten the kitty — *aumentar el pozo; hacer algo más atractivo.*

Would you buy it if I sweeten the kitty with chrome wheels? *¿Y lo compraría si se lo ofrezco con ruedas cromadas?*

to knock — *golpear*

to knock at the door — *llamar a la puerta.*

I knocked at the door. *Llamé a la puerta.*

to knock down — *derribar.*
He knocked down the door. *Derribó la puerta.*

to knock off — *rebajar.*
He knocked ten dollars off the price. *Rebajó el precio diez dólares.*

to knock off — *suspender.*
We knocked off the meeting at five. *Suspendimos la reunión a las cinco.*

to knock out — *poner fuera de combate.*
He knocked him out. *Lo puso fuera de combate.*

knot — *el nudo*
to tie the knot — *casar; casarse.*
I want to tie the knot, but Bob wants his freedom. *Yo quiero casarme, pero Bob desea su libertad.*

to know — *saber*
before one knows it — *sin darse cuenta.*
Before you know it, it's too late. *Sin darse cuenta es muy tarde.*

How do I know? — *¿Qué sé yo?*

to be in the know — *estar bien informado (enterado).*
Because he's such a friend of the president, he's always in the know. *Por ser tan amigo del presidente, siempre está bien informado.*

to know full well (only too well) — *saber de sobra.*
He knows full well (only to well) that his wife doesn't love him. *Sabe de sobra que su esposa no lo quiere.*

L

to label — *marcar; calificar*
to be labeled — *quedar considerado como.*
Don't label me as an ignoramus! ¡No me califique de ignorante!

lack — *la falta*

for lack of — *por falta de.*

She failed for lack of experience. *Fracasó por falta de experiencia.*

to lag — *retrasarse*

to lag behind — *ir atrasado a.*

He is lagging behind the others. *Va atrasado a los otros.*

lake — *el lago*

to tell (someone) to go jump in the lake — *mandar al diablo.*

When she refused to go out with him, he told her to go jump in the lake. *Cuando se negó a salir con él, la mandó al diablo.*

lam — *el escape; la fuga*

on the lam — *prófugo.*

He's been on the lam since he escaped from jail in 2006. *Ha sido un fugitivo desde que escapó de la cárcel en 2006.*

land — *la tierra*

to make land — *divisar tierra.*

We made land early in the morning. *Divisamos tierra temprano por la mañana.*

to see how the land lies — *tantear el terreno.*

We must check people's opinions to see how the land lies. *Debemos estudiar las opiniones de la gente para tantear el terreno.*

language — *el idioma, la lengua*

to use strong language — *expresarse en términos ofensivos.*

He used strong language. *Se expresó en términos ofensivos.*

lap — *el regazo*

in the lap of luxury — *rodeado de lujo.*

He won the lottery and lived in the lap of luxury ever since. *Ganó la lotería y desde entonces vivió rodeado de lujo.*

large — *grande*

by and large — *por regla general.*

By and large the supermarkets close at around nine. *Por regla general, los supermercados cierran alrededor de las nueve.*

to be at large — *estar en libertad (suelto).*

The criminal is still at large. *El criminal todavía está en libertad (suelto).*

lark — *la travesura*

for a lark — *para divertirse.*

Why so angry? We did it for a lark! *¿Por qué estás tan enojado? ¡Lo hicimos por divertirnos!*

last — *último*

at last — *por (al) fin.*

He's here at last. *Por (Al) fin está aquí.*

last but not least — *último en orden pero no en importancia.*

Last but not least, the house must have three bedrooms. *Ultimo en orden pero no en importancia, la casa debe tener tres alcobas (dormitorios).*

to see the last of — *no volver a ver.*

He saw the last of us. *No nos volvió a ver*

to the last — *hasta el fin.*

We stayed to the last. *(Nos) quedamos hasta el fin.*

late — *tarde*

late in life — *a una edad avanzada.*

She got married late in life. *Se casó a una edad avanzada.*

later on — *más adelante.*

Later on I'll explain it to you. *Más adelante te lo explicaré.*

to be late — *hacérsele tarde.*

I've got to leave because I'm late. *Tengo que marcharme porque se me hace tarde.*

to be late — *llegar tarde.*

I'm sorry I'm late. *Siento haber llegado tarde.*

latest — *último*

at the latest — *a más tardar.*

Come tomorrow at the latest. *Venga mañana a más tardar.*

the latest gossip — *el chisme de la última hora.*

The latest gossip is that she's divorced. *El chisme de la última hora es que está divorciada.*

---

to laugh — *reír*

He laughs best who laughs last. — *Al freír será el reír.*

to make one laugh — *causarle gracia.*

It made me laugh. *Me causó gracia.*

to laugh at — *reírse de.*

She's laughing at me. *Se ríe de mí.*

to laugh oneself sick — *tirarse al suelo de risa.*

I laughed myself sick. *Me tiré al suelo de risa.*

to laugh until one cries — *llorar de risa.*

They laughed until they cried. *Lloraron de risa.*

---

laurel — *el laurel*

to rest on one's laurels — *dormirse sobre sus laureles.*

He's resting on his laurels. *Se duerme sobre sus laureles.*

---

law — *la ley*

due process of law — *las debidas garantías procesales.*

Some inmates had been tried without the due process of law. *Algunos presos fueron juzgados sin las debidas garantías procesales.*

the rule of law — *el imperio de la ley; la legalidad.*

The rule of law should equally apply to all citizens. *Las normas jurídicas debieran aplicarse por igual a todos los ciudadanos.*

to lay down the law — *dar órdenes terminantes.*

Our professor laid down the law. *Nuestro profesor dio órdenes terminantes.*

to maintain law and order — *mantener la paz.*

They can't maintain law and order. *No pueden mantener la paz.*

to practice law — *ejercer la profesión de abogado.*

When he got out of jail he could not practice law anymore. *Cuando salió de la cárcel ya no pudo ejercer de abogado.*

to read law — *estudiar derecho.*

She reads law at Columbia University. *Estudia derecho en la Universidad de Columbia.*

to take the law into one's own hands — *hacerse justicia por sí mismo.*

The students took the law into their own hands. *Los estudiantes se hicieron justicia por sí mismos.*

---

to lay — *poner, colocar*

to lay aside — *poner a un lado; abandonar.*

He laid some money aside just in case. *Guardó algo de dinero por si acaso.*

to lay bare — *revelar; desnudar.*

Their plans were laid bare and thus they knew they could not escape. *Sus planes quedaron a la vista y así supieron que no podrían escapar.*

to lay down one's arms — *rendirse.*

They laid down their arms and ended up in a concentration camp. *Se rindieron y fueron a parar a un campo de concentración.*

to lay low — *esconderse temporalmente.*

We'll have to lay low until the police forget about us. *Nos esconderemos hasta que la policía se olvide de nosotros.*

to lay off — *despedir; dejar cesante.*

They laid off ten men. *Despidieron (Dejaron cesantes) a diez hombres.*

---

lead — *la delantera*

to play the lead — *tener el papel principal.*

She plays the lead. *Tiene el papel principal.*

to take the lead — *tomar la delantera.*

She took the lead in deciding. *Tomó la delantera en decidir.*

---

to lead — *conducir*

to lead one to — *llevarle a.*

It led me to doubt it. *Me llevó a dudarlo.*

leader — *el jefe*

to be a born leader — *nacer para mandar.*

Mr. López was a born leader. *El señor López nació para mandar.*

leaf — *la hoja*

to turn over a new leaf — *enmendarse; cambiar su modo de vivir.*

He turned over a new leaf. *Se enmendó (Cambió su modo de vivir).*

to leak — *salirse (un fluido); gotear*

to leak out — *trascender; descubrirse.*

The secret leaked out. *El secreto trascendió (se descubrió).*

to lean — *inclinarse*

to lean back — *echarse hacia atrás.*

She leaned back. *Se echó hacia atrás.*

leap — *el salto*

by leaps and bounds — *a pasos agigantados.*

He's growing by leaps and bounds. *Está creciendo a pasos agigantados.*

lease — *el alquiler*

to break a lease — *marcharse sin cumplir con el contrato de alquiler.*

They broke the lease two months after moving in. *Se marcharon sin cumplir con el contrato de alquiler dos meses después de haberse mudado.*

least — *menos*

at least — *a lo menos; por lo menos; al menos; cuando menos.*

He has at least three. *Tiene a lo menos (por lo menos, al menos, cuando menos) tres.*

in the least — *en lo más mínimo.*

I didn't like it in the least. *No me gustó en lo más mínimo.*

That's the least of it. — *Eso es lo de menos.*

leave — *el permiso; la despedida*

to take leave of — *despedirse de.*

He took leave of his friends. *Se despidió de sus amigos.*

to take leave of one's senses — *perder el juicio.*
She took leave of her senses. *Perdió el juicio.*

to leave — *salir, dejar*

to be left — *quedar.*
He was left crippled for life. *Quedó lisiado por toda la vida.*

to have left — *quedarle; restarle.*
I have a lot left to do. *Me queda (resta) mucho que hacer.*

to leave out — *omitir.*
We left out the first stanza. *Omitimos la primera estrofa.*

lecture — *la conferencia*

to give a good lecture to — *reprender.*
My father gave me a good lecture when he found out what I had done. *Mi padre me reprendió al saber lo que había hecho.*

leg — *la pierna*

not to have a leg to stand on — *no tener disculpa alguna.*
He doesn't have a leg to stand on. *No tiene disculpa alguna.*

to be on its last legs — *andar de capa caída; estar en las últimas.*
That company is on its last legs. *Esa compañía anda de capa caída (está en las últimas).*

to pull someone's leg — *tomarle el pelo.*
He likes to pull the public's leg. *Le gusta tomarle el pelo al público.*

to lend — *prestar*

to lend itself to — *prestarse a.*
What he said lends itself to various interpretations. *Lo que dijo se presta a diversas interpretaciones.*

length — *el largo, la largura*

at (great) length — *extensamente; por extenso.*
He examined it at (great) length. *Lo examinó extensamente (por extenso).*

to go to any length — *ser capaz de todo.*
He'll go to any length to get ahead. *Es capaz de todo para adelantarse.*

leopard — *el leopardo*

You can't get a leopard to change his spots. — *Genio y figura hasta la sepultura.*

lesson — *la lección*

to teach someone a lesson — *darle una lección.*

By refusing to see her he taught her a lesson. *Negándose a verla le dio una lección.*

to let — *dejar*

let alone — *y mucho menos.*

He can't read Spanish, let alone speak it. *No sabe leer español y mucho menos hablarlo.*

let it go — *déjelo.*

Let it go. It's too late now. *Déjelo. Ya es demasiado tarde.*

Let's face it. — *No hay que darle vueltas.*

to let alone — *dejar en paz.*

Let me alone. *Déjeme en paz.*

to let down — *desilusionar.*

She let him down. *Lo desilusionó.*

to let go — *despedir.*

The boss let him go. *El jefe lo despidió.*

to let go — *soltar.*

He let go of the rope. *Soltó la cuerda.*

to let on — *dejar saber.*

He didn't let on that he knew her. *No dejó saber que la conocía.*

to let out — *soltar.*

He let out a cry. *Soltó un grito.*

to let up — *disminuirse.*

The rain has let up a little. *La lluvia se ha disminuido un poco.*

to let up — *moderarse.*

The doctor told her to let up a little in her activities. *El médico le dijo que se moderara un poco en sus actividades.*

without letting up — *sin tregua.*

He studied all night without letting up. *Estudió toda la noche sin tregua.*

letter — *la letra*

to the letter — *al pie de la letra.*

He obeyed my instructions to the letter. *Obedeció mis instrucciones al pie de la letra.*

level — *el nivel*

on the level — *de buena fe.*

He told it to me on the level. *Me lo dijo de buena fe.*

lid — *la tapa*

to blow the lid off — *revelar un secreto.*

The journalist blew the lid off that business deal. *El periodista descubrió el pastel en ese convenio comercial.*

lie — *la mentira*

white lie — *la mentira inocente; la mentira piadosa.*

Telling her that she looked exactly like she did twenty years ago was a white lie. *Decirle que se veía igual que veinte años atrás fue una mentira piadosa.*

to lie — *echarse, acostarse*

to lie by — *estar cerca o a mano.*

The radio was lying by the pool. *La radio estaba cerca de la piscina.*

to lie in wait — *estar al acecho.*

She was lying in wait for the right man. *Estaba esperando la ocasión de encontrar al hombre indicado.*

to take it lying down — *aceptarlo con los brazos cruzados.*

He refused to take it lying down. *Se negó a aceptarlo con los brazos cruzados.*

life — *la vida*

life and limb — *la vida; la seguridad personal.*

And I am going to risk life and limb in this foolish adventure? *¿Y voy a arriesgar mi vida en esta tonta aventura?*

never in one's life — *en su vida.*
Never in my life have I read so much. *En mi vida he leído tanto.*

not on your life — *bajo ninguna circunstancia.*
I'm not going to marry her — not on your life. *No me voy a casar con ella bajo ninguna circunstancia.*

still life — *el bodegón; la naturaleza muerta.*
Do you prefer still life or portraiture? *¿Prefieres bodegones o retratos?*

the facts of life — *las verdades de la vida.*
Learning the facts of life is always interesting. *Aprender las verdades de la procreación es siempre interesante.*

the life of the party — *el alma de la fiesta.*
He's the life of the party. *Es el alma de la fiesta.*

to give a new lease on life — *dar nueva vida.*
That water pump will give the engine a new lease on life. *Esa bomba de agua le devolverá la vida al motor.*

to lay down one's life — *dar la vida.*
They laid down their lives for their country. *Dieron la vida por su patria.*

to lead a dog's life — *llevar una vida de perros.*
He leads a dog's life. *Lleva una vida de perros.*

to lead a . . . life — *hacer (llevar) una vida. . . .*
She leads a very secluded life. *Hace (Lleva) una vida muy solitaria.*

to make life miserable for — *amargarle la vida a.*
She made life miserable for her husband. *Le amargó la vida a su marido.*

to run for one's life — *salvarse por los pies.*
He ran for his life. *Se salvó por los pies.*

to take one's own life — *suicidarse.*
He took his own life. *Se suicidó.*

walks of life — *la clase social.*
A nation comprises people from all walks of life. *Una nación está compuesta de gente de todas las clases sociales.*

way of life — *el modo de vida; el modo de vivir.*
The European way of life seems less materialistic than ours. *El modo de vida europeo parece ser menos materialista que el nuestro.*

lifetime — *la vida; el curso de la vida.*

in a single lifetime — *en una sola vida.*

In a single lifetime you can't see it all. *En una sola vida no se puede verlo todo.*

light — *la luz*

in the light of — *teniendo en cuenta.*

In the light of what he said, perhaps it would be better to stay home. *Teniendo en cuenta lo que dijo, tal vez sea mejor quedarnos en casa.*

to bring to light — *sacar a luz.*

His investigations brought many new facts to life. *Sus investigaciones sacaron a luz muchos datos nuevos.*

to give someone a light — *darle fuego (lumbre).*

He gave me a light for my cigarette. *Me dio fuego (lumbre) para mi cigarrillo.*

to give someone the green light — *darle la autorización.*

We gave them the green light. *Les dimos la autorización.*

to make light of (to take lightly) — *tomar a broma.*

He made light of (took lightly) my problems. *Tomó a broma mis problemas.*

to see the light — *caer en la cuenta.*

After five explanations he saw the light. *Después de cinco explicaciones, cayó en la cuenta.*

to shed (throw) light on — *echar (arrojar) luz sobre.*

In his lecture he shed (threw) light on the mysteries of the universe. *En su conferencia echó (arrojó) luz sobre los misterios del universo.*

to turn (to switch) off the light — *apagar la luz.*

He turned (switched) off the light. *Apagó la luz.*

to turn (to switch) on the light — *encender (poner) la luz.*

Turn (switch) on the light. *Encienda (Ponga) la luz.*

like — *semejante*

and the like — *y cosas por el estilo.*

He brought books, newspapers, magazines, and the like. *Trajo libros, periódicos, revistas y cosas por el estilo.*

the likes of . . . — *otro semejante.*

I've never seen the likes of her. *Nunca he visto otra semejante.*

to like — *gustar, agradar*

how do you like . . . — *qué le parece. . . .*

How do you like Madrid? *¿Qué le parece Madrid?*

to like — *caerle bien; gustarle.*

I don't like him. *No me cae bien (gusta).*

to like better — *gustarle más.*

He likes Spanish better. *Le gusta más el español.*

likely — *probable*

(as) like(ly) as not — *a lo mejor.*

As likely as not (Like as not) it will snow. *A lo mejor nevará.*

it's likely — *es fácil.*

It's likely that they've eaten. *Es fácil que hayan comido.*

the most likely is — *lo más fácil es.*

The most likely is that it's too late. *Lo más fácil es que sea muy tarde.*

liking — *el gusto*

to be to one's liking — *ser de su agrado (gusto).*

It's to my liking. *Es de mi agrado (gusto).*

to take a liking to — *caerle en gracia.*

I took a liking to her. *Me cayó en gracia.*

lily — *el lirio*

to gild the lily — *adornar lo que no necesita adornos.*

Adding that vase is gilding the lily; the room looks good without it. *Añadir ese jarrón es sobrecargar el ambiente; el cuarto se ve bien como está.*

limb — *la rama de árbol*

out on a limb — *en situación peligrosa.*

A firefighter often has to go out on a limb. *Un bombero se encuentra a menudo en una situación peligrosa.*

limelight — *el haz luminoso del proyector*

to be in the limelight — *estar a la vista del público.*

Right now, he's in the limelight. *Por el momento está a la vista del público.*

limit — *el límite*

That's the limit. — *Es el colmo.*

to be off limits — *ser zona prohibida.*

That airport is off limits for commercial aircraft. *Ese aeropuerto está prohibido para aviones comerciales.*

to exceed the limits — *rebasar los límites.*

He had exceeded the limits of his capabilities. *Había rebasado los límites de sus capacidades.*

to go to the limit — *no dejar piedra por mover.*

He went to the limit to please her. *No dejó piedra por mover para complacerla.*

line — *la línea*

hot line — *la línea de emergencia.*

Kennedy called Khruschev on the hot line. *Kennedy llamó a Jruschov en la línea de emergencia.*

to draw the line — *detenerse.*

He doesn't know where to draw the line. *No sabe dónde detenerse.*

to drop someone a few lines — *ponerle unas (cuatro) líneas (letras).*

I dropped her a few lines. *Le puse unas (cuatro) líneas (cuatro letras).*

to stand in line; to line up — *hacer cola.*

We stood in line (We lined up) outside the cinema. *Hicimos cola fuera del cine.*

to toe the line — *observar las reglas.*

Knowing the consequences, the new recruit toed the line as much as he could. *Sabiendo las consecuencias, el nuevo recluta hacía lo posible por obedecer las reglas.*

to line — *alinear*

to line up — *ponerse en fila; hacer cola.*

We lined up. *Nos pusimos en fila (Hicimos cola).*

linen — *el lino*

to wash one's dirty linen in public — *sacar a relucir sus asuntos personales.*

She insists on washing her dirty linen in public. *Insiste en sacar a relucir sus asuntos personales.*

lip — *el labio*

to keep a stiff upper lip — *no desanimarse.*

It's hard to keep a stiff upper lip. *Es difícil no desanimarse.*

liquor — *el licor*

hard liquor — *licor de elevado contenido alcohólico.*

He switched from beer to hard liquor. *Cambió de la cerveza al trago fuerte.*

to live — *vivir*

to have to live with — *tener que aguantar.*

She has an illness she'll have to live with. *Tiene una enfermedad que tendrá que aguantar.*

to live and learn — *vivir para ver.*

We live and learn. *Vivimos para ver.*

to live it up — *darse buena vida.*

We spent the summer living it up. *Pasamos el verano dándonos buena vida.*

to live up to — *cumplir.*

He did not live up to his promises. *No cumplió sus promesas.*

living — *la vida*

to earn (make) a living — *ganarse la vida.*

He doesn't earn (make) a living. *No se gana la vida.*

lo — *mira; miren*

lo and behold — *me creerás que . . .*

I'm walking the dog, and lo and behold my old boyfriend is sitting on a bench. *Estoy paseando al perro y me creerás que ahí veo sentado en un banco a mi antiguo novio.*

load — *la carga*

Take a load off your feet. — *Siéntate.*

to take a load off one's mind — *quitarle un peso de encima.*

What they said took a load off my mind. *Lo que dijeron me quitó un peso de encima.*

location — *la ubicación; el sitio; la posición*

on location — *rodaje exterior; rodaje fuera de estudio.*

That movie was filmed on location in Bolivia. *Los exteriores de esa película fueron filmados en Bolivia.*

lock — *el cerrojo*

lock, stock and barrel — *por completo.*

We sold our grocery store, lock, stock and barrel. *Vendimos nuestra tienda de abarrotes con todo lo que tenía.*

under lock and key — *bajo llave.*

She keeps her diary under lock and key. *Ella guarda su diario muy celosamente bajo llave.*

to lock — *cerrar con llave*

to lock up (in) — *encerrar con llave.*

They locked him up (in). *Lo encerraron con llave.*

log — *el leño*

to sleep like a log — *dormir a pierna suelta.*

They slept like a log. *Durmieron a pierna suelta.*

long — *largo; mucho tiempo*

how long — *cuánto tiempo.*

How long have you been here? *¿Cuánto tiempo lleva usted aquí?*

long live — *viva.*

Long live the party! *¡Viva el partido!*

long since — *hace mucho (tiempo).*

They left long since. *Salieron hace mucho (tiempo).*

not to be long for this world — *estar cercano a la muerte.*

He's not long for this world. *Está cercano a la muerte.*

So long. — *Hasta la vista.*

the long and the short of it is — *en resumidas cuentas.*

The long and the short of it is that she prefers Spain. *En resumidas cuentas, prefiere a España.*

to take long — *tardar mucho.*

It won't take him long. *No tardará mucho.*

---

longer — *más tiempo*

no longer — *ya no.*

He no longer lives here. *Ya no vive aquí.*

---

look — *la mirada*

to give someone a dirty look — *darle (dirigirle) una mirada despectiva.*

He gave me a dirty look. *Me dio (dirigió) una mirada despectiva.*

to have a look about oneself — *tener aspecto de.*

She's pretty, but has a sad look about herself. *Es bonita, pero tiene un aire triste.*

to take a look at — *echarle (dar) un vistazo (una ojeada) a.*

We took a look at his new car. *Le echamos (Dimos) un vistazo (una ojeada) a su coche nuevo.*

---

to look — *mirar*

look out — *cuidado.*

Look out for the train! *¡Cuidado con el tren!*

to be looking up — *ir mejorando.*

Things are looking up. *Las cosas van mejorando.*

to look after — *cuidar a.*

Look after my child. *Cuide a mi hijo.*

to look at — *mirar.*

They looked at our garden. *Miraron nueslro jardín.*

to look down on — *despreciar a.*

She looks down on her little sister. *Desprecia a su hermanita.*

to look for — *buscar.*

She's looking for her key. *Busca su llave.*

to look forward to — *esperar con ansia.*

I'm looking forward to Christmas. *Espero con ansia la Navidad.*

to look good (bad) — *tener buena (mala) cara; tener buen (mal) aspecto.*

She looks good (bad). *Tiene buena (mala) cara; Tiene buen (mal) aspecto.*

to look into — *investigar.*

I'll look into the matter. *Investigaré el asunto.*

to look like — *parecerse a.*

She looks like her mother. *Se parece a su madre.*

to look out — *asomarse a.*

She's looking out the window. *Está asomada al balcón.*

to look out for — *ocuparse de.*

She looked out for her mother. *Se ocupó de su madre.*

to look out for — *tener cuidado (mucho ojo) con.*

Look out for the pickpockets. *Tenga cuidado (mucho ojo) con los rateros.*

to look out on — *dar a.*

My window looks out on the square. *Mi balcón da a la plaza.*

to look over — *examinar.*

He looked over my report. *Examinó mi informe.*

to look someone up — *venir a verle.*

Look us up when you come to Madrid. *Venga a vernos cuando llegue a Madrid.*

to look up — *buscar.*

I looked up the date of his birth. *Busqué la fecha de su nacimiento.*

to look up — *levantar la mirada.*

When I spoke he looked up. *Cuando hablé, levantó la mirada.*

to look up to — *respetar (admirar) a.*

She looks up to her older sister. *Respeta (Admira) a su hermana mayor.*

lookout — *la vigilancia*

to be on the lookout — *estar a la mira; estar alerta.*

We've got to be on the lookout for their arrival. *Hay que estar a la mira de (estar alerta por) su llegada.*

loose — *flojo, suelto*

to be on the loose — *andar suelto.*

The children are always on the loose. *Los niños siempre andan sueltos.*

lord — *el señor*

to be drunk as a lord — *estar hecho una cuba.*

He arrived home drunk as a lord. *Llegó a casa hecho una cuba.*

to lose — *perder*

Lost and found. — *Objetos perdidos.*

to get lost — *perderse.*

The child got lost. *El niño se perdió.*

to tell someone to get lost — *decirle que se vaya a freír espárragos.*

He told me to get lost. *Me dijo que me fuera a freír espárragos.*

loss — *la pérdida*

to cut one's losses — *perder lo menos posible.*

His investment had been awful, but he cut his losses by paying less taxes. *Su inversión había sido muy mala, pero logró reducir sus pérdidas pagando menos impuestos.*

your loss — *peor para ti.*

If you can't make it to my party, it's your loss. *Si no puedes venir a mi fiesta, peor para ti.*

lot — *la suerte*

to throw in (to cast) one's lot with — *decidir compartir la suerte de.*

I threw in (cast) my lot with John. *Decidí compartir la suerte de Juan.*

lot — *el lote*

a lot — *en extremo.*

I liked it a lot. *Me gustó en extremo.*

a lot of — *mucho.*

They sold a lot of wine. *Vendieron mucho vino.*

a whole lot — *una gran cantidad.*

I bought a whole lot. *Compré una gran cantidad.*

what a lot of — *cuántos.*
What a lot of fish! *¡Cuántos pescados!*

loud — *alto*

out loud — *en voz alta.*
She read the letter out loud. *Leyó la carta en voz alta.*

love — *el amor*

not for love nor money — *ni a tiros.*
I won't do it for love nor money. *No lo haré ni a tiros.*

There is no love lost between them. — *La antipatía es mutua.*

to be in love with — *estar enamorado de.*
She's in love with Charles. *Está enamorada de Carlos.*

luck — *la suerte*

as luck would have it — *por coincidencia; como lo quiso la suerte.*
As luck would have it, I kissed her just when Anna walked in. *La besé, y quiso la suerte que Ana entrara justo en ese momento.*

Best of luck. — *Que le vaya bien.*

to press one's luck — *tentar a la suerte; desafiar a la providencia.*
When he asked for another card, he really pressed his luck. *Cuando pidió otra carta, estaba realmente abusando de su suerte.*

to try one's luck — *probar fortuna.*
I tried my luck. *Probé fortuna.*

tough luck — *mala suerte; mala pata.*
You want to go on that train? Tough luck; the train left already. *¿Quiere ir en ese tren? Mala suerte, el tren ya se fue.*

lump — *el terrón*

to have a lump in one's throat — *tener un nudo en la garganta.*
He had a lump in his throat. *Tenía un nudo en la garganta.*

lurch — *la sacudida*

to leave in the lurch — *dejar en la estacada.*
He left her in the lurch. *La dejó en la estacada.*

M

mad — *enfadado, enojado; loco*

to be mad about — *tener locura por.*

He's mad about chess. *Tiene locura por el ajedrez.*

to get mad — *enfadarse.*

She got mad. *Se enfadó.*

to look mad — *tener cara de enfado.*

He looks mad. *Tiene cara de enfado.*

to make one mad — *darle rabia.*

It made us mad. *Nos dio rabia.*

---

mail — *el correo*

by return mail — *por vuelta de correo.*

Write me by return mail. *Escríbame por vuelta de correo.*

---

main — *principal*

in the main — *en general.*

In the main she's a happy person. *En general es una persona feliz.*

---

to make — *hacer*

make or break — *algo decisivo.*

That movie was a make or break for the company. *Esa película era decisiva para el futuro de la compañía.*

Make yourself at home. — *Está usted en su casa.*

to be able to make it — *poder ir.*

They invited me but I can't make it. *Me invitaron pero no puedo ir.*

to be made for — *tener madera para.*

I'm not made for traveling. *No tengo madera para viajar.*

to be on the make — *ser ambicioso.*

He's a young man on the make, and he'll go far. *Es un joven ambicioso y llegará lejos.*

to make away (off) with — *escaparse con.*

They made away (off) with our money. *Se escaparon con nuestro dinero.*

to make believe — *fingir.*

She made believe that she was ill. *Fingió estar enferma.*

to make clear — *aclarar; explicar.*

She made it clear that she wasn't going. *Aclaró (Explicó) que no iba.*

to make for — *dirigirse a.*

He made for the door. *Se dirigió a la puerta.*

to make good — *tener éxito.*

It's hard to make good in Hollywood. *Es difícil tener éxito en Hollywood.*

to make into — *convertir.*

I can easily make that closet into a bedroom. *Puedo transformar fácilmente ese clóset en un dormitorio.*

to make it — *llegar.*

We won't make it by ten. *No llegaremos para las diez.*

to make it — *no morirse.*

He's so ill that I'm afraid that he won't make it. *Está tan enfermo que temo que se muera.*

to make (it) known — *dar a conocer.*

Yesterday they made that news known. *Ayer dieron a conocer esa noticia.*

to make off — *largarse.*

He made off. *Se largó.*

to make out — *entender; descifrar.*

I couldn't make out the signature. *No pude entender (descifrar) la firma.*

to make out — *fingir.*

He's trying to make out that he knows her. *Está fingiendo que la conoce.*

to make out — *irle.*

How did you make out? *¿Cómo le fue?*

to make out — *preparar.*

Make out his tourist card. *Prepare su tarjeta de turista.*

to make out a check — *hacer un cheque.*

Make out a check for ten dollars. *Haga un cheque por diez dólares.*

to make over — *reformar.*

She made over her coat. *Reformó su abrigo.*

to make up — *inventar.*

He made up a lot of lies. *Inventó muchas mentiras.*

to make up for — *compensar.*

I didn't help today but I'll make up for it tomorrow. *No ayudé hoy pero lo compensaré mañana.*

to make up with — *hacer las paces (reconciliarse) con.*

She made up with her husband. *Hizo las paces (se reconcilió) con su esposo.*

man — *el hombre*

best man — *el padrino de boda.*

John was best man at my wedding. *Juan fue mi padrino de boda.*

con man — *el estafador.*

The con man cheated him out of a million dollars. *El estafador lo estafó por un millón de dólares.*

It's every man for himself. — *Cada cual se las arregle como pueda.*

Man alive! — *¡Hombre!*

man and wife — *marido y mujer.*

And they left the church as man and wife. *Y salieron de la iglesia como marido y mujer.*

Man overboard! — *¡Hombre al agua!*

Man proposes, God disposes. — *El hombre propone, Dios dispone.*

No man is an island. — *Nadie puede vivir aislado.*

the man in the street — *el hombre de la calle (hombre corriente).*

It's not for the man in the street. *No es para el hombre de la calle (hombre corriente).*

to a man — *sin faltar uno solo.*

They were there to a man. *Todos estaban sin faltar uno solo.*

to be a man of his word — *ser un hombre de palabra.*

He's a man of his word. *Es un hombre de palabra.*

to be a reputable man — *ser un hombre de bien.*

He's a reputable man. *Es un hombre de bien.*

to be the man for the job — *ser el hombre indicado.*

He's the man for the job. *Es el hombre indicado.*

manner — *la manera*

in a manner of speaking — *en cierto modo; hasta cierto punto.*

My sister was, in a manner of speaking, the cause of everything that happened. *Mi hermana fue en cierto modo (hasta cierto punto) la causa de todo lo ocurrido.*

to be just a manner of speaking — *ser sólo un decir.*

Don't get offended, it's just a manner of speaking. *No te ofendas, es sólo un decir.*

many — *muchos*

and as many more — *y otros tantos.*

He sold them five cows and as many more horses. *Les vendió cinco vacas y otros tantos caballos.*

map — *el mapa*

to put on the map — *hacer famoso; dar a conocer.*

With this gigantic skyscraper we'll put the city on the map. *Con este gigantesco rascacielos haremos famosa a esta ciudad.*

marbles — *las canicas*

not to have all one's marbles — *tener un tornillo suelto (flojo).*

It's obvious that he doesn't have all his marbles. *Se ve que tiene un tornillo suelto (flojo).*

march — *la marcha*

Forward march! — *¡En marcha!*

to steal a march on someone — *tomarle la delantera; ganarle por la mano.*

I stole a march on him. *Yo le tomé la delantera (le gané por la mano).*

market — *el mercado*

to play the market — *jugar a la bolsa.*

He plays the market. *Juega a la bolsa.*

marriage — *el matrimonio*

Marriages are made in heaven. — *Casamiento y mortaja, del cielo bajan.*

shotgun marriage — *matrimonio a la fuerza.*

With the Pill and legal abortion, shotgun marriages are getting scarce. *Con la píldora anticonceptiva y el aborto legalizado, los matrimonios a la fuerza están volviéndose escasos.*

master — *el maestro*

old master — *el pintor clásico.*

Rubens is an old master; Warhol is not. *Rubens es un pintor clásico, pero Warhol no lo es.*

match — *el igual*

to meet one's match — *hallar la horma de su zapato.*

He finally met his match. *Al fin halló la horma de su zapato.*

matter — *la materia*

a laughing matter — *cosa de risa.*

What they're demanding of us is not a (is no) laughing matter. *Lo que nos están exigiendo no es cosa de risa.*

as a matter of course — *como cosa normal.*

He accepted it as a matter of course. *Lo aceptó como cosa normal.*

as a matter of fact — *a decir verdad; en efecto; en realidad.*

As a matter of fact, I did it. *A decir verdad (En efecto, En realidad) lo hice yo.*

for that matter — *el caso es.*

For that matter, we didn't like it. *El caso es que no nos gustó.*

It doesn't matter. — *Es igual (No importa).*

to be a matter of — *ser cuestión de; consistir en.*

It's a matter of knowing how. *Es cuestión de (Consiste en) saber cómo.*

no matter how. . . . — *por más . . . que.*

No matter how cold it is, he goes swimming. *Por más frío que haga, va a nadar.*

no matter how — *sea como sea.*

No matter how, I'll do it. *Lo haré sea como sea.*

no matter when — *cuandoquiera que.*

No matter when we go there, they are watching television. *Cuandoquiera que vayamos allí están mirando (escuchando) la televisión.*

no matter where — *dondequiera que.*

No matter where he is, I'll find him. *Dondequiera que esté, lo encontraré.*

no matter who — *quienquiera que.*

No matter who tells you, don't believe it. *Quienquiera que se lo diga, no lo crea.*

that matter of — *eso (aquello) de.*

That matter of his accident is serious. *Eso (Aquello) de su accidente es grave.*

What's the matter? — *¿Qué hay?*

What's the matter with you? — *¿Qué tiene usted? (¿Qué le pasa)?*

---

maybe — *tal vez*

Maybe so (not). — *Puede que sí (no).*

---

meal — *la comida*

a square meal — *una comida abundante.*

He gets three square meals a day. *Tiene tres comidas abundantes al día.*

Enjoy your meal. — *Que le aproveche; Buen provecho.*

---

mean — *el medio; el punto medio*

the golden mean — *el justo medio.*

A prudent but interesting life is the golden mean. *Una vide prudente pero interesante representa al justo medio.*

---

to mean — *querer decir, significar*

to mean to — *pensar.*

He didn't mean to hurt me. *No pensaba lastimarme.*

to mean well — *tener buenas intenciones.*

She means well. *Tiene buenas intenciones.*

What do you mean? — *¿Qué quiere decir?*

What do you mean you don't know? — *¡Cómo que no sabe!*

meaning — *el sentido, el significado; la intención*

shade of meaning — *el matiz.*

In this book, the hero's personality had many shades of meaning. *El héroe en este libro tenía una personalidad de muchos matices.*

means — *la manera, el modo; los bienes*

beyond one's means — *por encima de sus posibilidades.*

They are living beyond their means. *Viven por encima de sus posibilidades.*

by all means — *sin falta.*

By all means go to the dance. *Vaya al baile sin falta.*

by means of — *mediante; por medio de.*

He was convinced by means of persuasion. *Fue convencido mediante (por medio de) mucha persuasión.*

by no means — *de (en) ningún modo; de (en) ninguna manera.*

By no means will we accept it. *No lo aceptaremos de (en) ningún modo (ninguna manera).*

to measure — *medir*

to measure up to one's expectations — *estar a la altura de sus esperanzas.*

He didn't measure up to our expectations. *No estaba a la altura de nuestras esperanzas.*

media — *los medios de difusión*

news media — *los órganos de información.*

News media from industrialized countries have been accused of a neocolonialistic approach to news. *Los órganos de información de los países industrializados han sido acusados de neocolonialismo informático.*

to meet — *encontrar*

to meet halfway — *partir(se) la diferencia con.*

He always meets his friends halfway. *Siempre (se) parte la diferencia con sus amigos.*

meeting — *la reunión*

to call a meeting — *convocar una junta.*

We called a meeting. *Convocamos una junta.*

memory — *la memoria*

from memory — *de memoria.*

He knows all their names from memory. *Sabe todos los nombres de memoria.*

if my memory serves me right — *si mal no recuerdo.*

If my memory serves me right, it's tomorrow. *Si mal no recuerdo, es mañana.*

mend — *el remiendo*

to be on the mend — *ir mejorando.*

He was very sick, but now he is on the mend. *Estaba muy enfermo, pero ya va mejorando.*

to mention — *mencionar*

Don't even mention it! — *¡Ni hablar!*

mercy — *la merced*

at . . . 's mercy — *a la merced de. . . .*

He's at his aunt's mercy. *Está a la merced de su tía.*

merit — *el mérito*

on one's own merits — *por su justo valor.*

He was judged on his own merits. *Lo juzgaron por su justo valor.*

mess — *el lío*

to be (in) a mess — *estar en desorden.*

His desk is (in) a mess. *Su escritorio está en desorden.*

to get into a mess — *meterse en un lío.*

We got into a mess. *Nos metimos en un lío.*

to make a mess — *estropear.*

They've made a mess of everything. *Lo han estropeado todo.*

method — *el método*

There is method in his madness. — *Nadie da palos de balde; Es más cuerdo de lo que parece.*

middle — *el centro, el medio*

about (around) the middle — *a mediados.*

He was born about (around) the middle of May. *Nació a mediados de mayo.*

in the middle of — *en medio de.*

It stopped in the middle of the street. *Se paró en medio de la calle.*

in the middle of — *en pleno.*

We got there in the middle of summer. *Llegamos en pleno verano.*

mildly — *suavemente*

to put it mildly — *sin exagerar.*

He said, to put it mildly, that he should have stayed home. *Dijo, sin exagerar, que debió quedarse en casa.*

milk — *la leche*

land of milk and honey — *Jauja; Utopia.*

You think this is the land of milk and honey? You must work hard here! *¿Tú crees que esto es Jauja? ¡Aquí debes trabajar duro!*

There's no use crying over spilt milk — *A lo hecho, pecho.*

mill — *el molino*

to have been through the mill — *saber por experiencia.*

I've been through the mill. *Lo sé por experiencia.*

mind — *la mente*

mind you — *por supuesto; eso sí.*

It is a good truck, mind you, but it has not passed all the tests yet. *Es un buen camión, por supuesto, pero todavía no ha pasado todas las pruebas.*

to be broad-minded — *tener amplio criterio.*

He's so broad-minded that he lets his wife go to bars alone. *Es de tan amplio criterio que permite a su mujer ir a los bares sola.*

to be in one's right mind — *estar en sus cabales (su juicio).*
He's not in his right mind. *No está en sus cabales (su juicio).*

to be out of one's mind — *haber perdido el juicio.*
He's out of his mind. *Ha perdido el juicio.*

to change one's mind — *cambiar (mudar; variar) de opinión.*
She changed her mind. *Cambió (Mudó; Varió) de opinión.*

to enter (cross) one's mind — *ocurrírsele.*
It never entered (crossed) his mind. *Nunca se le ocurrió.*

to have a dirty mind — *ser malicioso; ser mal pensado.*
With his dirty mind, he never looks at her as a person. *Con su mente sucia, nunca la mira como a una persona.*

to have a one-track mind — *ser de un solo interés.*
He has a one-track mind. *Es un hombre de un solo interés.*

to have an open mind about something — *no tener aún una opinión al respecto.*
I'll have an open mind until the end of the interview. *Me formaré una opinión después de haberlo entrevistado.*

to have in mind — *tener pensado (en la mente).*
I had in mind to go. *Tenía pensado (en la mente) ir.*

to have something on one's mind — *preocuparle algo.*
He's got something on his mind. *Algo le preocupa.*

to keep (to bear) in mind — *tener presente; tener en cuenta; recordar.*
Keep (Bear) in mind that I can't swim. *Tenga presente (Tenga en cuenta; Recuerde) que no sé nadar.*

to lose one's mind — *volverse loco.*
He lost his mind over Mary. *Se ha vuelto loco por María.*

to make up one's mind — *decidir; resolver.*
I made up my mind to stay. *Decidí (Resolví) quedarme.*

to slip one's mind — *olvidársele; pasársele de la memoria.*
It slipped my mind. *Se me olvidó (Se me pasó de la memoria).*

to speak one's mind freely — *hablar con toda franqueza.*
She spoke her mind freely to me. *Me habló con toda franqueza.*

to mind — *obedecer; tener inconveniente*

Do you mind if I smoke? — *¿Le molesta si fumo?*

to mind — *tener inconveniente.*

I don't mind your staying. *No tengo inconveniente en que se quede.*

---

mint — *la casa de moneda*

to cost a mint — *costar un ojo de la cara.*

That car must have cost him a mint. *Ese coche debió de costarle un ojo de la cara.*

---

minute — *el minuto*

at the last minute — *a última hora.*

He refused to go at the last minute. *Se negó a ir a última hora.*

Every minute counts. — *No hay tiempo que perder.*

---

miracle — *el milagro*

to work miracles — *hacer milagros.*

That plastic surgeon works miracles! Check how Anne looks now! *¡Ese cirujano plástico hace milagros! ¡Mira cómo luce Anne ahora!*

---

miserable — *miserable*

to make oneself miserable — *afligirse.*

She makes herself miserable by crying so much. *Se aflige llorando tanto.*

---

miss — *el tiro errado, el malogro*

A miss is as good as a mile. — *Lo mismo da librarse por poco que por mucho.*

---

to miss — *echar de menos; perder*

to be missing — *faltar.*

A book is missing from my shelf. *Falta un libro en mi estante.*

to miss — *escapársele.*

They missed what I said to them. *Se les escapó lo que les dije.*

---

mistake — *el error*

by mistake — *por equivocación.*

I did it by mistake. *Lo hice por equivocación.*

make no mistake about it — *no nos engañemos.*

Make no mistake about it; it's true. *No nos engañemos; es verdad.*

to mistake for — *confundir con; tomar por.*

They mistook me for my brother. *Me confundieron con (Me tomaron por) mi hermano.*

to mix — *mezclar*

to get mixed up — *confundirse.*

I couldn't hear and got mixed up. *No pude oír y me confundí.*

moment — *el momento*

at odd moments — *a (sus) ratos perdidos.*

I read at odd moments. *Leo a (mis) ratos perdidos.*

for the moment — *por el momento; de momento.*

For the moment it's all we have. *Por el (De) momento es todo lo que tenemos.*

one's shining moment — *el momento más glorioso de alguien.*

His shining moment was winning the trial. *Ganar el juicio fue el momento culminante de su vida.*

momentum — *el impulso*

to gain momentum — *agarrar impulso.*

The movement against the war has gained momentum. *El movimiento antibélico ha cobrado impulso.*

money — *el dinero*

tight money — *la escasez de dinero.*

Money for lending is tight as a result of the tight-money policy from the banks. *El dinero para préstamos escasea como resultado de la política de restricción de créditos por parte de los bancos.*

to be rolling in money — *rebosar en dinero.*

We had a cousin who was rolling in money. *Teníamos un primo que rebosaba en dinero.*

to have money to burn — *estar cargado de dinero.*

That family has money to burn. *Esa familia está cargada de dinero.*

to make good money — *ganar buen sueldo.*

He's making good money. *Está ganando buen sueldo.*

to throw good money after bad — *malgastar dinero al tratar de recuperar pérdidas.*

That business lost money from the start — don't continue throwing good money after bad. *Ese negocio siempre dejó pérdidas — no continúes malgastando dinero tratando de recuperar tu inversión.*

mood — *el humor*

to be in a good (bad) mood — *estar de buen (mal) humor (talante; genio).*

He's in a good (bad) mood. *Está de buen (mal) humor (talante; genio).*

to be in no mood to — *no estar en disposición de.*

I'm in no mood to sing. *No estoy en disposición de cantar.*

to be in the mood (feel inspired) (to) — *estar en vena (para).*

Poets aren't always in the mood (don't always feel inspired) to write. *Los poetas no siempre están en vena para escribir.*

moon — *la luna*

for the moon to shine — *hacer (haber) luna.*

The moon is shining. *Hace (Hay) luna.*

once in a blue moon — *muy de tarde en tarde.*

We go to a movie once in a blue moon. *Vamos al cine muy de tarde en tarde.*

moonlight — *la luz de la luna*

by moonlight — *a la luz de la luna.*

It's better seen by moonlight. *Se ve mejor a la luz de la luna.*

more — *más*

more and more — *cada vez más.*

They're getting more and more tired. *Se van cansando cada vez más.*

more often than not — *la mayoría de las veces.*

More often than not he doesn't eat breakfast. *La mayoría de las veces no se desayuna.*

the more . . . the more . . . — *cuanto más . . . , (tanto) más . . . ; mientras más . . . ., más . . . .*

The more one earns the more one spends. *Cuanto (Mientras) más se gana, (tanto) más se gasta.*

most — *más*

at most — *a lo sumo; cuando (a lo) más.*

We need five at most. *Nos hacen falta cinco a lo sumo (cuando más; a lo más).*

for the most part — *por lo general.*

For the most part, it's true. *Por lo general, es verdad.*

most — *la mayor parte de; los más.*

Most women marry. *La mayor parte de las (Las más) mujeres se casan.*

to make the most of — *sacar el mejor partido de.*

They make the most of their opportunities. *Sacan el mejor partido de sus oportunidades.*

motion — *el movimiento*

in slow motion — *a cámara lenta.*

They showed it in slow motion. *Lo proyectaron a cámara lenta.*

mountain — *la montaña*

to make a mountain out of a molehill — *hacer de una pulga un elefante (un camello).*

You're making a mountain out of a molehill. *Está haciendo de una pulga un elefante (un camello).*

mouth — *la boca*

for one's mouth to water — *hacérsele agua la boca.*

His mouth waters. *Se le hace agua la boca.*

It's straight from the horse's mouth. — *Lo sé de primera mano (de buena tinta).*

to have a big mouth — *írsele demasiado la lengua.*
He's got a big mouth. *Se le va demasiado la lengua.*

to keep one's mouth shut (keep still) — *no despegar los labios.*
No matter what they say, I'm going to keep my mouth shut (keep still). *Digan lo que digan, no voy a despegar los labios.*

to melt in one's mouth — *hacérsele (un) agua en la boca.*
It melts in my mouth. *Se me hace (un) agua en la boca.*

to say a mouthful — *decir una gran verdad; decir algo importante.*
He doesn't say much most of the time, but when he opens his mouth he says a mouthful. *Gran parte del tiempo no dice mucho, pero cuando abre la boca larga grandes verdades.*

move — *el movimiento*

to be on the move — *andar sin parar.*
He's always on the move. *Siempre anda sin parar.*

to be on the move — *estar en marcha.*
The enemy is on the move. *El enemigo está en marcha.*

to make a false move — *dar un paso en falso.*
He never makes a false move. *Nunca da un paso en falso.*

to move — *moverse*

to move (right) along — *ir a gran velocidad.*
They moved right along and arrived at ten. *Fueron a gran velocidad y llegaron a las diez.*

to move into — *instalarse en.*
A family just moved into that house. *Una familia acaba de instalarse en aquella casa.*

to move off — *alejarse.*
When he saw the policeman, the pickpocket moved off. *Al ver al policía el ratero se alejó.*

to move on — *marcharse.*
Move on! You can't park there. *¡Márchese! No se puede estacionar ahí.*

to move out (away) — *mudar(se) (de casa).*
Our neighbors moved out (away). *Nuestros vecinos (se) mudaron (de casa).*

much — *mucho*

How much does it sell for? — *¿A cómo se vende?*

not to think much of — *no tener un alto concepto de.*

He doesn't think much of our country. *No tiene un alto concepto de nuestro país.*

to make much of — *dar mucha importancia a.*

They made much of his performance. *Dieron mucha importancia a su actuación.*

---

mum — *callado*

Mum's the word! —*¡A callar!*

---

murder — *el asesinato*

to scream bloody murder — *gritar como si lo mataran.*

The victim was screaming bloody murder. *La víctima gritaba como si la mataran.*

---

music — *la música*

to face the music — *arrostrar las consecuencias.*

We had to face the music. *Tuvimos que arrostrar las consecuencias.*

---

must — *el deber*

to be a must — *ser indispensable.*

That play is a must. *Es indispensable ver esa comedia.*

---

to muster — *reunir; juntar; congregar*

to muster out — *dar de baja; licenciar.*

He was mustered out of the navy together with a million others. *Fue dado de baja de la marina junto a un millón más.*

to pass muster — *ser aceptado; ser adecuado.*

Ten years ago, this candidate would not have passed muster. *Diez años atrás, este candidato no habría sido aceptado.*

N

nail — *el clavo*

to drive a nail into one's coffin — *cavar uno su propia tumba.*

You are driving a nail into your coffin with every french fry you eat. *Con cada papa frita que comes vas cavando tu tumba.*

to hit the nail on the head — *dar en el clavo.*

You hit the nail on the head. *Dio en el clavo.*

---

name — *el nombre*

household name — *un nombre conocido por todos.*

Jihad has become a household name. Jihad *se ha convertido en un nombre que todos conocen.*

in . . . 's name — *en (a) nombre de. . . .*

He greeted us in the president's name. *Nos saludó en (a) nombre del presidente.*

maiden name — *nombre de soltera.*

She uses her maiden name. *Usa su nombre de soltera.*

to call someone names — *injuriar (insultar) a.*

She called her friend names. *Injurió (Insultó) a su amigo.*

to go by . . . 's name — *conocérsele con el nombre de . . . .*

He goes by his father's name. *Se le conoce con el nombre de su padre.*

to make a name for oneself — *hacerse famoso.*

He made a name for himself by studying hard. *Se hizo famoso estudiando mucho.*

What's in a name? — *El nombre es lo de menos.*

---

to name — *llamar*

for one's name to be (to be named) — *llamarse.*

His name is (He is named) Peter. *Se llama Pedro.*

to be named after (for) — *llevar el nombre de.*
He's named after (for) his uncle. *Lleva el nombre de su tío.*

You name it and we've got it. — *Lo que usted quiera lo tenemos.*

nap — *la siesta*

to catch napping — *coger desprevenido.*
We caught him napping. *Lo cogimos desprevenido.*

to take a nap — *echar un sueño (una siesta).*
If I get a chance, I'm going to take a nap. *Si tengo la oportunidad, voy a echar un sueño (una siesta).*

to take one's afternoon nap — *dormir la (echar una) siesta.*
She was taking her afternoon nap. *Estaba durmiendo la (echando una) siesta.*

necessity — *la necesidad*

of necessity — *por fuerza.*
I attended of necessity. *Asistí por fuerza.*

Necessity is the mother of invention. — *La necesidad es la madre de la inventiva.*

to make a virtue of necessity — *hacer de la necesidad virtud.*
Cigarettes are so expensive that I made a virtue of necessity and stopped smoking. *Los cigarrillos son tan caros que hice de la necesidad virtud y dejé de fumar.*

neck — *el cuello*

to break one's neck — *matarse.*
He broke his neck studying. *Se mató estudiando.*

to breathe down one's neck — *no dejar (ni) a sol ni a sombra.*
His creditors were breathing down his neck. *Sus acreedores no lo dejaban (ni) a sol ni a sombra.*

to get it in the neck — *recibir lo lindo.*
He got it in the neck. *Recibió lo lindo.*

to stick one's neck out — *arriesgarse.*
He's afraid to stick his neck out. *Tiene miedo de arriesgarse.*

needle — *la aguja*
It's like looking for a needle in a haystack. — *Es como buscar una aguja en un pajar.*

neither — *ni; tampoco*
neither am (have) I — *yo tampoco.*
"I didn't see that movie." — "Neither have I." *"No vi esa película." — "Yo tampoco."*

neither is (does, etc.) . . . . — *ni . . . tampoco.*
Neither is (does, etc.) he. *Ni él tampoco.*

neither . . . nor . . . — *ni . . . ni. . . .*
Neither the rain nor the snow stopped us. *Ni la lluvia ni la nieve nos pararon.*

nerve — *el nervio*
the nerve of it! — *¡qué desvergüenza!*
The nerve of it! He took it all! *¡Qué desvergüenza! ¡Se lo llevó todo!*

to get on one's nerves — *crisparle los nervios.*
He gets on my nerves. *Me crispa los nervios.*

nest — *el nido*
to feather one's nest — *forrarse el riñón.*
He's feathering his nest. *Se está forrando el riñón.*

to stir up a hornet's nest — *provocar indignación general.*
His action stirred up a hornet's nest. *Su acción provocó indignación general.*

never — *nunca; jamás*
Never fear. — *No hay cuidado.*

never mind — *no se moleste.*
Never mind. I'll do it. *No se moleste. Lo haré yo.*

never-never land — *un país de ensueños; un mundo de ilusiones.*
Instead of thinking realistically, your thoughts are always in never-never

land. *En vez de pensar en forma realista, tus pensamientos siempre vagan en un mundo de ilusiones.*

never to have had it so good — *nunca haberlo pasado tan bien.*
He's never had it so good. *Nunca lo ha pasado tan bien.*

news — *las noticias*

it's news to me — *no tenía idea; no lo sabía.*
"You are not supposed to smoke here" — "It's news to me." *"Tú no puedes fumar aquí." — "Yo no tenía idea."*

to break the news — *ser el primero en dar la noticia.*
He broke the news. *Fue el primero que dio la noticia.*

next — *siguiente; junto*

next to — *junto a; al lado de.*
They live next to the bakery. *Viven junto a (al lado de) la panadería.*

nick — *la mella*

in the nick of time — *en el momento crítico (a última hora).*
The ambulance arrived in the nick of time. *La ambulancia llegó en el momento crítico (a última hora).*

night — *la noche*

at night — *de noche.*
He works at night. *Trabaja de noche.*

at nightfall — *al anochecer.*
We'll stop at nightfall. *Nos pararemos al anochecer.*

for night to fall — *cerrar la noche.*
Night has now fallen. *Ya ha cerrado la noche.*

overnight (unexpectedly) — *de la noche a la mañana.*
He became famous overnight. *De la noche a la mañana se hizo famoso.*

to make a night of it — *divertirse hasta muy entrada la noche.*
They made a night of it. *Se divirtieron hasta muy entrada la noche.*

to say good night (good evening) — *dar las buenas noches.*
We said good night (good evening) to her. *Le dimos las buenas noches.*

to stay out all night — *trasnochar.*
He stayed out all night. *Trasnochó.*

nitty — *lendroso; piojoso*

nitty-gritty — *la parte más esencial de algo.*
Enough of details; let's get down to the nitty-gritty. *Basta de detalles; vamos ahora a lo verdaderamente importante.*

no — *ninguno*

no-nonsense — *serio; importante; práctico.*
Her no-nonsense attitude was respected by all students. *Su seriedad era respetada por todos los alumnos.*

No parking (smoking, etc.). — *Se prohibe estacionarse (fumar, etc.).*

not to take no for an answer — *no aceptar negativas.*
He doesn't take no for an answer. *No acepta negativas.*

to be of no account — *ser un cero a la izquierda.*
He's of no account. *Es un cero a la izquierda.*

to nod — *inclinar la cabeza*

to nod — *dar cabezadas.*
When he's sleepy, he nods. *Cuando tiene sueño, da cabezadas.*

to nod (yes) — *afirmar con la cabeza.*
I nodded (yes). *Afirmé con la cabeza.*

nook — *el rinconcito*

in every nook and cranny — *por todos los rincones.*
We looked in every nook and cranny. *Buscamos por todos los rincones.*

noon — *el mediodía*

at noon — *a (al) mediodía.*
We eat lightly at noon. *Comemos poco a (al) mediodía.*

nose — *la nariz*

right under one's nose — *delante de las narices.*
It's right under your nose. *Lo tiene delante de las narices.*

to count noses — *contar personas.*
The guide always counts noses before the tourists get on the bus. *El quía siempre cuenta los turistas antes que suban al autobús.*

to lead by the nose — *tener agarrado por las narices.*
She leads him by the nose. *Lo tiene agarrado por las narices.*

to pay through the nose — *costarle un ojo de la cara.*
Unfortunately, we had to pay through the nose. *Desafortunadamente, nos costó un ojo de la cara.*

to stick one's nose in someone else's business — *meter la nariz en asuntos no suyos.*
Don't stick your nose in my business. *No meta la nariz en asuntos míos.*

to turn up one's nose — *mirar con desprecio.*
She turned up her nose at my suggestion. *Miró con desprecio mi sugerencia.*

to win by a nose — *ganar con poca ventaja.*
He won by a nose. *Ganó con poca ventaja.*

To cut off one's nose to spite one's face. — *Tirar piedras contra el propio tejado.*

not — *no*

and what not — *tener de todo.*
The system has a receiver, DVD player and recorder, and what not. *El sistema cuenta con un receptor, un tocadiscos, una grabadora y un cuanto hay.*

if not — *en caso contrario.*
They want to go today; if not, they'll go tomorrow. *Quieren ir hoy; en caso contrario, irán mañana.*

not at all — *de nada; no hay de qué.*
Thank you. Not at all. *Gracias. De nada (No hay de qué).*

notch — *el grado*

to take someone down a notch — *bajarle los humos.*
She had to take him down a notch. *Ella tuvo que bajarle los humos.*

note — *la nota, el apunte*

to compare notes — *cambiar opiniones.*

We were comparing notes. *Cambiábamos opiniones.*

to make a note of — *tomar nota de; apuntar.*

I made a note of the address. *Tomé nota de (Apunté) la dirección.*

to take note of — *tomar nota de.*

I took note of what she said. *Tomé nota de lo que dijo.*

---

nothing — *nada*

for nothing — *gratis.*

He gave it to me for nothing. *Me lo dio gratis.*

next to nothing — *casi nada.*

The pain sensation was next to nothing. *La sensación de dolor fue insignificante.*

not . . . for nothing — *por algo.*

He's not the king for nothing. *Por algo es rey.*

there's nothing to it — *es sencillísimo.*

It's easy to do. There's nothing to it. *Es fácil de hacer. Es sencillísimo.*

to be nothing to complain about — *no ser para quejarse.*

It is nothing to complain about. *No es para quejarse.*

to be nothing to it — *carecer de fundamento.*

It's a rumor, but there's nothing to it. *Es un rumor, pero carece de fundamento.*

to be nothing to one — *no afectarle.*

That's nothing to me. *Eso a mí no me afecta.*

to be nothing to speak of — *no merecer la pena.*

The speech was nothing to speak of. *El discurso no merecía la pena.*

to be nothing to write home about — *no ser nada extraordinario.*

It's nothing to write home about. *No es nada extraordinario.*

to have nothing to do with — *no tener nada que ver con.*

He has nothing to do with the matter. *No tiene nada que ver con el asunto.*

to make nothing of it — *no concederle importancia.*

He found out but made nothing of it. *Lo supo pero no le concedió importancia.*

notice — *el aviso*

on short notice — *a la brevedad; en poco tiempo.*

I am sorry to have asked for a meeting on such short notice, but there's an urgent matter to discuss. *Siento haber dado tan poco tiempo para hacer la reunión, pero hay que tratar un tema muy urgente.*

to escape one's notice — *escapársele.*

It escaped my notice. *Se me escapó.*

to serve notice — *hacer saber; notificar.*

He served notice that our rent was due tomorrow. *Nos hizo saber (notificó) que la renta vencía mañana.*

to sit up and take notice — *parar la oreja.*

What she told me made me sit up and take notice. *Lo que me dijo me hizo parar la oreja.*

---

notion — *la noción*

to take a notion to — *antojársele.*

We took a notion to sell it. *Se nos antojó venderlo.*

---

now — *ahora*

from now on — *de ahora (aquí) en adelante.*

From now on, she'll stay home. *De ahora (aquí) en adelante se quedará en casa.*

just now — *por ahora.*

Just now, I can't go. *Por ahora, no puedo ir.*

now and again (then) — *de vez en cuando.*

I tell it to him now and again (then). *Se lo digo de vez en cuando.*

now then — *ahora bien.*

Now then, tell me the truth. *Ahora bien, dígame la verdad.*

only now — *apenas ahora.*

Only now did he receive the news. *Apenas ahora recibió las noticias.*

right now — *ahora mismo.*

Do it right now. *Hágalo ahora mismo.*

nowhere — *ninguna parte*

to get nowhere — *no haber logrado nada.*

So much work and we got nowhere! *¡Tanto trabajo y no logramos nada!*

nuisance — *la molestia*

to make a nuisance of oneself — *molestar.*

That boy is always making a nuisance of himself. *Ese chico siempre está molestando.*

null — *nulo*

null and void — *sin efecto.*

The agreement is null and void. *El acuerdo está sin efecto.*

number — *el número*

in round numbers — *en números redondos.*

They prefer us to express it in round numbers. *Prefieren que lo expresemos en números redondos.*

to have someone's number — *saber de qué pie cojea.*

I've got his number. *Sé de qué pie cojea.*

nut — *la tuerca*

nuts and bolts — *el aspecto práctico de algo.*

Jones provided the theory, but Walker managed all the nuts and bolts. *Jones aportó la teoría, pero Walker se encargó del lado práctico.*

nutshell — *la cáscara (de nuez)*

in a nutshell — *en pocas palabras.*

He told us in a nutshell. *Nos lo dijo en pocas palabras.*

O

oar — *el remo*

to put one's oar in — *meter su cuchara.*

In every conversation he has to put his oar in. *En cualquier conversación tiene que meter su cuchara.*

oath — *el juramento*

to administer an oath — *tomar juramento.*

The oath of allegiance was administered by the school principal. *El rector del colegio hizo tomar el juramento de fidelidad.*

to take (an) oath — *prestar juramento.*

The Representative took oath last week. *El diputado prestó juramento la semana pasada.*

oats — *la avena*

to sow one's wild oats — *pasar las mocedades.*

He's sowing his wild oats. *Está pasando las mocedades.*

object — *el objeto; la cosa*

no object — *algo que no es un obstáculo; algo que no es inconveniente.*

I would like that car, and price is no object. *Me gustaría ese carro, y el precio no es problema alguno.*

objection — *la objeción*

to raise objections to — *hacer objeciones (poner reparo) a.*

He is raising objections to the speech. *Está haciendo objeciones (poniendo reparo) al discurso.*

to see no objection — *no ver ningún inconveniente.*

We saw no objection. *No vimos ningún inconveniente.*

obligated — *obligado*

to be obligated to — *estar en el caso de.*

We're obligated to work there. *Estamos en el caso de trabajar allí.*

to oblige — *complacer*

to be obliged — *quedar agradecido.*

I'll be obliged if you lend me twenty dollars. *Le estaré agradecido si me presta veinte dólares.*

occasion — *la ocasión*

on other occasions — *otras veces.*

On other occasions we would paint. *Otras veces pintábamos.*

on the occasion of — *con motivo de.*
They invited us on the occasion of their daughter's wedding. *Nos invitaron con motivo de la boda de su hija.*

to rise to the occasion — *mostrarse a la altura de las circunstancias.*
He will rise to the occasion. *Se mostrará a la altura de las circunstancias.*

---

to occur — *ocurrir*

to occur to one — *ocurrírsele.*
It doesn't occur to me now. *No se me ocurre ahora.*

---

odds — *la ventaja*

for the odds to be against one — *no tener ventajas.*
He'll lose because the odds are against him. *Perderá porque no tiene ventajas.*

long odds — *condiciones desfavorables.*
The odds for a new world fair in New York are long. *Las probabilidades de una nueva feria mundial en Nueva York son escasas.*

oddly enough — *por extraño que parezca.*
The dogs, oddly enough, did not attack the trespasser. *Por extraño que parezca, los perros no atacaron al intruso.*

odds and ends — *cachivaches; cosas sueltas.*
All that remained at the radio shack were odds and ends that would not make a radio if put together. *Todo lo que quedaba en el taller de radio eran componentes sueltos que no harían una radio si fuesen ensamblados.*

the odds are — *lo probable es.*
The odds are that he'll lose. *Lo probable es que perderá.*

to be at odds with — *andar a la greña con.*
He's at odds with his father. *Anda a la greña con su padre.*

---

off — *de, desde; lejos, fuera*

off and on — *de vez en cuando.*
We skate off and on. *Patinamos de vez en cuando.*

to be off — *haber salido; haberse marchado.*
Are they off yet? *¿Han salido (¿Se han marchado)?*

to live off — *vivir a expensas de.*

He lives off his parents. *Vive a expensas de sus padres.*

offense — *la ofensa*

No offense meant. — *Lo dije sin mala intención.*

to take offense at — *ofenderse de.*

He took offense at what I said. *Se ofendió de lo que dije.*

offhand — *de improviso*

(right) offhand — *a primera vista; sin pensarlo.*

(Right) offhand, I'd say no. *A primera vista (Sin pensarlo), diría que no.*

office — *la oficina*

term of office — *el plazo del ejercicio de un cargo.*

Usually presidential terms of office are either four or six years. *Por lo general los plazos para la presidencia son de cuatro o seis años.*

to take office — *tomar posesión de su cargo.*

He takes office tomorrow. *Toma posesión de su cargo mañana.*

offing — *la lontananza*

to be in the offing — *estar en perspectiva.*

It's in the offing. *Está en perspectiva.*

often — *a menudo*

how often — *cada cuánto (tiempo).*

How often does it rain? *¿Cada cuánto (tiempo) llueve?*

so often — *tantas veces.*

He so often sleeps late. *Tantas veces duerme tarde.*

oil — *el aceite*

to pour oil on the flames — *echar leña al fuego.*

He only poured oil on the flames. *Sólo echó leña al fuego.*

to strike oil (to strike it rich) — *enriquecerse de súbito.*

They struck oil (struck it rich). *Se enriquecieron de súbito.*

old — *viejo*

to be . . . years old — *tener . . . años.*

She's sixteen years old. *Tiene dieciséis años.*

omelette — *la tortilla (de huevos)*

You can't make an omelette without breaking eggs. — *Lo que algo vale, algo cuesta.*

on — *en, sobre*

from . . . on — *desde . . . .*

From 1960 on, she's been in Spain. *Desde 1960, está en España.*

on or about — *alrededor de.*

The train arrives on or about four A.M. *El tren llega alrededor de las cuatro de la mañana.*

to be on to someone — *conocerle el juego.*

I'm on to him. *Le conozco el juego.*

to have on one — *llevar encima.*

I haven't any change on me. *No llevo suelto encima.*

once — *una vez*

at once — *inmediatamente; en seguida.*

He called at once. *Llamó inmediatamente (en seguida).*

at once (at the same time) — *a la vez; al mismo tiempo.*

How do you expect them to do five things at once (at the same time)? *¿Cómo quieres que hagan cinco cosas a la vez (al mismo tiempo)?*

not even once — *ni una sola vez.*

Not even once did I receive it. *Ni una sola vez lo recibí.*

once and for all — *por última vez; de una vez por todas (y para siempre)*

He told them once and for all to shut up. *Les dijo por última vez (de una vez por todas; de una vez y para siempre) que se callaran.*

once-over — *el vistazo*

to give the once-over — *dar un vistazo.*

He gave her the once-over. *Le echó un vistazo.*

one — *uno*

it's either one or the other — *una de dos.*

It's either one or the other: eat or leave the table. *Una de dos: o coma o deje la mesa.*

one by one — *uno a uno; de uno en uno.*

They passed one by one. *Pasaron uno a uno (de uno en uno).*

to pull a fast one — *engañar.*

He pulled a fast one on us. *Nos engañó.*

oneself — *uno mismo*

by oneself — *a solas.*

She went there by herself. *Fue allá a solas.*

by oneself — *solo.*

She lives in that house by herself. *Vive en esa casa sola.*

one-way — *de una sola dirección*

a one-way street — *una calle de dirección única.*

It's a one-way street. *Es una calle de dirección única.*

only — *sólo, solamente*

if only — *siquiera.*

You should stop smoking, if only to please your wife. *Debieras dejar de fumar, siquiera por complacer a tu esposa.*

open — *abierto*

in the open — *al descubierto.*

They were playing in the open. *Jugaban al descubierto.*

out in the open — *al aire libre.*

They like to be out in the open. *Les gusta estar al aire libre.*

wide open — *abierto de par en par.*

The door was wide open. *La puerta estaba abierta de par en par.*

to open — *abrir*

to open — *estrenarse.*

The play will open tomorrow. *La comedia se estrenará mañana.*

to open with — *dar principio con.*

The program opened with a song. *Se dio principio al programa con una canción.*

opener — *el abridor*

for openers — *para empezar.*

He scanned the entire script for openers, and then read it in detail. *Echó una mirada a todo el guión para empezar, y luego lo leyó en detalle.*

opera — *la ópera*

soap opera — *el novelón; la cebollera; el melodrama de televisión.*

Soap operas specialize in strong emotions. *Las cebolleras se especializan en emociones fuertes.*

opinion — *la opinión*

in one's opinion — *a su parecer (entender).*

In my opinion he's too young. *A mi parecer (entender) es muy joven.*

opposite — *opuesto*

just the opposite — *en sentido contrario.*

I understood just the opposite. *Lo entendí, en sentido contrario.*

opposition — *la oposición*

in opposition to — *en contra de.*

He spoke in opposition to the revolution. *Habló en contra de la revolución.*

to opt — *optar*

to opt in — *enrolarse; adherirse.*

You may opt in the dental insurance coverage if you wish. *Usted puede enrolarse al seguro dental de la empresa si lo desea.*

option — *la opción; la alternativa*

to keep one's options open — *no descartar ninguna posibilidad.*

Don't force me into anything final; I want to keep my options open. *No me fuerces a nada definitivo; quiero reservarme la posibilidad de elegir.*

order — *el (la) orden*

in order — *en regla.*

Everything seems to be in order. *Todo parece estar en regla.*

in order to — *para.*

We're here in order to learn. *Estamos aquí para aprender.*

in short order — *en breve plazo.*

They finished in short order. *Terminaron en breve plazo.*

on order — *por encargo.*

They sell only on order. *Venden sólo por encargo.*

That's a tall order. — *Eso es mucho pedir.*

to be made to order — *estar hecho a la medida; ser de encargo.*

It's made to order. *Está hecho a la medida (Es de encargo).*

to be out of order — *no funcionar.*

The elevator is out of order. *El ascensor no funciona.*

to call to order — *abrir; llamar al orden.*

The meeting was called to order. *Abrieron (Llamaron al orden) la reunión.*

to get out of order — *descomponerse.*

The motor got out of order. *El motor se descompuso.*

to put one's house in order — *arreglar uno sus asuntos.*

He realized that before preaching to others he had to put his own house in order. *Se dio cuenta de que antes de sermonear a otros debía resolver sus propias dificultades.*

---

out — *fuera*

Get out! (Scram!) — *¡Largo de aquí!*

out-and-out — *completo; total; absoluto.*

These violent actions are leading to out-and-out war. *Estas acciones de violencia están conduciendo a una guerra total.*

out of — *por.*

She locked the door out of fear. *Cerró la puerta con llave por temor.*

to outdo — *superar; vencer*

not to be outdone — *para no ser menos.*

He saw John's Rolex and, not to be outdone, bought himself a gold Omega. *Vio el Rolex de John y, para no ser menos, se compró un Omega de oro.*

to outdo oneself — *superarse.*

That was his masterpiece; now he had truly outdone himself. *Esa era su obra maestra; ahora había superado toda su creación previa.*

outset — *el principio*

at the outset — *al principio.*

At the outset I didn't like the idea. *Al principio no me gustó la idea.*

outside — *fuera*

at the outside — *cuando más; a lo más.*

It's going to cost us thirty dollars at the outside. *Nos va a costar treinta dólares cuando más (a lo más).*

on the outside — *por fuera.*

He dried it on the outside. *Lo secó por fuera.*

over — *de nuevo; excesivo*

all over (anywhere) — *por todas partes.*

You can get them all over (anywhere). *Se consiguen por todas partes.*

left over — *de sobra.*

They have money left over. *Tienen dinero de sobra.*

over and above — *por encima de; en exceso de.*

That was over and above anything we had expected. *Eso estaba por encima de cualquier cosa que hubiésemos esperado.*

over and over (again) — *una y otra vez.*

He called over and over (again). *Llamó una y otra vez.*

over there — *por allá.*

They're over there. *Están por allá.*

to be over — *pasar; acabarse*

It's over now. *Ya pasó (se acabó).*

overboard — *al agua*

to go overboard — *excederse.*

What a dinner! This time they have really gone overboard. *¡Qué cena! Esta vez se han excedido.*

overdue — *atrasado*

to be overdue — *estar retrasado.*

The train is overdue. *El tren está retrasado.*

own — *propio*

on one's own — *por (sus) puños.*

He achieved it on his own. *Lo realizó por (sus) puños.*

to be on one's own — *vivir por su propia cuenta.*

He's on his own. *Vive por su propia cuenta.*

to each his own — *sobre gustos no hay nada escrito.*

She is a PhD, but she married a common soldier — to each his own. *Tiene un doctorado, pero se casó con un simple soldado — sobre gustos no hay nada escrito.*

to hold one's own — *mantenerse firme.*

He held his own. *Se mantuvo firme.*

to own — *poseer*

to own up to the truth — *confesar la verdad.*

He won't own up to the truth. *No quiere confesar la verdad.*

P

p — *la p*

to mind one's p's and q's — *andar con cuidado con lo que dice (hace).*

She minds her p's and q's. *Anda con cuidado con lo que dice (hace).*

pace — *el paso*

to set the pace — *dar ejemplo.*

She set the pace for the rest. *Dio ejemplo para los demás.*

to pack — *empaquetar*

to pack off — *despachar.*

He packed his family off to the country. *Despachó a su familia al campo.*

to pack suitcases (bags) — *hacer las maletas (equipaje).*

We packed our suitcases (bags). *Hicimos las maletas (el equipaje).*

to send one packing — *despedir con cajas destempladas.*

She made a big scandal and sent him packing. *Hizo un gran escándalo y lo mandó a freír espárragos.*

---

pain — *el dolor*

growing pains — *las dificultades del comienzo.*

The new company is having the usual growing pains. *La nueva empresa experimenta los usuales trastornos del desarrollo.*

to be a pain in the neck — *ser una persona antipática.*

She's a pain in the neck. *Es una persona antipática.*

to take pains — *poner mucho cuidado (esmerarse) en.*

She took pains in writing the letter. *Puso mucho cuidado (Se esmeró) en escribir la carta.*

---

paint — *la pintura*

war paint — *los cosméticos.*

She put on her war paint and went to see her boyfriend. *Se puso sus cosméticos y fue a ver a su novio.*

---

pale — *el recinto; el límite; el margen*

beyond the pale — *fuera de los límites.*

Her statement went beyond the pale. *Su declaración se pasó de los límites.*

---

pan — *la cacerola*

Out of the frying pan into the fire. — *Huir del fuego y caer en las brasas.*

---

paradise — *el paraíso*

fool's paradise — *felicidad engañosa.*

She lives in a fool's paradise and doesn't want to see the truth. *Vive en un mundo de ilusiones y no quiere ver la verdad.*

---

pardon — *el perdón*

I beg your pardon — *Dispénseme (perdóneme).*

I beg your pardon? — *¿qué (cómo) dice usted?*

I beg your pardon. I didn't hear you. *¿Qué (Cómo) dice usted? No lo oí.*

parole — *la palabra de honor*

to be out on parole — *estar libre bajo palabra.*

He's out on parole. *Está libre bajo palabra.*

part — *la parte*

part and parcel — *parte integral; parte esencial.*

Being friendly is part and parcel of a politician's art. *Ser amistoso es parte esencial del arte de ser un político.*

to do one's part — *cumplir con su deber.*

In the war, we all had to do our part. *Durante la guerra todos debimos cumplir con nuestro deber.*

to look the part — *proyectar la imagen esperada.*

Pipe in hand, short beard, jacket with leather patches and pleasant manners: Professor Hornsby looked very much the part. *Pipa en mano, barba recortada, chaqueta con parches de cuero y agradables modales, el profesor Hornsby proyectaba la imagen esperada.*

particular — *particular, especial*

in particular — *en especial.*

I like the last chapter in particular. *Me gusta el último capítulo en especial.*

party — *la fiesta*

coming out party — *la presentación en sociedad.*

She went to her coming out party in a white dress. *Fue a presentarse en sociedad en un vestido blanco.*

housewarming party — *fiesta por el estreno de una casa.*

Yes, they bought a new house and now they are having the housewarming party. *Sí, compraron una casa y ahora tienen la fiesta del estreno.*

to throw a party — *dar una fiesta.*

We threw a party. *Dimos una fiesta.*

pass — *el paso*

to come to pass — *suceder; cumplirse.*

And the prophecy came to pass at last. *Y por fin se cumplió la profecía.*

to make a pass at — *hacer una propuesta amorosa.*

He made a pass at her. *Le hizo una propuesta amorosa.*

---

to pass — *pasar*

in passing — *de paso.*

He called to say goodbye and in passing told us that he would return in six months. *Llamó para despedirse y de paso nos dijo que volvería dentro de seis meses.*

to pass an exam — *aprobar (salir bien en) un examen.*

I passed my exam. *Aprobé (Salí bien en) mi examen.*

to pass as — *pasar por.*

He passed as an American. *Pasó por americano.*

to pass away — *morir(se).*

She passed away last night. *(Se) murió anoche.*

to pass by (without stopping) — *pasar de largo.*

He passed by (without stopping). *Pasó de largo.*

to pass out — *desmayarse.*

He passed out. *Se desmayó.*

to pass out — *distribuir.*

The teacher passed out the paper. *El maestro distribuyó el papel.*

to pass through — *pasar por.*

They passed through Madrid. *Pasaron por Madrid.*

---

pasture — *el pastizal; la dehesa*

greener pastures — *actividades más lucrativas.*

Matrax offers greener pastures. *Matrax ofrece mejor empleo.*

---

to pat — *dar golpecitos a*

to pat on the back — *darle palmadas en la espalda.*

He patted him gently on the back. *Le dio unas palmadas suavemente en la espalda.*

to pat on the back — *elogiar a.*

He patted his class on the back for its intelligence. *Elogió a su clase por su penetración.*

to patch — *remendar*

to patch up a quarrel — *hacer las paces.*

They patched up their quarrel. *Hicieron las paces.*

path — *la senda*

to beat a path — *asediar.*

He keeps beating a path to my office. *Sigue asediando mi despacho.*

to pay — *pagar; cancelar*

to pay back — *devolver; reembolsar.*

I'll pay you back as soon as my check arrives. *Te reembolsaré tan pronto llegue mi cheque.*

to pay off — *pagar y despedir a un empleado; compensar.*

He was too much trouble, so we paid him off. *Causaba demasiados problemas, así que le dimos su sueldo y lo despedimos.*

to pay off — *dar resultado.*

Our plans finally paid off and we found ourselves rich. *Nuestros planes finalmente dieron resultado y nos vimos ricos.*

pay — *el salario; el sueldo*

take-home pay — *salario neto (descontados los impuestos y otras obligaciones).*

My take-home pay is barely enough for survival. *Mi salario neto apenas basta para sobrevivir.*

payment — *el pago*

down payment — *el pago inicial.*

The down payment on a house is now too much for most people. *El pago inicial por una casa es ahora demasiado elevado para la mayoría de las personas.*

peace — *la paz*

peace of mind — *tranquilidad de espíritu.*

With more rest you'll have peace of mind. *Con un poco de descanso tendrá tranquilidad de espíritu.*

to be left in peace — *quedar en paz.*

We were left in peace. *Quedamos en paz.*

to disturb the peace — *perturbar (alterar) el orden público.*

They disturbed the peace. *Perturbaron (Alteraron) el orden público.*

to keep the peace — *mantener el orden público.*

They sent the soldiers to keep the peace. *Mandaron a los soldados para mantener el orden público.*

to make peace — *hacer las paces.*

We made peace. *Hicimos las paces.*

peacock — *el pavo real*

proud as a peacock — *engreído como un pavo real.*

After he got first prize in school, Bob walks as proud as a peacock. *Desde que ganó el primer premio en la escuela, Bob anda más engreído que un pavo real.*

peak — *la cima*

to reach its peak — *llegar a su punto cumbre.*

It has reached its peak. *Ha llegado a su punto cumbre.*

pearl — *la perla*

to cast pearls before swine — *echar margaritas a los cerdos.*

This is casting pearls before swine. *Esto es echar margaritas a los cerdos.*

peg — *el gancho; el colgador; la clavija; la estaca*

off the peg — *ropa hecha de confección.*

Few can afford dressmakers nowadays; most women buy off the peg. *Pocas mujeres pueden hoy darse el lujo de ir a la modista; la mayoría compran ropa de confección.*

square peg — *persona inadaptada.*

That poor devil is a square peg in any group of people. *Ese pobre diablo es incapaz de adaptarse a ningún grupo de personas.*

to take someone down a peg or two — *bajarle los humos a alguien.*
Joe has been too loud lately; we'll have to take him down a peg or two. *José ha estado muy vocinglero últimamente; habrá que bajarle los humos.*

penchant — *la afición*
to have a penchant for — *ser atraído por.*
I have a penchant for languages. *Las lenguas me atraen.*

pencil — *el lápiz*
to sharpen a pencil — *sacar punta a un lápiz.*
I sharpened the pencils. *Saqué punta a los lápices.*

penniless — *sin dinero*
to be left penniless — *quedarse con el día y la noche.*
She was left penniless. *Se quedó con el día y la noche.*

penny — *el centavo*
A penny saved is a penny earned. — *Alquimia probada, tener renta y no gastar nada.*

to cost one a pretty penny — *costarle un ojo de la cara (un dineral).*
It cost him a pretty penny. *Le costó un ojo de la cara (un dineral).*

perfect — *perfecto*
Practice makes perfect. — *El ejercicio hace maestro al novicio.*

to phase — *ejecutar en fases; planear por fases*
to phase out — *eliminar por fases; suprimir gradualmente.*
We will phase out the old equipment as we buy new. *A medida que vamos comprando nuevos equipos, iremos eliminando los antiguos.*

pick — *lo mejor; lo más escogido; la cosecha*
to take one's pick — escoger uno a su gusto.
We have quite an assortment of sandwiches; take your pick. *Tenemos todo un surtido de emparedados, puedes escoger a gusto.*

to pick — *escoger*

to pick and choose — *ser quisquilloso al escoger.*

There is no time to pick and choose. *No hay tiempo para ser quisquilloso al escoger.*

picnic — *la merienda campestre*

to be no picnic — *no ser cosa fácil.*

It's no picnic to organize a team. *Organizar un equipo no es cosa fácil.*

picture — *el cuadro*

Get the picture? — *¿Entiende?*

to fit into the picture — *venir a.*

I don't see how that fits into the picture. *No veo a qué viene eso.*

to present a gloomy picture — *hablar en términos muy pesimistas.*

He presented a gloomy picture of the war. *Habló de la guerra en términos muy pesimistas.*

to take a picture — *sacar una foto.*

He took a picture of the tree. *Sacó una foto del árbol.*

piece — *el pedazo*

to break into pieces — *hacer añicos.*

I broke the pitcher into pieces. *Hice añicos la jarra.*

to fall to pieces — *venirse abajo.*

The government is falling to pieces. *El gobierno se viene abajo.*

to give someone a piece of one's mind — *decirle cuántas son cinco.*

She gave me a piece of her mind. *Me dijo cuántas son cinco.*

to speak one's piece — *decir todo lo que quiere decir.*

He spoke his piece. *Dijo todo lo que quería decir.*

pig — *el cerdo, el puerco*

to buy a pig in a poke — *comprar a ciegas.*

We bought a pig in a poke. *Lo compramos a ciegas.*

pill — *la píldora*

to sugarcoat the pill — *dorar la píldora.*

Tell me the truth and don't sugarcoat the pill. *Dígame la verdad y no dore la píldora.*

pin — *el alfiler*

to be on pins and needles — *estar en ascuas (espinas).*

They're all on pins and needles. *Todos están en ascuas (espinas).*

to pin — *prender con un alfiler*

to pin down — *precisar.*

We couldn't pin down who it was who started the fire. *No pudimos precisar quién fue el que empezó el incendio.*

to pin someone down — *obligarle a decirlo.*

They tried to pin him down but he refused to explain. *Trataron de obligarle a decirlo pero él no quiso explicar.*

to pinch — *pellizcar*

in a pinch — *en un aprieto.*

In a pinch you can use our car. *En un aprieto pueden usar nuestro coche.*

to feel the pinch — *pasar estrecheces.*

He's been out of work for six months and is beginning to feel the pinch. *Lleva seis meses sin trabajo y ya empieza a pasar estrecheces.*

piper — *el flautista*

He who pays the piper calls the tune. — *Quien paga, manda.*

to pitch — *lanzar*

to pitch in — *cooperar.*

If we all pitch in, we'll finish by five. *Si todos cooperamos, lo terminaremos para las cinco.*

pitchfork — *la horca*

to rain pitchforks — *llover a cántaros.*

It's raining pitchforks. *Está lloviendo a cántaros.*

pity — *la piedad, la lástima*

It's a pity (too bad). — *Es (una) lástima.*

to take pity on — *tenerle lástima.*

They took pity on us. *Nos tuvieron lástima.*

place — *el lugar*

high places — *las altas esferas.*

He gets the contracts because he has friends in high places. *Él obtiene los contratos porque tiene conexiones con gente importante.*

in place of — *en lugar de.*

He came in place of his sister. *Vino en lugar de su hermana.*

in the first place — *en primer lugar.*

In the first place, it's not mine. *En primer lugar, no es mío.*

to be going places — *llegar lejos.*

He's going places. *Llegará lejos.*

to be out of place — *estar de más.*

Will it be out of place to invite her? *¿Estará de más invitarla?*

to know one's place — *saber cuál es su sitio.*

Our maid knows her place. *Nuestra criada sabe cuál es su sitio.*

to take first place — *quedar primero.*

This horse took first place. *Este caballo quedó primero.*

to take place — *celebrarse; tener lugar.*

The meeting will take place in my office. *La reunión se celebrará (tendrá lugar) en mi oficina.*

plague — *la peste*

to avoid someone like the plague — *huir de alguien como de la peste.*

We avoid him like the plague. *Huimos de él como de la peste.*

play — *el juego*

fair play — *el juego limpio.*

And do you expect fair play from that team? *¿Y tú esperas juego limpio de ese equipo?*

foul play — *un hecho delictivo.*

It failed because of foul play. *Fracasó a causa de un hecho delictivo.*

to play — *jugar*

to play down the merit of — *darle poca importancia.*

He played down its merit. *Le dio poca importancia.*

to play dumb — *hacerse el tonto.*

He won't gain anything by playing dumb. *No gana nada con hacerse el tonto.*

to play up to — *bailarle el agua a.*

She played up to her professor. *Le bailó el agua al profesor.*

---

to please — *gustar*

please — *haga el favor de; tenga la bondad de.*

Please come in. *Haga el favor (Tenga la bondad) de pasar.*

---

plenty — *suficiente*

to go through plenty — *pasar grandes apuros.*

They went through plenty in the beginning. *Pasaron grandes apuros al principio.*

---

plot — *la trama.*

The plot thickens. — *La madeja se enreda.*

---

point — *el punto*

a case in point — *un ejemplo de eso.*

Man is violent, and a case in point are our endless wars. *El hombre es violento, y prueba de ello son nuestras incesantes guerras.*

a turning point — *un punto crucial.*

Her marriage was a turning point in her life. *Su matrimonio fue un punto crucial en su vida.*

at this point — *a estas alturas.*

Why stop studying at this point? *¿Para qué dejar de estudiar a estas alturas?*

It's beside the point. — *No viene al caso.*

moot point — *algo que no ha sido demostrado; algo discutible.*

The presence of life on other planets is a moot point. *La presencia de vida en otros planetas es tema de discusión.*

point blank — *a quemarropa.*
He fired at him point blank. *Disparó contra él a quemarropa.*

That's not the point. — *No se trata de eso.*

to be on (at) the point of — *estar a punto de.*
We're on (at) the point of moving. *Estamos a punto de mudarnos.*

to get (come) to the point — *ir al grano.*
He talks a lot but doesn't get (come) to the point. *Habla mucho pero no va al grano.*

to make a point of — *dar mucha importancia a.*
She made a point of her beauty. *Dio mucha importancia a su belleza.*

to make one's point — *hacerse entender.*
He made his point. *Se hizo entender.*

to miss the point — *no caer en la cuenta.*
He missed the point. *No cayó en la cuenta.*

to press one's point — *insistir en su argumento.*
No need to press your point. *No vale la pena insistir en su argumento.*

to score a point — *apuntarse un tanto.*
You scored a point with the boss when you solved the lost-books mystery. *Te apuntaste un tanto con el jefe cuando resolviste el misterio de los libros perdidos.*

to see the point — *ver el objeto.*
I don't see the point of buying two. *No veo el objeto de comprar dos.*

to speak to the point — *hablar al caso.*
He spoke to the point. *Habló al caso.*

to stretch a point — *hacer una concesión.*
They stretched a point and hired her. *Hicieron una concesión y la emplearon.*

up to a point — *hasta cierto punto.*
Up to a point I agree with you. *Hasta cierto punto estoy de acuerdo contigo.*

---

pole — *el poste; el palo*

wouldn't touch it with a ten-foot pole — *no querer saber nada de eso.*
I wouldn't touch that funny contract with a ten-foot pole. *No quiero saber nada de ese contrato sospechoso.*

policy — *la política*

the carrot and stick policy — *la política de tentar y amenazar.*

First we offer tax incentives, then we pass tough laws — the carrot and stick policy. *Primero ofrecemos incentivos tributarios y luego aprobamos leyes duras — la política de tentar y amenazar.*

---

to polish — *pulir*

to polish off — *acabar con.*

He polished off two bottles of beer. *Acabó con dos botellas de cerveza.*

---

poll — *la encuesta*

to take a poll — *hacer una encuesta.*

They took a poll to find out which program was the most popular. *Hicieron una encuesta para saber cuál programa era el más popular.*

---

pooh — *¡Bah!*

to pooh-pooh — *restar importancia a; desdeñar.*

Our father pooh-poohed our fear of bankruptcy. *Nuesto padre no dio importancia a nuestro temor de una bancarrota.*

---

poor — *pobre*

Poor me! — *¡Pobre (Ay) de mí!*

---

to pop — *estallar; reventar; saltar*

to pop in — *irrumpir; entrar de sopetón.*

That guy pops in at any moment. *Ese tipo se aparece en cualquier momento.*

---

possible — *posible*

as far as possible — *en cuanto sea posible; en lo posible.*

I'll follow it as far as possible. *Lo seguiré en cuanto sea posible (en lo posible).*

as soon as possible — *lo más pronto posible; lo antes posible; cuanto antes.*

Come as soon as possible. *Vengan lo más pronto posible (lo antes posible; cuanto antes).*

---

posted — *enterado*

to keep posted — *tener al corriente.*

Keep us posted on the outcome. *Ténganos al corriente de los resultados.*

pot — *la caldera*

A watched pot never boils. — *Quien espera desespera.*

It's the pot calling the kettle black. — *Dijo la sartén al cazo: quítate allá que me tiznas.*

to hit the jackpot — *ponerse las botas; sacar el gordo.*

We hit the jackpot. *Nos pusimos las botas (Sacamos el gordo).*

potato — *la papa*

hot potato — *un asunto delicado.*

Genetic engineering is a hot potato for the senate. *La ingeniería genética es un tema delicado para el senado.*

potluck — *la comida ordinaria.*

to take potluck — *comer lo que haya; aceptar lo que venga.*

We'll have to take potluck with that project in Japan. *Con ese proyecto en Japón deberemos aceptar lo que venga.*

premium — *el premio*

to be at a premium — *estar muy solicitado.*

It's at a premium. *Está muy solicitado.*

present — *el presente*

at present — *en el momento actual.*

At present it's open. *En el momento actual está abierto.*

press — *la prensa*

yellow press — *la prensa sensacionalista.*

Every six months the yellow press mentions aliens from other planets. *Cada seis meses la prensa sensacionalista menciona seres de otros planetas.*

to press — *apretar; compeler; obligar; exprimir; persuadir; urgir*

to press for — *insistir en.*

The prosecutor pressed for a guilty verdict. *El fiscal insistía en un veredicto de culpable.*

to press on — *avanzar de prisa.*

We pressed on and arrived on time. *Avanzamos de prisa y llegamos a tiempo.*

to press through — *abrirse paso.*

The tourists pressed through the crowd of vendors. *Los turistas se abrieron paso entre la muchedumbre de vendedores.*

pretty — *bonito; hermoso; bueno; excelente*

to sit pretty — *estar en posición ventajosa.*

If I get that promotion, I'll sit pretty in a sea of subordinates. *Si obtengo ese ascenso, estaré en la punta del cerro y con un montón de subordinados.*

prevention — *la prevención*

An ounce of prevention is worth a pound of cure. — *Más vale prevenir que curar.*

price — *el precio*

to set a price — *poner un precio.*

They set a very low price. *Pusieron un precio muy bajo.*

pride — *el orgullo*

to swallow one's pride — *tragarse el orgullo.*

Sometimes it's best to swallow your pride. *A veces es mejor tragarse el orgullo.*

prime — *el estado de mayor perfección*

in the prime of life — *en la flor de la vida (de edad).*

He died in the prime of life. *Murió en la flor de la vida (de edad).*

print — *la impresión, la estampa*

to be out of print — *estar agotado.*

The book is out of print. *El libro está agotado.*

probation — *la prueba*

to put on probation — *poner en libertad vigilada.*

His offense was minor, so they put him on probation. *Su delito fue de poca cuantía y por eso lo pusieron en libertad vigilada.*

problem — *el problema*

That's your problem. — *Eso es cosa suya (Allá usted).*

production — *la producción*

to step up production — *incrementar la producción.*

The factory stepped up production during the war. *La fábrica incrementó la producción durante la guerra.*

profile — *el perfil; el contorno*

to keep a low profile — *tratar de pasar desapercibido.*

After all the disturbances you have caused, it's better if you keep a low profile. *Después de todos los disturbios que causaste, será mejor que trates de pasar desapercibido.*

to profit — *aprovechar*

to profit from — *sacar provecho de.*

He profits from her advice. *Saca provecho de su consejo.*

promise — *la promesa*

to have a lot of promise — *prometer mucho.*

She's got a lot of promise. *Promete mucho.*

prophecy — *la profecía*

self-fufilling prophecy — *profecía de realización asegurada.*

The forecast that every one of us will be bald in a hundred years is a self-fulfilling prophecy. *La predicción de que todos seremos calvos en cien años es una profecía de complimiento automático.*

provocation — *la provocación*

on the slightest provocation — *por cualquier cosa.*

He gets mad on the slightest provocation. *Se enoja por cualquier cosa.*

proxy — *el poder*

by proxy — *por poder.*

He voted by proxy. *Votó por poder.*

pull — *el tirón, el estirón*

to have lots of pull — *tener gran influencia.*

He has lots of pull. *Tiene gran influencia.*

to pull — *tirar*

to pull apart — *separar.*

They pulled the two fighters apart. *Separaron a los dos contrincantes.*

to pull down — *bajar.*

He pulled down the metal curtain. *Él bajó la cortina metálica.*

to pull in — *entrar; llegar a la estación.*

The train had just pulled in when we arrived. *El tren acababa de llegar a la estación cuando llegamos.*

to pull off — *quitarse.*

She pulled her blouse off. *Se quitó la blusa.*

to pull on — *ponerse.*

She pulled her panties on. *Se puso las bragas.*

to pull oneself together — *componerse.*

She pulled herself together. *Se compuso.*

to pull out — *partir; salir de la estación.*

The boat pulled out of the harbor. *El bote salió del puerto.*

to pull through — *salir de sus apuros (su enfermedad).*

I think he'll pull through. *Creo que saldrá de sus apuros (su enfermedad).*

to pull up — *arrimar.*

Pull up a chair. *Arrime una silla.*

punch — *el puñetazo; el puñete*

to pull one's punches — *obrar con moderación.*

This time the union representative didn't pull his punches in attacking management. *Esta vez el representante del sindicato no se anduvo con miramientos al atacar a la gerencia.*

purpose — *el propósito*

on purpose — *adrede; intencionadamente.*

He did it on purpose. *Lo hizo adrede (intencionadamente).*

to talk at cross purposes — *hablar sin comprenderse uno a otro.*

They are talking at cross purposes. *Están hablando sin comprenderse uno a otro.*

---

purse — *la bolsa*

You can't make a silk purse out of a sow's ear. — *Aunque la mona se vista de seda, mona se queda.*

---

pursuit — *la busca, la persecución*

to be in pursuit of — *ir en pos de.*

He's in pursuit of the enemy. *Va en pos del enemigo.*

---

to push — *empujar*

to push one's way through — *abrir paso a empujones (empellones).*

He pushed his way through. *Se abrió paso a empujones (empellones).*

---

to put — *poner, colocar*

to be hard put — *verse apurado.*

He's very hard put. *Se ve muy apurado.*

to put across — *hacer entender.*

He can't put across his ideas to us. *No puede hacernos entender sus ideas.*

to put away — *guardar.*

He put away his toys. *Guardó sus juguetes.*

to put down — *sofocar.*

They put down the insurrection. *Sofocaron la insurrección.*

to put off — *aplazar.*

We put off our trip. *Aplazamos nuestro viaje.*

to put on — *ponerse.*

He put on his jacket. *Se puso la chaqueta.*

to put one beside oneself — *sacar a uno de sus casillas.*

His bad manners put him beside himself. *Sus malos modales le causaron una enorme irritación.*

to put oneself out — *deshacerse.*

She put herself out to please us. *Se deshizo por complacernos.*

to put out — *apagar.*

They put out the fire (light). *Apagaron el fuego (la luz).*

to put someone up — *darle cama; dar donde pasar . . . .*

They put us up for the night. *Nos dieron cama para pasar la noche (Nos dieron donde pasar la noche).*

to put together — *armar.*

They put together the motor. *Armaron el motor.*

to put up — *construir.*

They put up the building in two months. *Construyeron el edificio en dos meses.*

to put up with — *aguantar (soportar).*

She put up with a lot. *Aguantó (Soportó) mucho.*

Q

quandary — *la incertidumbre*

to be in a quandary — *verse ante un dilema.*

We're in a quandary. *Nos vemos ante un dilema.*

quarrel — *la disputa*

to pick fights (quarrels) — *tomarse (meterse) con.*

He likes to pick a fight (quarrel) with his wife. *Le gusta tomarse (meterse) con su esposa.*

quarters — *la morada*

at (in) close quarters — *muy pegados.*

They work at (in) close quarters. *Trabajan muy pegados.*

question — *la pregunta, la cuestión*

beyond all question — *indudable.*

He's beyond all question a rebel. *Es un rebelde indudable.*

It's out of the question. — *¡Eso ni pensarlo (Es imposible)!*

That's beside the question. — *Eso no viene al caso.*

to ask a question — *hacer una pregunta.*
I asked a question. *Hice una pregunta.*

to be a question of — *tratarse de.*
It's a question of money. *Se trata de dinero.*

to be an open question — *ser una cuestión discutible.*
It's an open question. *Es una cuestión discutible.*

to call into question — *poner en tela de juicio.*
He called into question his colleague's conclusions. *Puso en tela de juicio las conclusiones de su colega.*

to pop the question — *declararse.*
Only after a long time did he finally pop the question. *Se declaró sólo al cabo de largo tiempo.*

without question — *sin más vueltas.*
It was John, without question. *Fue Juan, sin más vueltas.*

---

quick — *la carne viva*

to cut to the quick — *herir en lo vivo.*
His criticism cut me to the quick. *Su crítica me hirió en lo vivo.*

---

quite — *completamente, bastante*

quite a few — *bastantes.*
Quite a few came. *Vinieron bastantes.*

to be quite a woman — *ser toda una mujer.*
She's quite a woman. *Es toda una mujer.*

---

quits — *la tregua*

to call it quits — *abandonar la partida.*
We called it quits. *Abandonamos la partida.*

---

to quote — *citar*

not to be quoted — *decir una suposición.*
Don't quote me, but it seems that the senator will vote in favor of the project. *No estoy seguro, pero parece que el senador votará a favor del proyecto.*

R

race — *la carrera*

rat race — *competencia incesante.*

To get to the top you must always compete in the rat race. *Para llegar a la cumbre debes subordinarte a la competencia incesante.*

rag — *el trapo*

to be in rags — *andar en andrajos.*

He's in rags. *Anda en andrajos.*

to go from rags to riches — *pasar de la miseria a la riqueza.*

He's gone from rags to riches. *Ha pasado de la miseria a la riqueza.*

rage — *la rabia*

to be all the rage — *hacer furor.*

Those hats were all the rage last year. *Esos sombreros hicieron furor el año pasado.*

rain — *la lluvia*

rain or shine — *con buen o mal tiempo.*

We're going to work there rain or shine. *Vamos a trabajar allí con buen o mal tiempo.*

to rain — *llover*

It never rains but it pours. — *Siempre llueve sobre mojado; Las desgracias nunca vienen solas.*

to rake — *rastrillar; barrer*

to rake in — *ganar en abundancia.*

He sells genetically modified seeds and rakes in millions. *Vende semillas genéticamente modificadas y gana millones.*

random — *casual*

at random — *al azar.*

They were chosen at random. *Se les escogió al azar.*

range — *la escala*

at close range — *de cerca.*

I want to see it at close range. *Deseo verlo de cerca.*

to be within range — *estar a tiro.*

The animal is within range. *El animal está a tiro.*

to range with — *estar en la misma altura o el mismo nivel.*

The Soviet MiG ranged with the American Sabre Jet. *El MiG soviético era comparable al Sabre Jet norteamericano.*

rank — *la fila*

the rank and file — *las masas; el pueblo.*

We must educate the rank and file. *Debemos educar a las masas (al pueblo).*

to join the ranks — *darse de alta.*

He joined the ranks. *Se dio de alta.*

to rank — *tener posición*

to rank high — *ocupar una alta posición.*

Our city ranks high. *Nuestra ciudad ocupa una alta posición.*

rap — *golpecito*

to take the rap — *sufrir las consecuencias.*

I took the rap for his negligence. *Sufrí yo las consecuencias de su descuido.*

rat — *la rata*

to smell a rat — *olerle mal el asunto.*

I smell a rat. *Me huele mal el asunto.*

rate — *la razón; el paso*

at any rate — *de todos modos; de todas maneras.*

At any rate, he's the one who has it. *De todos modos (De todas maneras) es él quien lo tiene.*

at the rate of — *a razón de.*
We were traveling at the rate of 100 kilometers an hour. *Viajábamos a razón de cien kilómetros la hora.*

at this rate — *a este paso.*
At this rate we won't get there. *A este paso no llegaremos.*

second-rate — *de calidad inferior.*
These are second-rate shoes. *Estos son zapatos bastante mal hechos.*

---

rather — *más bien*

would rather — *preferir.*
I would rather go. *Preferiría ir.*

---

to rave — *delirar*

to rave about — *deshacerse en elogios de.*
He raved about his children. *Se deshizo en elogios de sus hijos.*

---

reach — *el alcance*

to be out of (within) one's reach — *estar fuera de (estar a) su alcance.*
It's out of (within) our reach. *Está fuera de (está a) nuestro alcance.*

---

to reach — *alcanzar*

to reach an understanding — *llegar a un acuerdo.*
We've reached an understanding. *Hemos llegado a un acuerdo.*

to reach for — *esforzarse por coger.*
He reached for the bread. *Se esforzó por coger el pan.*

---

to read — *leer*

to read over — *echar una ojeada a.*
I read over his exam. *Eché una ojeada a su examen.*

to read up on — *leer sobre; informarse de.*
I'm reading up on Pérez Galdós. *Estoy leyendo sobre (Me estoy informando de) Pérez Galdós.*

---

ready — *listo*

ready-made — *de confección.*
She always goes to the stores and buys ready-made dresses. *Ella siempre va a las tiendas y se compra los trajes hechos.*

ready, willing, and able — *totalmente dispuesto a algo.*
He was ready, willing, and able to do anything to win her heart. *Estaba listo para todo con tal de ganar su corazón.*

to get ready to — *disponerse (prepararse) a.*
I'm getting ready to study. *Me dispongo (Me preparo) a estudiar.*

real — *real*
for real — *de verdad; realmente.*
Is that coin for real or is it a fake? *¿Es esa moneda de verdad o una falsificación?*

reason — *la razón*
for no reason — *sin ningún motivo.*
He insulted her for no reason. *La insultó sin ningún motivo.*

it stands to reason — *es lógico.*
It stands to reason that he must go. *Es lógico que tenga que ir.*

to have reason to — *tener por qué.*
You have no reason to criticize. *No tiene por qué criticar.*

to listen to reason — *entrar en razón.*
She refused to listen to reason. *No quiso entrar en razón.*

to lose one's reason — *perder la razón.*
She lost her reason. *Perdió la razón.*

to recall — *hacer volver*
beyond recall — *irrevocable.*
He is still conscious, but his memory is beyond recall. *Todavía está consciente, pero su memoria no tiene remedio.*

receipt — *el recibo*
to acknowledge receipt — *acusar recibo.*
He acknowledged receipt of the money order. *Acusó recibo del giro.*

record — *el registro*
for the record — *para que conste en acta.*
He said it for the record. *Lo dijo para que constara en acta.*

off the record — *en confianza.*

What he said is off the record. *Lo que dijo lo dijo en confianza.*

to keep a record — *llevar cuenta.*

She keeps a record of all the family expenses. *Lleva cuenta de todos los gastos de familia.*

red — *rojo*

in the red — *en déficit; endeudado.*

His business is always in the red. *Su negocio está siempre en déficit (endeudado).*

to see red — *encolerizarse.*

I see red when he beats her. *Me encolerizo cuando él le pega.*

red-handed (in the act) — *con las manos en la masa.*

He was caught red-handed (in the act). *Lo cogieron con las manos en la masa.*

red-hot — *calentado al rojo*

red-hot — *al rojo (vivo) (al rojo blanco).*

The iron was red-hot. *El hierro estaba al rojo (vivo) (al rojo blanco).*

reed — *la caña*

slender as a reed — *delgado como un junco.*

She dieted and now she's as slender as a reed. *Estuvo en dieta y ahora está tan delgada como una espiga.*

to refuse — *rehusar*

to refuse flatly — *negarse rotundamente.*

He flatly refused to accept it. *Se negó rotundamente a aceptarlo.*

to refuse to — *resistirse a.*

She refused to get old. *Se resistía a envejecer.*

regalia — *atavío de gala*

in full regalia (all dressed up) — *de punta en blanco.*

At the banquet everybody was in full regalia. *En el banquete todos estaban de punta en blanco.*

rein — *la rienda*

to give free rein to — *dar rienda suelta a.*

He always gives free rein to his feelings. *Siempre da rienda suelta a sus sentimientos.*

repair — *la reparación*

to be beyond repair — *no poder repararse (componerse).*

This car is beyond repair. *Este coche no puede repararse (componerse).*

to be in bad (good) repair — *estar en malas (buenas) condiciones.*

The roads are always in bad (good) repair. *Los caminos siempre están en malas (buenas) condiciones.*

to report — *hacer informe, informar*

to report for — *presentarse para.*

He reported for work on Monday. *Se presentó para trabajar el lunes.*

to report on — *dar cuenta de.*

He always reports on his trips. *Siempre da cuenta de sus viajes.*

reputation — *la reputación, la fama*

to have the reputation of — *tener fama de.*

They have the reputation of being honest. *Tienen fama de ser honrados.*

to live up to one's reputation — *hacer honor a su fama.*

He'll have to live up to his reputation. *Tendrá que hacer honor a su fama.*

request — *la petición*

at . . . 's request — *a petición (instancia) de. . . .*

We sent it at John's request. *Lo mandamos a petición (instancia) de Juan.*

requirement — *la exigencia*

to meet all the requirements — *reunir (llenar) todos los requisitos.*

He met all the requirements for his doctorate. *Reunió (Llenó) todos los requisitos para su doctorado.*

to resign — resignar

to resign oneself to — *conformarse con.*

I have resigned myself to staying. *Me he conformado con quedarme.*

resistance — *la resistencia*

the line of least resistance — *la solución más fácil.*

Following the line of least resistance soon leads to moral dilemmas. *Escoger siempre la solución más fácil asegura la aparición de dilemas morales.*

resort — *el recurso*

as a last resort — *en último caso; como último recurso.*

As a last resort, use this one. *En último caso (Como último recurso), sírvase de éste.*

to rest — *descansar*

to come to rest — *venir a parar.*

It came to rest in front of our house. *Vino a parar en frente de nuestra casa.*

to rest assured — *tener la seguridad.*

Rest assured that we'll come. *Tenga la seguridad de que vendremos.*

respect — *el respecto, el respeto*

with respect to — *(con) respecto a.*

He wrote with respect to the earthquake. *Escribió (con) respecto al terremoto.*

return — *el retorno*

point of no return — *punto en que el regreso o retirada es ya impráctico o imposible.*

The airplane passed the point of no return. *El avión sobrepasó la mitad de su ruta.*

to revert — *revertir*

to revert to — *recaer en.*

After his wife died, he reverted to his old vices. *Después de la muerte de su esposa, recayó en sus antiguos vicios.*

rhyme — *la rima*

without rhyme or reason — *sin ton ni son.*

His statement was without rhyme or reason. *Su declaración fue sin ton ni son.*

rib — *la costilla*

rib-tickling — *cómico; humorístico.*

That rib-tickling magazine specialized in political satire. *Esa revista cómica se especializaba en sátira política.*

to poke one in the ribs — *darle un codazo.*

As soon as he mentioned that sensitive subject, his wife poked him in the ribs. *Tan pronto como mencionó ese delicado tema, su esposa le dio un codazo.*

rich — *rico*

to be rich in — *tener mucho . . .*

This medicine is rich in vitamin C. *Este medicamento tiene mucha vitamina C.*

riches — *las riquezas*

an embarrassment of riches — *no saber por dónde empezar.*

So much Halloween candy was an embarrassment of riches. *Con tantas golosinas en Halloween uno no sabía por dónde empezar.*

to rid — *librar*

to get rid of — *deshacerse (librarse) de.*

I got rid of my car. *Me deshice (libré) de mi coche.*

ride — *el paseo*

to go for a ride — *dar un paseo (en coche).*

They went out for a ride. *Salieron a dar un paseo (en coche).*

to take for a ride — *llevar de paseo (en coche).*

He took us for a ride. *Nos llevó de paseo (en coche).*

ridiculous — *ridículo*

to make look ridiculous — *poner en ridículo.*

He made me look ridiculous. *Me puso en ridículo.*

right — *el derecho; la derecha; la razón*

right and left — *a diestra y siniestra.*

Snow was falling right and left. *Caía la nieve a diestra y siniestra.*

to be in the right — *estar en lo firme (tener razón).*
He told me I was in the right when I wouldn't accept the money.
Me dijo que estaba en lo firme (tenía razón) al no querer aceptar el dinero.

to be right — *tener razón.*
He's right. *Tiene razón.*

to have a right to — *tener derecho a.*
He has a right to talk. *Tiene derecho a hablar.*

to (on) the right — *a la derecha.*
It's to (on) the right. *Está a la derecha.*

---

right — *correcto; bien; mismo*

right away (off) — *en seguida.*
He refused right away (off). *Rehusó en seguida.*

right here — *aquí mismo.*
It's right here. *Está aquí mismo.*

right now — *ahora mismo.*
Come right now. *Venga ahora mismo.*

Right on! — *¡Muy bien!*
"We must fight for our rights!" — "Right on!" *"¡Debemos luchar por nuestros derechos!" — "¡Muy bien!"*

right then and there — *en el acto.*
I bought it right then and there. *Lo compré en el acto.*

That's right. — *Así es; Eso es.*

to be all right with — *con el permiso de.*
If it's all right with you, I won't stay. *Con su permiso no me quedaré.*

to be right back — *volver en seguida.*
I'll be right back. *Vuelvo en seguida.*

to serve one right — *tenerlo bien merecido.*
He went to jail? Serves him right for cheating so many people. *¿Fue a parar a la cárcel? Pues lo tuvo bien merecido por haber engañado a tanta gente.*

rightly — *correctamente*

rightly or wrongly — *mal que bien; con razón o sin ella.*

Rightly or wrongly, they won. *Mal que bien (Con razón o sin ella), ganaron.*

rightly so — *a justo título.*

He said no, and rightly so. *Dijo que no y a justo título.*

ring — *la llamada*

to give someone a ring — *llamarle por teléfono (darle un telefonazo).*

He gave me a ring. *Me llamó por teléfono (Me dio un telefonazo).*

to have a familiar ring — *sonarle a algo conocido.*

It has a familiar ring. *Me suena a algo conocido.*

rise — *la subida*

to give rise to — *dar lugar (origen) a.*

It gave rise to many problems. *Dio lugar (origen) a muchos problemas.*

risk — *el riesgo*

a calculated risk — *un riesgo previsto.*

I took a calculated risk by welding the pipe on that spot. *Soldé el caño en ese punto después de prever el riesgo.*

to afford a risk — *correr un riesgo.*

We can't afford the risk of crossing this bridge. *No podemos correr el riesgo de atravesar este puente.*

to run the risk — *correr el riesgo (peligro).*

We ran the risk of being discovered. *Corrimos el riesgo (peligro) de ser descubiertos.*

river — *el río*

to sell someone down the river — *traicionarle.*

We've been sold down the river. *Nos han traicionado.*

road — *el camino*

one for the road — *el trago de despedida.*

Let's have one for the road, unless you are driving. *Tomemos un trago de despedida, a menos que estés manejando.*

The road to hell is paved with good intentions. — *El infierno está lleno de buenos propósitos, y el cielo de buenas obras.*

to be on the road — *estar de viaje.*

My work forces me to be on the road almost all the time. *Mi trabajo me obliga a estar de viaje casi todo el tiempo.*

to hit the road — *ponerse en camino.*

It's time for us to hit the road. *Ya es hora de ponernos en camino.*

rock — *la piedra*

on the rocks — *solo con hielo.*

He took his rum on the rocks. *Tomó su ron solo con hielo.*

to be on the rocks — *andar mal.*

Their friendship is on the rocks. *Su amistad anda mal.*

rocker — *la mecedora*

to be off one's rocker — *estar loco.*

He lost everything and now he's off his rocker. *Lo perdió todo y ahora anda loco.*

role — *el papel*

to play one's role — *representar su papel.*

He plays his role well. *Representa bien su papel.*

Rome — *Roma*

Rome was not built in a day. — *No se ganó Zamora en una hora.*

When in Rome do as the Romans do. — *Donde fueres, haz lo que vieres.*

roof — *el techo*

to raise the roof — *armar un alboroto.*

Every time we did not bring our homework, the teacher raised the roof. *El profesor siempre armaba la grande cuando no traíamos los deberes.*

room — *el cuarto; el espacio*

room and board — *pensión completa.*

We'd like to have room and board. *Nos gustaría tener pensión completa.*

There's always room for one more. — *Donde comen seis comen siete.*

to make room for — *dejar sitio.*

They made room for us in the car. *Nos dejaron sitio en el coche.*

to take up room — *ocupar espacio.*

This table takes up too much room. *La mesa ocupa demasiado espacio.*

---

roost — *la percha de gallinero*

to rule the roost — *mandar.*

In that house the mother rules the roost. *En esa casa manda la madre.*

---

root — *la raíz*

grass roots — *la población rural; el campo.*

Grass root voters were his main support base. *Los votantes rurales eran su apoyo más grande.*

to take root — *echar raíces; arraigar.*

It's taking root. *Está echando raíces (arraigando).*

---

rope — *la cuerda*

to give someone too much rope — *darle demasiada libertad.*

His parents gave him too much rope. *Sus padres le dieron demasiada libertad.*

to know the ropes — *saber cuántas son cinco; estar al tanto de las cosas.*

He knows the ropes. *Sabe cuántas son cinco (Está al tanto de las cosas).*

to reach the end of one's rope — *no poder más.*

He had reached the end of his rope. *No podía más.*

---

rough — *agitado*

to be rough on — *estropear.*

This soap is rough on hands. *Este jabón estropea las manos.*

to have a rough idea — *tener una idea aproximada.*

I have a rough idea. *Tengo una idea aproximada.*

to have a rough time of it — *pasarlas muy duras.*

We had a rough time of it. *Las pasamos muy duras.*

row — *la pelea*

to have a row — *armarse un bochinche.*

There was quite a row near our house. *Se armó un bochinche bastante grande cerca de nuestra casa.*

row — *la fila*

in a row — *seguidos.*

We went two days in a row. *Fuimos dos días seguidos.*

rub — *el busilis*

to be the rub — *ser lo malo.*

The rub is that he can't speak it. *Lo malo es que no sabe hablarlo.*

to rub — *frotar*

to rub against — *codearse con.*

At the Waldorf we rubbed against all the beautiful people. *En el Waldorf nos codeamos con toda la gente linda.*

to rub it in — *machacar.*

When I'm wrong, he always rubs it in. *Cuando estoy equivocado, siempre machaca.*

rule — *la regla*

a hard and fast rule — *una regla inflexible.*

It's a hard and fast rule. *Es una regla inflexible.*

as a general rule — *por regla general.*

As a general rule, I walk. *Por regla general voy a pie.*

to rule — *gobernar*

to rule out — *excluir, descartar.*

They have ruled out that possibility. *Han excluido (Han descartado) esa posibilidad.*

to rumor — *rumorearse*

it is rumored — *es fama.*

It is rumored that she poisoned her husband. *Es fama que envenenó a su esposo.*

run — *el curso, la carrera*

also-ran — *entre los demás participantes.*

Robert always was an also-ran; he never won any prizes. *Roberto nunca obtuvo premios; nunca pasó de mero participante.*

dry run — *la prueba.*

Let's have a dry run with this system before we get it on line. *Pongamos este sistema a prueba antes de conectarlo a la red.*

in the long run — *a la larga; a largo plazo; a la postre.*

In the long run it will cost less. *A la larga (A largo plazo; A la postre) costará menos.*

on the run — *a la carrera.*

If I don't want to be late, I'll have to eat on the run. *Si no quiero llegar tarde, tendré que comer a la carrera.*

run-of-the-mill — *ordinario; mediocre.*

Despite the great promotion, it was a run-of-the-mill musical. *Pese a la tremenda promoción, fue una comedia musical muy ordinaria.*

to give someone a run for his money — *darle una competencia fuerte.*

I gave him a run for his money. *Le di una competencia fuerte.*

to run — *correr*

to run across — *tropezar (dar) con.*

I ran across an old friend. *Tropecé (Di) con un viejo amigo.*

to run after — *ir detrás.*

He runs after blondes. *Va detrás de las rubias.*

to run around with — *asociarse con.*

He runs around with young people. *Se asocia con los jóvenes.*

to run away — *escaparse; huirse.*

The thief ran away. *El ladrón se escapó (huyó).*

to run down — *parar.*

My watch has run down. *Mi reloj ha parado.*

to run dry — *secarse.*

The well ran dry. *El pozo se secó.*

to run into — *tropezar (encontrarse) con.*
I ran into him. *Tropecé (Me encontré) con él.*

to run low on (short of) — *írsele acabando.*
We're running low on (short of) paper. *Se nos va acabando el papel.*

to run out — *acabársele.*
I've run out of money. *Se me acabó el dinero.*

to run over (down) — *atropellar (derribar) a.*
He ran over (down) a pedestrian. *Atropelló (Derribó) a un peatón.*

to run smoothly — *ir sobre ruedas.*
The business is running smoothly. *El negocio va sobre ruedas.*

to run up (down) to — *correr a.*
Run up (down) to the corner and get a paper. *Corra a la esquina y compre un periódico.*

---

runner — *el corredor; la corredora*

runner-up — *el subcampeón; el corredor o jugador o equipo que llega en segundo lugar.*
He managed to be the runner-up, but his dream of Olympic gold was shattered. *Logró el segundo puesto, pero su sueño de lograr el oro olímpico quedó roto.*

---

to rush — *darse prisa*

for blood to rush to one's face — *ponerse colorado (sonrojarse).*
Blood rushed to his face. *Se puso colorado (Se sonrojó).*

to rush things — *precipitar las cosas.*
You're rushing things. *Está precipitando las cosas.*

to rush through — *hacer de prisa.*
He rushed through his work. *Hizo de prisa su trabajo.*

---

rush — *la prisa*

in a mad rush — *precipitadamente.*
He left me in a mad rush. *Me dejó precipitadamente.*

S

sack — *el saco*

to be left holding the sack (bag) — *quedarse con la carga en las costillas.*

I was left holding the sack (bag). *Me quedé con la carga en las costillas.*

to give someone the sack (to sack someone) — *despedirlo.*

They gave him the sack (They sacked him). *Lo despidieron.*

---

safe — *salvo, seguro*

safe and sound — *sano y salvo.*

They arrived safe and sound. *Llegaron sanos y salvos.*

to be on the safe side — *para mayor seguridad.*

To be on the safe side, let's take ten. *Para mayor seguridad tomemos diez.*

to be safe — *estar a salvo.*

He's safe. *Está a salvo.*

to play it safe — *andar con precaución.*

He tried to play it safe. *Trató de andar con precaución.*

---

safety — *la seguridad*

safety first — *la seguridad ante todo.*

Our motto is "Safety First." *Nuestro lema es "La seguridad ante todo."*

to reach safety — *ponerse a salvo.*

They reached safety. *Se pusieron a salvo.*

---

sail — *la vela*

to trim one's sails — *adaptarse; amoldarse.*

I have a lot of opposition . . . perhaps I should trim my sails a bit. *Tengo mucha oposición . . . quizás será mejor amoldarme un poquito.*

---

saintly — *santo*

to act saintly — *hacerse el santo.*

He acts so saintly. *Se hace el santo.*

---

sake — *el motivo*

For Heaven's sake! — *¡Por Dios!*

for one's sake — *para su propio bien.*

It's for your sake. *Es para su propio bien.*

for the sake of — *por ganas (motivo) de.*

He argues for the sake of arguing. *Disputa por ganas (motivo) de disputar.*

---

sale — *la venta*

on sale — *a la venta.*

They put them on sale. *Los pusieron a la venta.*

---

salt — *la sal*

to be worth one's salt — *valer el pan que come.*

He's not worth his salt. *No vale el pan que come.*

to take with a grain of salt — *acoger con reserva(s).*

You have to take what he says with a grain of salt. *Hay que acoger con reserva(s) todo lo que dice.*

---

to salt — *salar*

to salt away — *ahorrar.*

He salts away all he earns. *Ahorra todo lo que gana.*

---

same — *mismo*

It's all the same. — *Es lo mismo (Lo mismo da).*

The same to you. — *Igualmente (Lo mismo digo).*

to be all the same — *ser igual.*

It's all the same to me. *A mí me es igual.*

---

say — *el decir*

to have one's say — *decir su parecer; dar su opinión.*

He had his say. *Dijo su parecer (Dio su opinión).*

---

to say — *decir*

It is easier said than done. — *Una cosa es decirlo y otra hacerlo.*

It's no sooner said than done. — *Dicho y hecho.*

so to say — *por decirlo así.*
He is, so to say, a bit slow. *Él es, por decirlo así, un poco tardo.*

that is to say — *es decir.*
Our friends, that is to say, the Joneses, came. *Nuestros amigos, es decir los Jones, vinieron.*

there's no saying — *no hay modo de saber.*
There's no saying when the next tornado will arrive. *No hay manera de saber cuándo llegará el próximo tornado.*

to go without saying — *holgar decir; entenderse.*
It goes without saying that she's intelligent. *Huelga decir (Se entiende) que es inteligente.*

to say nothing of — *sin mencionar.*
Taxes are terrible here, to say nothing of the environmental problems. *Los impuestos aquí son terribles, sin mencionar los problemas ambientales.*

to say the least — *por lo menos.*
It's interesting, to say the least. *Es interesante, por lo menos.*

when all is said and done — *al fin y al cabo.*
When all is said and done, it's an excellent university. *Al fin y al cabo es una universidad excelente.*

You can say that again. — *Bien puede usted decirlo.*

You don't say! — *¡No me digas!*

---

saying — *el dicho*

as the saying goes (as they say) — *como dijo el otro.*
Well, Rome wasn't built in a day, as the saying goes (as they say). *Bueno, no se ganó Zamora en una hora, como dijo el otro.*

---

scale — *la escala; la balanza*

on a large scale — *en gran escala; en grande.*
They're bought on a large scale. *Se compran en gran escala (en grande).*

to tip the scales — *decidirlo.*
His recommendation tipped the scales in my favor. *Su recomendación lo decidió a mi favor.*

to scale — *escalar*

to scale down — *reducir.*

He scaled down his prices. *Redujo sus precios.*

scapegoat — *víctima propiciatoria*

to be made the scapegoat — *pagar los vidrios rotos.*

He's going to have to be made the scapegoat, even though we know he's not the guilty one. *Va a tener que pagar los vidrios rotos, aunque sabemos que no es el culpable.*

scarce — *escaso*

to make oneself scarce — *irse; no dejarse ver.*

Make yourself scarce. *Váyase (No se deje ver).*

scene — *la escena*

behind the scenes — *entre bastidores.*

It was decided behind the scenes. *Se decidió entre bastidores.*

to make a scene — *armar (causar) un escándalo.*

She made a scene when her husband didn't return. *Armó (Causó) un escándalo cuando no volvió su esposo.*

schedule — *el horario*

to be behind schedule — *traer (llevar) retraso.*

That train is an hour behind schedule. *Ese tren trae (lleva) una hora de retraso.*

score — *marca; línea; cuenta; resultado; nota; tantos*

on that score — *en tanto a eso.*

Records must be maintained; on that score, you should hire a secretary. *Los documentos deben registrarse; en tanto a eso, usted debiera emplear una secretaria.*

to keep score — *apuntar los tantos.*

John and I play, and Bob keeps score. *John y yo jugamos, mientras Bob apunta los tantos.*

to know the score — *conocer la verdadera situación.*

The general knows the score — we're beaten! *El general conoce la verdadera situación y sabe que hemos perdido.*

to settle a score — *ajustar cuentas.*

I'll settle the score with Jimmy as soon as I leave this jail. *Ajustaré las cuentas con Jimmy tan pronto como salga de esta cárcel.*

to scrape — *raspar*

to scrape along — *ir tirando.*

She scrapes along on five dollars a week. *Va tirando con cinco dólares a la semana.*

to scrape together — *reunir (dinero).*

He scraped together enough (money) to buy bread and milk. *Reunió (dinero) para comprar pan y leche.*

scratch — *el arañazo, el rasguño*

to start from scratch — *empezar desde el principio.*

He started from scratch in his profession. *Empezó desde el principio en su profesión.*

screw — *el tornillo*

to have a screw loose — *faltarle un tornillo.*

Sometimes I think that Ricardo has a screw loose. *A veces me parece que a Ricardo le falta un tornillo.*

sea — *el (la) mar*

on the high seas — *en alta mar.*

They collided on the high seas. *Se chocaron en alta mar.*

search — *la busca*

to go out in search of — *salir a la (en) busca de.*

We went out in search of our cat. *Salimos a la (en) busca de nuestro gato.*

season — *la estación*

off season — *fuera de temporada.*

We were in Acapulco off season. *Estuvimos en Acapulco fuera de temporada.*

seat — *el asiento*

to take a back seat — *perder mucha influencia.*

After losing the championship, he had to take a back seat. *Después de perder el campeonato, perdió mucha influencia.*

to take a seat — *tomar asiento.*

Take a seat. *Tome asiento.*

---

second — *segundo*

to be second to none — *no tener rival.*

As a teacher he's second to none. *Como maestro no tiene rival.*

---

secret — *el secreto*

an open secret — *un secreto conocido de todos.*

Her bad conduct is an open secret. *Su mala conducta es un secreto conocido de todos.*

to let someone in on the secret — *decirle el secreto.*

He let me in on the secret. *Me dijo el secreto.*

---

security — *la seguridad*

to give security — *dar fianza.*

They couldn't give security. *No pudieron dar fianza.*

---

to see — *ver*

as one sees it — *a su modo de ver.*

As I see it, it's a mistake. *A mi modo de ver, es un error.*

let's see — *a ver.*

Let's see. Which is yours? *A ver. ¿Cuál es el suyo?*

See you later. — *Hasta luego.*

Seeing is believing. — *Santo Tomás, ver y creer.*

to see off — *despedirse de.*

We went to the station to see him off. *Fuimos a la estación para despedirnos de él.*

to see to it — *encargarse de.*

I'll see to it that she knows it. *Me encargaré de que lo sepa.*

to see to the door — *acompañar a la puerta.*

She saw me to the door. *Me acompañó a la puerta.*

seed — *la semilla*

to go to seed — *envejecer; gastarse; arruinarse.*

Since his wife died, he went to seed very fast. *Desde que su esposa murió, él envejeció rápidamente.*

to sow the seeds of — *dar principio a.*

Jones had sown the seeds of this empire. *Jones había empezado este imperio.*

to sell — *vender*

to be sold out — *estar agotado.*

The tickets are sold out. *Las entradas están agotadas.*

to sell out — *liquidar.*

They sold out all their stock. *Liquidaron todas sus existencias.*

to sell someone out — *traicionarle.*

He sold us out. *Nos traicionó.*

to send — *mandar*

to send for — *hacer venir.*

He sent for his parents. *Hizo venir a sus padres.*

to send out — *enviar.*

He has not sent out the monthly invoices yet. *Todavía no ha enviado las facturas mensuales.*

send-off — *la despedida*

to give a big send-off — *dar una despedida suntuosa.*

We gave my aunt a big send-off. *Dimos a mi tía una despedida suntuosa.*

sense — *el sentido*

horse sense — *buen sentido común.*

He's got horse sense. *Tiene buen sentido común.*

in a sense — *en cierto sentido.*

In a sense it's your own fault. *En cierto sentido tú mismo tienes la culpa.*

to come to one's senses — *entrar en razon.*
Some day he'll come to his senses. *Algún día entrará en razón.*

to make sense — *tener sentido.*
It doesn't make sense. *No tiene sentido.*

service — *el servicio*

At your service. — *Para servirle a usted (Servidor de usted).*

to be of service — *ser útil (servir).*
This book is of no service to me. *Este libro no me es útil (no me sirve).*

to pay lip service to — *fingir respetar.*
We paid lip service to his rules. *Fingimos respetar sus reglas.*

set — *la colección*

a set of teeth — *dentadura.*
She has a new set of teeth. *Tiene dentadura nueva.*

to set — *poner, colocar*

to be set — *estar listo.*
They are set to travel to Mexico. *Están listos para viajar a México.*

to set (the sun) — *ponerse (el sol).*
The sun sets early. *El sol se pone temprano.*

to set about — *ponerse a.*
He set about organizing a new company. *Se puso a organizar una nueva compañía.*

to set aside — *poner a un lado.*
I put my work aside. *Puse a un lado mi trabajo.*

to set back — *aplazar.*
Her illness caused her to set back the date of her wedding. *Su enfermedad le hizo aplazar la fecha de su boda.*

to set forth — *presentar.*
He set forth some interesting ideas. *Presentó unas ideas interesantes.*

to set forth — *salir.*
We set forth on our trip. *Salimos de viaje.*

to set forward (ahead) — *hacer adelantar.*
I set my watch forward (ahead). *Hice adelantar mi reloj.*

to set off — *hacer estallar.*

They set off the bomb. *Hicieron estallar la bomba.*

to set off (out) — *ponerse en camino.*

They set off (out) after breakfast. *Se pusieron en camino después del desayuno.*

to set right — *aclarar.*

In his speech he set things right. *En su discurso aclaró las cosas.*

to set straight — *poner en su punto.*

We set things straight. *Pusimos las cosas en su punto.*

to set up — *establecer.*

My father set me up in business. *Mi padre me estableció en un negocio.*

to set up — *levantar.*

They set up their equipment in the park. *Levantaron su equipo en el parque.*

---

to settle — *establecer; solucionar*

to settle — *ir a cuentas.*

Let's settle this! *¡Vamos a cuentas!*

to settle down — *arraigar; establecerse.*

My father settled down in the U.S. *Mi padre arraigó (se estableció) en los Estados Unidos.*

to settle down — *ponerse a.*

He settled down to study. *Se puso a estudiar.*

to settle down — *sentar la cabeza.*

My son refuses to settle down. *Mi hijo se niega a sentar la cabeza.*

to settle for — *conformarse con.*

He settled for fifty dollars. *Se conformó con cincuenta dólares.*

to settle on — *ponerse de acuerdo.*

They settled on how much to charge. *Se pusieron de acuerdo sobre cuánto cobrar.*

---

sex — *el sexo*

the fair sex — *el bello sexo.*

It is believed that the fair sex is afraid of mice. *Se cree que el bello sexo teme a los ratones.*

shake — *la sacudida; el meneo*

to be no great shakes — *no ser nada del otro mundo.*

She may have had two PhDs, but as a teacher she was no great shakes. *Puede haber tenido dos doctorados, pero como profesora no era gran cosa.*

to shake off — *arrojar o desprender con sacudidas.*

I shook the dandruff off the jacket, but more fell on it. *Sacudí la caspa de la chaqueta, pero más caspa le cayó encima.*

to shake one's head — *menear la cabeza.*

He shook his head in disbelief. *Meneó la cabeza con extrañeza.*

to shake up — *remover; mezclar; agitar.*

Take these three ingredients, shake them up, and you'll get great ice-cream. *Toma estos tres ingredientes, mézclalos bien y obtendrás un excelente helado.*

---

shame — *la vergüenza*

It's a crying shame. — *Es una verdadera vergüenza.*

It's a shame. — *Es una lástima (¡Qué pena!).*

Shame on you! — *¡Vergüenza debería darte!*

What? You didn't apologize? Shame on you! — *¿Cómo? ¿No te disculpaste? ¡Vergüenza debiera darte!*

---

shape — *la forma*

to be in the shape of — *tener la forma de.*

It's in the shape of a bird. *Tiene la forma de un pájaro.*

to be in tip-top shape — *estar en excelentes condiciones.*

It's in tip-top shape. *Está en excelentes condiciones.*

to put in final shape — *darle forma a.*

It took them a long time to put their plans in final shape. *Tardaron mucho en darle forma a sus planes.*

to take shape — *comenzar a formarse.*

His plans for the future were taking shape. *Sus planes para el futuro comenzaban a formarse.*

share — *la parte*

the lion's share — *la parte del léon.*

He got the lion's share. *El recibió la parte del león.*

sharp — *agudo*

at . . . sharp — *a la(s) . . . en punto.*

Come at four o'clock sharp. *Venga a las cuatro en punto.*

to be sharp — *cortar.*

The wind is very sharp today. *El viento corta mucho hoy.*

shave — *el afeitado*

to have a close shave — *salvarse por los pelos.*

We had a close shave. *Nos salvamos por los pelos.*

sheep — *la oveja*

the black sheep of the family — *la oveja negra de la familia; el garbanzo negro de la familia.*

He's the black sheep of the family. *Es la oveja negra (el garbanzo negro) de la familia.*

to separate the sheep from the goats — *distinguir entre los buenos y los malos.*

Our boss separated the sheep from the goats. *Nuestro jefe distinguió entre los buenos y los malos.*

to shift — *ayudarse, cambiar*

to shift for oneself — *arreglárselas (por sí) solo.*

He left home to shift for himself. *Abandonó su casa para arreglárselas (por sí) solo.*

shirt — *la camisa*

to keep one's shirt on — *no perder la paciencia.*

Keep your shirt on. *No pierda la paciencia.*

to lose one's shirt — *perder hasta la camisa.*

He lost his shirt in that deal. *Perdió hasta la camisa en ese negocio.*

shoe — *el zapato*

to be in someone else's shoes — *estar (hallarse) en su lugar (pellejo).*

If I were in your shoes, I'd stay. *Si estuviera (Si me hallara) en su lugar (pellejo), me quedaría.*

to get along on a shoe string — *vivir con muy poco dinero.*

He gets along on a shoe string. *Vive con muy poco dinero.*

---

to shoot — *disparar*

to shoot down — *derribar.*

I'll shoot down every argument you have to marry her. *Echaré por tierra todos los argumentos que tengas para casarte con ella.*

---

shop — *la tienda*

to go shopping — *ir de compras (tiendas).*

Let's go shopping. *Vamos de compras (tiendas).*

to talk shop — *hablar de su trabajo.*

He always talks shop. *Siempre habla de su trabajo.*

---

shore — *la costa*

to be . . . off shore — *estar a . . . de la costa.*

It's two miles off shore. *Está a dos millas de la costa.*

---

short — *corto*

in short — *en resumen; en fin.*

In short, we spent it all. *En resumen (En fin), lo gastamos todo.*

the short and long of it — *el total; el resumen.*

The short and the long of it is that she's marrying Joe instead of Bob. *En resumidas cuentas, decidió casarse con Joe en vez de Bob.*

There is no shortcut to success. — *No hay atajo sin trabajo.*

to be short of — *andar escaso de.*

I am short of cash. *Ando escaso de efectivo (dinero).*

to sell short — *subestimar el valor de alguien o algo.*

Don't sell your hopes and dreams short; after a while you'll be sorry. *No subestimes tus esperanzas y sueños; después de un tiempo te arrepentirás.*

shortly — *en breve*

shortly after — *a poco de.*

Shortly after seeing her, he fell. *A poco de verla, se cayó.*

shortly before (after) — *poco antes (después).*

I had received it shortly before (after). *Lo había recibido poco antes (después).*

shot — *el tiro*

not by a long shot — *ni con (por) mucho.*

Our team didn't win. Not by a long shot. *Nuestro equipo no ganó. Ni con (por) mucho.*

random shot — *un intento al azar.*

He didn't know the subject, so his comment was just a random shot. *No conocía el tema; por eso, su comentario fue un intento al azar.*

to be a big shot — *ser un pez gordo.*

He's a big shot. *Es un pez gordo.*

to be a good shot — *ser buen tirador.*

He's a good shot. *Es buen tirador.*

to call all the shots — *hacer todas las decisiones.*

He's calling all the shots. *Está haciendo todas las decisiones.*

to take a shot at — *hacer una tentativa (un intento) de.*

He took a shot at solving the problem. *Hizo una tentativa (un intento) de resolver el problema.*

shoulder — *el hombro*

straight from the shoulder — *con toda franqueza; sin rodeos.*

She let us have it straight from the shoulder. *Nos lo dijo con toda franqueza (sin rodeos).*

to give someone the cold shoulder — *volverle las espaldas; tratarle con frialdad.*

She gave him the cold shoulder. *Le volvió las espaldas (Le trató con frialdad).*

to shrug one's shoulders — *encogerse de hombros.*

He shrugged his shoulders. *Se encogió de hombros.*

show — *el espectáculo*

a one-man show — *una exposición individual.*

We saw her sketches at her one-man show. *Vimos sus dibujos en su exposición individual.*

floor show — *el programa de espectáculos.*

There are floor shows at 8 and 10 P.M. *Hay espectáculos a las 8 y 10 de la noche.*

to make a great show of — *hacer alarde (ostentación) de.*

He made a great show of his knowledge. *Hizo alarde (ostentación) de sus conocimientos.*

to run the show — *llevar la voz cantante.*

Despite his shortcomings, he manages to run the show all by himself. *Pese a sus defectos, se las arregla para ser el encargado de todo.*

to steal the show — *ser la sensación de la fiesta.*

The baby stole the show. *El nene fue la sensación de la fiesta.*

to show — *mostrar*

to show around — *mostrar.*

He showed us around town. *Nos mostró la ciudad.*

to show into — *hacer pasar a.*

He showed us into his office. *Nos hizo pasar a su oficina.*

to show off — *presumir.*

She likes to show off. *Le gusta presumir.*

to show up — *presentarse.*

He showed up late. *Se presentó tarde.*

showing — *la demostración*

to make a good (poor) showing — *hacer buen (mal) papel.*

They made a good (poor) showing in the contest. *Hicieron buen (mal) papel en el concurso.*

shrift — *la confesión*

to give short shrift — *despachar de prisa.*

He gave it short shrift. *Lo despachó de prisa.*

to shut — *cerrar*

to shut down — *clausurar.*

They have shut down the university. *Han clausurado la universidad.*

to shut (up) in — *encerrar en.*

They shut him (up) in the garage. *Lo encerraron en el garage.*

to shut off — *cerrar; cortar.*

They shut off the water. *Cerraron (Cortaron) el agua.*

to shut out — *cerrar la puerta a.*

He shut out the cat. *Le cerró la puerta al gato.*

to shut up — *callarse.*

He refused to shut up. *No quiso callarse.*

---

sick — *enfermo*

to be sick and tired of — *estar harto y cansado.*

I'm sick and tired of this place. *Estoy harto y cansado de este lugar.*

to get sick — *enfermar(se).*

He gets sick when he eats too much. *(Se) enferma cuando come demasiado.*

to make one sick — *hacerle mal.*

That fruit will make you sick. *Esa fruta le hará mal.*

to make one sick (fig.) — *reventarle.*

Her ideas make me sick. *Sus ideas me revientan.*

---

side — *el lado*

on all sides — *por todas partes.*

It's surrounded by mountains on all sides. *Está rodeado de montañas por todas partes.*

on the other side — *al otro lado.*

On the other side it's red. *Al otro lado es rojo.*

on the other side of — *más allá de.*

It's on the other side of the station. *Está más allá de la estación.*

right side up — *boca arriba.*

Put the trunk right side up. *Ponga el baúl boca arriba.*

to get up on the wrong side of the bed — *levantarse por los pies de la cama (del lado izquierdo).*

I don't know what's the matter with him today. He must have gotten up on the wrong side of the bed. *No sé qué tiene hoy. Se habrá levantado por los pies de la cama (del lado izquierdo).*

to take sides — *tomar partido.*
I decided not to take sides. *Decidí no tomar partido.*

sight — *la vista*

at first sight — *a primera vista.*
They recognized each other at first sight. *Se reconocieron a primera vista.*

Out of sight, out of mind. — *Ojos que no ven, corazón que no siente.*

sight unseen — *sin verlo.*
I bought it sight unseen. *Lo compré sin verlo.*

to be in sight — *estar a la vista.*
It's in sight. *Está a la vista.*

to get out of sight — *perderse de vista.*
He wants us to get out of his sight. *Quiere que nos perdamos de vista.*

to know by sight — *conocer de vista.*
I know him by sight. *Lo conozco de vista.*

to lose sight of — *perder de vista.*
I lost sight of them. *Los perdí de vista.*

to lower one's sights — *moderar las aspiraciones.*
We had to lower our sights. *Tuvimos que moderar nuestras aspiraciones.*

to see the sights — *ver los puntos de interés.*
We went out to see the sights. *Salimos para ver los puntos de interés.*

sign — *el signo; la señal*

to give a sign — *hacer seña.*
He gave me a sign to come in. *Me hizo seña para que entrara.*

to show signs of — *dar muestras de.*
He showed signs of uneasiness. *Dio muestras de inquietud.*

to sign — *firmar*

to sign off — *terminar las emisiones.*
The station signed off. *La estación terminó sus emisiones.*

to sign up — *alistarse.*
He signed up for the trip. *Se alistó para el viaje.*

silence — *el silencio*
Silence is consent. — *Quien calla otorga.*
Silence is golden. — *En boca cerrada no entran moscas.*

silent — *silencioso*
to remain silent — *guardar silencio.*
He's remaining silent. *Guarda silencio.*

sin — *el pecado*
as ugly as sin — *más feo que una araña.*
The poor boy was as ugly as sin. — *El pobre niño era más feo que un demonio.*

to sit — *sentarse*
to sit back — *recostarse.*
He sat back in his chair. *Se recostó en su silla.*
to sit down — *sentarse; tomar asiento.*
He sat down. *Se sentó (tomó asiento).*
to sit out — *pasar por alto.*
Let's sit this one out. *Pasemos éste por alto.*
to sit up — *incorporarse.*
I can hardly sit up. *Apenas puedo incorporarme.*

sitting — *la sentada*
at a sitting — *de una sentada.*
He used to eat a kilo of meat at a sitting. *Comía un kilo de carne de una sentada.*

six — *seis*
It's six of one and half a dozen of the other. — *Lo mismo da.*

to size — *medir el tamaño*

to cut down to size — *reducir a proporciones normales.*

It is time to cut his ambitious plans down to size. *Es tiempo de reducir sus ambiciosos planes a su justa medida.*

to size up — *medir con la vista.*

He sized us up and then invited us in. *Nos midió con la vista y luego nos invitó a pasar.*

sketch — *el boceto*

a thumb-nail sketch — *un resumen muy breve.*

He gave us a thumb-nail sketch of the plot. *Nos dio un resumen muy breve de la trama.*

skin — *la piel*

by the skin of one's teeth — *por los pelos.*

I got here by the skin of my teeth. *Llegué por los pelos.*

to be nothing but skin and bones — *estar en los huesos.*

I almost didn't recognize John; he was nothing but skin and bones. *Por poco no reconozco a Juan; estaba en los huesos.*

to be soaked to the skin — *estar calado (mojado) hasta los huesos.*

We're soaked to the skin. *Estamos calados (mojados) hasta los huesos.*

to get under one's skin — *irritarle.*

The noise got under our skin. *El ruido nos irritó.*

to nearly jump out of one's skin — *por poco morirse de susto.*

He nearly jumped out of his skin when he heard it. *Por poco se muere de susto al oírlo.*

sky — *el cielo*

pie in the sky — *promesas falsas.*

Politicians always promise pie in the sky. *Los políticos siempre prometen cosas inverosímiles.*

to go sky high — *ponerse por las nubes.*

Prices went sky high. *Los precios se pusieron por las nubes.*

to praise to the skies — *poner por (sobre) las nubes.*

We praised him to the skies. *Lo pusimos por (sobre) las nubes.*

to slap — *dar una palmada*

to slap someone — *arrimarle una bofetada.*
She slapped me. *Me arrimó una bofetada.*

to slap someone on the back — *palmotearle la espalda.*
He slapped me on the back. *Me palmoteó la espalda.*

slate — *la pizarra*

to have a clean slate — *tener las manos limpias.*
We have a clean slate. *Tenemos las manos limpias.*

to wipe the slate clean — *empezar de nuevo.*
They wiped the slate clean. *Empezaron de nuevo.*

to sleep — *dormir*

to sleep away — *pasarse durmiendo.*
He slept the afternoon away. *Se pasó la tarde durmiendo.*

to sleep it off — *dormir la mona.*
He's sleeping it off. *Está durmiendo la mona.*

to sleep on it — *consultarlo con la almohada.*
I'll sleep on it. *Lo consultaré con la almohada.*

sleepy — *soñoliento*

to be sleepy — *tener sueño.*
He's sleepy. *Tiene sueño.*

sleeve — *la manga*

in (one's) shirtsleeves — *en mangas de camisa.*
He went out in the garden in (his) shirtsleeves. *Salió al jardín en mangas de camisa.*

to have something up one's sleeve — *tener algo en reserva (tramado).*
He's got something up his sleeve. *Tiene algo en reserva (tramado).*

to laugh up one's sleeve — *reír para sí (para sus adentros).*
He's laughing up his sleeve. *Está riéndose para sí (para sus adentros).*

slip — *la falta, el error, el desliz*

a slip of the tongue — *error de lengua (lapsus linguae).*

If she said it, it was just a slip of the tongue. *Si lo dijo, fue sólo un error de lengua (lapsus linguae).*

Freudian slip — *el desliz subconsciente.*
Calling her "Honey" instead of "Bonny" was a Freudian slip. *Llamarla "Teta" en vez de "Tita" fue un desliz del subconsciente.*

to give someone the slip — *escaparse de.*
She gave them the slip. *Se escapó de ellos.*

---

to slip — *escapar*

to slip away — *escurrirse.*
It slipped away. *Se escurrió.*

---

to slip — *deslizar*

to be slipping — *perder la habilidad acostumbrada.*
Another mistake? You've been slipping lately! *¿Otro error? ¡Últimamente no has sido el que eras!*

to slip one over on — *jugar una mala pasada.*
She won by slipping one over on her opponent. *Ganó jugándole una mala pasada a su contrario.*

to slip through one's fingers — *írsele (escurrirse) de entre las manos.*
Money just slips through my fingers. *El dinero se me va (se me escurre) de entre las manos.*

---

to slow — *ir más despacio*

to slow down (up) — *tomar las cosas con más calma.*
The doctor told me to slow down (up). *El médico me dijo que tomara las cosas con más calma.*

---

sly — *secreto, astuto*

on the sly — *a escondidas.*
She would visit him on the sly. *Lo visitaba a escondidas.*

---

smile — *la sonrisa*

to give someone a smile — *hacerle una sonrisa.*
I gave her a pitying smile. *Le hice una sonrisa de lástima.*

---

smoke — *el humo*

Where there's smoke there's fire. — *Cuando el río suena, agua lleva.*

to go up in smoke — *quedar en nada.*

His plans went up in smoke. *Sus planes quedaron en nada.*

to have a smoke — *echar un cigarrillo (cigarro).*

We went out and had a smoke. *Salimos y echamos un cigarrillo (cigarro).*

---

smoker — *fumador*

to be a chain-smoker — *fumar un cigarrillo tras otro.*

He's a chain-smoker. *Fuma un cigarrillo tras otro.*

---

snag — *el tropiezo*

to hit (strike) a snag — *tropezar con un obstáculo.*

We hit (struck) a snag in our plans. *Tropezamos con un obstáculo con nuestros planes.*

---

snail — *el caracol*

at a snail's pace — *a paso de tortuga.*

The procession was advancing at a snail's pace. *La procesión avanzaba a paso de tortuga.*

---

snappy — *enérgico*

Make it snappy. — *Dese prisa.*

---

to sneak — *mover(se) a hurtadillas*

to sneak into — *entrar sin pagar.*

He sneaked into the movie. *Entró en el (al) cine sin pagar.*

to sneak off (away, out) — *irse a hurtadillas.*

He sneaked off (away, out). *Se fue a hurtadillas.*

---

to sneeze — *estornudar*

not to be sneezed at — *no ser cualquier cosa.*

His paintings are not to be sneezed at. *Sus cuadros son cosa seria.*

---

so — *así*

and so — *y así es que; de modo que; por lo cual.*

He went, and so I have to remain. *El fue, y así es que (de modo que, por lo cual) yo tengo que quedarme.*

and so on — *y así sucesivamente; y así por el estilo.*

They discussed economics, politics, money, and so on. *Discutieron la economía, la política, el dinero y así sucesivamente (y así por el estilo).*

so as to — *para.*

So as not to waste time, let's begin right now. *Para no perder tiempo, empecemos ahora mismo.*

so be it — *así sea.*

If that is really what you want, so be it. *Si de veras es lo que tú quieres, así sea.*

So do (did, will, etc.) I. — *Yo también.*

so far — *hasta ahora.*

So far no one has called. *Hasta ahora, no ha llamado nadie.*

So far so good. — *Hasta ahora todo va bien.*

So much for that. — *Asunto concluido.*

so much so — *hasta tal punto; tanto es así.*

She likes the movies, so much so that she goes every week. *Le gusta el cine, hasta tal punto (tanto es así) que va todas las semanas.*

So much the better (worse). — *Tanto mejor (peor).*

so-so — *así así.*

She feels so-so. *Se siente así así.*

so-and-so — *fulano*

so-and-so — *fulano de tal.*

So-and-so called. *Fulano de tal llamó.*

soap — *el jabón*

to soft-soap — *adular; lisonjear.*

If you soft-soap her enough, you'll get into her bed. *Con suficientes adulaciones, te meterás en su cama.*

to sock — *pegar; golpear*

to sock it to somebody — *alentar a alguien a la violencia física u oral.*
Sock it to him, baby! Don'l let him do that! *¡Duro con él compadre! ¡No le dejes que haga eso!*

some — *algún*

and then some — *y mucho más; con creces.*
I got what I wanted, and then some. *Obtuve lo que quise y mucho más.*

some . . . (some . . . -odd) — *. . . y tantos; y pico.*
Some fifty (Some fifty-odd) students came. *Vinieron cincuenta y tantos (y pico) alumnos.*

some . . . or other — *no sé qué. . . .*
He gave me some book or other on bullfighting. *Me dio no sé qué libro sobre el toreo.*

something — *algo*

for there to be something . . . about it — *tener algo de. . . .*
There was something boring about it. *Tenía algo de aburrido.*

for there to be something . . . about someone — *tener un no sé qué. . . .*
There's something likeable about her. *Tiene un no sé qué simpático.*

. . . or something? — *¿ . . . o qué?*
Are you deaf or something? *¿Estás sordo o qué?*

something else — *otra cosa.*
I want something else. *Deseo otra cosa.*

something like that — *algo por el estilo.*
He said that she was his cousin, or something like that. *Dijo que era su prima, o algo por el estilo.*

to be into something — *dedicarse a.*
Now he's into hunting. *Ahora está dedicado a la caza.*

to be something of — *tener algo de.*
He's something of a painter. *Tiene algo de pintor.*

to give something to drink (to eat) — *dar a (de) beber (comer).*
He gave us something to drink (to eat). *Nos dio a (de) beber (comer).*

You can't get something for nothing. — *Lo que algo vale, algo cuesta.*

song — *la canción*

song and dance — *la historia de siempre; las consabidas excusas.*

Late again! And now the usual song and dance about the boss not letting you go? *¡Tarde de nuevo! ¿Y ahora la historia de siempre, que el jefe no te deja irte?*

swan song — *el canto del cisne.*

Yesterday's class was his swan song. *La clase de ayer fue su canto del cisne.*

to buy for a song — *comprar regalado.*

They bought it for a song. *Lo compraron regalado.*

soon — *pronto*

as soon as — *en cuanto; así que.*

As soon as we eat, we'll go. *En cuanto (Así que) comamos, iremos.*

not a moment too soon — *justo a tiempo.*

The girlfriend left not a moment too soon before his wife entered. *Su amiga se fue justo a tiempo antes de entrar la esposa.*

sooner — *más pronto*

no sooner — *no bien.*

He no sooner got the money than be bought the car. *No bien recibió el dinero, compró el coche.*

No sooner said than done. — *Dicho y hecho.*

sooner or later — *tarde o temprano.*

Sooner or later he'll know. *Tarde o temprano sabrá.*

sorrow — *el dolor*

to drown one's sorrows — *ahogar las penas.*

He drowned his sorrows in drink. *Ahogó sus penas en vino.*

sorry — *apenado*

Better safe than sorry. — *Más vale prevenir que curar.*

to feel sorry for — *tenerle lástima.*

He feels sorry for her. *Le tiene lástima.*

sort — *la clase, la especie*

something of the sort — *algo por el estilo.*

She said something of the sort. *Dijo algo por el estilo.*

sort of — *un poco.*

He's sort of stupid. *Es un poco estúpido.*

to be out of sorts — *estar de mal humor.*

He's out of sorts. *Está de mal humor.*

soul — *el alma*

every living soul — *todo bicho viviente.*

I imagine every living soul knows about it by now. *Supongo que ya lo sabe todo bicho viviente.*

not a living soul — *no . . . alma nacida (viviente).*

There's not a living soul who's capable of doing that. *No hay alma nacida (viviente) que sea capaz de hacer eso.*

spade — *la pala*

to call a spade a spade — *llamar al pan, pan y al vino, vino.*

He calls a spade a spade. *Llama al pan, pan, y al vino, vino.*

to spare — *pasar sin*

to have time to spare — *tener tiempo que perder.*

I have no time to spare. *No tengo tiempo que perder.*

to have . . . to spare — *sobrarle . . .*

I have two to spare. *Me sobran dos.*

to speak — *hablar*

so to speak — *por decirlo así.*

He's a rabble rouser, so to speak. *Es un alborotapueblos, por decirlo así.*

to be speaking to each other (to be on speaking terms) — *hablarse.*

They aren't speaking to each other (on speaking terms). *No se hablan.*

to be spoken for — *estar comprometido.*

The car is already spoken for. *El coche ya está comprometido.*

to be well spoken of — *tener muy buena reputación.*

That surgeon is well spoken of by his colleagues. *Ese cirujano goza de excelente reputación entre sus colegas.*

to speak for itself — *hablar por sí mismo.*

That the world is getting warmer speaks for itself. *Que el mundo se está calentando es evidente por sí mismo.*

to speak for oneself — *decirlo por uno mismo; personalmente.*

Speaking for myself I believe that the union has gone too far. *Personalmente, creo que al sindicato se le pasó la mano.*

to speak for oneself — *hablar en defensa propia.*

She will speak for herself at the right time. *Hablará en defensa propia en el momento indicado.*

to speak highly of — *decir mil bienes de.*

He spoke highly of my daughter. *Dijo mil bienes de mi hija.*

to speak out — *hablar.*

He didn't dare speak out. *No se atrevió a hablar.*

to speak up — *hablar más alto.*

Please speak up. *Haga el favor de hablar más alto.*

to speak up for — *salir en defensa de.*

He always spoke up for me. *Siempre salía en mi defensa.*

---

speed — *la velocidad*

at breakneck speed — *a todo correr.*

The rider was traveling at breakneck speed. *El jinete iba a todo correr.*

at full speed — *a toda carrera (vela; prisa).*

He came running at full speed. *Vino a toda carrera (vela; prisa).*

to travel at a speed of — *llevar una velocidad de.*

He often travels at a speed of 90 miles an hour. *A menudo lleva una velocidad de 90 millas la hora.*

---

spic-and-span — *nuevo, bien arreglado*

spic-and-span — *limpio como una patena.*

They left the house spic-and-span. *Dejaron la casa limpia como una patena.*

spirit — *el espíritu*

in high spirits — *de muy buen humor.*

They arrived in high spirits. *Llegaron de muy buen humor.*

spite — *el despecho*

in spite of — *a pesar de; a despecho de.*

They came in spite of the rain. *Vinieron a pesar de (a despecho de) la lluvia.*

in spite of the fact that — *y eso que.*

She's tired in spite of the fact that she slept 10 hours. *Está cansada, y eso que durmió diez horas.*

sponge — *la esponja*

to throw in the sponge — *darse por vencido.*

Toward the end, he decided to throw in the sponge. *Hacia el final, decidió darse por vencido.*

to sponge — *limpiar con esponja*

to sponge off someone — *vivir de gorra; vivir a costa de alguien.*

He sponges off his friends. *Vive de gorra (Vive a costa de sus amigos).*

spoon — *la cuchara*

To be born with a silver spoon in one's mouth. — *Nacer en la opulencia; Nacer de pie.*

spot — *la mancha*

on the spot — *en el acto.*

He sold it to me on the spot. *Me lo vendió en el acto.*

to have a soft spot in one's heart for — *tenerle mucho cariño.*

I have a soft spot in my heart for her. *Le tengo mucho cariño.*

to put someone on the spot — *ponerle en un aprieto (una situación comprometida).*

He put us all on the spot. *Nos puso a todos en un aprieto (una situación comprometida).*

to touch a sore spot — *poner el dedo en la llaga.*

He touched a sore spot. *Puso el dedo en la llaga.*

spree — *la juerga*

to go out on a spree — *irse de juerga (parranda).*

We went out on a spree. *Nos fuimos de juerga (parranda).*

spur — *la espuela*

on the spur of the moment — *impulsivamente.*

I decided on the spur of the moment. *Decidí impulsivamente.*

square — *la casilla*

to be back to square one — *volver al punto de partida.*

All our attempts failed and we are back to square one. *Todos nuestros intentos han fallado y hemos vuelto al punto de partida.*

stab — *la puñalada*

a stab in the back — *una puñalada trapera.*

His comment was a stab in the back. *Su comentario fue una puñalada trapera.*

stage — *la etapa; el estado; la fase; la escena de teatro*

at this stage — *a estas alturas; como están las cosas.*

Yes, at this stage it is possible. *Sí, tal como están las coas, es posible.*

backstage — *en privado.*

All this was arranged backstage, without us knowing anything about it. *Todo esto se tramó calladamente, sin que nosotros supiéramos nada al respecto.*

stake — *la estaca; la (a)puesta*

to be at stake — *estar en juego.*

His life is at stake. *Su vida está en juego.*

to die at the stake — *morir en la hoguera.*

They died at the stake. *Murieron en la hoguera.*

to pull up stakes — *mudar(se de casa).*

They pulled up stakes. *(Se) Mudaron (de casa).*

stamp — *el sello*

to rubber-stamp — *aprobar rutinariamente.*

Chinese bureaucrats rubber-stamp any decision from their superiors. *Los burócratas chinos aprueban automáticamente cualquier decisión tomada por sus superiores.*

---

stand — *la opinión, el puesto*

to take a stand — *adoptar una actitud.*

Our club refused to take a stand. *Nuestro club no quiso adoptar una actitud.*

---

to stand — *poner derecho; estar; soportar*

not to be able to stand the sight of — *no poder ver ni en pintura.*

I can't stand the sight of her. *No la puedo ver ni en pintura.*

to be standing — *estar de (en) pie.*

She's standing. *Está de (en) pie.*

to know where one stands — *saber a qué atenerse.*

I wish we knew where we stand. *Ojalá que supiéramos a qué atenernos.*

to stand aside — *mantenerse apartado.*

He stood aside. *Se mantuvo apartado.*

to stand back — *retirarse (al fondo).*

He asked us to stand back. *Nos pidió que nos retiráramos (al fondo).*

to stand behind (back of) — *garantizar.*

He stood behind (back of) his offer. *Garantizó su oferta.*

to stand behind (back of) — *respaldar a.*

He stood behind (back of) his son in the argument. *Respaldó a su hijo en la discusión.*

to stand for — *significar; representar.*

What does that symbol stand for? *¿Qué significa (representa) ese símbolo?*

to stand for — *tolerar.*

He won't stand for her foolishness. *No quiere tolerar sus tonterías.*

to stand on one's own two feet — *valerse de sí mismo.*

He stands on his own two feet. *Se vale de sí mismo.*

to stand out — *ser prominente.*

His red hair stands out in any crowd. *Su pelo rojo es prominente en cualquier grupo.*

to stand still — *estarse quieto.*

Stand still! *¡Estése quieto!*

to stand up — *ponerse de pie; pararse.*

They stood up. *Se pusieron de pie (Se pararon).*

to stand . . . up — *dejar plantado.*

We had an appointment for four but they stood me up. *Estábamos citados para las cuatro pero me dejaron plantado.*

to stand up against — *resistir.*

The wall has stood up against the flood. *El muro ha resistido la inundación.*

to stand up and be counted — *expresar los principios de uno; dar la cara.*

Although it may be dangerous, one must stand up and be counted. *Aunque pueda ser peligroso, uno debe defender su posición.*

to stand up for — *defender.*

He stood up for his rights. *Defendió sus derechos.*

to stand up to — *hacer frente a.*

He stood up to his accusers. *Hizo frente a sus acusadores.*

standard — *la norma*

by any standard — *en modo alguno.*

They're not as good as these by any standard. *No son tan buenos como éstos en modo alguno.*

double standard — *dos medidas distintas.*

Often we use double standards to judge what we like and what we don't. *A menudo usamos dos medidas distintas para juzgar los que nos gusta y lo que no nos gusta.*

to meet the standards — *estar al nivel deseado.*

His work doesn't meet the standards. *Su trabajo no está al nivel deseado.*

standing — *la reputación*

to be in good standing — *estar al corriente de sus obligaciones.*

He's not in good standing. *No está al corriente de sus obligaciones.*

standstill — *la parada*

to come to a standstill — *pararse.*

Traffic has come to a standstill. *El tránsito se ha parado.*

to stare — *mirar fijamente*

to stare at — *mirar de hito en hito.*

She's staring at him. *Lo está mirando de hito en hito.*

start — *el principio; el sobresalto*

right from the start — *desde un principio.*

We realized his intentions right from the start. *Nos dimos cuenta de sus intenciones desde un principio.*

to get one's start — *empezar.*

He got his start in his father's store. *Empezó en la tienda de su padre.*

to give one a start — *darle un susto.*

The noise gave me a start. *El ruido me dio un susto.*

to start — *empezar*

to start — *poner en marcha.*

She started the motor. *Puso en marcha el motor.*

to start out — *ponerse en camino.*

We started out. *Nos pusimos en camino.*

state — *el estado*

to get oneself into a state — *ponerse muy nervioso.*

Don't get yourself into a state just because of a storm. *No te pongas tan nervioso por una tormenta.*

to lie in state — *yacer en capilla ardiente.*

The senator lay in state in Washington. *El senador yacía en capilla ardiente en Washington.*

to stay — *quedar(se)*

to be here to stay — *estar destinado a perdurar.*

Football is here to stay. *El futbol está destinado a perdurar.*

to stay in — *quedarse en casa.*

The doctor told him to stay in. *El médico le dijo que se quedara en casa.*

to stay out — *quedarse fuera (de casa).*

They stayed out all night. *Se quedaron fuera (de casa) toda la noche.*

to stay put — *estarse quieto.*

Despite the bombing, he stayed put in his apartment. *Pese al bombardeo, no se movió de su apartamento.*

to stay up — *no acostarse.*

I stayed up all night. *No me acosté en toda la noche.*

---

stead — *el lugar*

to stand one in good stead — *serle muy útil.*

It will stand you in good stead. *Le será muy útil.*

---

steam — *el vapor*

to blow off steam — *desahogarse.*

He blew off steam. *Se desahogó.*

to run out of steam — *agotarse.*

The runner started full of energy, but soon he was running out of steam. *El corredor comenzó con gran energía, pero pronto comenzó a agotarse.*

under one's own steam — *por sí mismo; por sus propias fuerzas.*

He was able to do the work under his own steam. *Pudo llevar a cabo el trabajo por sí mismo (por sus propias fuerzas) .*

---

step — *el paso*

step by step — *paso a paso.*

He described it step by step. *Lo describió paso a paso.*

to be a step away from — *estar a un paso de.*

He's a step away from death. *Está a un paso de la muerte.*

to retrace one's steps — *volver sobre sus pasos.*

We retraced our steps. *Volvimos sobre nuestros pasos.*

to take a step — *dar un paso.*
The child took two steps. *El niño dio dos pasos.*

Watch your step. — *Tenga usted cuidado.*

to step — *dar un paso*

to step down — *renunciar.*
The manager is going to step down. *El gerente va a renunciar.*

to step in — *pasar.*
Step in. *Pase.*

to step out — *salir.*
He stepped out. *Salió.*

to step up — *acelerar.*
They stepped up their activities. *Aceleraron sus actividades.*

to step up — *acercarse.*
Step up when your name is called. *Acérquese cuando llamen su nombre.*

to stick — *pegar*

Stick 'em up! — *¡Manos arriba!*

to be stuck-up — *ser muy presuntuosa.*
She's stuck-up. *Es muy presuntuosa.*

to be stuck with — *no poder deshacerse.*
I'm stuck with these five copies. *No puedo deshacerme de estos cinco ejemplares.*

to stick by — *ser fiel a.*
He'll stick by us forever. *Nos será fiel para siempre.*

to get stuck — *ser engañado (estafado).*
I paid five dollars and got stuck. *Pagué cinco dólares y me engañaron (estafaron).*

to stick it out (till the end) — *perseverar hasta el final.*
He stuck it out (till the end). *Perseveró hasta el final.*

to stick one's head out — *asomarse.*
He stuck his head out the window. *Se asomó a la ventana.*

to stick to — *atenerse a.*
Stick to the book. *Aténgase al libro.*

stir — *la agitación*

to cause a stir — *llamar la atención.*

He entered without causing a stir. *Entró sin llamar la atención.*

to stir — *agitar*

to stir up — *incitar.*

He's always stirring up his colleagues. *Siempre está incitando a sus colegas.*

to stir up — *provocar.*

Her death stirred up a lot of rumors. *Su muerte provocó muchos rumores.*

stock — *el surtido*

to be out of stock — *estar agotado.*

The book is out of stock. *El libro está agotado.*

to have in stock — *tener en existencia.*

We don't have hammers in stock. *No tenemos martillos en existencia.*

to take stock — *hacer inventario.*

The store is closed because they are taking stock. *La tienda está cerrada porque están haciendo inventario.*

to take stock in — *confiar en.*

I take no stock in his ideas. *No confío en sus ideas.*

to take stock of — *hacer un estudio de.*

Take stock of what his capabilities are. *Haga un estudio de sus capacidades.*

to stomach — *tragar*

not to be able to stomach — *no poder soportar.*

I can't stomach him. *No lo puedo soportar.*

stone — *la piedra*

A rolling stone gathers no moss. —*Hombre de muchos oficios, pobre seguro.*

It's a stone's throw from here. — *Está a un tiro de piedra de aquí.*

to leave no stone unturned — *mover cielo y tierra.*

Leave no stone unturned and keep looking until you find the girl! *¡Muevan cielo y tierra y no dejen de buscar hasta encontrar la niña!*

to stoop — *inclinarse, encorvarse.*

to stoop to — *rebajarse a.*

She would never stoop to (lower herself to) begging on the street. *Nunca sa rebajaría a pedir limosna por la calle.*

stop — *la parada; el fin*

to put a stop to — *poner fin (término) a.*

He put a stop to the shouting. *Puso fin (término) a los gritos.*

to stop — *parar*

to stop at nothing — *ser capaz de todo.*

He'll stop at nothing to get what he wants. *Es capaz de todo para conseguir lo que quiere.*

to stop dead — *detenerse repentinamente (de repente).*

They stopped dead when they saw the tiger. *Su detuvieron repentinamente al ver al tigre.*

to stop over — *hacer escala.*

He stopped over in Madrid to see us. *Hizo escala en Madrid para vernos.*

store — *la tienda*

to have . . . in store for one — *tener . . . que le espera.*

He's got a lot of work in store for him. *Tiene mucho trabajo que le espera.*

storm — *la tormenta*

to take by storm — *asaltar.*

The students took the bookstore by storm. *Los estudiantes asaltaron la librería.*

to weather the storm — *capear el temporal.*

Yes, she saw me with Dorothy, and now I must weather the storm before I talk to her again. *Sí, me vio con Dorothy, y ahora debo capear el temporal antes de volverle a hablar.*

story — *el cuento*

a cock-and-bull story — *un cuento chino.*

He told us a cock-and-bull story. *Nos contó un cuento chino.*

to make a long story short — *en resumidas cuentas.*

To make a long story short, he died. *En resumidas cuentas, murió.*

sob story — *la historia lacrimosa.*

He gave me a sob story and hit me for a twenty. *Me contó una historia lacrimosa y me pidió un billete de veinte.*

straight — *derecho*

straight ahead — *derecho; hacia aelante.*

Go straight ahead and then turn right. *Anda derecho y luego tuerces a la derecha.*

to get it straight — *entenderlo bien.*

I never got it straight. *Nunca lo entendí bien.*

to go straight — *enmendarse.*

He got out of jail and went straight. *Salió de la cárcel y se enmendó.*

to set someone straight — *mostrar a alguien la situación tal como es.*

Larry set him straight about Laura's "friend." *Larry le dijo un par de verdades sobre el "amigo" de Laura.*

to set the record straight *aclarar las cosas.*

She set the record straight by declaring that she would run in the next elections. *Aclaró las cosas al afirmar que iba a ser candidata en las elecciones próximas.*

to shoot straight — *actuar con honradez.*

That car dealer shoots straight, so it will be better to deal with him. *Ese concesionario actúa honradamente, así que será mejor tratar con él.*

strategist — *el estratega*

armchair strategist — *estadista de café.*

For the armchair strategists, all problems can be solved. *Para los estadistas de café todos los problemas se pueden resolver.*

straw — *la paja*

It's the last straw. — *¡Es el colmo (No faltaba más)!*

It's the straw that breaks the camel's back. — *La última gota es la que hace rebosar el vaso.*

street — *la calle*

across the street — *enfrente.*

The building across the street is new. *El edificio de enfrente es nuevo.*

to go down (up) the street — *seguir calle abajo (arriba).*

He went down (up) the street. *Siguió calle abajo (arriba).*

to live on easy street — *estar en buena situación económica.*

They are living on easy street. *Están en buena situación económica.*

---

stretch — *el trecho; el tramo*

home stretch — *la recta final.*

He was on the home stretch: one final exam and the diploma would be his. *Estaba en la recta final: un examen final y el diploma sería suyo.*

---

stride — *zancada; tranco; adelanto; avance*

to make great strides — *progresar a grandes pasos.*

He made great strides in the new company. *Hizo grandes progresos en la nueva empresa.*

to take in one's stride — *vencer un obstáculo sin esfuerzo.*

The exams seemed difficult, but she took them in her stride. *Los exámenes parecían ser difíciles, pero ella los pasó sin esfuerzo.*

---

strike — *la huelga*

to go on strike — *declararse en huelga.*

They went on strike. *Se declararon en huelga.*

wildcat strike — *una huelga no autorizada por el sindicato.*

If the union doesn't back us up, we'll go on a wildcat strike. *Si el sindicato no nos apoya, igual iremos a la huelga.*

---

to strike — *golpear*

to strike — *dar.*

It struck five. *Dieron las cinco.*

to strike back — *defenderse.*

The accused struck back with new evidence. *El acusado se defendió con nueva evidencia.*

to strike down — *derribar.*

He struck him down with a blow to his chin. *Lo derribó con un golpe en el mentón.*

to strike it rich — *tener un golpe de fortuna.*

Have you seen his new car? He must have struck it rich. *¿Has visto su coche nuevo? Habrá tenido un golpe de fortuna.*

to strike out — *suprimir; tachar.*

We had to strike out the last word. *Tuvimos que suprimir (tachar) la última palabra.*

to strike up — *empezar a tocar.*

The band struck up a march. *La banda empezó a tocar una marcha.*

string — *la cuerda*

to be tied to one's mother's apron strings — *estar pegado a las faldas de su madre.*

She's been tied to her mother's apron strings all her life. *Ha estado pegada a las faldas de su madre toda la vida.*

to pull strings — *tocar todos los resortes.*

I had to pull strings to get it. *Tuve que tocar todos los resortes para conseguirlo.*

with no strings attached — *sin compromiso.*

He gave it to us with no strings attached. *Nos lo dio sin compromiso.*

stroke — *el golpe*

a stroke of luck — *un golpe de suerte.*

He won by a sheer stroke of luck. *Ganó a puro golpe de suerte.*

finishing strokes — *los toques finales.*

He put the finishing strokes on the painting. *Dio los toques finales al cuadro.*

with one stroke of the pen — *de un plumazo.*

Centuries of servitude were finished with one stroke of the pen. *Siglos de esclavitud terminaron de un plumazo.*

stuff — *la materia*

to know one's stuff — *ser experto.*

He really knows his stuff. *Es muy experto.*

style — *el estilo*

in a modern style — *a lo moderno.*

She dresses in a modern style. *Se viste a lo moderno.*

. . . style — *a la . . . .*

Love, Italian style. *Amor a la italiana.*

to be in style — *estar de moda.*

It's not in style any more. *Ya no está de moda.*

to go out of style — *pasarse de moda.*

They've gone out of style. *Se han pasado de moda.*

---

subject — *el tema*

to broach a subject — *plantear un asunto.*

How can we broach that subject to him when he's so sick? *¿Cómo podemos plantearle ese asunto cuando está tan enfermo?*

---

success — *el éxito.*

to be a howling success — *tener un éxito clamoroso.*

The play was a howling success. *La comedia tuvo un éxito clamoroso.*

---

successful — *exitoso*

to be successful — *tener (buen) éxito.*

He went into business but he wasn't successful. *Se dedicó a los negocios pero no tuvo (buen) éxito.*

---

sudden — *súbito*

all of a sudden — *de repente; de pronto, de golpe.*

All of a sudden he fell. *De repente (De pronto; De golpe) se cayó.*

---

suit — *el palo (de la baraja)*

to follow suit — *seguir el ejemplo.*

He refused to follow suit. *Se negó a seguir el ejemplo.*

---

to suit — *satisfacer*

Suit yourself. — *Haga lo que quiera.*

---

suitcase — *la maleta*

to live out of a suitcase — *vivir con la maleta hecha.*

For nine months we lived out of a suitcase. *Por nueve meses vivimos con la maleta hecha.*

to sum — *sumar*

to sum up — *para resumir.*

To sum up, the trip was too short. *Para resumir, el viaje fue demasiado corto.*

summer — *el verano*

Indian summer — *el veranillo de San Martín.*

We like to travel in Indian summer. *Nos gusta viajar en el veranillo de San Martín.*

sun — *el sol*

a place in the sun — *la oportunidad de prosperar.*

All he wanted with his little business was a place in the sun. *Todo lo que quería con su pequeño negocio era la oportunidad de prosperar.*

to be (right) out in the sun — *estar al (a pleno) sol.*

They're (right) out in the sun. *Están al (a pleno) sol.*

to sun — *asolear*

to sun oneself — *tomar el sol.*

They're sunning themselves. *Están tomando el sol.*

sure — *seguro*

as sure as two and two are four — *como dos y dos son cuatro.*

As sure as two and two are four, they'll not arrive on time. *Como dos y dos son cuatro, no van a llegar a tiempo.*

for sure — *a punto fijo.*

I don't know for sure. *No sé a punto fijo.*

to make sure — *no dejar de.*

Make sure that you sign it. *No deje de firmarlo.*

sure enough — *efectivamente.*

I thought she was going to buy the car and sure enough she did. *Creía que iba a comprar el coche y efectivamente lo compró.*

surprise — *la sorpresa*

to take by surprise — *sorprender.*

The news took me by surprise. *La noticia me sorprendió.*

swallow — *el trago; la golondrina*

One swallow does not make a summer. — *Una golondrina no hace verano.*

to down in one swallow — *tomar de un golpe.*

He downed it in one swallow. *Lo tomó de un golpe.*

to swear — *jurar*

to be sworn in — *prestar juramento.*

The senators will be sworn in tomorrow. *Los senadores prestarán juramento mañana.*

to swear by — *tener una fe ciega en; poner toda su confianza en.*

She swears by this medicine. *Tiene una fe ciega (Pone toda su confianza) en esta medicina.*

to swear off — *renunciar a.*

He swore off smoking. *Renunció a fumar.*

to sweep — *barrer*

a new broom sweeps clean — *una escoba nueva barre mejor.*

The new boss reduced red tape and fired a couple of lazy employees — a new broom sweeps clean. *El nuevo jefe redujo la burocracia y echó a un par de empleados vagos — una escoba nueva barre mejor.*

to swim — *nadar*

to swim (across) — *cruzar (atravesar) a nado (nadando).*

He swam (across) the river. *Cruzó (Atravesó) el río a nado (nadando).*

swing — *la oscilación*

to be in full swing — *estar en plena actividad.*

Things are in full swing. *Las cosas están en plena actividad.*

to switch — *cambiar; desviar*

to switch off — *cortar (la corriente); apagar (las luces).*

She switched the lights off and went to bed. *Apagó las luces y se fue a acostar.*

to switch on — *conectar la corriente; encender (las luces).*

He switched the lamp on and got out of bed. *Encendió la lámpara y se bajó de la cama.*

symbol — *el símbolo*

status symbol — *signo de distinción.*

The new rich are fond of status symbols, such as race horses and huge jewels. *Los nuevos ricos aprecian símbolos de prestigio social como los caballos de carrera y enormes joyas.*

to sympathize — *compadecer*

to sympathize with — *compadecer (se de).*

I sympathize with your bad luck. *(Me) compadezco (de) su mala fortuna.*

sympathy — *la compasión, la condolencia*

to extend one's sympathy — *dar el pésame.*

He extended me his sympathy. *Me dio el pésame.*

system — *el sistema*

to get something out of one's system — *quitarse algo de encima; satisfacer un deseo.*

It seems that Argentineans will never get the tango out of their system. *Parece que los argentinos nunca se quitarán el tango de encima.*

T

t — *la t*

to suit to a T — *satisfacer a la perfección.*

Our new home suits us to a T. *Nuestra casa nueva nos satisface a la perfección.*

tab — *la cuenta*

to keep tabs on — *tener a la vista.*

She keeps tabs on her husband. *Tiene a la vista a su esposo.*

to pick up the tab — *pagar la cuenta.*

My friend picked up the tab. *Mi amigo pagó la cuenta.*

---

table — *la mesa*

to clear the table — *levantar (quitar) la mesa.*

I cleared the table. *Levanté (Quité) la mesa.*

to end up under the table — *acabar borracho.*

He drank so much that he ended up under the table. *Tomó tanto que acabó borracho.*

to set the table — *poner la mesa.*

She set the table. *Puso la mesa.*

to turn the tables — *volver las tornas.*

He turned the tables on us. *Nos volvió las tornas.*

to wait on tables — *servir (a) la mesa.*

They wait on tables. *Sirven (a) la mesa.*

---

to table — *poner sobre la mesa*

to table the motion — *aplazar la discusión de la moción.*

We tabled the motion. *Aplazamos la discusión de la moción.*

---

tack — *la tachuela*

to get down to brass tacks — *ir al grano.*

Let's get down to brass tacks. *Vamos al grano.*

---

take — *el botín; la parte; la participación*

to be on the take — *recibir soborno.*

That judge has been on the take for years. *Ese juez ha recibido sobornos por años.*

---

to take — *tomar; llevar*

take it from me — *hágame caso; se lo digo yo.*

Genny, take it from me and pack your raincoat, because it always rains in Seattle. *Genny, hazme caso y lleva tu impermeable, porque en Seattle siempre llueve.*

to be taken aback — *quedarse asombrado.*
He was taken aback. *Se quedó asombrado.*

to be taken in — *ser engañado.*
He got taken in by the salesman. *Fue engañado por el vendedor.*

to take after — *parecerse a; ser de la pasta de.*
He takes after his father. *Se parece a (Es de la pasta de) su padre.*

to take amiss — *tomar (llevar) a mal.*
He took what I said amiss. *Tomó (Llevó) a mal lo que dije.*

to take apart — *desarmar.*
He took the toy apart. *Desarmó el juguete.*

to take aside — *llevar aparte.*
He took us aside. *Nos llevó aparte.*

to take away — *llevarse.*
He took away the desk. *Se llevó la mesa.*

to take back — *llevarse de vuelta.*
He took back what he gave me. *Se llevó lo que me dio.*

to take back — *retractarse de.*
He took back what he said. *Se retractó de lo que dijo.*

to take down — *bajar.*
He took the picture down to the lobby. *Bajó el cuadro al vestíbulo.*

to take down — *descolgar.*
He took down the picture. *Descolgó el cuadro.*

to take down — *tomar nota de; apuntar.*
He took down what I said. *Tomó nota de (Apuntó) lo que dije.*

to take for — *tomar por.*
She took him for a doctor. *Lo tomó por médico.*

to take in — *ir a ver.*
We took in a play. *Fuimos a ver una comedia.*

to take it — *tener entendido.*
I take it that you're leaving. *Tengo entendido que sale.*

to take it out on — *desquitarse a costa de.*

He lost his job and is taking it out on his boss. *Perdió su trabajo y se está desquitando a costa de su jefe.*

to take off — *despegar.*

The plane took off in the snow. *El avión despegó en la nieve.*

to take off — *marcharse.*

They took off at dawn. *Se marcharon al amanecer.*

to take off — *quitarse.*

He took off his hat. *Se quitó el sombrero.*

to take on — *echarse encima; tomar sobre sí.*

He took on more work. *Se echó encima (Tomó sobre sí) más trabajo.*

to take on — *emplear.*

They took on a new secretary. *Emplearon a una nueva secretaria.*

to take on — *luchar con.*

He took me on single-handed. *Luchó conmigo mano a mano.*

to take out — *sacar.*

He took it out of the box. *Lo sacó de la caja.*

to take over — *hacer cargo.*

He took over when she became ill. *El se hizo cargo cuando ella (se) enfermó.*

to take to — *entregarse a; darle por.*

He took to gambling. *Se entregó al juego (Le dio por jugar).*

to take to — *lanzarse a.*

We all took to the streets. *Todos nos lanzamos a la calle.*

to take to — *tomarle cariño.*

He took to my sister immediately. *Le tomó cariño a mi hermana en seguida.*

to take up — *acortar.*

He took up the sleeves of the coat a little. *Acortó las mangas del saco.*

to take up — *discutir; preocuparse de.*

He took up the matter of the flights. *Discutió el (Se preocupó del) asunto de los vuelos.*

to take up with — *ir con; relacionarse con.*
He's taken up with a group of doctors. *Va (Se ha relacionado) con un grupo de médicos.*

to take wrong — *interpretar mal.*
She took him wrong. *Lo interpretó mal.*

tale — *el cuento*

old wives' tales — *cuentos de viejas.*
Rubbing an onion on your scalp to grow hair is an old wives' tale. *Restregar una cebolla sobre el cuero cabelludo para hacer crecer el cabello es un cuento de viejas.*

talk — *la charla*

now you're talking — *eso sí; eso es otra cosa.*
You offer the loan at 5 percent? Now you're talking! *¿Ofrece el préstamo con un interés del 5 por ciento? ¡Pues eso es ya otra cosa!*

pillow talk — *conversaciones de alcoba; intimidades.*
More than one spy got information by way of pillow talk. *Más de un espía obtuvo información mediante intimidades obtenidas en la alcoba.*

to be all talk — *ser puras palabras.*
His promises are all talk. *Sus promesas son puras palabras.*

to engage in small talk — *hablar de trivialidades.*
They engaged in small talk to kill time. *Hablaron de trivialidades para matar el tiempo.*

to talk — *hablar*

to be all talked out — *haber hablado hasta no poder más.*
By evening I was all talked out. *Para la noche había hablado hasta no poder más.*

to talk back to — *replicar a.*
He talked back to his mother. *Replicó a su madre.*

to talk big — *exagerar.*
He likes to talk big. *Le gusta exagerar.*

to talk into — *persuadir a.*
He talked her into going. *La persuadió a que fuera.*

to talk out of — *disuadir de.*
He talked me out of buying it. *Me disuadió de comprarlo.*

to talk over — *discutir.*
We talked over our plans. *Discutimos nuestros planes.*

talker — *el hablador*

to be a loose talker — *ser muy ligero de palabra.*
She's a very loose talker. *Es muy ligera de palabra.*

talking-to — *la reprensión*

to give a (good) talking-to — *dar una amonestación.*
When she arrived home late, her father gave her a (good) talking-to. *Cuando llegó tarde a casa, su padre le dio una amonestación.*

tape — *la cinta*

red tape — *papeleo.*
There's a lot of red tape. *Hay mucho papeleo.*

target — *el blanco*

to hit the target — *dar en el blanco.*
She hit the target. *Dio en el blanco.*

task — *la tarea*

to take to task — *reprender.*
He took them to task for being lazy. *Los reprendió por ser perezosos.*

to undertake the task — *darse a la tarea.*
She undertook the task of learning Russian. *Se dio a la tarea de aprender ruso.*

taste — *el gusto*

to acquire a taste for — *aficionarse a; tomar gusto a.*
I have acquired a taste for ballet. *Me he aficionado (He tomado gusto) al ballet.*

to be in poor taste — *ser de mal gusto.*
What he said was in very poor taste. *Lo que dijo fue de muy mal gusto.*

to taste — *gustar*

to taste like (of) — *saber a.*

It tastes like (of) garlic. *Sabe a ajo.*

---

to team — *enyugar*

to team up with — *aliarse con.*

They teamed up with our president. *Se aliaron con nuestro presidente.*

---

teapot — *la tetera*

a storm in a teapot — *una tormenta en un vaso de agua.*

The so-called revolution was merely a storm in a teapot. *La llamada revolución no pasó de ser una tormenta en un vaso de agua.*

---

tear — *la lágrima*

to move to tears — *conmover a (mover a) lágrimas.*

His story moved me to tears. *Su relato me conmovió (movió) a lágrimas.*

to shed bitter tears — *llorar a lágrima viva.*

She's shedding bitter tears. *Está llorando a lágrima viva.*

to shed crocodile tears — *llorar lágrimas de cocodrilo.*

She shed crocodile tears. *Lloró lágrimas de cocodrilo.*

---

to tear — *romper*

to tear down — *derribar.*

They are tearing down the building. *Están derribando el edificio.*

to tear up — *romper.*

He tore up the contract. *Rompió el contrato.*

---

to tell — *decir*

Tell me! — *¡Cuénteme!*

to tell apart — *distinguir entre.*

I can't tell the two apart. *No puedo distinguir entre los dos.*

to tell it like it is — *hablar sin rodeos.*

He likes to tell it like it is. *Le gusta hablar sin rodeos.*

to tell . . . off — *decirle cuántas son cinco.*

If he keeps bothering me I'm going to tell him off. *Si me sigue molestando le voy a decir cuántas son cinco.*

to tell on — *denunciar.*

He always tells on his sister. *Siempre denuncia a su hermana.*

temper — *el temple, el humor, la condición*

to keep one's temper — *no perder la paciencia (calma).*

Try to keep your temper. *Trate de no perder la paciencia (calma).*

to lose one's temper — *perder la paciencia; encolerizarse.*

He lost his temper. *Perdió la paciencia (Se encolerizó).*

tempest — *la tempestad*

It's a tempest in a teapot. — *Es una tempestad en un vaso de agua.*

term — *el término*

in terms of — *desde el punto de vista de.*

Please explain this in their terms. *Por favor explique esto desde el punto de vista de ellos.*

to be on good terms — *estar en buenas relaciones.*

They are on good terms. *Están en buenas relaciones.*

to come to terms — *llegar a (concertar) un acuerdo.*

They came to terms. *Llegaron a (Concertaron) un acuerdo.*

to serve a term — *cumplir condena.*

He served a term in jail. *Cumplió condena en la cárcel.*

test — *la prueba*

acid test — *la prueba decisiva.*

The exam will be the acid test. *El examen será la prueba decisiva.*

to put to a test — *poner a prueba(s).*

I put her to a test. *La puse a prueba(s).*

that — *eso*

that is — *es decir.*

She is living in the capital of Venezuela, that is, in Caracas. *Vive en la capital de Venezuela, es decir, en Caracas.*

That'll do. — *Ya está bien.*

That's it! — *¡Eso es!*

That's that. — *Así es. Fin.*

to be as bad as (all) that — *ser para tanto.*

It wasn't as bad as (all) that. *No fue para tanto.*

two can play at that — *donde las dan las toman.*

Be careful with those funny contracts, remember that two can play at that. *Cuidado con esos contratos raros, recuerda que donde las dan las toman.*

there — *allí*

out there — *por ahí; por allí; por el mundo.*

He just sits out there, doing nothing. *Está por ahí sentado, sin hacer nada.*

to be all there — *estar en sus cabales.*

She's not all there. *No está en sus cabales.*

thick — *grueso*

through thick and thin — *por las buenas y las malas.*

She stuck with him through thick and thin. *Se quedó con él por las buenas y las malas.*

to thin — *adelgazar*

to thin out — *reducir el número.*

We thinned out our employees. *Redujimos el número de empleados.*

thing — *la cosa*

a many-splendored thing — *algo magnífico; algo maravilloso.*

A vacation in Monaco is a many-splendored thing, but it's expensive. *Una vacación en Mónaco es algo maravilloso, pero sale caro.*

all things being equal — *en igualdad de circunstancias.*

All things being equal, we should win the race. *La situación siendo la misma, debiéramos ganar la carrera.*

a sure thing — *algo cierto; ningún problema.*

Don't worry, that deal is a sure thing. *No te preocupes, ese negocio no será ningún problema.*

for one thing — *en primer lugar.*

For one thing, I don't have any. *En primer lugar, no tengo ninguno.*

It's a good thing! — *¡Menos mal!*

It's (just) one of those things. — *Son cosas de la vida.*

It's the same old thing. — *Es lo de siempre.*

not to know the first thing about — *no saber nada de.*
He doesn't know the first thing about chemistry. *No sabe nada de química.*

not to understand a thing — *no entender ni papa (jota).*
They didn't understand a thing! *¡No entendieron ni papa (jota)!*

Of all things! — *¡Qué sorpresa!*

such a thing — *tal cosa.*
I can't believe such a thing. *No puedo creer tal cosa.*

that very thing — *eso mismo.*
That very thing disturbs us. *Eso mismo nos molesta.*

the first thing in the morning — *a primera hora.*
Let's leave the first thing in the morning. *Salgamos mañana a primera hora.*

the next best thing to — *lo que más se acerca a.*
HDTV is the next best thing to seeing the real world. *La televisión de alta definición es lo más parecido a ver el mundo real.*

the only thing — *lo único.*
It's the only thing he said. *Es lo único que dijo.*

the shape of things to come — *el mundo del futuro.*
Global warming and famine may be the shape of things to come. *El calentamiento global y la hambruna universal pueden ser parte del mundo futuro.*

Things are humming around here. — *Hay mucha actividad por aquí.*

Things are not what they used to be. — *Los tiempos han cambiado.*

to be quite the thing — *ser lo indicado.*
Westerners believe that nurseries are quite the thing for their children. *Los occidentales creen que los jardines infantiles son lo indicado para sus niños.*

to be seeing things — *ver visiones.*
She's seeing things. *Ve visiones.*

to be the real thing — *ser auténtico.*
This diamond isn't false; it's the real thing. *Este diamante no es falso; es auténtico.*

to do one's own thing — *hacer uno lo suyo.*
I left my family and now I'm doing my own thing. *Dejé a mi familia y ahora hago lo que me dé la gana.*

to know a thing or two about — *saber algo de.*
I know a thing or two about Spain. *Sé algo de España.*

to manage things all right — *arreglárselas.*
He managed things all right. *Se las arregló.*

to take things in one's stride — *tomarse todo con calma.*
He takes things in his stride. *Se toma todo con calma.*

to tell someone a thing or two — *decirle cuántos son cinco.*
I told her a thing or two. *Le dije cuántos son cinco.*

You can't have too much of a good thing. — *Lo que abunda no daña.*

to think — *pensar*

I should think so! — *¡Así lo creo!*

not to think much of — *tener en poco.*
He didn't think much of his son's friends. *Tenía en poco a los amigos de su hijo.*

to think a lot of oneself — *tener muy buena opinión de sí mismo.*
He thinks a lot of himself. *Está muy pagado (Tiene buena opinión) de sí mismo.*

to think about — *pensar en.*
He's thinking about (of) his future. *Está pensando en su porvenir.*

to think highly of — *tener un alto concepto de.*
She thinks highly of her teacher. *Tiene un alto concepto de su maestro.*

to think it over — *pensarlo.*
I was thinking it over when he entered. *Lo estaba pensando cuando entró.*

to think twice — *pensar dos veces.*
I thought twice before I did it. *Pensé dos veces antes de hacerlo.*

to think up — *inventar.*
I have to think up an excuse. *Tengo que inventar una excusa.*

What do you think of it? — *¿Qué le parece?*

Who would have thought it! — *¡Quién había de creerlo!*

thinking — *el pensamiento*

wishful thinking — *castillos en el aire.*

He does too much wishful thinking. *Pasa mucho tiempo construyendo castillos en el aire.*

thirst — *la sed*

to be thirsty — *tener sed.*

He's thirsty. *Tiene sed.*

this — *esto; tan*

this — *así de.*

They have a son this tall. *Tienen un hijo así de alto.*

Thomas — *Tomás*

doubting Thomas — *incrédulo.*

If you don't show it to that doubting Thomas, he'll never believe you. *Si no se lo muestras a ese incrédulo, nunca te va a creer.*

thought — *el pensamiento*

A penny for your thoughts. — *¿En qué estás pensando?*

You are distracted today; a penny for your thoughts. *Hoy andas distraído, ¿en qué estás pensando?*

on second thought — *pensándolo bien.*

On second thought he decided to go. *Pensándolo bien, decidió ir.*

schools of thought — *teorías; corrientes de opinión.*

There are different schools of thought regarding the origins of life, including creationism and evolution. *Hay distintas teorías respecto al origen de la vida, incluyendo el creacionismo y la evolución.*

the very thought of it — *sólo pensarlo.*

They very thought of it made her cry. *Sólo pensarlo la hizo llorar.*

to be lost in thought — *estar abstraído.*

He couldn't answer because he was deeply lost in thought. *No supo contestar porque estaba muy abstraído.*

without a thought — *sin pensarlo.*

They did it without a thought. *Lo hicieron sin pensarlo.*

thread — *el hilo*

to break the thread — *cortar el hilo.*

He broke the thread of my story. *Me cortó el hilo del cuento.*

to lose the thread — *perder el hilo.*

He lost the thread of the conversation. *Perdió el hilo de la conversación.*

throat — *la garganta*

to be at each other's throat — *pelear.*

Those inmates are at each other's throat every day. *Esos presos pelean todos los días entre ellos.*

through — *a través*

through and through — *de pies a cabeza.*

He's a patriot through and through. *Es un patriota de pies a cabeza.*

to be through with — *haber terminado con.*

I'm through with your book. *He terminado con su libro.*

to throw — *echar*

to throw a party — *dar una fiesta.*

They threw a party for us. *Nos dieron una fiesta.*

to throw away — *botar; tirar.*

He threw away the rest. *Botó (Tiró) lo demás.*

to throw it up to someone — *echárselo en cara.*

She keeps throwing it up to me. *Sigue echándomelo en cara.*

to throw out — *echar; expulsar.*

He was thrown out of the club. *Lo echaron (expulsaron) del club.*

to throw up — *vomitar.*

He threw up. *Vomitó.*

to throw up one's hands — *desesperarse.*

When he told me to wait five hours, I threw up my hands. *Cuando me dijo que esperara cinco horas, me desesperé.*

thumb — *el dedo pulgar*

by rule of thumb — *aproximadamente.*

That, by rule of thumb, will require two tons of cement. *Eso requerirá aproximadamente dos toneladas de cemento.*

to be all thumbs — *tener manos torpes; caérsele todo de las manos.*
He's all thumbs. *Tiene manos torpes (Todo se le cae de las manos).*

to have a green thumb — *tener don de jardinería.*
He's got a green thumb. *Tiene don de jardinería.*

to have under one's thumb — *tener dominado.*
She has him under her thumb. *Lo tiene dominado.*

to twiddle one's thumbs — *estar ocioso.*
He's twiddling his thumbs. *Está ocioso.*

to thumb — *hojear*

to thumb through — *hojear.*
I only had time to thumb through the book. *Sólo tuve el tiempo para hojear el libro.*

to tick — *hacer tictac*

to make someone tick — *impulsar, mover.*
What makes him tick? Money! *¿Qué es lo que lo motiva? ¡El dinero!*

ticket — *la entrada, el boleto, el billete*

a one-way ticket — *un billete (boleto) de ida.*
We have a one-way ticket. *Tenemos un billete (boleto) de ida.*

a round-trip ticket — *un billete (boleto) de ida y vuelta.*
He has a round-trip ticket. *Tiene un billete (boleto) de ida y vuelta.*

tidings — *las noticias*

the glad tidings — *las buenas noticias.*
They announced the glad tidings. *Anunciaron (Dieron) las buenas noticias.*

tie — *la corbata*

black tie — *el traje de etiqueta.*
Will the cocktail party be black tie or is a common suit OK? *¿Requiere traje de etiqueta el cóctel, o basta con un traje corriente?*

tight — *apretado*

Hold tight. — *Agárrese bien.*

to sit tight — *no hacer nada.*

Let's sit tight for awhile. *No hagamos nada por un rato.*

---

time — *el tiempo; la hora*

a long time — *mucho tiempo.*

She worked a long time. *Trabajó mucho tiempo.*

a long time before — *desde mucho antes.*

They had gone to Spain a long time before. *Se habían ido a España desde mucho antes.*

a short time ago — *hace poco.*

He entered a short time ago. *Entró hace poco.*

ahead of time — *con anticipación; con anterioridad; de antemano.*

It came ahead of time. *Vino con anticipación (con anterioridad, de antemano).*

any time (now) — *de un momento a otro; de hoy a mañana.*

It will start any time (now). *Comenzará de un momento a otro (de hoy a mañana).*

around that time — *por esos días; por esa época.*

Around that time she got married. *Por eso días (esa época) se casó.*

at a set time — *a hora fija.*

We eat at a set time. *Comemos a hora fija.*

at all times — *en todo tiempo.*

We were helping them at all times. *Los ayudábamos en todo tiempo.*

at one time — *en algún tiempo; un tiempo.*

At one time I had ten. *En algún (Un) tiempo tenía diez.*

at that time — *en aquel momento (tiempo; entonces).*

At that time he was sixteen. *En aquel momento (tiempo; entonces) tenía diez y seis años.*

at the present time — *en la actualidad.*

At the present time we haven't any. *En la actualidad no tenemos ninguno.*

at the same time — *a la vez; al mismo tiempo.*
She was laughing and crying at the same time. *(Se) reía y lloraba a la vez (al mismo tiempo).*

at the time — *a la sazón; por la época.*
At the time she was fifty. *A la sazón (Por la época) tenía 50 años.*

at times — *a veces; en ocasiones.*
At times she feels lonesome. *A veces (En ocasiones) se siente sola.*

before one's time — *antes de que uno existiera.*
Silent movies? That was before my time. *¿Películas mudas? Eso fue antes de que yo naciera.*

behind the times — *atrasado de noticias.*
As far as political matters are concerned, they are behind the times. *En cuanto a asuntos políticos están atrasados de noticias.*

by that time — *para entonces; para esa época.*
By that time he had retired. *Para entonces (Para esa época) se había jubilado.*

for the time being — *por el momento.*
For the time being, I'm busy. *Por el momento estoy ocupado.*

from time to time — *de vez en cuando; de cuando en cuando.*
We see each other from time to time. *Nos vemos de vez en cuando (de cuando en cuando).*

in due time — *a su tiempo.*
I'll have it in due time. *Lo tendré a su tiempo.*

in no time — *en un abrir y cerrar de ojos.*
He did it in no time. *Lo hizo en un abrir y cerrar de ojos.*

in one's spare time — *a ratos perdidos.*
I read Spanish in my spare time. *Leo el español a ratos perdidos.*

in recent times (years) — *en los últimos tiempos (años).*
In recent times (years) he has gotten fat. *En los últimos tiempos (años) ha engordado.*

it is high time — *ya es hora.*
It is high time that they all learn to drive. *Ya es hora que todos ellos aprendan a manejar.*

It's about time! — *¡A buenas horas! (¡Ya era hora!).*

many is the time — *muchas veces.*

Many is the time that I wanted to go there. *Muchas veces quería ir allí.*

most of the time — *la mayor parte del tiempo.*

It's hot most of the time. *Hace calor la mayor parte del tiempo.*

of that time — *de entonces.*

The kids of that time knew less. *Los chicos de entonces sabían menos.*

on time — *a la hora; a tiempo.*

It started on time. *Empezó a la hora (a tiempo).*

once upon a time there was — *érase una vez.*

Once upon a time there was a wolf. *Erase una vez un lobo.*

part-time — *por horas (trabajo, estudio, empleado).*

He got a part-time job. *Obtuvo un trabajo pagado por hora.*

small-time — *insignificante.*

Those small-time crooks would not commit murder. *Esos ladroncitos no serían capaces de asesinar a nadie.*

There is a time for all things. — *Cada cosa a su tiempo.*

time and tide — *tiempo y sazón.*

Time and tide come and go, and you had your chance and didn't take it. *La oportunidad viene y se va, y hubo una vez que tú pudiste aprovecharla y no lo hiciste.*

Time is a great healer. — *El tiempo todo lo cura.*

Time is money. — *El tiempo es oro.*

Time is up. — *Ya es la hora; Ha llegado la hora.*

to be (to arrive) on time — *llegar a tiempo.*

I was (arrived) on time. *Llegué a tiempo.*

to be time to — *ser (la) hora de.*

It's time to go to bed. *Es la hora de acostarse.*

to go with the times — *estar al día.*

You must be part of the digital age to go with the times. *Para estar al día debes participar en la era digital.*

to have a good time — *pasarlo bien; divertirse.*

They had a good time. *Lo pasaron bien (Se divirtieron).*

to have a hard time of it — *pasar muchos apuros.*
He had a hard time of it. *Pasó muchos apuros.*

to have a whale of a time — *divertirse como loco.*
We had a whale of a time in Paris. *Nos divertimos como locos en París.*

to have the time of one's life — *divertirse en grande.*
We went to the party and had the time of our life. *Fuimos a la fiesta y nos divertimos en grande.*

to keep good time — *marcar bien la hora; andar bien.*
This watch does not keep good time. *Este reloj no marca bien la hora (no anda bien).*

to keep time — *llevar el compás.*
He keeps time with his foot. *Lleva el compás con el pie.*

to last a short time — *durar poco tiempo.*
It lasted a short time. *Duró poco tiempo.*

to live on borrowed time — *estar vivos de pura suerte.*
Considering nuclear proliferation, we are living on borrowed time. *Considerando la proliferación nuclear, estamos vivos de pura suerte.*

to make good time — *ganar tiempo.*
We made good time on the highway. *Ganamos tiempo por la carretera.*

to make up for lost time — *recuperar el tiempo que se perdió.*
We made up for lost time. *Recuperamos el tiempo que perdimos.*

to spend one's time — *pasar el tiempo.*
He spends his time gambling. *Pasa el tiempo jugando (por dinero).*

to take one's time — *tomar su tiempo.*
He takes his time. *Toma su tiempo.*

to take time — *costar tiempo.*
It takes time. *Cuesta tiempo.*

to take time off — *tomar tiempo libre.*
She took time off. *Tomó tiempo libre.*

to take up someone's time — *quitarle el tiempo.*
She took up our time. *Nos quitó el tiempo.*

to tell time — *decir la hora.*
He doesn't know how to tell time. *No sabe decir la hora.*

to waste time — *perder tiempo.*

He's wasting time. *Está perdiendo tiempo.*

---

tip — *la punta, la propina*

from tip to toe — *de pies a cabeza.*

He jumped from the diving board and soaked me from tip to toe. *Saltó del trampolín y me bañó de pies a cabeza.*

to have at one's finger tips — *saber al dedillo.*

She has it at her finger tips. *Lo sabe al dedillo.*

to have on the tip of one's tongue — *tener en la punta de la lengua.*

I have it on the tip of my tongue. *Lo tengo en la punta de la lengua.*

---

to tip — *dar propina*

to tip over — *volcar.*

The child tipped over the chair. *El niño volcó la silla.*

to tip someone — *darle una propina.*

He tipped her. *Le dio una propina.*

to tip someone off — *informarle bajo cuerda.*

He tipped us off. *Nos informó bajo cuerda.*

---

tiptoe — *la punta del pie*

on tiptoe(s) — *de (en) puntillas.*

She entered on tiptoe(s). *Entró de (en) puntillas.*

---

tit

to give tit for tat — *pagar en la misma moneda.*

He insulted me and I gave him tit for tat. *El me insultó y yo le pagué en la misma moneda.*

---

toe — *el dedo del pie*

to be on one's toes — *estar alerta.*

He's always on his toes. *Siempre está alerta.*

to keep on one's toes — *mantener alerto.*

He keeps his students on their toes. *Mantiene alertos a sus alumnos.*

to tread on someone's toes — *ofenderle.*
He changed it without treading on our toes. *Lo cambió sin ofendernos.*

together — *juntos*

to drink a toast together — *brindar a coro.*
We drank a toast together. *Brindamos a coro.*

to pull oneself together — *calmarse.*
Pull yourself together. *Cálmese.*

token — *la muestra*

by the same token — *por la misma razón.*
If we invite Mary, by the same token we must invite Bob. *Si invitamos a María, por la misma razón debemos invitar a Roberto.*

in token of — *como expresión de; como muestra de.*
We sent flowers in token of appreciation. *Mandamos flores como expresión (muestra) de gratitud.*

Tom — *Tomás*

every Tom, Dick and Harry — *cualquier persona.*
This is my private office, and I won't allow every Tom, Dick and Harry to walk in! *¡Este es mi despacho privado y no permito que cualquiera entre!*

tomorrow — *mañana*

See you tomorrow. — *Hasta mañana.*

tone — *el tono*

in a very sour tone — *hecho un vinagre.*
He spoke to us in a very sour tone. *Nos habló hecho un vinagre.*

tongue — *la lengua*

native (mother) tongue — *la lengua materna.*
It's his native (mother) tongue. *Es su lengua materna.*

slip of the tongue — *un desliz de la lengua.*
My tongue slipped and I said "slaves" instead of "Slavs." *Me traicionó la lengua cuando dije "esclavos" en vez de "eslavos".*

to hold one's tongue — *morderse la lengua; callar.*
He held his tongue. *Se mordió la lengua (Calló).*

to talk with one's tongue in one's cheek — *no hablar en serio.*
I hope he's talking with his tongue in his cheek. *Ojalá que no hable en serio.*

tongue twister — *el trabalenguas.*
It's a tongue twister. *Es un trabalenguas.*

tooth — *el diente*

set of teeth — *la dentadura.*
His set of teeth looks nice, but are the teeth real? *Su dentadura luce muy bien, ¿pero son verdaderos esos dientes?*

to be long in the tooth — *ser viejo.*
I am too long in the tooth to run after her. *Estoy demasiado viejo para andar persiguiéndola.*

to fight tooth and nail — *luchar a brazo partido.*
We fought tooth and nail. *Luchamos a brazo partido.*

to have a sweet tooth — *ser muy goloso.*
She has a sweet tooth. *Es muy golosa.*

top — *la cumbre*

at the top of one's voice — *a gritos.*
I called out at the top of my voice. *Llamé a gritos.*

from top to bottom — *de arriba abajo.*
We painted it from top to bottom. *Lo pintamos de arriba abajo.*

on top of — *encima de.*
On top of all his troubles, he's ill. *Encima de todas sus penas, está enfermo.*

to be (sitting) on top of the world — *sentirse dueño del mundo.*
Now that he's won the prize, he's (sitting) on top of the world. *Habiendo ganado el premio, se siente dueño del mundo.*

to be tops — *ser lo mejor.*
As far as Pepe is concerned, Sylvia's tops. *Para Pepe, Silvia es lo mejor.*

to blow one's top — *poner el grito en el cielo.*
I blew my top. *Puse el grito en el cielo.*

to top — *coronar*

to top it off — *rematarlo.*

We topped it off with a glass of wine. *Lo rematamos con una copa de vino.*

to top someone — *aventajarle.*

He topped me. *Me aventajó.*

torch — *la antorcha*

to carry the torch for — *estar enamorado de.*

She is still carrying the torch for him. *Todavía está enamorada de él.*

to toss — *arrojar, echar*

to toss (flip a coin) — *echar a cara o cruz.*

Let's toss (flip a coin) to see who pays. *Echemos a cara o cruz para ver quién paga.*

to toss about — *dar vueltas.*

I tossed about all night. *Di vueltas toda la noche.*

touch — *el toque*

to be out of touch — *no comunicarse.*

We're out of touch. *No nos comunicamos.*

to be touch and go — *ser cosa de suerte; depender de la suerte.*

For three days it was touch and go with her fever. *Por tres días de fiebre todo dependió de la suerte.*

to get (keep) in touch — *ponerse en contacto; comunicarse con.*

I got in touch with him. *Me puse en contacto (Me comuniqué) con él.*

to lose one's touch — *perder el tiento.*

She's lost her touch. *Ha perdido el tiento.*

to put the touch on someone — *darle un sablazo.*

He put the touch on me. *Me dio un sablazo.*

to touch — *tocar*

to be touched (in the head) — *estar tocado (de la cabeza).*

He's a little touched (in the head). *Está un poco tocado (de la cabeza).*

to touch down — *aterrizar.*

It touched down at five. *Aterrizó a las cinco.*

to touch off — *provocar.*
It touched off World War II. *Provocó la segunda Guerra Mundial.*

to touch on — *referirse a.*
He touched on the Peruvian Indians. *Se refirió a los indios peruanos.*

to touch up — *retocarse.*
She touched up her face. *Se retocó la cara.*

---

tow — *el remolque*

to take in tow — *encargarse de.*
The father took his son in tow. *El padre se encargó de su hijo.*

to take in tow — *llevarse a remolque.*
They took our car in tow. *Se llevaron nuestro coche a remolque.*

---

towel — *la toalla*

to throw in the towel — *darse por vencido (abandonar la partida).*
He finally had to throw in the towel. *Por fin tuvo que darse por vencido (abandonar la partida).*

---

tower — *la torre*

to live in an ivory tower — *vivir en una torre de marfil.*
He lives in an ivory tower. *Vive en una torre de marfil.*

---

town — *el pueblo*

one-horse town — *un pueblito insignificante.*
Regardless of recent developments, our city remains a one-horse town. *Pese a su reciente desarrollo, nuestra ciudad sigue siendo un pueblito de mala muerte.*

to be the talk of the town — *dar mucho que hablar (ser la comidilla de la ciudad).*
Her divorce is the talk of the town. *Su divorcio da mucho que hablar (es la comidilla de la ciudad).*

to paint the town red — *ir de juerga (parranda).*
They painted the town red. *Fueron de juerga (parranda).*

to toy — *jugar*

to toy with the idea — *acariciar la idea.*

He's been toying with the idea all year. *Ha estado acariciando la idea todo el año.*

track — *la huella*

off the beaten track — *fuera del camino trillado.*

They travel off the beaten track. *Viajan fuera del camino trillado.*

the wrong side of the tracks — *el barrio más pobre.*

He comes from the wrong side of the tracks and wants to marry my daughter? *¿Viene de ese barrio maloliente y pretende casarse con mi hija?*

to be off (the) track — *andar despistado.*

That's not right. You're off (the) track. *No tiene usted razón. Anda usted despistado.*

to be on the right track — *andar por buen camino.*

You're on the right track. *Anda por buen camino.*

to keep track — *preocuparse; estar al corriente.*

He keeps track of everything. *Se preocupa (Está al corriente) de todo.*

to lose track of — *perder de vista.*

I've lost track of that family. *He perdido de vista a esa familia.*

to make tracks — *ir(se) de prisa.*

They were really making tracks. *(Se) iban muy de prisa.*

to track — *rastrear*

to track down — *seguir el rastro.*

They weren't able to track him down. *No pudieron seguirle el rastro.*

trap — *la trampa*

booby trap — *la trampa explosiva.*

Mac didn't see the wire of the booby trap and died in the explosion. *Mac no vio el alambre de la trampa explosiva y murió en la explosión.*

to tread — *pisar*

to tread softly — *proceder con prudencia.*

We trod softly when we first arrived. *Al principio procedimos con prudencia.*

treatment — *el tratamiento*

to give someone the red-carpet treatment — *recibirlo a cuerpo de rey.*

They gave him the red-carpet treatment. *Lo recibieron a cuerpo de rey.*

tree — *el árbol*

to bark up the wrong tree — *ir (andar) descaminado.*

You're barking up the wrong tree. *Va (Anda) descaminado.*

trick — *la maña*

to be up to one's old trick — *hacer de las suyas.*

It's evident that he's up to his old tricks. *Se ve que está haciendo de las suyas.*

to do the trick — *arreglarse.*

A little soap will do the trick. *Con un poco de jabón se arreglará.*

to play a dirty trick on someone — *jugarle una mala pasada (mala jugada).*

She played a dirty trick on me. *Me jugó una mala pasada (mala jugada).*

to play a trick on someone — *hacerle una broma.*

She played a trick on me. *Me hizo una broma.*

trip — *el viaje*

ego trip — *la autosatisfacción.*

That expensive party is just one more of John's ego trips. *Esa fiesta tan cara es sólo una manera más que tiene John de satisfacer su ego.*

round-trip — *el viaje de ida y vuelta.*

We bought a round-trip ticket to Brazil. *Compramos un boleto de ida y vuelta a Brasil.*

to be on a trip — *estar de viaje.*

They're on a trip. *Están de viaje.*

to leave (to go) on a trip — *salir de viaje.*
They're leaving (going) on a trip. *Salen de viaje.*

to take a trip — *hacer (realizar) un viaje.*
We took a trip. *Hicimos (Realizamos) un viaje.*

trouble — *el apuro*

That's the trouble. — *Ese es el inconveniente.*

to be in trouble — *estar en un aprieto.*
We're in trouble. *Estamos en un aprieto.*

to cause trouble — *dar guerra.*
They were always causing trouble. *Siempre daban guerra.*

to look for trouble — *buscarle tres pies al gato.*
He goes around looking for trouble. *Le anda buscando tres pies al gato.*

to stay out of trouble — *no meterse en líos.*
It's best to stay out of trouble. *Es mejor no meterse en líos.*

to take the trouble to — *tomarse la molestia (el trabajo) de.*
He took the trouble to thank me. *Se tomó la molestia (el trabajo) de darme las gracias.*

What's the trouble? — *¿Qué le pasa?*

true — *verdadero*

It's too good to be true. — *¿Será verdad tanta belleza?*

to be true to one's word — *ser fiel a su palabra.*
He's always true to his word. *Siempre es fiel a su palabra.*

to come true — *convertirse en realidad.*
At last his plans came true. *Por fin sus planes se convirtieron en realidad.*

to try — *tratar*

to try hard — *hacer todo lo posible.*
He tried hard but couldn't. *Hizo todo lo posible pero no pudo.*

to try on — *probarse.*
He tried on the hat. *Se probó el sombrero.*

to try one's patience — *poner a prueba su paciencia.*
This child tries my patience. *Este chico pone a prueba mi paciencia.*

to try out — *practicar.*

He tried out his Spanish in Mexico. *Practicó su español en México.*

try as he might — *por más que trató.*

Try as he might he couldn't hit the target. *Por más que trató, no pudo acertar al blanco.*

tune — *la melodía*

to be in (out of) tune — *estar (des)afinado.*

The guitar is in (out of) tune. *La guitarra está (des)afinada.*

to call the tune — *llevar el control.*

The accountant insists on calling the tune at the meetings. *El contador insiste en controlar las reuniones.*

to change one's tune — *cambiar de disco (actitud).*

He used to talk against the president but now he has changed his tune. *Antes hablaba contra el presidente pero ahora ha cambiado de disco (actitud).*

to pay to the tune of — *pagar la friolera de.*

I had to pay to the tune of a hundred dollars. *Tuve que pagar la friolera de cien dólares.*

to tune — *afinar*

to tune in — *sintonizar.*

I can't tune in that program. *No puedo sintonizar ese programa.*

Turk — *el turco*

Young Turk — *el rebelde; el idealista.*

Many politicians start as Young Turks, but with time they become conservative. *Muchos políticos comienzan como rebeldes e idealistas, pero con el tiempo se vuelven conservadores.*

turkey — *el pavo*

cold turkey — *parar en seco.*

He went cold turkey with the cigarettes. *Paró en seco con los cigarrillos.*

turn — *la vuelta*

at every turn — *a cada paso.*

At every turn there was a truck. *A cada paso había un camión.*

in turn — *a su vez.*

They all tasted it in turn. *Todos la probaron a su vez.*

One good turn deserves another. — *Bien con bien se paga.*

to be one's turn — *tocarle; corresponderle.*

It's your turn. *Le toca (corresponde) a usted.*

to speak out of turn — *meter su cuchara.*

He spoke out of turn again. *Metió su cuchara otra vez.*

to take a new turn — *tomar nuevo aspecto.*

The news took a new turn. *Las noticias tomaron nuevo aspecto.*

to take a turn for the better (worse) — *mejorarse (empeorarse).*

He took a turn for the better (worse). *El se mejoró (se empeoró).*

to take turns (at) — *turnarse.*

We take turns (at) answering the phone. *Nos turnamos para contestar el teléfono.*

---

to turn — *dar vuelta, volverse; doblar*

not to know where to turn (for help) — *no saber a quién dirigirse (por ayuda).*

He doesn't know where to turn (for help). *No sabe a quién dirigirse (por ayuda).*

to turn around — *dar una vuelta.*

He turned around and saw her. *Dio una vuelta y la vio.*

to turn down — *bajar.*

Turn down the radio. *Baje la radio.*

to turn down — *rechazar.*

He turned down my request. *Rechazó mi petición.*

to turn in — *entregar.*

He turned in his equipment. *Entregó su equipo.*

to turn in — *irse a la cama.*

He turned in at ten. *Se fue a la cama a las diez.*

to turn in(to) — *entrar en.*
He turned in(to) our driveway. *Entró en nuestra calzada.*

to turn into — *convertirse en.*
The wine turned into vinegar. *El vino se convirtió en vinagre.*

to turn off — *cerrar.*
Turn off the water. *Cierre la llave del agua.*

to turn off — *doblar.*
He turned off to the left. *Dobló a la izquierda.*

to turn on — *atacar.*
The bear turned on the tourist. *El oso atacó al turista.*

to turn on — *poner.*
Turn on the gas (light). *Ponga el gas (la luz).*

to turn out — *apagar (cerrar).*
They turned out the light. *Apagaron (Cerraron) la luz.*

to turn out — *presentarse.*
All his friends turned out for the wedding. *Todos sus amigos se presentaron para la boda.*

to turn out — *producir.*
The factory turned out ten airplanes in one day. *La fábrica produjo diez aviones en un día.*

to turn out — *resultar.*
It turned out well. *Resultó bien.*

to turn over (upside down) — *darle vuelta.*
He turned it over (upside down). *Le dio vuelta.*

to turn over — *transferir.*
He turned over his money to his son. *Transfirió su dinero a su hijo.*

to turn over — *volcarse.*
The car turned over. *El coche se volcó.*

to turn pale — *ponerse pálido.*
He turned pale. *Se puso pálido.*

to turn to — *recurrir a.*
He turned to his father for his help. *Recurrió a su padre por su ayuda.*

to turn up — *aparecer.*

They turned up at our house. *Aparecieron en nuestra casa.*

to turn up — *poner más alto.*

Turn up the radio. *Ponga la radio más alto.*

twinkling — *el centelleo*

in the twinkling of an eye — *en un abrir y cerrar de ojos; en un santiamén.*

He answered in the twinkling of an eye. *Contestó en un abrir y cerrar de ojos (en un santiamén).*

two — *dos*

by twos (two by two) — *de dos en dos; dos a dos.*

They entered by twos (two by two). *Entraron de dos en dos (dos a dos).*

that makes two of us — *ya somos dos.*

That makes two of us. I arrived late too. *Ya somos dos. Yo también llegué tarde.*

to divide in two (half) — *dividir por la mitad.*

We divided it in two (half). *Lo dividimos por la mitad.*

to put two and two together — *atar cabos.*

By putting two and two together, I understood. *Atando cabos, comprendí.*

U

unaware — *inconsciente*

to be unaware — *ignorar; estar ajeno a.*

I am unaware of the problem. *Ignoro el (Estoy ajeno al) problema.*

to understand — *entender*

to make oneself understood — *hacerse entender.*

She couldn't make herself understood. *No pudo hacerse entender.*

understanding — *el entendimiento.*

with the understanding that — *con la condición de que.*

We bought the apartment with the understanding that we would share the expenses. *Compramos el apartamento con la condición de que compartiríamos los gastos.*

undertone — *la voz baja*

in an undertone — *por lo bajo.*

He said it in an undertone. *Lo dijo por lo bajo.*

up — *arriba*

the game is up — *todo está perdido; no hay nada que hacer.*

When she found me in bed with Helen, I understood that the game was up. *Cuando me encontró en cama con Elena, comprendí que no había nada que hacer.*

Time's up. — *Ya es la hora.*

to be up — *haberse levantado.*

He's not up yet. *Todavía no se ha levantado.*

to be up and about — *haberse restablecido.*

She had the flu last week, but she's up and about now. *Estaba con la gripe la semana pasada, pero ya se ha restablecido.*

to be up and about — *estar levantado.*

At five in the morning, she was already up and about. *A las cinco de la mañana ya estaba levantada.*

to be up for — *haber sido presentado para.*

The motion is up for a vote. *La proposición ha sido presentada para votación.*

to be up on — *estar al corriente de.*

He's up on world news. *Está al corriente de las noticias mundiales.*

to be up to — *sentirse capaz de.*

I'm not up to working today. *No me siento capaz de trabajar hoy.*

to be up to one — *depender de (tocarle a) uno.*

It's up to you. *Depende de (Le toca a) usted.*

to go up — *subir.*
He went up the stairs. *Subió la escalera.*

to keep up — *continuar.*
He couldn't keep up. *No pudo continuar.*

to keep up with — *correr parejas con.*
He couldn't keep up with his class. *No pudo correr parejas con su clase.*

to look up and down — *mirar de arriba abajo.*
We looked up and down. *Miramos de arriba abajo.*

to move upstream (downstream) — *ir aguas arriba (abajo).*
It was moving upstream (downstream). *Iba aguas arriba (abajo).*

up there — *allá arriba.*
It's up there. *Está allá arriba.*

up to now — *hasta ahora; hasta la fecha.*
Up to now, I don't know. *Hasta ahora (la fecha) no sé.*

What are you up to? — *¿Qué está haciendo?*

What's up? — *¿Qué pasa?*

---

use — *el uso*

it's no use — *es inútil.*
It's no use trying to solve it. *Es inútil tratar de resolverlo.*

to be of no use — *no servir de (para) nada.*
It's of no use to us. *No nos sirve de (para) nada.*

to have no use for — *no gustarle.*
I have no use for that girl. *Esa chica no me gusta.*

to make use of — *servirse de.*
He made use of them. *Se sirvió de ellos.*

what's the use of — *para (a) qué.*
What's the use of crying? *¿Para (A) qué llorar?*

---

used — *usado*

to get used to — *acostumbrarse a.*
We get used to working hard. *Nos acostumbramos a trabajar mucho.*

usual — *usual*

as usual — *como de costumbre.*

She arrived late, as usual. *Llegó tarde, como de costumbre.*

utmost — *el más alto grado*

to do one's utmost — *desvivirse; hacer todo lo posible.*

She did her utmost to find us. *Se desvivió (Hizo todo lo posible) por encontrarnos.*

V

vacation — *las vacaciones*

to be on vacation — *estar de vacaciones.*

He's on vacation. *Está de vacaciones.*

value — *el valor; el mérito; el aprecio*

to take at face value — *aceptar sin dudar; aceptar por las apariencias.*

And you took at face value all he said, knowing that he is a liar? *¿Y tú aceptaste sin dudar todo lo que dijo, sabiendo que es un mentiroso?*

variety — *la variedad*

Variety is the spice of life. — *En la variedad está el gusto.*

vengeance — *la venganza*

with a vengeance — *con todas sus fuerzas.*

He studied with a vengeance. *Estudió con todas sus fuerzas.*

to venture — *aventurarse*

Nothing ventured, nothing gained. — *El que no se arriesga no pasa la mar.*

verge — *el borde*

to be on the verge of — *estar a punto (al borde) de.*

They're on the verge of reaching an agreement. *Están a punto (al borde) de ponerse de acuerdo.*

very — *muy*

not very — *poco.*

It was not very interesting. *Fue poco interesante.*

the very one — *precisamente.*

He's the very one I'm looking for. *Es precisamente él a quien busco.*

view — *la vista*

exchange of views — *un intercambio de ideas.*

The president and I had an exchange of views at the meeting. *El presidente y yo intercambiamos ideas en la reunión.*

in view of this — *en vista de esto.*

In view of this, you can't go. *En vista de esto no puede ir.*

to be on view — *estar en exhibición.*

The painting is on view. *La pintura está en exhibición.*

to take a dim view of — *parecerle mal; no entusiasmarse de.*

He took a dim view of our missing class. *Le pareció mal (No se entusiasmó de) que faltáramos a la clase.*

with a view to — *con miras a; con el propósito de.*

He signed it with a view to earning more money. *Lo firmó con miras a (con el propósito de) ganar más dinero.*

virtue — *la virtud*

by virtue of — *en virtud de.*

He presented it by virtue of his authority. *Lo presentó en virtud de su autoridad.*

vision — *la visión*

to have visions of — *imaginar.*

I had visions of being late. *Me imaginaba llegando tarde.*

visit — *la visita*

to pay someone a visit — *hacerle una visita.*

We paid them a visit. *Les hicimos una visita.*

voice — *la voz*

at the top of one's voice — *a voz en cuello.*

He was yelling at the top of his voice. *Gritaba a voz en cuello.*

in a low (loud) voice — *en voz baja (alta).*

She spoke in a low (loud) voice. *Habló en voz baja (alta).*

to lower one's voice — *apagar la voz.*

She lowered her voice. *Apagó la voz.*

to raise one's voice — *alzar la voz.*

He raised his voice. *Alzó la voz.*

with one voice — *a una voz; por unanimidad.*

The strikers roared their approval with one voice. *Los huelguistas rugieron su aprobación a una voz.*

to vote — *votar*

to vote in — *elegir por votación.*

He was voted in. *Fue elegido por votación.*

to vouch — *comprobar; verificar*

to vouch for — *responder de; garantizar algo.*

I vouch for my friend. *Respondo de mi amigo.*

voyage — *el viaje*

maiden voyage — *la primera travesía; el viaje inaugural.*

It was the ship's maiden voyage. *Fue la primera travesía (el viaje inaugural) del barco.*

W

wagon — *el carretón*

to be on the wagon — *dejar de beber.*

He's been on the wagon for half a year. *No ha bebido en medio año.*

to fall off the wagon — *volver a beber.*

He didn't touch a drop for a month, and then he fell off the wagon. *No probó una gota por un mes, pero luego recayó en la bebida.*

wait — *espera*

to have a long wait — *tener que esperar mucho.*

We had a long wait. *Tuvimos que esperar mucho.*

to lie in wait — *estar al (en) acecho.*

He's lying in wait. *Está al (en) acecho.*

to wait — *esperar*

not to be able to wait — *arder en deseos de.*

I have not seen Mary in five years, and I can't wait until she arrives! *¡Hace cinco años que no he visto a María, y ardo en deseos de que llegue!*

to wait for — *esperar.*

He's waiting for us. *Nos espera.*

to wait on — *servir.*

She waited on us. *Nos sirvió.*

to wait up for — *desvelarse esperando a.*

He waited up for his children. *Se desveló esperando a sus hijos.*

wait and see — *ya lo veremos.*

His attitude is "wait and see." *Su actitud es "ya lo veremos."*

wake — *la estela*

in the wake of — *a consecuencia de.*

They abandoned their home in the wake of the flood. *A consecuencia de la inundación abandonaron su casa.*

to wake — *despertar*

to wake up — *despertarse.*

She woke up at six. *Se despertó a las seis.*

walk — *el paseo*

all walks of life — *todas las clases sociales.*

They come from all walks of life. *Son de todas las clases sociales.*

to take a walk — *dar un paseo (una vuelta).*
He likes to take a walk. *Le gusta dar un paseo (una vuelta).*

to walk — *caminar*

to walk (to stroll) around — *dar vueltas (pasearse) por.*
I walked (strolled) around the garden. *Di vueltas (Me paseé) por el jardín.*

to walk around the block — *dar (la) vuelta a la manzana.*
He walked around the block. *Dio (la) vuelta a la manzana.*

to walk back — *volver a pie.*
We walked back. *Volvimos a pie.*

to walk off with — *llevarse; robar.*
He walked off with our typewriter. *Se llevó (Robó) nuestra máquina de escribir.*

to walk out — *abandonar el trabajo.*
The employees walked out when the boss insulted them. *Los empleados abandonaron el trabajo cuando el jefe los insultó.*

to walk up (down) — *subir (bajar) andando (a pie).*
She walked up (down). *Subió (Bajó) andando (a pie).*

to walk up and down — *pasearse de arriba abajo.*
They were walking up and down. *Se paseaban de arriba abajo.*

wall — *la pared*

hole in the wall — *una tienda o un cuarto demasiado pequeño; cuchitril.*
That business is a miserable hole in the wall. *Ese negocio es un cuchitril miserable.*

the writing on the wall — *la advertencia de peligro.*
He saw the writing on the wall and left the company before it went bankrupt. *Comprendió lo que iba a suceder y dejó la compañía antes de que ésta se fuera a la bancarrota.*

to drive up the wall — *enfurecer a alguien.*
They drove me up the wall with their demands! *¡Me volvieron furioso con sus exigencias!*

to have one's back to the wall — *estar entre la espada y la pared.*
We have our backs to the wall. *Estamos entre la espada y la pared.*

wall to wall — *de un extremo a otro.*
People were wall to wall in the market. *Había gente de una extremo a otro del mercado.*

Walls have ears. — *Las paredes oyen.*

to wall — *murar*

to be walled in — *estar encerrado (con muro).*
We were walled in. *Estábamos encerrados (con muro).*

want — *la necesidad*

for want of — *por falta de; por carecer de.*
For want of sugar, I couldn't bake the cake. *Por faltarme el azúcar, no pude hornear la torta.*

to be in want — *estar necesitado.*
They are in want of shelter. *Necesitan un refugio.*

war — *la guerra*

to wage war — *hacer (la) guerra.*
He waged war. *Hizo (la) guerra.*

to ward — *resguardar; vigilar*

to ward off — *parar; detener; desviar.*
We must ward this attack off, or we will lose. *O detenemos este ataque, o perdemos.*

warm — *caliente*

It's warm. — *Hace calor.*

to be warm — *tener calor.*
I'm warm. *Tengo calor.*

to send warm greetings (regards) — *mandar saludos cariñosos.*
We all send warm greetings (regards). *Todos mandamos saludos cariñosos.*

to warm — *calentar*

to warm up — *calentar.*
They warmed up the meat. *Calentaron la carne.*

to warm (oneself) up — *calentarse.*

Let's warm up near the fire before we leave. *Calentémonos cerca del fuego antes de salir.*

to warm up to — *entrar en confianza con.*

The lost cat soon warmed up to us. *El gato perdido pronto entró en confianza con nosotros.*

waste — *el derroche, el despilfarro*

to go to waste — *malgastarse; desperdiciarse.*

It would be a shame for all that money to go to waste. *Sería una lástima que se malgastara (se desperdiciara) todo ese dinero.*

watch — *la guardia, la vigilancia; el reloj*

to be on the watch for — *estar a la mira de.*

Be on the watch for my dog. *Esté a la mira de mi perro.*

to keep (to stand) watch — *hacer la (estar de) guardia.*

He kept (stood) watch all night. *Hizo la (Estuvo de) guardia toda la noche.*

to wind up a watch — *dar cuerda a un reloj.*

I wound up my watch. *Di cuerda a mi reloj.*

to watch — *mirar*

to watch out for — *tener cuidado con.*

Watch out for the train. *Tenga cuidado con el tren.*

to watch over — *guardar.*

The dog watched over his master. *El perro guardó a su amo.*

Watch it! — *¡Cuidado!*

Watch it! A car is coming! *¡Cuidado! ¡Que viene un auto!*

water — *el agua*

not to hold water — *caerse por su base.*

That explanation doesn't hold water. *Esa explicación se cae por su base.*

Still waters run deep. — *Del agua mansa me libre Dios, que de la brava me libro yo.*

That's water under the bridge now. — *Lo hecho hecho está.*

to be in hot water — *estar en un aprieto.*

He's in hot water. *Está en un aprieto.*

to pour oil on troubled waters — *apaciguar los ánimos.*

Somebody must pour oil on these troubled waters, or our country will go to war. *Alguien debe calmar los ánimos, o nuestro país irá a la guerra.*

to fish in troubled waters — *pescar en agua turbia (revuelta).*

They are fishing in troubled waters. *Pescan en agua turbia (revuelta).*

to throw cold water on — *echar una jarra de agua fría a.*

He threw cold water on our plans. *Echó una jarra de agua fría a nuestros planes.*

to tread water — *pedalear en el agua.*

He's treading water. *Está pedaleando en el agua.*

to water — *regar*

for one's mouth to water — *hacérsele agua la boca.*

My mouth waters. *Se me hace agua la boca.*

to make one's eyes water — *hacerle llorar.*

It made my eyes water. *Me hizo llorar.*

to water down — *suavizar; moderar.*

His speech was watered down because he didn't want to annoy the Chinese delegation. *Su discurso fue suavizado porque no quiso irritar a la delegación china.*

way — *la manera, el modo; el camino*

any way one likes — *como quiera.*

I'll make them any way you like. *Los haré como usted quiera.*

by the way — *a propósito (entre paréntesis).*

By the way, do you have it? *A propósito (Entre paréntesis), ¿lo tiene?*

by way of — *a guisa de.*

By way of explanation, he read the letter to us. *A guisa de explicación, nos leyó la carta.*

by way of — *pasando por.*

We came by way of Chicago. *Vinimos pasando por Chicago.*

either way — *en uno u otro caso.*

Either way, I'll manage. *En uno u otro caso, me las arreglaré.*

halfway through — *a mitad de.*

They got up from the table halfway through the meal. *Se levantaron de la mesa a mitad de la comida.*

in a big way — *en grande.*

She always celebrates her birthday in a big way. *Siempre celebra su cumpleaños en grande.*

in a way — *en cierto modo; hasta cierto punto.*

In a way, it will be difficult. *En cierto modo (Hasta cierto punto) será difícil.*

in one's way — *a su manera.*

In his way he tries to help. *A su manera, trata de ayudar.*

in such a way — *de tal modo.*

She said it in such a way that I didn't understand. *Lo dijo de tal modo que no comprendí.*

in the same way — *en la misma forma; de la misma manera.*

He does it in the same way. *Lo hace en la misma forma (de la misma manera).*

in the way of — *en.*

What do you have in the way of a piano? *¿Qué tiene en pianos?*

It's all in the way you say it. — *Todo depende de cómo se dice (diga).*

no way — *imposible; de ninguna manera.*

No way you can go to the theater tomorrow. *De ninguna manera puedes ir al teatro mañana.*

on the way — *de camino.*

On the way, buy some milk. *De camino, compre leche.*

on the way — *por el camino.*

I saw him on the way. *Lo vi por el camino.*

one way or another — *de algún modo.*

We'll do it one way or another. *Lo haremos de algún modo.*

somewhere along the way — *por el camino.*

Somewhere along the way I may find happiness. *Quizás encuentre la felicidad por el camino.*

way of life — *manera (estilo) de vivir.*
He doesn't like our way of life. *No le gusta nuestra manera (nuestro estilo) de vivir.*

the hard way — *el modo más difícil.*
He does it the hard way. *Lo hace del modo más difícil.*

the other way (a)round (just the opposite) — *al revés; al contrario.*
It's the other way (a)round (just the opposite). *Es al revés (al contrario).*

the way in — *la entrada.*
We couldn't find the way in. *No pudimos encontrar la entrada.*

the way out — *la salida.*
Here's the way out. *Aquí está la salida.*

There are no two ways about it. *No hay que darle vueltas.*

this way — *de este modo; de esta manera.*
This way we'll pay less. *De este modo (De esta manera) pagaremos menos.*

this way — *por acá (aquí).*
This way, please. *Por acá (aquí), por favor.*

to be in the way — *estorbar; estar de sobra.*
He's always in the way. *Siempre estorba (está de sobra).*

to be on one's way — *marcharse, irse.*
We ought to be on our way if we want to arrive by ten. *Debemos marcharnos (irnos) si queremos llegar para las diez.*

to block the way — *cerrar el paso.*
It blocked our way. *Nos cerró el paso.*

to find its way to — *ir a parar a.*
Very little food finds its way to the houses of the poor. *Muy poco de la comida va a parar a las casas de los pobres.*

to force (to make) one's way through — *abrir paso.*
They forced (made) their way through. *Abrieron paso.*

to get in each other's way — *estorbarse.*
In that narrow aisle, the other hostess and I kept getting in each other's way. *En ese angosto pasillo, la otra azafata y yo continuábamos estorbándonos.*

to get one's way — *salir(se) con la suya.*
He always gets his way. *Siempre (se) sale con la suya.*

to get out of the way — *quitarse de en medio.*
Get out of the way! *¡Quítese de en medio!*

to get that way — *ponerse así.*
He gets that way often. *Se pone así a menudo.*

to get under way — *ponerse en marcha.*
We got under way late. *Nos pusimos en marcha tarde.*

to give way — *ceder.*
The dam gave way. *La presa cedió.*

to go a long way — *alcanzar para mucho.*
You can go a long way with what you have if you're careful. *Si tiene cuidado, lo que tiene alcanzará para mucho.*

to go a long way — *hacer muchos esfuerzos.*
He goes a long way to help his students. *Hace muchos esfuerzos para ayudar a sus alumnos.*

to go one's separate ways — *irse cada uno por su lado.*
After the movie, they went their separate ways. *Después de la película, cada uno se fue por su lado.*

to go out of one's way — *desvivirse.*
They went out of their way to help us. *Se desvivieron por ayudarnos.*

to have a (nice) way with people — *saber manejar a la gente.*
She has a (nice) way with people. *Sabe manejar a la gente.*

to have come a long way — *haber adelantado mucho.*
Building has come a long way in Mexico City. *La construcción ha adelantado mucho en México.*

to have it both ways — *querer tenerlo todo.*
Save money and go on vacation? You can't have it both ways! *¿Ahorrar e irte de vacaciones? ¡No puedes tenerlo todo!*

to look the other way — *hacer la vista gorda.*
I looked the other way. *Hice la vista gorda.*

to one's way of thinking — *a su modo de ver.*
To my way of thinking, it's a bargain. *A mi modo de ver es una ganga.*

to pave the way for — *abrirle el camino a.*

We paved the way for the new boss. *Le abrimos el camino al nuevo jefe.*

to return to one's old ways — *volver a las andadas.*

He returned to his old ways. *Volvió a las andadas.*

to rub one the wrong way — *irritarle.*

He rubs me the wrong way. *Me irrita.*

to see one's way to — *ver el modo de.*

We can't see our way to insure your ship. *No vemos de qué modo podríamos asegurar su barco.*

to work one's way up — *progresar.*

He has worked his way up until he became manager. *Ha progresado en su trabajo hasta hacerse gerente.*

way off — *muy lejos.*

They live way off at the edge of town. *Viven muy lejos, en las afueras de la ciudad.*

way off — *muy equivocado.*

His calculations are way off. *Sus cálculos son muy equivocados.*

ways and means — *medios y arbitrios.*

Ways and means must be found to convince them. *Deben encontrarse los medios para convencerlos.*

---

wear — *el uso*

wear and tear — *desgaste (por el uso).*

There was a lot of wear and tear on the car. *Hubo mucho desgaste (por el uso) del coche.*

---

to wear — *usar, llevar*

to be worn out — *estar agotado.*

I'm worn out. *Estoy agotado.*

to be worn out — *estar gastado.*

The motor is worn out. *Este motor está gastado.*

to wear off — *pasar.*

Your headache will wear off. *Su dolor de cabeza pasará.*

to wear well — *durar mucho.*

This material wears well. *Este género dura mucho.*

weather — *el tiempo*

to be under the weather — *estar indispuesto; no sentirse bien.*

He's under the weather today. *Está indispuesto (No se siente bien) hoy.*

weather permitting — *si el tiempo lo permite.*

Weather permitting, we'll walk. *Si el tiempo lo permite, iremos a pie.*

weight — *el peso*

to carry one's weight — *dar uno lo necesario de su parte.*

Despite all difficulties, he carried his weight and finished the course. *Pese a las dificultades, dio de sí cuanto fue necesario y terminó el curso.*

to put on weight — *ponerse gordo; engordar.*

He's putting on weight. *Se está poniendo gordo (Está engordando).*

welcome — *la bienvenida*

to be welcome to — *estar a su disposición.*

You are welcome to stay at our house. *Nuestra casa está a su disposición.*

to outstay one's welcome — *abusar de la hospitalidad de otros.*

He outstayed his welcome and then we couldn't make him leave. *Abusó de nuestra hospitalidad y después no podíamos lograr que se fuera.*

Welcome! — *¡Bienvenido!*

You are welcome. — *De nada; No hay de qué.*

well — *bien*

as well as — *así como (tanto . . . como . . .).*

The cat as well as the dog sleeps in the house. *El gato así como el perro (Tanto el gato como el perro) duerme en la casa.*

just as well — *más vale así.*

I didn't go to the exhibition, but it's just as well because the main company didn't show up. *No fui a la exhibición, pero mejor así porque la empresa más importante no se presentó.*

pretty well — *medianamente.*

"How are you?" — "Pretty well." *"¿Cómo estás?" — "Así así."*

to be well and good, but . . . — *estar todo muy bien pero . . .*

This is all well and good, but I'm still waiting for the rent money. *Todas esas razones son excelentes, pero yo todavía no veo la plata de la renta.*

to be well off — *ser rico.*

He's well off. *Es rico.*

to know only too well — *saber de sobra.*

I know it only too well. *Lo sé de sobra.*

to think well of — *tener buena impresión de.*

He thinks well of them. *Tiene buena impresión de ellos.*

Well now! — *¡Vaya!*

well then — *pues bien.*

Well then! How goes it? *¡Pues bien! ¿Cómo le va?*

---

wet — *mojado*

to be all wet — *estar completamente equivocado.*

They are all wet! Those aren't ducks, they are geese! *¡Esos no ven una! ¡Esos son gansos, no patos!*

to be soaking wet — *estar hecho una sopa.*

He's soaking wet. *Está hecho una sopa.*

---

whale — *la ballena*

to be a whale of a . . . — *ser un . . . tremendo.*

It was a whale of a party. *Fue una fiesta tremenda.*

---

what — *qué*

So what? — *¿Qué más da?*

to know what is what — *saber cuántas son cinco.*

She knows what is what. *Sabe cuántas son cinco.*

what about — *qué hay de.*

What about that house you were going to build? *¿Qué hay de la casa que iba a construir?*

What can I do for you? — *¿Qué se le ofrece?*

What for? — *¿Para qué?*

What will you have (to drink)? — *¿Qué va a tomar?*

what with — *a causa de; debido a; con eso de.*

House sales are down — what with higher taxes and mortgages it's not surprising. *Las ventas de casas han disminuido, y no es de sorprender viendo como crecieron los impuestos e hipotecas.*

What's it all about? — *¿De qué se trata?*

what's it to . . . ? — *¿Qué le importa a . . . ?*

If I like to live in the country, what's it to you? *Si a mí me gusta vivir en el campo, ¿qué te importa a ti?*

What's new? — *¿Qué hay de nuevo?*

What's up? — *¿Oué sucede (ocurre; pasa)?*

what's what — *la verdad.*

All too often we don't see what's what until it's too late. *Muy a menudo no vemos la verdad hasta que es demasiado tarde.*

---

whatever — *lo que*

whatever it may be — *sea lo que sea.*

Whatever it may be, I can't believe it. *Sea lo que sea, no lo puedo creer.*

---

wheel — *la rueda*

to be a big wheel — *ser un pez gordo.*

He's a big wheel. *Es un pez gordo.*

---

while — *el rato*

a (little) while ago — *hace un rato.*

I saw her a (little) while ago. *La vi hace un rato.*

a while back — *hace un rato.*

I would have gone a while back, but not now. *Habría ido hace un rato, pero ahora no.*

after a (little) while — *al cabo de un rato.*

After a (little) while it began. *Al cabo de un rato empezó.*

every little while — *cada poco; a cada rato.*

Every little while the sun came out. *Cada poco (A cada rato) salía el sol.*

in a little while — *dentro de poco.*

We'll arrive in a little while. *Llegaremos dentro de poco.*

whistle — *el silbato*

to wet one's whistle — *echarse un trago.*

They stopped by the bar to wet their whistle. *Pasaron por el bar para echarse un trago.*

to whiz — *moverse rápidamente*

to whiz by — *pasar como una flecha.*

I saw her whiz by in her convertible. *La vi pasar como una flecha en su convertible.*

who — *quién; quien*

Who cares? — *¿Qué más da?*

whole — *entero*

on the whole — *en general.*

On the whole, he's cooperative. *En general es cooperativo.*

why — *por qué*

that's why — *por eso.*

That's why she's crying. *Por eso está llorando.*

why — *pero si.*

Why, I always greet you! *¡Pero si siempre lo saludo!*

widow — *la viuda*

football widow — *esposa cuya soledad es causada por la afición del marido por el fútbol.*

Every woman is a football widow during the championship game. *Todas las mujeres quedan de viudas durante el partido por el campeonato.*

wig — *la peluca*

to be a big wig — *ser un pez gordo.*

He's a big wig. *Es un pez gordo.*

wildfire — *el fuego griego*

to spread like wildfire — *correr como pólvora en reguera.*

The news spread like wildfire. *La noticia corrió como pólvora en reguera.*

will — *la voluntad*

against one's will — *a la fuerza; de mala voluntad.*

He came against his will. *Vino a la fuerza (de mala voluntad).*

at will — *a voluntad.*

They fired at will. *Dispararon a voluntad.*

Where there's a will there's a way. — *Querer es poder.*

to win — *ganar*

to win out over — *poder más que.*

Love won out over hate. *El amor pudo más que el odio.*

wind — *el viento*

There's something in the wind. — *Algo está pendiente; Se está tramando algo.*

to fly into the wind — *volar contra el viento.*

They flew into the wind. *Volaron contra el viento.*

to get wind of — *enterarse de.*

I got wind of their arrival. *Me enteré de su llegada.*

to take the wind out of one's sails — *desanimarle.*

It took the wind out of my sails. *Me desanimó.*

to wind — *enrollar*

to wind up — *acabar.*

He wound up in court. *Acabó en el tribunal.*

to wind up — *cerrar.*

We are winding up our school year. *Estamos cerrando nuestro año académico.*

window — *la ventana*

to go window shopping — *mirar los escaparates.*

She likes to go window shopping. *Le gusta mirar los escaparates.*

wine — *el vino*

to wine and dine — *agasajar.*

They were very happy to wine and dine the new ambassador. *Les complació mucho tratar con hospitalidad al nuevo embajador.*

wing — *el ala (f.)*

to clip someone's wings — *cortarle las alas.*

They clipped his wings. *Le cortaron las alas.*

to take under one's wing — *tomar bajo su protección.*

His professor took him under his wing. *Su profesor lo tomó bajo su protección.*

to wait in the wings — *esperar la entrada en escena; esperar el momento de actuar.*

He waited in the wings for three years, but now the post was his. *Esperó su oportunidad por tres años, pero ahora el cargo era suyo.*

wink — *el guiño*

not to sleep a wink — *no pegar (un) ojo.*

She didn't sleep a wink. *No pegó (un) ojo.*

to take forty winks — *echar una siesta.*

He took forty winks before leaving. *Echó una siesta antes de salir.*

to wipe — *secar*

to wipe out — *destruir.*

The bombs wiped out the town. *Las bombas destruyeron el pueblo.*

wisdom — *la sabiduría*

conventional wisdom — *la creencia popular.*

Conventional wisdom says that all dogs are loyal. *La creencia popular dice que todos los perros son fieles.*

wise — *sabio*

to be wise to — *conocerle el juego.*

Be careful. She's wise to you. *Ten cuidado. Te conoce el juego.*

to wish — *desear*

I wish I could. — *ojalá; me gustaría.*

to wish it off on someone else — *endosárselo.*

She wished it off on me. *Me lo endosó.*

wit — *el ingenio*

to be at one's wit's end — *no saber qué hacer.*

He's at his wit's end. *No sabe qué hacer.*

to be out of one's wits — *haber perdido el juicio.*

He's out of his wits. *Ha perdido el juicio.*

to keep one's wits about one — *conservar su presencia de ánimo.*

He kept his wits about him. *Conservó su presencia de ánimo.*

---

with — *con*

to be with it — *estar al día.*

He's always with it. *Siempre está al día.*

---

wolf — *el lobo*

to cry wolf — *dar una falsa alarma.*

They cried wolf. *Dieron una falsa alarma.*

---

wonder — *la maravilla*

nine days' wonder — *la maravilla de un día.*

The first edition was sold out, but I still believe that this book is a nine days' wonder. *La primera edición se agotó, pero yo todavía creo que este libro será un éxito pasajero.*

no wonder — *no es de extrañar; no es extraño.*

No wonder he's ill. *No es de extrañar (No es extraño) que esté enfermo.*

---

woods — *el bosque*

to be out of the woods — *estar fuera de peligro.*

The doctor says that he's out of the woods. *El médico dice que está fuera de peligro.*

---

wool — *la lana*

to pull the wool over one's eyes — *engañarlo como a un chino.*

They pulled the wool over his eyes. *Lo engañaron como a un chino.*

---

word — *la palabra*

beyond words — *indecible.*

I was grieved beyond words. *Mi pena fue indecible.*

by word of mouth — *de palabra.*

We were informed by word of mouth. *Nos informaron de palabra.*

for words to fail one — *quedarse sin palabras.*

Words fail me. *Me quedo sin palabras.*

four-letter word — *la palabra soez.*

His speech was loaded with four-letter words. *Su discurso estaba lleno de palabras soeces.*

in so many words — *sin rodeos.*

He told me in so many words that he considered me an idiot. *Me dijo sin rodeos que me consideraba como un idiota.*

not to utter a word — *no despegar los labios.*

He never utters a word. *Nunca despega los labios.*

not to mince words — *hablar sin rodeos (sin morderse la lengua).*

He was the only one who didn't mince words. *Fue el único que habló sin rodeos (sin morderse la lengua).*

to eat one's words — *tragarse las palabras.*

We made him eat his words. *Lo hicimos tragarse las palabras.*

to get a word in edgewise — *meter baza.*

They don't let him get a word in edgewise. *No lo dejan meter baza.*

to have a word with — *hablar dos palabras con.*

He'd like to have a word with us. *Quisiera hablar dos palabras con nosotros.*

to keep one's word — *cumplir con su palabra.*

He keeps his word. *Cumple con su palabra.*

to leave word — *dejar recado (dicho).*

He left word that he couldn't come. *Dejó recado (dicho) que no podía venir.*

to mark someone's words — *advertir lo que se le dice.*

Mark my words. *Advierta lo que le digo.*

to put in a good word for — *interceder por.*

I put in a good word for her. *Yo intercedí por ella.*

to put into words — *encontrar palabras.*

I can't put into words my gratitude. *No puedo encontrar palabras para expresar mi gratitud.*

to put words in someone's mouth — *atribuirle algo que no dijo.*

You're putting words in my mouth. *Me está atribuyendo algo que no he dicho.*

to say (give) the word — *avisar, dar permiso.*

We were waiting for him to give the word. *Esperábamos a que nos avisara (diera permiso).*

to send word — *mandar recado.*

He sent word that I was to come. *Mandó recado que debía venir.*

to take someone at his word — *tomar en serio lo que dice.*

She took me at my word. *Tomó en serio lo que dije.*

to take someone's word for it — *creerle.*

He wouldn't take my word for it. *No quiso creerme.*

word for word — *palabra por palabra.*

He recited it to me word for word. *Me lo recitó palabra por palabra.*

---

work — *el trabajo*

at work — *trabajando; realizando trabajos u obras.*

My masons are at work here. *Mis albañiles están trabajando aquí.*

in the works — *en preparación; en perspectiva.*

One project is finished and another is in the works. *Un proyecto está terminado y otro está en preparación.*

to make short work of — *terminar rápidamente con algo.*

She made short work of the steak and potatoes. *Se comió la carne y las papas en un dos por tres.*

---

to work — *trabajar*

to get all worked up — *excitarle.*

We got all worked up over the idea. *La idea nos excitó.*

to work one's way — *abrirse paso.*

We worked our way into the house. *Nos abrimos paso hasta la casa.*

to work one's way through college — *trabajar para costear sus estudios universitarios.*

He's working his way through college. *Está trabajando para costear sus estudios universitarios.*

to work out — *preparar; planear.*
We worked out the details. *Preparamos (Planeamos) los detalles.*

to work out — *resolver.*
We worked out the problem. *Resolvimos el problema.*

to work out — *ejercitarse (entrenarse).*
She works out in the gym every day. *Se ejercita (Se entrena) en el gimnasio todos los días.*

to work out well — *salir (resultar) bien.*
It worked out well. *Salió (Resultó) bien.*

---

world — *el mundo*

to set the world on fire — *hacerse famoso.*
He'll never set the world on fire. *Nunca se hará famoso.*

not for (anything in) the world — *por nada del mundo.*
I wouldn't accept it for (anything in) the world. *No lo aceptaría por nada del mundo.*

to be a man of the world — *ser un hombre de mundo.*
He's a man of the world. *Es un hombre de mundo.*

to be out of this world — *ser algo de sueño.*
Her cooking is out of this world. *Su cocina es algo de sueño.*

to come down in the world — *venir a menos.*
The family came down in the world. *La familia vino a menos.*

to have the best of two worlds — *beneficiarse por ambos lados.*
The job at the airline allows me to travel for free, so I'm having the best of both worlds. *El empleo en la aerolínea me permite viajar gratis, así que me beneficio por ambos lados.*

---

worst — *el peor*

at its worst — *de lo peor.*
His behavior was at its worst today. *Hoy su comportamiento fue peor que nunca.*

if worst comes to worst — *en el peor de los casos.*
If worst comes to worst, we'll buy another one. *En el peor de los casos, compraremos otro.*

worth — *el valor*

for all one is worth — *a (hasta) más no poder; con todas sus fuerzas.*

They're playing for all they're worth. *Están jugando a (hasta) más no poder (con todas sus fuerzas).*

Take it for what it is worth. — *Lléveselo por el valor que pueda tener.*

to be worthwhile — *valer (merecer) la pena.*

It's worthwhile. *Vale (Merece) la pena.*

to get one's money worth — *sacar el valor de lo que pagó.*

We didn't get our money's worth. *No sacamos el valor de lo que pagamos.*

---

wreck — *la ruina*

to be a nervous wreck — *ser un manojo (saco) de nervios.*

She's a nervous wreck. *Es un manojo (saco) de nervios.*

---

writer — *el escritor*

ghost writer — *el colaborador anónimo.*

He's the ghost writer of the book authored by the senator. *Él es el colaborador anónimo del libro que supuestamente escribió el senador.*

---

writing — *la escritura*

in writing — *por escrito.*

He complained in writing. *Se quejó por escrito.*

to commit to writing — *poner por escrito.*

He committed it to writing. *Lo puso por escrito.*

---

wrong — *equivocado*

to be in the wrong — *ser (el) culpable.*

He was in the wrong. *Era (el) culpable.*

to go wrong — *salir mal.*

Things went wrong. *Las cosas salieron mal.*

to take one wrong — *entender, interpretar mal a alguien.*

Please don't take me wrong, I would lend you the money if I had any. *Por favor, no me entiendas mal, yo te prestaría el dinero si lo tuviera.*

to take the wrong . . . — *equivocarse de. . . .*
I took the wrong street. *Me equivoqué de calle.*

Y

yarn — *el cuento; la historieta*
to spin a yarn — *contar cuentos increíbles.*
Grandpa was always spinning yarns after a couple of beers. *El abuelo siempre contaba historias fantásticas después de un par de cervezas.*

year — *el año*
all year round — *todo el año.*
They live here all year round. *Viven aquí todo el año.*

to be well along in years — *estar muy entrado (metido) en años.*
He's well along in years. *Está muy entrado (metido) en años.*

yellow — *amarillo*
to be yellow — *ser cobarde.*
If you're not yellow, you'll fight me. *Si no eres un cobarde, pelearás conmigo.*

Modismos Españoles Corrientes

Las palabras inglesas entre paréntesis representan a la palabra clave que ha de buscarse para encontrar el modismo español deseado. Los números revelan la página en que se halla dicha palabra.

A

a cada paso 304 (*turn*)
a cada rato 323 (*while*)
a cámara lenta 181 (*motion*)
a cambio de 87 (*exchange*)
a causa de 21 (*because*)
a ciencia cierta 45 (*certain*)
¡A comer! 53 (*to come*)
¿A cómo se vende? 183 (*much*)
a consecuencia de 312 (*wake*)
a costa de 87 (*expense*)
a crédito 61 (*credit*)
a cuestas 15 (*back*)
a diestra y siniestra 228 (*right*)
a duras penas 71 (*difficulty*)
a escondidas 255 (*sly*)
a eso de la(s) 13 (*at*)
a estas alturas 263 (*stage*)
a estas alturas 211 (*point*)
a este paso 222 (*rate*)
a expensas de 87 (*expense*)
a fondo 69 (*depth*)
a fuerza de 71 (*dint*)
a gritos 297 (*top*)
a guisa de 316 (*way*)
a hora fija 291 (*time*)
a instancia de 226 (*request*)
a justo título 230 (*rightly*)
a juzgar por 144 (*to judge*)
a la brevedad 191 (*notice*)
a la carrera 234 (*run*)
a la fuerza 325 (*will*)
a la hora 293 (*time*)
a la hora de la verdad 76 (*down*)
a la larga 234 (*run*)
a la merced de . . . 175 (*mercy*)
a la puerta de la casa 75 (*doorstep*)
a la sazón 292 (*time*)
a la vez 196 (*once*)
a la(s) . . . en punto 246 (*sharp*)
a lo lejos 72 (*distance*)
a lo mejor 160 (*likely*)
a mano 121 (*hand*)
a manos llenas 123 (*handful*)
a más no poder 331 (*worth*)
a más tardar 152 (*latest*)
a mediados 176 (*middle*)
a medias 120 (*half*)
a medio cerrar 120 (*half*)
a mitad de 317 (*way*)
a pasos agigantados 154 (*leap*)
a pesar de 262 (*spite*)
a petición de 226 (*request*)
a pie 102 (*foot*)
a poco de 248 (*shortly*)
a primera vista 111 (*glance*)
a propósito 316 (*way*)
a punto fijo 275 (*sure*)
a quemarropa 212 (*point*)
A quien le corresponda. 56 (*to concern*)
a ratos perdidos 292 (*time*)
a razón de 223 (*rate*)
a solas 9 (*alone*)
a solas 197 (*oneself*)
a su manera 317 (*way*)
a su modo 93 (*fashion*)
a su modo de ver 241 (*to see*)
a su parecer 198 (*opinion*)
a su vez 304 (*turn*)
a sus anchas 130 (*heart*)

a tal punto 88 (*extent*)
a tiempo 291 (*time*)
a toda carrera 261 (*speed*)
a toda costa 59 (*cost*)
a toda hora 137 (*hour*)
a todo lo que da 8 (*all*)
a toda prisa 125 (*haste*)
a todo trance 59 (*cost*)
a última hora 178 (*minute*)
a una voz 311 (*voice*)
a ver 241 (*to see*)
a viva fuerza 103 (*force*)
a voz en cuello 311 (*voice*)
a vuelo de pájaro 62 (*crow*)
abierto de par en par 197 (*open*)
abogado del diablo 5 (*advocate*)
abrirle el apetito 11 (*appetite*)
abrirse paso 215 (*to press*)
acabar por 84 (*to end*)
aceptarlo con los brazos cruzados 157 (*to lie*)
acercarse rodeando 51 (*to close*)
aclarar las cosas 271 (*straight*)
acostarse con las gallinas 22 (*bed*)
aficionarse a 282 (*taste*)
agarrar impulso 179 (*momentum*)
ahí será el diablo 70 (*devil*)
ahogar las penas 259 (*sorrow*)
ahora bien 191 (*now*)
ahora mismo 229 (*right*)
aires renovadores 46 (*change*)
ajustar cuentas 240 (*score*)
al aire libre 6 (*air*)
al alcance de la voz 41 (*call*)
al amanecer 65 (*dawn*)
al anochecer 187 (*night*)
al azar 222 (*random*)
al contrario 57 (*contrary*)
al cuidado de 42 (*care*)
al descubierto 197 (*open*)
al fiado 61 (*credit*)
al fin y al cabo 238 (*to say*)
al menos 154 (*least*)
al mismo tiempo 196 (*once*)
al oído 80 (*ear*)
al principio 99 (*first*)
Al que madruga. Dios le ayuda. 26 (*bird*)
al rayar el alba 65 (*dawn*)
al revés 318 (*way*)
al rojo (vivo) 225 (*red-hot*)
al romper el alba 60 (*crack*)
alcanzar para mucho 319 (*way*)
algo por el estilo 260 (*sort*)
alrededor de 196 (*on*)
alzar el vuelo 101 (*flight*)
alzarse en armas 12 (*arm*)
Allá él (ella, etc.) 39 (*business*)
Allá usted. 216 (*problem*)
¡Allá voy! 53 (*to come*)
andar a la greña con 194 (*odds*)
andar con rodeos 39 (*bush*)
andar de capa caída 155 (*leg*)
andar de prisa 138 (*hurry*)
andar en andrajos 221 (*rag*)
andar en quisquillas 120 (*hair*)
andar escaso de 247 (*short*)
andar por buen camino 300 (*track*)
andar por las ramas 39 (*bush*)
anque parezca mentira 23 (*to believe*)
ante todo 7 (*all*)
apaciguar los ánimos 316 (*water*)
apalear a alguien 21 (*to beat*)
aparte de 13 (*aside*)
aprender de memoria 130 (*heart*)
apuntar los tantos 239 (*score*)

apuntarse un tanto 212 (*point*)
aquí dentro 131 (*here*)
aquí mismo 131 (*here*)
armar camorra 106 (*fur*)
armar un alboroto 40 (*Cain*)
armar un escándalo 239 (*scene*)
armarse la grande 130 (*hell*)
armarse un bochinche 233 (*row*)
arrebatar a uno 102 (*foot*)
así así 257 (*so*)
así como 321 (*well*)
así de 288 (*this*)
así es 23 (*to believe*)
así y todo 85 (*even*)
asomarse a 10 (*to appear*)
Asunto terminado. 42 (*care*)
atacar a fondo 145 (*jugular*)
atajar por 64 (*to cut*)
atar cabos 306 (*two*)
Aunque la mona se vista de seda, mona se queda. 218 (*purse*)
avivar uno el seso 41 (*cap*)

B

bailarle el agua a 211 (*to play*)
bajarle los humos 189 (*notch*)
bajarle los humos a alguien 207 (*peg*)
bajo llave 163 (*lock*)
bajo ningún pretexto 1 (*account*)
¡Bien hecho! 115 (*good*)
boca abajo 89 (*face*)
boca arriba 89 (*face*)
brillar por su ausencia 56 (*conspicuous*)
buenos tiempos pasados 66 (*day*)
burlarse de 106 (*fun*)
buscarle tres pies al gato 302 (*trouble*)
buscárselas 36 (*to bring*)

C

cada cuánto (tiempo) 195 (*often*)
cada poco 323 (*while*)
cada vez más 180 (*more*)
caer de bruces 90 (*face*)
caer de plano 100 (*flat*)
caer de redondo 100 (*flat*)
caer en la cuenta 159 (*light*)
caerle bien 160 (*to like*)
caerse por su base 315 (*water*)
caérsele las alas 71 (*discouraged*)
cambiar de opinión 177 (*mind*)
cambiar opiniones 190 (*note*)
capear el temporal 270 (*storm*)
cara a cara 89 (*eyeball*)
cara mitad 120 (*half*)
castillo de naipes 42 (*card*)
causa de todos los males 86 (*evil*)
cavar uno su propia tumba 184 (*nail*)
cerrar el paso 318 (*way*)
cerrarle la puerta en las narices 74 (*door*)
cifrar sus esperanzas en 135 (*hope*)
cobro revertido 46 (*charge*)
cocer en su propia salsa 145 (*juice*)
codearse con 233 (*to rub*)
como alma que lleva el diablo 19 (*bat*)
como caído de las nubes 29 (*blue*)
como de costumbre 309 (*usual*)
como lo quiso la suerte 167 (*luck*)
como nadie 53 (*come*)
cómo no 59 (*course*)
como quien dice 126 (*to have*)

como si esto fuera poco 142 (*insult*)
comprar a ciegas 208 (*pig*)
comprar regalado 259 (*song*)
con arreglo a 1 (*according*)
con el propósito de 310 (*view*)
con el sombrero en la mano 125 (*hat*)
con el transcurso del tiempo 59 (*course*)
con las manos en la masa 3 (*act*)
con miras a 310 (*view*)
con motivo de 194 (*occasion*)
con mucho 93 (*far*)
con pulso firme 123 (*hand*)
con todo 85 (*even*)
concertar un acuerdo 284 (*term*)
conciliar el sueño 13 (*asleep*)
conformarse con 244 (*to settle*)
confundir con 179 (*mistake*)
conocer a fondo 31 (*book*)
conocerle el juego 20 (*to be*)
consultarlo con la almohada 254 (*to sleep*)
contar con 59 (*to count*)
contra viento y marea 130 (*hell*)
conversaciones de alcoba 281 (*talk*)
corrientes de opinión 288 (*thought*)
cortar de raíz 38 (*bud*)
cortarle las alas 325 (*wing*)
cosa de niños 33 (*boy*)
costar trabajo 124 (*hard*)
costarle un dineral 207 (*penny*)
costarle un ojo de la cara 189 (*nose*)
crisparle los nervios 186 (*nerve*)
Cuando el río suena, agua lleva. 256 (*smoke*)
cuando más 181 (*most*)
cuando menos 154 (*least*)
cuando menos se piense 87 (*expected*)
cuanto antes 213 (*possible*)
cuanto más . . . (tanto) más . . . 181 (*more*)
cuánto tiempo 163 (*long*)
cuentos de viejas 281 (*tale*)
cueste lo que cueste 59 (*cost*)
¡Cuidado! 315 (*to watch*)
cuidado con . . . 43 (*careful*)
cuidar a cuerpo de rey 123 (*hand*)

D

dadas las circunstancias 49 (*circumstance*)
dar a 90 (*to face*)
dar a conocer 171 (*map*)
dar a entender 111 (*to give*)
dar alcance 44 (*to catch*)
dar cabezadas 188 (*to nod*)
dar cuenta de 226 (*to report*)
dar de baja 183 (*to muster*)
dar el pésame 277 (*sympathy*)
dar en el clavo 184 (*nail*)
dar fin a 83 (*end*)
dar guerra 302 (*trouble*)
dar la mano a 123 (*hand*)
dar la razón a 2 (*to acknowledge*)
dar lugar a 230 (*rise*)
dar nueva vida 158 (*life*)
dar origen a 230 (*rise*)
dar palmadas 122 (*hand*)
dar principio a 242 (*seed*)
dar principio con 198 (*to open*)
dar que pensar 102 (*food*)
dar rienda suelta a 226 (*rein*)
dar un paseo 313 (*walk*)
dar un paseo (en coche) 228 (*ride*)
dar un paso 268 (*to step*)
dar un portazo 74 (*door*)

dar un vistazo 196 (*once-over*)
dar una vuelta 304 (*to turn*)
dar vueltas 298 (*to toss*)
darle con la puerta en las narices 74 (*door*)
darle escalofríos 61 (*creeps*)
darle lo suyo 69 (*desert*)
darle por 280 (*to take*)
darle rabia 168 (*mad*)
darse buena vida 162 (*to live*)
darse la gran vida 133 (*hog*)
darse por aludido 132 (*hint*)
darse por vencido 110 (*to give*)
darse tono 6 (*air*)
de . . . en . . . 105 (*from*)
de acuerdo con 1 (*according*)
de algún modo 317 (*way*)
de aquí en adelante 191 (*now*)
de arriba abajo 297 (*top*)
de balde 104 (*free*)
de beuna fe 91 (*faith*)
de cabeza 128 (*head*)
de cerca 222 (*range*)
de cuando en cuando 292 (*time*)
de dos en dos 306 (*two*)
de golpe 274 (*sudden*)
de la noche a la mañana 187 (*night*)
de lo peor 330 (*worst*)
de mala fe 91 (*faith*)
De noche todos los gatos son pardos. 44 (*cat*)
de momento 179 (*moment*)
De nada 321 (*welcome*)
de ningún modo 49 (*circumstance*)
de ninguna manera 174 (*means*)
de noche 187 (*night*)
de oído 80 (*ear*)
de palabra 327 (*word*)
de pies a cabeza 289 (*through*)
de pies a cabeza 295 (*tip*)
de pronto 7 (*all*)
de punta en blanco 225 (*regalia*)
de puntillas 295 (*tiptoe*)
de repente 274 (*sudden*)
de sobra 200 (*over*)
De tal palo, tal astilla. 48 (*chip*)
de todas formas 43 (*case*)
de todas maneras 85 (*event*)
de todos modos 222 (*rate*)
de un extremo a otro 314 (*wall*)
de un momento a otro 291 (*time*)
de un plumazo 273 (*stroke*)
de un salto 100 (*flash*)
de una vez 72 (*to do*)
de una vez por todas 196 (*once*)
de uno en uno 197 (*one*)
de vez en cuando 292 (*time*)
decir mil bienes de 261 (*to speak*)
decirle cuántas son cinco 208 (*piece*)
decirle que se vaya a freír espárragos 166 (*to lose*)
decirlo por uno mismo 261 (*to speak*)
defenderse bien 108 (*to get*)
dejar cesante 153 (*to lay*)
dejar colgado 52 (*cold*)
dejar con la carga en las costillas 16 (*bag*)
dejar en paz 156 (*to let*)
dejar en paz 9 (*alone*)
dejar huella 140 (*impression*)
dejar recado 328 (*word*)
dejarle boquiabierto 35 (*breath*)
Del agua mansa me libre Dios, que de la brava me libro yo. 315 (*water*)
delante de las narices 188 (*nose*)
delgado como un junco 225 (*reed*)
depender de 69 (*to depend*)

desde luego 59 (*course*)
desde el punto de vista de 284 (*in terms of*)
desde un principio 9 (*along*)
¿Desea alguien? 10 (*anyone*)
deshacerse de 228 (*to rid*)
deshacerse en lágrimas 34 (*to break*)
despedir con cajas destempladas 202 (*to pack*)
despedirse de 154 (*leave*)
Dicho y hecho. 259 (*sooner*)
Díos los cría y ellos se juntan. 26 (*bird*)
distar mucho de ser 62 (*cry*)
doblar la cabeza 110 (*to give*)
Donde comen seis comen siete. 232 (*room*)
Donde fueres, haz lo que vieres. 231 (*Rome*)
donde las dan las toman 285 (*that*)
dorar la píldora 209 (*pill*)
dormir a pierna suelta 163 (*log*)
dormir la mona 254 (*to sleep*)
dormir la siesta 185 (*nap*)
dormirse sobre sus laureles 152 (*laurel*)
dos a dos 306 (*two*)
dudoso bien 28 (*blessing*)

E

echar aceite al fuego 105 (*fuel*)
echar chispas 135 (*to hop*)
echar la casa por la ventana 113 (*to go*)
echar la vista encima 88 (*eye*)
echar leña al fuego 195 (*oil*)
echar margaritas a los cerdos 206 (*pearl*)
echar raíces 232 (*root*)
echar tierra al escándalo 139 (*to hush*)
echar una mano 123 (*hand*)
echar una ojeada a 223 (*to read*)
echar una siesta 185 (*nap*)
echarle la culpa a 27 (*blame*)
echarse encima 280 (*to take*)
echárselas de 30 (*to boast*)
echárselo en la cara 289 (*to throw*)
ejecutar en fases 207 (*to phase*)
el alma de la fiesta 158 (*life*)
el bello sexo 244 (*sex*)
el día menos pensado 87 (*expected*)
El ejercicio hace maestro al novicio. 207 (*perfect*)
el séptimo cielo 51 (*cloud*)
empeñarse en 24 (*bent*)
empezar la casa por el tejado 43 (*cart*)
en absoluto 8 (*all*)
en algún tiempo 291 (*time*)
en alta mar 240 (*sea*)
En boca cerrada no entran moscas. 252 (*silence*)
en broma 144 (*joke*)
en cambio 121 (*hand*)
en caso contrario 189 (*not*)
en cierto modo 317 (*way*)
en confianza 224 (*record*)
en contra de 198 (*opposition*)
en cuanto a 12 (*as*)
en cuanto sea posible 213 (*possible*)
en cueros 18 (*bare*)
en demasía 87 (*excess*)
en efecto 172 (*matter*)
en el acto 262 (*spot*)
en el fondo 75 (*down*)
en el mejor de los casos 24 (*best*)

en el momento actual 214 (*present*)
en el peor de los casos 330 (*worst*)
en el quinto infierno 83 (*end*)
en especial 203 (*particular*)
en fecha próxima 65 (*date*)
en fila india 97 (*file*)
en flagrante 3 (*act*)
en gran parte 88 (*extent*)
en grande 238 (*scale*)
en igualdad de circunstancias 285 (*thing*)
en la actualidad 291 (*time*)
en la cara 90 (*face*)
en la flor de la vida (de edad) 215 (*prime*)
en lo más mínimo 154 (*least*)
en lo posible 213 (*possible*)
en lo que va de 93 (*far*)
en mangas de camisa 254 (*sleeve*)
en masa 103 (*force*)
en medio de 176 (*middle*)
en nombre de 22 (*behalf*)
en números redondos 192 (*number*)
en obras 56 (*construction*)
en pie 82 (*effect*)
en pleno día 67 (*daylight*)
en primer lugar 210 (*place*)
en privado 263 (*stage*)
en puntillas 295 (*tiptoe*)
en punto 75 (*dot*)
¿En qué estás pensando? 288 (*thought*)
en regla 199 (*order*)
en resumidas cuentas 271 (*story*)
en seguida 196 (*once*)
en su vida 158 (*life*)
en tanto a eso 239 (*score*)
en todas partes 8 (*all*)
en todo caso 85 (*event*)
en total 8 (*all*)
en último caso 227 (*resort*)
en un abrir y cerrar de ojos 292 (*time*)
en un dos por tres 143 (*jiffy*)
en un principio 99 (*first*)
en un santiamén 306 (*twinkling*)
en uno u otro caso 316 (*way*)
en vigor 82 (*effect*)
en virtud de 310 (*virtue*)
en voz baja 311 (*voice*)
enamorarse de 92 (*to fall*)
encargarse de 241 (*to see*)
encogerse de hombros 248 (*shoulder*)
encontrarse entre la espada y la pared 15 (*back*)
engreído como un pavo real 206 (*peacock*)
entenderse bien 132 (*to hit*)
enterarse de 97 (*to find*)
entiendo que 139 (*I*)
entrar de sopetón 213 (*to pop*)
entrar en razón 243 (*sense*)
entrar en vigor 82 (*effect*)
entre bastidores 239 (*scene*)
entre la espada y la pared 70 (*devil*)
entregar el alma 110 (*ghost*)
érase una vez 293 (*time*)
escoger uno a su gusto 207 (*pick*)
Es como buscar una aguja en un pajar. 186 (*needle*)
es decir 238 (*to say*)
¡Es el colmo! 271 (*straw*)
Es igual. 70 (*difference*)
Eso es cosa suya. 216 (*problem*)
Eso es harina de otro costal. 136 (*horse*)
Eso es lo de menos. 154 (*least*)

Eso es. 229 (*right*)
¡Eso ni pensarlo! 220 (*question*)
eso sí 281 (*talk*)
Eso sí. 141 (*indeed*)
Eso sí que no. 141 (*indeed*)
esperar la entrada en escena 326 (*wing*)
estar a cargo 46 (*charge*)
estar a la altura de 84 (*equal*)
estar a la mira 165 (*lookout*)
estar a la mira de 315 (*watch*)
estar a mano 157 (*to lie*)
estar abatido 76 (*downcast*)
estar a punto de 1 (*about*)
estar a salvo 236 (*safe*)
estar a su alcance 223 (*reach*)
estar a tiro 222 (*range*)
estar a un paso de 267 (*step*)
estar agotado 215 (*print*)
estar agotado 242 (*to sell*)
estar agotado 320 (*to wear*)
estar al acecho 157 (*to lie*)
estar al acecho 312 (*wait*)
estar al borde de 309 (*verge*)
estar al corriente 65 (*date*)
estar al corriente de 141 (*informed*)
estar al día 293 (*time*)
estar al frente 46 (*charge*)
estar al sol 275 (*sun*)
estar al tanto 65 (*date*)
estar al tanto de 15 (*aware*)
estar bajo sospecha 51 (*cloud*)
estar de buen humor 180 (*mood*)
estar de mal humor 180 (*mood*)
estar de moda 140 (*in*)
estar de servicio 79 (*duty*)
estar de turno 79 (*duty*)
estar de vuelta 15 (*back*)
estar en ascuas 209 (*pin*)
estar en blanco 27 (*blank*)
estar en buenas relaciones 284 (*term*)
estar en desorden 175 (*mess*)
estar en el caso de 193 (*obligated*)
estar en juego 263 (*stake*)
estar en la misma altura 222 (*to range*)
estar en las últimas 155 (*leg*)
estar en lo firme 118 (*ground*)
estar en los huesos 253 (*skin*)
estar en marcha 182 (*move*)
estar en perspectiva 195 (*offing*)
estar en plena actividad 276 (*swing*)
estar en su juicio 177 (*mind*)
estar en su pellejo 247 (*shoe*)
estar en sus cabales 177 (*mind*)
estar en vena (para) 180 (*mood*)
estar en vigor 104 (*force*)
estar en vísperas de 85 (*eve*)
estar fuera de sí 24 (*beside*)
estar fuera de su alcance 223 (*reach*)
estar hasta la coronilla de 95 (*fed*)
estar hecho a la medida 199 (*order*)
estar hecho una sopa 322 (*wet*)
estar libre de palabra 203 (*parole*)
estar mojado hasta los huesos 253 (*skin*)
estar muy de moda 9 (*all*)
estar muy entrado en años 332 (*year*)
estar otra vez con las mismas 19 (*to be*)
estar para 1 (*about*)
estar que arde 128 (*head*)
estar rendido 9 (*all*)
estar sin aliento 35 (*breath*)

estar sin blanca 34 (*to break*)
estar sobre aviso 119 (*guard*)
estar todo muy bien pero . . . 322 (*well*)
estirar la pata 38 (*bucket*)
estrechar la mano a 123 (*hand*)
estrechar manos 101 (*flesh*)
estrellarse contra 21 (*to beat*)

F

faltar a 91 (*to fail*)
faltar a clase 63 (*to cut*)
forma de proceder 3 (*action*)
forrarse el riñón 186 (*nest*)
freír en su aceite 145 (*juice*)
frente a 2 (*across*)
frente a frente 89 (*face*)
frisar en los . . . años 51 (*close*)
fruncir el ceño 37 (*brow*)
fruncir el entrecejo 105 (*to frown*)
fuera de los límites 202 (*pale*)

G

ganarle la acción 145 (*jump*)
ganarse la vida 162 (*living*)
Genio y figura hasta la sepultura. 156 (*leopard*)
gozar del favor 31 (*book*)
guardar cama 22 (*bed*)
guardar rencor 118 (*grudge*)
guardar silencio 252 (*silent*)
gustarle más 160 (*to like*)

H

haber agotado todos los recursos 18 (*barrel*)
haber perdido el juicio 327 (*wit*)
hablar hasta por los codos 80 (*ear*)
hablar por sí mismo 261 (*to speak*)
hace poco 291 (*time*)
hacer acto de presencia 11 (*appearance*)
hacer acto de presencia 100 (*flag*)
hacer alarde de 249 (*show*)
hacer añicos 208 (*piece*)
hacer calor 137 (*hot*)
hacer caso 130 (*heed*)
hacer cola 161 (*line*)
hacer de la necesidad virtud 185 (*necessity*)
hacer dinero rápidamente 37 (*buck*)
hacer el papel 231 (*role*)
hacer el ridículo 102 (*fool*)
hacer el tonto 102 (*fool*)
hacer escala 270 (*to stop*)
hacer frío 52 (*cold*)
hacer furor 221 (*rage*)
hacer honor a su fama 226 (*reputation*)
hacer juego con 115 (*to go*)
hacer la vista gorda 89 (*eye*)
hacer las maletas 202 (*to pack*)
hacer las paces 206 (*peace*)
hacer las paces con 170 (*to make*)
hacer las veces de 3 (*to act*)
hacer lo posible 24 (*best*)
hacer pasar por control 47 (*to check*)
hacer su agosto 148 (*killing*)
hacer una mueca 90 (*face*)
hacer una pregunta 220 (*question*)
hacer uno lo suyo 287 (*thing*)
hacerle compañía 55 (*company*)
hacerle daño 139 (*to hurt*)
hacerle quedar bien 61 (*credit*)

hacerle tragar saliva 62 (*crow*)
hacerse de rogar 124 (*hard*)
hacerse el muerto 67 (*dead*)
hacerse el santo 236 (*saintly*)
hacerse el sordo 80 (*ear*)
hacerse el tonto 211 (*to play*)
hacerse entender 306 (*to understand*)
hacérsele agua la boca 181 (*mouth*)
hacérsele tarde 151 (*late*)
hágame caso 278 (*to take*)
hallar la horma de su zapato 172 (*match*)
hasta cierto punto 69 (*degree*)
hasta cierto punto 81 (*extent*)
hasta el día del juicio 131 (*hell*)
hasta la médula 58 (*core*)
hasta la muerte 84 (*end*)
hasta las altas horas de la noche 93 (*far*)
hasta los ojos 81 (*ear*)
hasta quemar el último cartucho 72 (*ditch*)
hasta tal punto 257 (*so*)
Hay muchos modos de matar pulgas. 44 (*cat*)
hecho un vinagre 296 (*tone*)
herir en lo vivo 220 (*quick*)
historia de siempre 259 (*song*)
holgar decir 238 (*to say*)
¡Hombre al agua! 170 (*man*)
hoy mismo 66 (*day*)
huir de alguien como de la peste 210 (*plague*)
Huir del fuego y caer en las brasas. 202 (*pan*)
humo de pajas 100 (*flash*)

I

igual que 145 (*just*)
imperio de la ley 152 (*law*)
intento al azar 248 (*shot*)
interesarse por 142 (*interest*)
interpretar mal a alguien 331 (*wrong*)
ir a medias 96 (*fifty*)
ir al grano 212 (*point*)
ir con destino 32 (*bound*)
ir de capa caída 76 (*downhill*)
ir de compras 247 (*shop*)
ir de juerga 26 (*binge*)
ir de tiendas 247 (*shop*)
ir en pos de 218 (*pursuit*)
ir por cuenta de la casa 137 (*house*)
ir por mal camino 115 (*to go*)
ir rumbo a 32 (*bound*)
ir sobre ruedas 235 (*to run*)
ir tirando 109 (*to get*)
ir tras de 112 (*to go*)
irlo pasando 108 (*to get*)
irse cada uno por su lado 319 (*way*)
irse de juerga 263 (*spree*)
írsele de entre las manos 255 (*to slip*)
írsele demasiado la lengua 182 (*mouth*)

J

juego limpio 210 (*play*)
jugarle una mala pasada 301 (*trick*)
jugarlo todo a una carta 82 (*egg*)
jugarse el todo por el todo 114 (*to go*)
junto a 187 (*next*)
justicia divina 146 (*justice*)
justo a tiempo 259 (*soon*)
justo medio 173 (*mean*)
juzgar a la ligera 56 (*conclusion*)

L

La confianza hace perder el respeto. 57 (*contempt*)
la manzana de la discordia 30 (*bone*)
la mar de 83 (*end*)
la mayor parte de 181 (*most*)
la niña de sus ojos 11 (*apple*)
la oveja negra de la familia 246 (*sheep*)
la parte del león 246 (*share*)
la prueba irrefutable 119 (*gun*)
la recta final 272 (*stretch*)
La suerte está echada. 48 (*chip*)
lanzar una indirecta 132 (*hint*)
¡Largo de aquí! 199 (*out*)
las altas esferas 210 (*place*)
Las apariencias engañan. 21 (*beauty*)
Le da la mano y se toma el brazo (pie). 140 (*inch*)
levantarse por los pies de la cama 250 (*side*)
limpio como una patena 261 (*spic-and-span*)
llamar a filas 53 (*color*)
llamar al pan, pan y al vino, vino 260 (*spade*)
llamar la atención 56 (*conspicuous*)
llamarle la atención (sobre) 14 (*attention*)
llegar a las manos 29 (*blow*)
llegar a su punto cumbre 206 (*peak*)
llegar a una inteligencia 223 (*to reach*)
llegar tarde 151 (*late*)
llevar a cabo 43 (*to carry*)
llevar a la novia al altar 36 (*bride*)
llevar adelante 6 (*ahead*)
llevar de paseo (en coche) 228 (*ride*)
llevar el compás 294 (*time*)
llevar el nombre de 185 (*to name*)
llevar encima 196 (*on*)
llevar la voz cantante 249 (*show*)
llevar una ventaja 4 (*advantage*)
llevar una vida . . . 158 (*life*)
llevarle la ventaja 81 (*edge*)
llevarse a rastras 76 (*to drag*)
llevarse bien con 108 (*to get*)
llorar a mares 88 (*eye*)
llorar lágrimas de cocodrilo 283 (*tear*)
llover a cántaros 44 (*cat*)
lo antes posible 213 (*possible*)
Lo dije sin mala intención. 195 (*offense*)
lo más pronto posible 213 (*possible*)
lo mejor de lo mejor 61 (*crop*)
lo mismo . . . que . . . 32 (*both*)
Lo mismo da. 8 (*all*)
lo mismo que 145 (*just*)
lo pasado, olvidado 40 (*bygone*)
lo que es 12 (*as*)
lo que más se acerca a 286 (*thing*)
lo que se estila 107 (*game*)

M

mala pata 167 (*luck*)
mano derecha 104 (*Friday*)
¡Manos arriba! 268 (*to stick*)
mantener el rumbo 60 (*course*)
mantenerse firme 133 (*to hold*)
marido y mujer 170 (*man*)
más allá 93 (*farther*)
más allá de 250 (*side*)
más ciego que un topo 19 (*bat*)

más feo que una araña 252 (*sin*)
más vale así 321 (*well*)
Más vale prevenir que curar. 259 (*sorry*)
Más vale tarde que nunca. 25 (*better*)
matar a palos 68 (*death*)
matar dos pájaros de un tiro 26 (*bird*)
matrimonio a la fuerza 172 (*marriage*)
me creerás que . . . 162 (*lo*)
medios de difusión 174 (*media*)
medios y arbitrios 320 (*way*)
mejor que mejor 8 (*all*)
mejor que nunca 86 (*ever*)
menear la cabeza 245 (*to shake*)
mentira piadosa 157 (*lie*)
merecer la pena 311 (*worth*)
meter la pata 103 (*foot*)
meter su cuchara 192 (*oar*)
meterse en gastos 87 (*expense*)
meterse en un lío 175 (*mess*)
metérsele en la cabeza 129 (*head*)
mientras más . . . más . . . 181 (*more*)
mirar de hito en hito 266 (*to stare*)
mirar de reojo 58 (*corner*)
modo de vida 158 (*life*)
moratoria fiscal 134 (*holiday*)
morder el polvo 79 (*dust*)
morderse la lengua 297 (*tongue*)
morir al pie del cañón 31 (*boot*)
morir en la hoguera 263 (*stake*)
morir vestido 31 (*boot*)
mostrarse a la altura de las circunstancias 194 (*occasion*)
mover cielo y tierra 269 (*stone*)
Mucho ruido y pocas nueces. 4 (*ado*)
mucho tiempo 291 (*time*)
muerto de envidia 84 (*envy*)
¡Muy bien! 229 (*right*)
muy de tarde en tarde 180 (*moon*)
muy entrada la mañana 151 (*late*)

N

nada de eso 148 (*kind*)
nadar en la abundancia 94 (*fat*)
nadie como él 86 (*ever*)
naturaleza muerta 158 (*life*)
ni a tiros 167 (*love*)
ni aunque me maten 67 (*dead*)
¡Ni con mucho! 93 (*far*)
¡Ni hablar! 175 (*to mention*)
ni lo uno ni lo otro 99 (*fish*)
¡Ni mucho menos! 93 (*far*)
ni pizca 27 (*bit*)
ni siquiera 85 (*even*)
ni soñarlo 73 (*to do*)
no . . . alma nacida 260 (*soul*)
no bien 259 (*sooner*)
no caer en la cuenta 212 (*point*)
no concederle importancia 190 (*nothing*)
no dejar piedra por mover 161 (*limit*)
no descartar ninguna posibilidad 198 (*option*)
no despegar los labios 328 (*word*)
no entender ni papa (jota) 286 (*thing*)
no es de extrañar 327 (*wonder*)
No es para tanto. 106 (*fuss*)
¡No faltaba más! 271 (*straw*)
No hay de qué. 321 (*welcome*)

No hay mal que por bien no venga. 51 (*cloud*)
no hay modo de saber 238 (*to say*)
¡No hay pero que valga! 40 (*but*)
No hay que darle vueltas. 318 (*way*)
No hay remedio. 131 (*to help*)
¡No me digas! 147 (*to kid*)
¡No me digas! 238 (*to say*)
no merecer la pena 190 (*nothing*)
no meterse en lo que no le toca 39 (*business*)
no obstante 8 (*all*)
no pegar ojo 326 (*wink*)
no pintar nada 140 (*ice*)
no poder más 112 (*to go*)
no poder menos de 131 (*to help*)
no saber por dónde empezar 228 (*riches*)
no se moleste 186 (*never*)
no sé qué . . . 258 (*some*)
no ser cualquier cosa 256 (*to sneeze*)
no ser nada del otro mundo 245 (*shake*)
no servir de (para) nada 308 (*use*)
No te hagas ilusiones de . . . 140 (*idea*)
no tener donde caerse muerto 75 (*down*)
no tener nada que ver con 190 (*nothing*)
no tener pelo de tonto 102 (*fool*)
no tenía idea 187 (*news*)
No tiene más remedio. 131 (*to help*)
¡No tocar! 121 (*hand*)
no venir al caso 131 (*here*)
no ver ningún inconveniente 193 (*objection*)
No viene al caso. 211 (*point*)

O

¿...o qué? 258 (*something*)
o si no ya verás 83 (*else*)
obedecer a 11 (*to arise*)
olerle mal el asunto 222 (*rat*)
ojalá que así fuera 20 (*to be*)
órganos de información 174 (*media*)
oscurantismo medioeval 5 (*age*)

P

pagar a plazos 141 (*installment*)
pagar al contado 44 (*cash*)
pagar en la misma moneda 109 (*to get*)
pagar los vidrios rotos 239 (*scapegoat*)
palmo a palmo 140 (*inch*)
para entonces 292 (*time*)
para los tontos 26 (*bird*)
para mayor seguridad 236 (*safe*)
para no ser menos 200 (*to outdo*)
para resumir 275 (*to sum*)
para siempre 115 (*good*)
parar en seco 303 (*turkey*)
pararse en pelillos 120 (*hair*)
parecerse a 165 (*to look*)
partir(se) la diferencia con 174 (*to meet*)
pasar como una flecha 324 (*to whiz*)
pasar de largo 204 (*to pass*)
pasar de moda 94 (*fashion*)
pasar las mocedades 193 (*oats*)
pasar por 88 (*expose*)
pasar por 204 (*to pass*)
pasar sin 73 (*to do*)

pasarlas muy duras 232 (*rough*)
pasarlo bien 84 (*to enjoy*)
pasarlo en grande 17 (*ball*)
pasarse de listo 120 (*half*)
pasarse sin 108 (*to get*)
pase lo que pase 48 (*chip*)
paso a paso 69 (*degree*)
paso a paso 267 (*step*)
pedir la palabra 101 (*floor*)
pegar fuego a 98 (*fire*)
pensándolo bien 288 (*thought*)
pensión completa 231 (*room*)
peor para ti 166 (*loss*)
peor que peor 8 (*all*)
perder el juicio 155 (*leave*)
perder la ocasión 45 (*chance*)
perder la razón 141 (*insane*)
perder los estribos 128 (*head*)
perder tiempo 295 (*time*)
persuadir engañosamente 55 (*to con*)
peso de la ley 12 (*arm*)
pintor clásico 172 (*master*)
pisarle los tacones 130 (*heel*)
plantear un asunto 274 (*subject*)
poner a prueba 284 (*test*)
poner a un lado 153 (*to lay*)
poner a un lado 243 (*to set*)
poner al corriente de 65 (*date*)
poner al descubierto 18 (*bare*)
poner atención 14 (*attention*)
poner el dedo en la llaga 262 (*spot*)
poner el grito en el cielo 45 (*ceiling*)
poner en claro 50 (*to clear*)
poner en duda 75 (*doubt*)
poner en libertad 104 (*free*)
poner en ridículo 228 (*ridiculous*)
poner en su punto 244 (*to set*)
poner la mano encima 98 (*finger*)
poner la mesa 278 (*table*)
poner las cartas boca arriba 42 (*card*)
poner las cartas sobre la mesa 42 (*card*)
poner los pies en 103 (*foot*)
poner manos a la obra 71 (*to dig*)
poner pies en polvorosa 130 (*heel*)
poner sobre las nubes 253 (*sky*)
poner un huevo 82 (*egg*)
ponerle en ridículo 102 (*fool*)
ponerle los pelos de punta 120 (*hair*)
ponerse de moda 94 (*fashionable*)
ponerse de pie 265 (*to stand*)
ponerse en camino 244 (*to set*)
ponerse en contacto 298 (*touch*)
ponerse en fila 161 (*to line*)
ponerse en marcha 109 (*to get*)
ponerse las botas 214 (*pot*)
ponerse por las nubes 253 (*sky*)
por ahí 285 (*there*)
por algo 190 (*nothing*)
por allá 200 (*over*)
por casualidad 1 (*accident*)
por casualidad 45 (*chance*)
por completo 163 (*lock*)
por conducto reglamentario 46 (*channel*)
por consideración a 56 (*consideration*)
por decirlo así 238 (*to say*)
por decirlo así 260 (*to speak*)
por demás 14 (*at*)
por escrito 331 (*writing*)
por el menor motivo 125 (*hat*)

por encima de 200 (*over*)
por eso 324 (*why*)
por extraño que parezca 194 (*odds*)
por fas o por nefas 135 (*hook*)
por fin 151 (*last*)
por ganas de 237 (*sake*)
por gusto 106 (*fun*)
por las buenas y las malas 285 (*thick*)
por lo menos 66 (*day*)
por lo menos 154 (*least*)
por lo que a mí me toca 55 (*to concern*)
por los pelos 253 (*skin*)
por más . . . que 172 (*matter*)
por motivo de 2 (*account*)
por nada del mundo 330 (*world*)
por poder 217 (*proxy*)
por regla general 151 (*large*)
por regla general 233 (*rule*)
por rumores 117 (*grapevine*)
por si acaso 43 (*case*)
por si las moscas 43 (*case*)
por supuesto 59 (*course*)
por supuesto 176 (*mind*)
por término medio 15 (*average*)
por todas partes 200 (*over*)
por vuelta de correo 168 (*mail*)
preguntar por 141 (*to inquire*)
prender fuego a 98 (*fire*)
prescindir de 72 (*to dispense*)
prestar atención 14 (*attention*)
prestar juramento 193 (*oath*)
prestar juramento 276 (*to swear*)
probar fortuna 167 (*luck*)
proceder sin miramientos 94 (*fast*)
proyectar la imagen esperada 203 (*part*)
prueba decisiva 284 (*test*)
Puede que sí (no). 173 (*maybe*)
punto medio 173 (*mean*)

Q

qué diablos 131 (*hell*)
qué ha sido de 22 (*to become*)
qué le parece. . . 160 (*to like*)
Que le vaya bien. 167 (*luck*)
¿Qué más da? 324 (*who*)
¿Qué más quieres? 86 (*ever*)
¿Qué mosca le ha picado? 110 (*to get*)
qué se ha hecho 22 (*to become*)
¡Qué tiempos aquellos! 66 (*day*)
quedar agradecido 193 (*to oblige*)
quedar lucido 53 (*color*)
quedarse con el día y la noche 207 (*penniless*)
quedarse con la carga en las costillas 236 (*sack*)
querer decir 77 (*to drive*)
Querer es poder. 325 (*will*)
Quien calla otorga. 252 (*silence*)
quitarle un peso de encima 163 (*load*)
quitarse algo de encima 277 (*system*)
quitarse de en medio 319 (*way*)

R

rebosar de felicidad 7 (*air*)
recibirlo a cuerpo de rey 301 (*treatment*)
refugio fiscal 127 (*haven*)
reírse de 152 (*to laugh*)
representar su papel 231 (*role*)
respecto a 227 (*respect*)
restar importancia 213 (*to pooh-pooh*)

romper a reír (llorar) 38 (*to burst*)
romper el hielo 140 (*ice*)

S

saber a 283 (*to taste*)
saber a ciencia cierta 91 (*fact*)
saber a qué atenerse 264 (*to stand*)
saber al dedillo 295 (*tip*)
saber cuántas son cinco 322 (*what*)
saber de memoria 129 (*heart*)
saber de qué pie cojea 192 (*number*)
saber de sobra 322 (*well*)
sacar (a alguien) del apuro 135 (*hook*)
sacar a relucir 37 (*to bring*)
sacar a uno de sus casillas 218 (*to put*)
sacar del aislamiento 52 (*cold*)
sacar el pecho 48 (*chest*)
sacar en claro 50 (*clear*)
sacar provecho de 216 (*to profit*)
sacar punta a un lápiz 207 (*pencil*)
sacar una foto 208 (*picture*)
sacarle de sus casillas 78 (*to drive*)
sacarle las castañas del fuego 48 (*chestnut*)
salir de viaje 301 (*trip*)
salir ganando 54 (*to come*)
salirse con la suya 319 (*way*)
salvar las apariencias 90 (*face*)
salvarse por los pelos 41 (*call*)
sano y salvo 236 (*safe*)
se comprende 97 (*to figure*)
sea como fuere 19 (*to be*)
sea como sea 172 (*matter*)
sea lo que sea 323 (*whatever*)
seguir adelante 112 (*to go*)
seguir algo al pie de la letra 31 (*book*)
seguir su curso 60 (*course*)
Según y conforme. 69 (*to depend*)
sentar la cabeza 244 (*to settle*)
ser aficionado a 92 (*fan*)
ser conocido por 113 (*to go*)
ser cosa de coser y cantar 76 (*downhill*)
ser de encargo 199 (*order*)
ser de la pasta de 279 (*to take*)
ser de su agrado 160 (*liking*)
ser difícil de tratar 124 (*hard*)
ser el blanco de algo 83 (*end*)
ser el hombre indicado 170 (*man*)
ser el ojo derecho de. . . 64 (*darling*)
ser gallina 48 (*chicken*)
ser hora de 293 (*time*)
ser lobos de una misma camada 37 (*brush*)
ser mal pensado 177 (*mind*)
ser más bueno que el pan 115 (*gold*)
ser mayor de edad 5 (*age*)
ser muy ligero de palabra 282 (*talker*)
ser para tanto 285 (*that*)
ser sólo un decir 171 (*manner*)
ser tal para cual 148 (*kind*)
ser un buen partido 44 (*catch*)
ser un caso de fuerza mayor 3 (*act*)
ser un cero a la izquierda 188 (*no*)
ser un pez gordo 248 (*shot*)
ser una desgracia para 136 (*hopeless*)

ser uña y carne 121 (*hand*)
¿Será verdad tanta belleza? 302 (*true*)
si hubiera uno 10 (*any*)
si mal no recuerdo 175 (*memory*)
Siempre llueve sobre mojado. 221 (*to rain*)
sin duda 75 (*doubt*)
sin efecto 192 (*null*)
sin más ni más 4 (*ado*)
sin más vueltas 220 (*question*)
sin pestañear 89 (*eye*)
sin rodeos 328 (*word*)
sin ton ni son 227 (*rhyme*)
sin tregua 157 (*to let*)
situación imperante 5 (*affair*)
Sobre gustos no hay nada escrito. 21 (*beauty*)
sobre gustos no hay nada escrito 201 (*own*)
sobre todo 7 (*all*)
sonarle (a algo conocido) 23 (*bell*)
su media naranja 25 (*better*)
subírsele a la cabeza 128 (*head*)
superar una etapa 58 (*corner*)

T

tan claro como el agua 66 (*day*)
tantear el terreno 150 (*land*)
tanto . . . como . . . 32 (*both*)
tanto es así 257 (*so*)
tanto lo bueno como lo malo 9 (*all*)
tanto mejor 8 (*all*)
tanto peor 8 (*all*)
tarde o temprano 259 (*sooner*)
tener . . . años 196 (*old*)
tener a bien 99 (*fit*)
tener a menos 23 (*beneath*)
tener a raya 19 (*bay*)
tener a raya 47 (*to check*)
tener al corriente 214 (*posted*)
tener algo de 258 (*something*)
tener algo de . . . 258 (*something*)
tener algo tramado 254 (*sleeve*)
tener amplio criterio 176 (*mind*)
tener buen aspecto 165 (*to look*)
tener buena cara 165 (*to look*)
tener calor 314 (*warm*)
tener cara de enfado 168 (*mad*)
tener carta blanca 122 (*hand*)
tener corazón de piedra 124 (*hard-hearted*)
tener cuidado con 315 (*to watch*)
tener de todo 189 (*not*)
tener delante sí 126 (*to have*)
tener derecho a 229 (*right*)
tener el corazón en la mano 129 (*heart*)
tener el corazón en un puño 129 (*heart*)
tener el papel principal 153 (*lead*)
tener en cuenta 2 (*account*)
tener en existencia 269 (*stock*)
tener en la punta de la lengua 295 (*tip*)
tener en su poder 122 (*hand*)
tener entre algodones 111 (*glove*)
tener éxito 169 (*to make*)
tener fama de 226 (*reputation*)
tener frío 52 (*cold*)
tener ganas de 95 (*to feel*)
tener gracia 106 (*funny*)
tener hambre 138 (*hunger*)
tener inconveniente 178 (*to mind*)
tener la bondad de 116 (*good*)
tener la culpa 27 (*blame*)
tener la forma de 245 (*shape*)

tener la mira puesta en 6 (*to aim*)
tener los días contados 66 (*day*)
tener lugar 210 (*place*)
tener madera para 168 (*to make*)
tener mal aspecto 165 (*to look*)
tener mala cara 165 (*to look*)
tener muy buena opinión de sí mismo 287 (*to think*)
tener por qué 224 (*reason*)
tener presente 177 (*mind*)
tener prisa 138 (*hurry*)
tener puesto 126 (*to have*)
tener que 126 (*to have*)
tener que ver con 126 (*to have*)
tener razón 229 (*right*)
tener sed 288 (*thirst*)
tener sentido 243 (*sense*)
tener sueño 254 (*sleepy*)
tener un alto concepto de 284 (*to think*)
tener un nudo en la garganta 167 (*lump*)
tener vergüenza 13 (*ashamed*)
tenerle lástima 259 (*sorry*)
tenerlo bien merecido 229 (*right*)
¡Tenga cuidado! 42 (*careful*)
tentar a la suerte 167 (*luck*)
terminar por 84 (*to end*)
tiempo y sazón 293 (*time*)
Tirar piedras contra el propio tejado. 189 (*nose*)
tirarse al suelo de risa 152 (*to laugh*)
tocar a su fin 50 (*close*)
todo depende de 8 (*all*)
todo lo que se pueda 20 (*bear*)
tomar a broma 159 (*light*)
tomar a mal 279 (*to take*)
tomar a pecho 130 (*heart*)
tomar de un golpe 276 (*swallow*)
tomar el fresco 6 (*air*)
tomar el rábano por las hojas 43 (*cart*)
tomar el sol 275 (*to sun*)
tomar gusto a 282 (*taste*)
tomar juramento 193 (*oath*)
tomar la delantera 153 (*lead*)
tomar la palabra 101 (*floor*)
tomar nota de 190 (*note*)
tomar partido 251 (*side*)
tomar por 279 (*to take*)
tomar sobre sí 280 (*to take*)
tomarle el pelo 155 (*leg*)
tomarle la delantera 171 (*march*)
tomarlo a pecho 124 (*hard*)
tomarse el trabajo de 302 (*trouble*)
tomarse la molestia de 302 (*trouble*)
tomarse un descanso 34 (*break*)
toques finales 273 (*stroke*)
tormenta en un vaso de agua 283 (*teapot*)
trabar amistad 105 (*friendship*)
tragar el anzuelo 135 (*hook*)
tragarse las palabras 328 (*word*)
tratar de 1 (*about*)
tratar de 4 (*to address*)
tratarse de 220 (*question*)
Trato hecho. 68 (*deal*)
¡Tremenda cosa! 68 (*deal*)

U

un . . . sí y otro no 86 (*every*)
un callejón sin salida 9 (*alley*)
un círculo vicioso 49 (*circle*)
un cuanto hay 126 (*to have*)
un cuento chino 270 (*story*)
un sin fin de 83 (*end*)
un tal 45 (*certain*)
una de dos 197 (*one*)
una y otra vez 200 (*over*)

unir la acción a la palabra 3 (*action*)
uno a uno 197 (*one*)
unos y otros 8 (*all*)

V

valer el pan que come 237 (*salt*)
valer la pena 331 (*worth*)
valerse de 14 (*avail*)
vencer el primer obstáculo 18 (*base*)
venderse como pan bendito 137 (*hot*)
venderse como pan caliente 40 (*cake*)
venir a menos 330 (*world*)
venir a parar 227 (*to rest*)
venirse abajo 117 (*grief*)
venirse abajo 208 (*piece*)
ver el modo de 320 (*way*)
verdades de la vida 158 (*life*)
¡Vergüenza debería darte! 245 (*shame*)
verse obligado a 55 (*to compel*)
vestido de veinticinco alfileres 147 (*to kill*)
vivir a expensas de 195 (*off*)
vivir al día 123 (*hand*)
vivir con la maleta hecha 275 (*suitcase*)
vivir de gorra 262 (*to sponge*)
vivir en una torre de marfil 299 (*tower*)
vivir para ver 162 (*to live*)
vivir por su propia cuenta 201 (*own*)
vivito y coleando 7 (*alive*)
volver a las andadas 320 (*way*)
volver al punto de partida 49 (*circle*)
volver en sí 54 (*to come*)
volver la espalda 15 (*back*)
volver sobre sus pasos 267 (*step*)
volverse loco 61 (*crazy*)

Y

y así sucesivamente 257 (*so*)
y cosas por el estilo 159 (*like*)
y eso que 262 (*spite*)
y mucho más 258 (*some*)
y otros tantos 171 (*many*)
¿Y tú crees eso? 102 (*foot*)
ya es hora 292 (*time*)
Ya lo creo. 141 (*indeed*)
ya no 164 (*longer*)
ya se acabó 8 (*all*)
ya veo 139 (*I*)
yacer en capilla ardiente 266 (*state*)
yo tampoco 186 (*neither*)

Z

zona de desastre 11 (*area*)

Indice

A

a 1
a calculated risk 230
a case in point 211
a friend in court 60
a has-been 126
a laughing matter 172
a many-splendored thing 285
a new ball game 107
a new broom sweeps clean 276
A penny for your thoughts. 288
a place in the sun 275
A rolling stone gathers no moss. 269
a shot in the arm 11
a sure thing 285
a ticklish job 143
a ward of the court 60
about 1
about-face 90
about the middle 176
above all 7
accident 1
accord 1
according 1
according to 1
according to Hoyle 138
account 1
to account 2
to account for 2
acid test 284
to acknowledge 2
to acknowledge . . . to be right (to agree with) 2
to acknowledge receipt 224
acre 2
across 2
across from 2
across the board 29
across the street 272
act 3
to act 3
to act as 3
to act high and mighty 132
to act one's age 5
to act saintly 236
to act up 3
action 3
to add fuel to the flames 105
to add insult to injury 142
addition 4
to address 4
to address as 4
to administer an oath 193
ado 4
advance 4
advantage 4
to advise 5
advocate 5
affair 5
to afford a risk 230
after a fashion 93
after a (little) while 323
after all 7
after hours 137
after one's own heart 129
against 5
against one's better judgment 145
against one's will 325
age 5
to agree 6
ahead 6
ahead of time 291
to aim 6
to aim to 6
air 6

to align 7
alive 7
alive and kicking 7
all 7
all alone 9
all along 9
all at once (all of a sudden) 7
all but 7
all day long 7
all hands 120
all hell to break loose 130
all in all 8
all in one breath 35
all of a sudden 274
all of them 8
all out 8
all over 8
all right 8
All the better (worse) 8
all the same 8
all things being equal 285
an all-time high 8
all told 8
all walks of life 158
all year round 332
alley 9
to allow 9
to allow for 9
alone 9
along 9
also-ran 234
to amount 10
to amount to 10
an embarrassment of riches 228
an exercise in futility 107
an open and shut case 43
and as many more 171
and be done with it 72
and so 257
and so on 257
and the like 159
and then some 258
and what have you 126
and what not 189
to answer 10
to answer one's purpose 10
any 10
any minute (time) now 10
any time (now) 291
any way one likes 316
anyone 10
anyone for? 10
anything 10
anything goes 112
to appear 10
to appear at (in) 10
appearance 11
appetite 11
apple 11
the apple of one's eye 11
to apply 11
argument 11
area 11
to arise 11
to arise from 11
arm 11
armchair strategist 271
arm in arm 11
army 12
around 12
around here 131
around that time 291
around the clock 50
arrangement 12
to arrive on time 293
as 12
as a child 12
as a general rule 233

as a joke (jokingly) 144
as a last resort 227
as a matter of course 172
as a matter of fact 172
as blind as a bat 19
as far as I'm concerned 55
as far as one knows 93
as far as possible 213
as for 12
as it were 19
as likely as not 160
as luck would have it 167
as one sees it 241
as plain as day 66
as soon as 259
as sure as two and two are four 275
as the case may be 43
as the crow flies 62
as the saying goes (as they say) 238
as they come 53
as ugly as sin 252
as usual 309
as well as 321
as yet 12
ashamed 13
aside 13
aside from 13
to ask 13
to ask a question 220
to ask for it 13
to ask for the floor 101
asleep 13
assassination 13
astonished 13
astray 13
at 13
at a set time 291
at a sitting 252
at a snail's pace 256
at about 13
at all cost 59
at all hours 137
at all times 291
at an early date 65
at any rate 222
at arm's length 12
at best 24
at breakneck speed 261
at close quarters 219
at close range 222
at (the break of) dawn 65
at every turn 304
at first 99
at first glance 111
at first sight 251
at full speed 261
at heart 129
at intervals 142
at its worst 330
at last 151
at least 154
at length 155
at less than 13
at . . . 's mercy 175
at most 181
at night 187
at nightfall 187
at noon 188
at odd moments 179
at once (at the same time) 196
at one time 291
at one's best 24
at one's doorstep 75
at one's earliest convenience 57
at present 214

at random 222
at . . .'s request 226
at . . . sharp 246
at that 14
at that time 291
at the bottom of the ladder 32
at the bottom of the page 32
at the crack of dawn 60
at the drop of a hat 125
at the end of 83
at the end of nowhere 83
at the expense of 87
at the head 128
at the last minute 178
at the latest 152
at the outset 200
at the outside 200
at the present time 291
at the rate of 223
at the same time 292
at the time 292
at the top of one's voice 311
at this point 211
at this rate 233
at this stage 263
at times 292
at will 325
at work 329
At your service. 243
to attend 14
to attend to 14
attention 14
to attract one's attention 14
avail 14
to avail oneself of 14
to be of no avail 14
available 14
average 15
to avoid someone like the plague 210
awake 15
aware 15
axe 15

B

back 15
backstage 263
to back 16
to back down 16
to back out 16
to back someone up 16
to back up 16
bacon 16
bad 16
bag 16
to balance the account 2
balancing act 3
ball 16
bandwagon 17
bang 17
to bank 17
to bank on 17
to bar 17
to bar from 17
to bar in 17
bare 18
bare-assed 18
to bare one's heart 129
bargain 18
to bark up the wrong tree 301
barrel 18
base 18
to base 18
to base oneself (one's opinion) on 18
basis 19
bat 19

to bat 19
to bawl 19
to bawl out 19
bay 19
to be 19
. . . -to-be 19
to be a big shot 248
to be a big wheel 323
to be a big wig 324
to be a born leader 154
to be a chain-smoker 256
to be a chip off the old block 48
to be a dead duck 79
to be a dime a dozen 71
to be a fan of 92
to be a good catch 44
to be a good shot 248
to be a howling success 274
to be a loose talker 282
to be a man of his word 170
to be a man of the world 330
to be a matter of 172
to be (in) a mess 175
to be a must 183
to be a nervous wreck 331
to be a pain in the neck 202
to be a question of 220
to be a reputable man 170
to be a step away from 267
to be a whale of a . . . 322
to be able to do it blindfolded 28
to be able to make it 168
to be about 1
to be about to 1
to be advised 5
to be ahead of 6
to be aiming at (to have designs on) 6
to be all ears 80
to be all for 9
to be all in 9
to be all right with 229
to be all set 9
to be all talk 281
to be all talked out 281
to be all the rage 9
to be all the same 237
to be all there 285
to be all thumbs 290
to be all wet 322
to be an act of God 3
to be an old hand 121
to be an open question 220
to be around 12
to be as bad as (all) that 285
to be as fit as a fiddle 96
to be as good as done 116
to be as good as gold 115
to be ashamed 13
to be astonished at 13
to be at a premium 214
to be at death's door 68
to be at each other's throat 289
to be (ill) at ease 81
to be at fault 94
to be at it again 19
to be at large 151
to be at odds with 194
to be at one's wit's end 324
to be at stake 264
to be aware of 15
to be back 15
to be back to square one 263
to be becoming 20
to be becoming to 22

to be behind schedule 239
to be bent on 24
to be beside oneself 24
to be better off 25
to be beyond repair 226
to be blank 27
to be born lucky 32
To be born with a silver spoon in one's mouth. 262
to be born yesterday 32
to be bound for 32
to be bound to 33
to be broad-minded 176
to be broke 34
Be careful! 42
be careful not to 43
to be chicken 48
to be cold 52
to be cold comfort 55
to be compelled to 55
to be conspicuous by one's absence 56
to be convinced 57
to be crushed by 62
to be cut out for 63
to be . . .'s darling 64
to be dead set against 67
to be dead to the world 67
to be down and out 75
to be downcast 76
to be downhill all the way 76
to be drunk as a lord 166
to be dumbfounded 79
to be dying to 70
to be eager to 80
to be enough 84
to be enough to go around 112
to be equal to 84
to be even 85
to be exposed as 88
to be fed up with 95
to be fond of 102
to be for 103
to be frowned upon 105
to be full of oneself 106
to be funny 106
to be glad to see someone 111
to be going on 112
to be going places 210
to be gone 112
to be good enough to 116
to be good for 116
to be gratified 117
to be had 126
to be hand in glove 121
to be hard 124
to be hard on one's heels 130
to be hard put 218
to be hard to deal with 124
to be head and shoulders above one 128
to be head over heels in love 128
to be here to stay 267
to be (at) home 134
to be homesick 134
to be hopeless at 136
to be hot 137
to be hungry 138
to be in 140
to be in a good frame of mind 104
to be in a good (bad) mood 180
to be in a hurry 138
to be in a jam 143
to be in a quandary 219
to be in bad (good) repair 226

to be in charge 46
to be in conformity with 56
to be in doubt 75
to be in for 140
to be in force 103
to be in full swing 276
to be in good standing 266
to be in hot water 316
to be in love with 167
to be in no mood to 180
to be in one's element 82
to be in one's good (bad) book 31
to be in one's right mind 177
to be in poor taste 282
to be in pursuit of 218
to be in rags 221
to be in sight 251
to be in someone else's shoes 247
to be in style 274
to be in the bag 16
to be in the clear 50
to be (up) in the clouds 51
to be in the doghouse 74
to be in the know 149
to be in the limelight 161
to be in the mood (feel inspired) 180
to be in the offing 195
to be in the right 229
to be in the same boat 30
to be in the shape of 245
to be in the way 318
to be in the wrong 331
to be in tip-top shape 245
to be in trouble 302
to be in (out of) tune 303
to be in want 314
to be informed about 141
to be instrumental in 141
to be into something 258
to be involved in 142
to be just a manner of speaking 171
to be keen about 146
to be labeled 149
to be late 151
to be left 155
to be left holding the sack (bag) 236
to be left in peace 206
to be left penniless 207
to be long in the tooth 297
to be looking up 164
to be lost in thought 288
to be mad about 168
to be made for 168
to be made the scapegoat 239
to be made to order 199
to be missing 178
to be more than enough 84
to be named after (for) 185
to be no good 16
to be no great shakes 245
to be no picnic 208
to be nobody's fool 102
to be nothing but skin and bones 253
to be obliged 193
to be off limits 161
to be off one's rocker 231
to be out of this world 330
to be nothing to complain about 190
to be nothing to it 190
to be nothing to one 190
to be nothing to speak of 190

to be nothing to write home about 190
to be obligated to 193
to be of age 5
to be of benefit 23
to be of no account 2
to be of no avail 14
to be of no use 308
to be of service 243
to be off 194
to be . . . off shore 246
to be off (the) track 300
to be old hat 125
to be on a collision course 59
to be on a first-name basis 19
to be on a trip 301
to be on duty 79
to be on edge 81
to be on firm ground 118
to be on good terms 284
to be on one's guard 119
to be on hand 122
to be on its last legs 155
to be on one's own 201
to be on one's toes 295
to be on one's way 318
to be on pins and needles 209
to be on speaking terms 260
to have a lot on the ball 17
to be on the ball 16
to be on the eve of 85
to be on the fence 96
to be on the go 112
to be on the house 137
to be on the lookout 165
to be on the loose 166
to be on the make 168
to be on the mend 175
to be on the move 182
to be on (at) the point of 212
to be on the receiving end 83
to be on the right track 300
to be on the rocks 231
to be on the road 231
to be on the safe side 236
to be on the verge of 309
to be on the wagon 311
to be on the watch for 315
to be (to arrive) on time 293
to be onto someone 196
to be (sitting) on top of the world 297
to be on vacation 309
to be on view 310
to be one of a kind 148
to be one's affair 5
to be one's turn 304
to be (right) out in the sun 275
to be out of breath 35
to be out of one's mind 177
to be out of (within) one's reach 223
to be out of one's wits 327
to be out of order 199
to be out of place 210
to be out of print 215
to be out of sorts 260
to be out of stock 269
to be out of the woods 327
to be out of this world 330
to be out of touch 298
to be out on parole 330
to be over 200
to be overdue 201
to be pushing daisies 64
to be quite a character 46
to be quite a woman 220
to be quite the thing 286

to be rich in 228
to be right 229
to be right back 229
to be rolling in money 180
to be rough on 232
to be safe 236
to be second to none 241
to be seeing things 286
to be set 243
to be sharp 246
to be short of 247
to be sick and tired of 250
to be sick of the whole business 39
to be sleepy 254
to be slipping 255
to be soaked to the skin 253
to be soaking wet 322
to be sold out 242
to be someone's fair-haired boy 33
to be something of 258
to be speaking to each other 260
to be spoken for 260
to be standing 264
to be stone deaf 67
to be stuck with 268
to be successful 274
to be sworn in 276
to be taken aback 279
to be taken in 279
to be the dog in the manger 73
to be the man for the job 170
to be the real thing 286
to be the rub 233
to be the talk of the town 299
to be thirsty 288
to be through with 289
to be tied to one's mother's apron strings 273
to be time to 293
to be to blame 27
to be to one's advantage 4
to be to one's liking 160
to be too clever by half 120
to be tops 297
to be touch and go 298
to be touched (in the head) 298
to be true to one's word 302
to be two of a kind 148
to be unaware 306
to be under a cloud 51
to be under control 57
to be under the weather 321
to be up 307
to be up against 5
to be up and about 307
to be up for 307
to be up for grabs 116
to be up on 307
to be up to 307
to be up to no good 116
to be up to one 307
to be up to one's old trick 301
to be walled in 314
to be warm 314
to be welcome to 321
to be well along in years 332
to be well and good, but . . . 322
to be well heeled 130
to be well off 322
to be well spoken of 261
to be wide awake 15
to be willing to 20
to be wise to 326
to be with it 327

to be within range 222
to be worn out 320
to be worth one's salt 237
to be worthwhile 331
to be yellow 332
to be . . . years old 196
bean 20
to bear 20
to bear (to hold) a grudge 118
to bear fruit 105
to bear in mind 177
to bear the brunt 37
to bear with someone 20
bearing 20
to beat 21
to beat a path 205
to beat against 21
to beat around the bush 39
to beat back 21
to beat down 21
to beat it 21
to beat one to it 21
to beat one's brains out 33
to beat one's head against a wall 128
to beat someone up 21
to beat to death 68
to beat up 21
beauty 21
Beauty is but skin deep. 21
Beauty is in the eye of the beholder. 21
because 21
because of 21
to become 22
to become fashionable 94
becoming 22
bed 22
bedfellow 22
bee 22
beeline 22
before one knows it 149
before one's time 292
behalf 22
behind 23
behind the scenes 239
behind the times 292
to believe 23
believe it or not 23
bell 23
to belong 23
beneath 23
benefit 23
the benefit of the doubt 23
bent 24
beside 24
besides 24
best 24
best man 170
Best of luck. 167
to bet 25
better 25
better half 120
one's better half 25
Better late than never. 25
better safe than sorry 259
better than ever 86
Between the devil and the deep blue sea. 70
beyond all question 219
beyond one's means 174
beyond recall 224
beyond the pale 202
beyond the shadow of a doubt 75
beyond words 327
big 25
big deal 68

Big deal! 68
big hand 121
bill 26
bind 26
binge 26
bird 26
A bird in the hand is worth two in the bush. 26
birds of a feather 26
Birds of a feather flock together. 26
birth 26
bit 26
to bite 27
to bite off more than one can chew 27
to bite the dust 79
black 27
the black sheep of the family 246
black tie 290
blame 27
blank 27
blanket 28
to blast 28
to blast off 28
to bleed 28
to bleed white (dry) 28
blessing 28
blessing in disguise 71
a blind alley 9
blind date 28
to blindfold 28
block 28
to block the way 318
blood 29
blow 29
to blow 29
a blow-by-blow description 69
to blow down 29
to blow hot and cold 29
to blow off steam 267
to blow one's own horn 136
to blow one's top 297
to blow out 29
to blow over 29
to blow the lid off 157
to blow to kingdom come 148
to blow up 29
blue 29
board 29
to boast 30
to boast of 30
boat 30
body 30
bogey man 30
to boil down to 30
bone 30
a bone of contention 30
boner 31
booby trap 300
book 31
boot 31
to bore 32
to bore to death (bore stiff) 32
born 32
both 32
both . . . and . . . 32
to bother 32
bottom 32
Bottoms up! 32
bound 32
to bow 33
to bow out 33
bowl of cherries 48
Boxing Day 33
boy 33
boys will be boys 33

brain 33
brain drain 76
brand 33
brand new 33
bread 33
break 34
to break a lease 154
to break down 34
to break even 34
to break into 34
to break into pieces 208
to break loose 34
to break off 34
to break one's back 15
to break one's neck 185
to break one's spirit 34
to break out 34
to break out in tears 34
to break the ice 140
to break the news 187
to break the thread 289
breakdown 34
breast 35
breath 35
to breathe down one's neck 185
breeze 35
to breeze through 35
bride 36
bridge 36
to bring 36
to bring about 36
to bring back 36
to bring closer 36
to bring down the house 36
to bring home 134
to bring home the bacon 16
to bring in from (out of) the cold 52
to bring it on oneself 36
to bring someone to (around) 36
to bring to an end 83
to bring to light 159
to bring up 36
to bring up to date 65
to broach a subject 274
brow 37
brunt 37
brush 37
to brush 37
to brush up on 37
buck 37
to buck 37
Buck up! 37
bucket 38
bud 38
to bug 38
to build 38
to build up 38
bull 38
to bump 38
to bump into 38
to bump off 38
to burn one's bridges behind one 36
to burn the candle at both ends 41
to burst 38
to burst into flames 100
to burst out laughing (crying) 38
to bury one's head in the sand 128
to bury the hatchet 125
bush 39
business 39
but 40

to butter 40
to butter up 40
to buy 40
to buy a pig in a poke 208
to buy for a song 259
to buy out 40
to buy up 40
by a good deal 68
by accident 1
by air 6
by all means 174
by and large 151
by any standard 265
by chance 45
by coincidence 52
by degrees 69
by dint of 71
by ear 80
by far 93
by fits and starts 99
by hand 121
by hook or by crook 135
by leaps and bounds 154
by means of 174
by mistake 179
by moonlight 180
by no means 174
by oneself 197
by proxy 217
by return mail 168
by rule of thumb 289
by that time 292
by the day 66
by the handful 123
by the same token 296
by the skin of one's teeth 253
by the way 316
by twos (two by two) 306
by virtue of 310
by way of 316
by word of mouth 328
bygone 40

C

Cain 40
cake 40
call 41
to call 41
to call a meeting 175
to call a spade a spade 260
to call all the shots 248
to call down 41
to call into question 220
to call it a day 66
to call it quits 220
to call on 41
to call one's attention to 14
to call someone names 184
to call the tune 303
to call to order 199
to call to the colors 53
to call up 41
candle 41
canoe 41
cap 41
capacity 42
to capitalize 42
to capitalize on 42
card 42
care 42
to care 42
careful 42
the carrot and stick policy 213
to carry 43
to carry one's heart on one's sleeve 129
to carry one's weight 321
to carry out 43

to carry the ball 43
to carry the day 66
to carry the torch for 298
cart 43
case 43
cash 44
cash on the barrel head 44
to cast 44
to cast doubt on 75
to cast one's lot with 166
to cast pearls before swine 206
cat 44
catch 44
to catch 44
to catch cold 52
to catch fire 98
to catch hold of 44
to catch napping 185
to catch on 44
to catch on to 44
to catch one off one's guard 119
to catch one's eye 88
to catch up with 45
to cause a commotion 55
to cause a stir 269
to cause trouble 302
to cave 45
to cave in 45
ceiling 45
certain 45
a certain 45
chance 45
chances are that 45
change 46
to change hands 122
to change one's mind 177
to change one's tune 303
channel 46
character 46
character assassination 13
charge 46
charity 46
Charity begins at home. 46
charter flight 101
chase 46
check 46
to check 47
to check against 47
to check in (out) 47
to check oneself 47
to check through 47
to check up on 47
to check with 47
to cheer 47
to cheer up 47
cherry 48
chest 48
chestnut 48
chicken 48
chicken feed 95
chin 48
chip 48
the chips are down 48
circle 49
circumstance 49
citizen 49
to clap one's hands 122
clean 49
to clean 49
to clean out 49
cleaners 50
clear 50
to clear 50
to clear the table 278
to clear up 50
climber 50
to clip someone's wings 325

clock 50
close 50
to close 51
to close down 51
to close in 51
closet 51
cloth 51
cloud 51
cloud nine 51
coast 52
The coast is clear. 52
cock 52
a cock-and-bull story 270
the cock of the walk 52
cocktail 52
coincidence 52
cold 52
cold turkey 303
collar 52
color 53
to come 53
to come about 53
to come across 53
to come along 54
Come and get it! 53
to come back 54
to come clean 49
to come down in the world 330
to come down to 54
to come down to earth 81
to come first 99
to come from 54
to come from far and wide 93
to come from far away 93
to come full circle 49
come hell or high water 130
to come in handy 54
to come of age 5
to come off 54
Come on! 53
to come out ahead 54
to come out well (badly) 54
to come to 54
to come to a bad end 83
to come to a head 128
to come to a standstill 266
to come to an end 83
to come to an untimely end 83
to come to blows 29
to come to grief 117
to come to grips with 118
to come to one's senses 243
to come to pass 204
to come to pass 54
to come to rest 227
to come to terms 284
to come to the point 212
come to think of it 53
to come true 54
to come true 302
Come what may 53
comfort 54
coming out party 203
command 55
to commit to writing 331
commotion 55
company 55
to compare notes 190
to compel 55
competitive examination 86
to con 55
con game 107
to con into 55
con man 170
to concern 55
conclusion 56
condition 56
to confide 56

to confide in 56
conformity 56
consideration 56
conspicuous 56
construction 56
to contain 57
contempt 57
contrary 57
control 57
convenience 57
conventional wisdom 326
conversation 57
to convince 57
to cook 57
to cook one's goose 57
cookie 58
cool 58
to cool 58
cool as a cucumber 63
Cool off! 58
to cool off 58
to cool one's heels 130
copycat 44
core 58
corner 58
cost 59
to cost a mint 178
to cost one a pretty penny 207
to count 59
to count noses 189
to count on 59
to count one's blessings 28
to count out 59
counter 59
courage 59
course 59
course of action 3
court 60
courtesy 60
crack 60
to crack a book 31
to crack jokes 144
to crawl 60
to crawl in 60
crazy 60
cream 61
creature comforts 54
credibility gap 108
credit 61
creeps 61
crime 61
Crime doesn't pay. 61
crop 61
to cross 61
cross-country 62
to cross out 61
crow 62
to crow 62
to crow over (or about) 62
crush 62
to crush 62
crust 62
cry 62
to cry 62
to cry one's eyes out 88
to cry out 62
to cry wolf 327
cucumber 63
cuff 63
cup 63
to cure 63
custom 63
to cut 63
to cut a fine figure 96
to cut away 63
cut and dried 63
to cut class 63
to cut corners 58

to cut down 63
to cut down to size 253
to cut in 63
to cut in half 120
to cut it fine 98
to cut no ice 140
to cut off 63
To cut off one's nose to spite one's face. 189
to cut one's losses 166
to cut out 64
to cut short 64
to cut to the quick 220
to cut through 64
to cut up 64

D

dark 64
dark ages 5
dark horse 136
to darken one's door 74
darling 64
date 65
to date 65
to date back to 65
dawn 65
to dawn on 65
day 66
day in and day out 67
daylight 67
dead 67
dead tired 67
deaf 67
deal 67
Dear John letter 144
death 68
decision 68
deck 68
deep down 75
degree 69
delivery 69
to depend 69
to depend on 69
depth 69
description 69
desert 69
to deserve credit for something 61
despair 70
detour 70
devil 70
devil's advocate 5
to die 70
to die at the stake 263
to die away (down) 70
to die out 70
to die with one's boots on 31
difference 70
difficulty 71
dig 71
to dig 71
to dig in 71
to dig up 71
to dig up the hatchet 125
dime 71
dint 71
dirt 71
disaster area 11
discouraged 71
disguise 71
dish 72
dispense 72
to dispense with 72
disposal 72
distance 72
district 72
to disturb the peace 206
ditch 72

to divide in two (half) 306
to do 72
to do a halfway job 143
to do away with 73
to do better than that 25
to do credit 61
to do one good (harm) 116
to do one's best 24
to do one's bit 27
to do one's heart good 129
to do one's own thing 287
to do one's part 203
to do one's utmost 309
to do over 73
to do something the hard way 124
to do the dishes 72
to do the trick 301
to do well 73
to do with 73
to do without 73
dog 73
dog days 66
doghouse 74
to doll 74
to doll up 74
domain 74
Don't bite the hand that feeds you. 121
don't bother 32
Don't count your chickens before they are hatched. 48
Don't even mention it! 175
Don't get any ideas . . . 140
door 74
doorstep 75
dot 75
double 75
to double back 75
double date 65
double standard 265
doubt 75
doubting Thomas 288
down 75
to down in one swallow 276
down payment 205
downcast 76
downhill 76
to drag 76
to drag off 76
to drag one's feet 103
drain 76
to draw 76
to draw a blank 27
to draw interest 142
to draw someone out 76
to draw the line 161
to draw to a close 50
to draw up 76
to dress 77
to dress down 77
to dress in 77
dressed fit to kill (all dressed up) 147
drib 77
dribs and drabs 77
drink 77
to drink 77
to drink a toast together 296
to drive 77
to drive a nail into one's coffin 184
to drive at 77
to drive away 77
to drive back 77
to drive by 78
to drive from 78
to drive on 78

to drive one crazy (mad) 78
to drive through 78
to drive up the wall 313
drive-in 77
driver 78
to drop 78
to drop a line 78
to drop in on 78
to drop out 78
to drop someone a few lines 161
to drown one's sorrows 259
drunk 78
dry run 234
to dry 79
to dry out 79
to dry up 79
duck 79
due process of law 152
dumbfounded 79
dust 79
Dutch 79
duty 79

E

to each his own 201
eager 80
ear 80
The early bird gets the worm. 26
to earn (make) a living 162
to earn one's keep 146
earnest 80
earth 81
ease 81
easy 81
Easy come, easy go. 81
easy does it 72
to eat 81
to eat one's heart out 129
to eat one's words 328
to eat out 81
edge 81
to edge 82
to edge in 82
effect 82
egg 82
ego trip 301
either way 316
elbow 82
to elbow 82
to elbow one's way through 82
elbow grease 117
element 82
elephant 83
eleventh 83
else 83
end 83
to end 84
to end up by 84
to end up under the table 278
to engage in small talk 281
English 84
to enjoy 84
to enjoy oneself 84
Enjoy your meal. 173
enough 84
Enough is enough! 84
to enter (cross) one's mind 177
envy 84
equal 84
equally 85
errand 85
to escape one's notice 191
estate 85
eve 85
even 85
even so 85

event 85
ever 86
ever since 86
every 86
every bit 27
Every cloud has a silver lining. 51
Every dog has his day. 73
every little while 323
every living soul 260
Every minute counts. 178
every other . . . 86
every Tom, Dick and Harry 296
evil 86
examination 86
example 87
to exceed the limits 161
excess 87
exchange 87
exchange of views 310
excuse 87
to excuse 87
excuse me 87
expected 87
expense 87
to expose 88
to extend one's sympathy 277
extent 88
eye 88
eyeball 89
eyeball to eyeball 89
eyebrow 89
eyelid 89

F

face 89
to face 90
face down 89
to face (up to) it 90
to face the music 183
face to face 89
face up 89
fact 91
fact-finding group 118
the facts of life 158
fail 91
to fail 91
fail-safe 91
to fail to 91
to fail to show up for 91
fair 91
fair and square 91
fair game 107
fair play 210
the fair sex 244
faith 91
to fall 92
to fall apart 92
to fall asleep 13
to fall behind 92
to fall flat 92
to fall flat on one's face 90
to fall for 92
to fall in love with 92
to fall off 92
to fall off the wagon 312
to fall short 92
to fall through 92
to fall to pieces 208
Familiarity breeds contempt. 57
fan 92
fancy 92
far 93
far and near 93
Far from it! 93
far into the night 93

far-out 93
farther 93
farther on 93
fashion 93
fashionable 94
fast 94
fat 94
The fat is in the fire. 94
fate 94
fault 94
favor 95
feather 95
to feather one's nest 186
feature 95
fed 95
feed 95
to feel 95
to feel bad 95
to feel fit 99
to feel for someone 95
to feel free 95
to feel it beneath one 23
to feel like 95
to feel sorry for 259
to feel the pinch 209
feelings 95
fence 96
fiddle 96
to fiddle 96
to fiddle with 96
fifty 96
to fight tooth and nail 297
figure 96
to figure 97
to figure on 97
to figure out 97
to figure up (out) 97
file 97
fill 97
to fill 97
to fill in (out) 97
to fill in for 97
to fill the gap 97
to find 97
to find fault with 94
to find its way to 318
to find out 97
finder 98
Finders keepers, losers weepers. 98
fine 98
fine and dandy 98
finger 98
finishing strokes 273
fire 98
to fire 99
Fire away! 99
first 99
first and foremost 99
First come, first served. 99
the first thing in the morning 286
to fish in troubled waters 316
fit 99
to fit 99
fit for 99
fit for a king 148
to fit in 99
to fit into the picture 208
to fit like a glove 111
five 100
flag 100
flame 100
flash 100
a flash in the pan 100
flat 100
to refuse flatly 225
flesh 100

flight 101
to flip 101
to flip over 101
to flock 101
to flock together 101
to flog a dead horse 136
floor 101
floor show 249
to fly 101
to fly by 101
fly-by-night 101
to fly in 102
to fly into the wind 325
to follow suit 274
fond 102
food 102
fool 102
to fool 102
to fool around 102
foolproof 102
a foolproof method 102
fool's paradise 202
foot 102
to foot the bill 26
football widow 324
for a lark 151
for all I know 8
for all intents and purposes 142
for all one is worth 331
for better or for worse 25
for blood to rush to one's face 235
for certain 45
for form's sake (as a matter of form) 104
for fun 106
for good 115
For heaven's sake! 237
for kicks 147
for lack of 150
for night to fall 187
for no reason 224
for nothing 190
for one thing 285
for one's days to be numbered 66
for one's feelings to be hurt 96
for one's mouth to water 181
for one's name to be 184
for one's sake 237
for openers 198
for real 224
for sure 275
for that matter 172
for the birds 26
for the moment 179
for the moon to shine 180
for the most part 181
for the odds to be against one 194
for the record 224
for the sake of 237
for the time being 292
for there to be something . . . about it 258
for there to be something . . . about someone 258
for want of 314
for words to fail one 328
force 103
to force one's way through 318
forest 104
forever and ever 86
Forward march! 171
form 104
foul play 210
four-letter word 328

frame 104
free 104
free-for-all 104
Freudian slip 255
Friday 104
friend 105
A friend in need is a friend indeed. 105
friendship 105
from 105
from bad to worse 16
from behind 23
from day to day 66
from memory 175
from now on 191
from . . . on 196
from time to time 292
from tip to toe 295
from . . . to . . . 105
from top to bottom 297
to frown 105
fruit 105
fry 105
fuel 105
full 105
full of beans 20
full time 105
full-fledged 106
fun 106
funny 106
fur 106
fuss 106
futility 107

G

to gain 107
to gain momentum 179
to gain on 107
game 107
the game is up 307
gap 108
gas 108
gate 108
gate-crasher 108
general delivery 69
the generation gap 108
to get 108
(to get) a bee in one's bonnet 22
to get a breath of fresh air 6
to get a kick out of 147
to get a raw deal 68
to get a word in edgewise 328
to get ahead 108
to get all balled up 17
to get all worked up 329
to get along 108
to get along on a shoe string 247
to get along well 108
to get along with 108
to get along without 108
to get away 109
to get away with it 109
to get back 109
to get back at 109
to get behind the eight ball 17
to get better 25
to get by 109
to get by one 109
to get cheaply 109
to get close to 51
to get cold feet 103
to get dark 64
to get dead drunk 78
to get discouraged 71
to get down to brass tacks 278
to get down to business 39

to get down to the facts 91
to get down to work 76
to get even with 85
to get going 109
to get hooked on 135
to get hot 137
to get hot under the collar 52
to get in a bind 26
to get in each other's way 318
to get in touch 298
to get into a mess 175
to get into arguments 11
to get involved in 109
to get it 109
to get it in the neck 185
Get it out of your head! 108
to get it straight 271
to get lost 166
to get mad 168
to get mixed up 179
to get nowhere 192
to get off 109
to get (someone) off the hook 135
to get on 109
to get on one's high horse 136
to get on one's nerves 186
to get on the bandwagon 17
to get oneself into a state 266
to get one's fingers burnt 98
to get one's money's worth 331
to get one's start 266
to get one's way 319
Get out! 199
to get out of a jam 143
to get out of hand 122
to get out of order 199
to get out of sight 251
to get out of the way 319
to get ready 109
to get ready to 224
to get red in the face 90
to get rid of 228
to get sick 250
to get something out of one's system 77
to get stuck 268
to get that way 319
to get the ball rolling 17
to get the better of 25
to get the jump on someone 145
Get the picture? 208
to get there 109
to get through 109
to get to 110
to get to first base 18
to get to the bottom 32
to get to the bottom of the barrel 18
to get to the heart of the problem 129
to get (come) to the point 212
to get together 110
to get under one's skin 253
to get under way 319
to get up 110
to get up on the wrong side of the bed 250
to get used to 308
to get what is coming to one 110
to get wind of 325
ghost 110
ghost writer 331
gift 110
to gild the lily 160

to give 110
to give a good lecture to 155
to give a (good) talking-to 282
to give a hand 123
to give a new lease on life 158
to give a sign 251
give-and-take 110
to give away 110
to give birth to 26
to give credit 61
to give food for thought 102
to give free rein to 226
Give him an inch and he'll take a mile. 140
to give him the business 39
to give in 110
to give off 110
to give one a start 266
to give one an appetite 11
to give one the creeps 61
to give out 111
to give rise to 230
to give security 241
to give short shrift 249
to give someone a big hand 122
to give someone a break 34
to give someone a dirty look 164
to give someone a light 159
to give someone a piece of one's mind 208
to give someone a ring 230
to give someone a run for his money 234
to give someone a smile 255
to give someone a wide berth 24
to give someone his just deserts 69
to give someone the air 6
to give someone the cold shoulder 248
to give someone the green light 159
to give someone the red-carpet treatment 301
to give someone the sack 236
to give someone the slip 255
to give someone too much rope 232
to give something to drink (to eat) 258
to give the bride away 36
to give the devil his due 70
to give tit for tat 295
to give to understand 111
to give up 111
to give up the ghost 110
to give way 319
glad 111
the glad tidings 290
glance 111
to glance 111
to glance over 111
glove 111
to go 112
to go a long way 319
to go after 112
to go against the grain 117
to go ahead 112
to go ahead with 6
to go all out 113
to go along with 113
to go around 113
to go around in circles 49
to go as far as to say 113

to go astray 113
to go away 113
to go back on one's word 113
to go better 113
to go by 113
to go by the book 31
to go by . . .'s name 184
to go crazy 61
to go down 113
to go down the drain 76
to go down (up) the street 272
to go down with 113
to go downhill 76
to go Dutch 79
to go far 93
Go fly a kite. 148
to go for 114
to go for a ride 228
to go for broke 114
to go for the jugular 145
to go from hand to hand 122
to go from rags to riches 221
to go get 114
to go haywire 127
to go in for 114
to go insane 141
to go into effect 82
to go it alone 9
to go off 114
Go on! 112
to go on 114
to go on a binge 26
to go on a trip 302
to go on strike 272
to go one's separate ways 319
to go out 114
to go out in search of 240
to go out of fashion 94
to go out of one's way 319
to go out of style 274
to go out on a spree 263
to go over 114
to go over to 114
to go over with a bang 17
to go overboard 201
to go past 114
to go scot free 104
to go shopping 247
to go sky high 253
to go smoothly 114
to go straight 114
to go through 114
to go through plenty 211
to go to any length 153
to go to bat for 19
to go to bed with the chickens 22
to go to one's head 128
to go to seed 242
to go to the dogs 73
to go to the expense 87
to go to the limit 161
to go to waste 315
to go under 115
to go up in smoke 256
to go window shopping 325
to go with 115
to go with the times 293
to go without saying 238
to go wrong 115
God 115
God willing 115
God's acre 2
gold 115
the golden mean 173
good 115
good and . . . 115
a good bit 26

the good book 31
Good for you! 115
Good heavens! 130
the good old days 66
grab 116
grade 116
grain 117
to grant 117
grape 117
grapevine 117
grass roots 232
to gratify 117
grease 117
green with envy 84
greener pastures 204
grief 117
to grin 118
to grin and bear it 118
grip 118
ground 118
group 118
to grow 118
to grow on one 118
to grow out of it 118
growing pains 202
grudge 118
guard 119
to guard against 119
guess 119
to guess 119
gun 119

H

habit 119
had better 126
had rather 126
hair 120
half 120
half . . . and half . . . 120
half closed 120
half done 120
half-hearted 120
halfway through 317
hand 120
to hand 123
to hand down 123
to hand in 123
hand in hand 121
handful 123
hand-me-down 121
to hand over 123
to handle with kid gloves 111
hands down 121
Hands off! 121
to hang 124
to hang on someone's words 124
hard 124
hard and fast 124
a hard and fast rule 233
hard-boiled 124
hard core 58
hard feelings 95
hard liquor 162
the hard way 318
haste 125
Haste makes waste. 125
hat 125
hat in hand 125
hatchet 125
haul 125
to have 126
to have a bad effect 82
to have a ball 17
to have a big mouth 182
to have a case 43
to have a chip on one's shoulder 48

to have a clean slate 254
to have a close call 41
to have a close shave 246
to have a crush on 62
to have a day off 66
to have a dirty mind 177
to have a familiar ring 230
to have a field day 67
to have a fit 99
to have a free hand 122
to have a go at it 112
to have a good break 34
to have a good command 55
to have a good time 293
to have a green thumb 290
to have a hard time of it 294
to have a long wait 312
to have a look about oneself 164
to have a lot of promise 216
to have a lump in one's throat 167
to have a (nice) way with people 319
to have a one-track mind 177
to have a penchant for 207
to have a right to 229
to have a rough idea 232
to have a rough time of it 232
to have a row 233
to have a screw loose 240
to have a smoke 256
to have a soft spot in one's heart for 262
to have a sweet tooth 297
to have a whale of a time 294
to have a word with 328
to have an advantage over 4
to have an axe to grind 15
to have an eye for 88
to have an open mind about something 177
to have at hand 122
to have at one's finger tips 295
to have been through the mill 176
to have before one 126
to have come a long way 319
to have someone's ear 80
to have fun 106
to have had it 126
to have in mind 177
to have in one's hands 122
to have in stock 269
to have . . . in store for one 270
to have it both ways 319
to have it coming 54
to have it in for 126
to have it out 126
to have just 146
to have left 155
to have lots of go 112
to have lots of pull 217
to have money to burn 180
to have no use for 308
to have nothing to do with 190
to have on 126
to have on one 196
to have on the tip of one's tongue 295
to have one's back to the wall 313
to have one's back turned 15
to have one's feet on the ground 103
to have one's fill of 97
to have one's hands full 122

to have one's heart in one's mouth 129
to have one's heart set on 129
to have one's say 237
to have (hold) open house 137
to have over a barrel 18
to have reason to 224
to have someone's number 192
to have something on one's mind 177
to have something up one's sleeve 254
to have the best of two worlds 330
to have the blues 29
to have the edge on someone 81
to have the gift of gab 110
to have the reputation of 226
to have the time of one's life 294
to have the upper hand 122
to have time to spare 260
to have to 126
to have to do with 127
to have . . . to go 115
to have to live with 162
to have . . . to spare 260
to have under one's thumb 290
to have visions of 310
haven 127
haves 127
the haves and the have-nots 127
havoc 127
hawk 127
hawks and doves 127
hay 127
haywire 127
He laughs best who laughs last. 152
He who pays the piper calls the tune. 209
head 128
head first (on one's head) 128
head on 128
Heads or tails? 128
heart 129
heaven 130
Heaven forbid! 130
heavy duty 79
heed 130
heel 130
hell 130
to help 131
to help out 131
to help someone out 131
here 131
here is 131
herring 131
to hide 132
hide-and-seek 132
high 132
high places 210
hint 132
hip 132
hit 132
to hit 132
to hit (strike) a snag 256
a hit-and-run driver 78
to hit it off well 132
to hit on the idea of 133
hit or miss 132
to hit the ceiling 45
to hit the deck 68
to hit the hay 127
to hit the jackpot 214
to hit the nail on the head 184

to hit the road 231
to hit the target 282
hog 133
hold 133
to hold 133
to hold a grudge 118
to hold at bay 19
to hold fast 94
to hold good 133
Hold it! 133
to hold on 133
to hold on to 133
to hold one's course 60
to hold one's own 133
to hold one's own 201
to hold one's tongue 297
to hold out 133
to hold out for 133
to hold over 133
to hold still 134
Hold tight. 291
hole 134
hole in the wall 313
holiday 134
home 134
home delivery 69
home stretch 272
homesick 134
to honor 135
hook 135
to hook 135
to hook up 135
hooky 135
to hop 135
hope 135
to hope 135
hopeless 136
horn 136
horse 136
horse sense 242
horseback 136
host 136
hot 137
hot air 6
hot line 161
hot potato 214
hour 137
house 137
house of cards 42
household name 184
housewarming party 203
how 138
How about that? 138
How are you doing? 73
How come? 53
How do I know? 149
How do you do? 73
how do you like . . . 160
how else 138
however it may be 19
How glad we are! 111
How goes it? 112
how long 163
How much does it sell for? 183
how often 195
how on earth 81
howl 138
Hoyle 138
to humble 138
to humble oneself 138
hunger 138
hurry 138
Hurry back. 138
Hurry up. 138
to hurt 139
to hurt one's feelings 96
to hurt someone 139

to hush 139
to hush up the scandal 139

I

i 139
I 139
I, for one 139
I beg your pardon. 203
I guess so. 119
I say 139
I see 139
I should hope so! 135
I should think so! 287
I take it 139
I wish I could 326
I would rather 139
ice 139
idea 140
if any 10
if ever 86
if ever there was one 86
if he (she) is a day 66
if my memory serves me right 175
if not 189
if only 197
if worst comes to worst 330
ill 140
I'll bet. 25
I'm coming! 53
I'm game. 107
impression 140
in a big way 317
in a body 30
in a flash 100
in a jiffy 143
in a little while 323
in a low (loud) voice 311
in a mad rush 235
in a manner of speaking 171
in a modern style 274
in a nutshell 192
in a pinch 209
in a row 233
in a sense 242
in a single lifetime 159
in a very sour tone 296
in a way 317
in addition to 4
in advance 4
in an undertone 307
in any case 43
in any event 85
in black and white 27
in broad daylight 67
in care of 42
in case 43
in close quarters 219
in cold blood 29
in depth 69
in doing so 73
in due course 59
in due time 292
in earnest 80
in effect 82
in every nook and cranny 188
in exchange for 87
in fact 91
in force 103
in full regalia (all dressed up) 225
in good (bad) faith 91
in great haste 125
in here 131
in high spirits 262
in mint condition 56
in my book 31
in . . .'s name 184

in no time 292
in one's favor 317
in one's opinion 198
in one's spare time 292
in one's way 317
in opposition to 198
in order 199
in order to 199
in particular 203
in passing 204
in place of 210
in plain English 84
in recent times (years) 292
in round numbers 192
in (one's) shirtsleeves 254
in short 247
in short order 199
in single file 97
in slow motion 181
in so many words 328
in spite of 262
in spite of the fact that 262
in such a way 317
in terms of 284
in the act 3
in the air 6
in the black 27
in the capacity of 42
in the course of time 59
in the dead of winter 67
in the distance 72
in the face 89
in the face of . . . 90
in the first place 210
in the flesh 100
in the lap of luxury 150
in the least 154
in the light of 159
in the long run 234
in the main 168
in the middle of 176
in the nick of time 187
in the open 197
in the prime of life 215
in the public eye 88
in the red 225
in the same breath 35
in the same way 317
in the twinkling of an eye 306
in the wake of 312
in the way of 317
in the works 329
in token of 296
in turn 304
in view of this 310
in writing 331
inch 140
to inch 141
to inch along 141
inch by inch 140
indeed 141
Indian summer 275
informed 141
to inquire 141
to inquire about 141
the ins and outs 140
insane 141
inside 141
inside and out 141
installment 141
instrumental 141
insult 142
intent 142
interest 142
interval 142
to involve 142
to iron 142

to iron out one's difficulties 142
it beats me 21
It can't be helped. 131
It doesn't matter. 172
it figures 97
It is easier said than done. 237
it is high time 292
it is I 139
it is rumored 233
It makes no difference. 70
It never rains but it pours. 221
it stands to reason 224
It's a crying shame. 245
It's a deal. 68
It's a good thing! 285
It's a pity (too bad). 210
It's a shame. 245
It's a stone's throw from here. 269
It's a tempest in a teapot. 284
It's about time! 293
it's all in... 8
It's all in the way you say it. 317
It's all over. 8
It's all the same. 237
It's beside the point. 211
it's either one or the other 197
It's enough to make you cry (laugh). 84
It's every man for himself. 170
It's his (her, etc.) business. 39
It's like looking for a needle in a haystack. 186
it's likely 160
It's my business. 39
it's news to me 187
It's no sooner said than done. 237
it's no use 308
it's none of . . .'s business 39
It's not worth making such a fuss over. 106
It's (just) one of those things. 286
It's out of the question. 220
It's six of one and half a dozen of the other. 252
It's straight from the horse's mouth. 181
It's the last straw. 271
It's the straw which breaks the camel's back. 271
It's the pot calling the kettle black. 214
It's the same old thing. 286
it's too bad 16
It's too good to be true. 302
It's warm. 314

J

jack 142
to jack 143
Jack of all trades, master of none. 142
to jack up the prices 143
jam 143
jazz 143
to jazz up 143
jiffy 143
job 143
John 144
to join 144
to join the army 12
to join the ranks 222
joke 144

Joneses 144
to jot 144
to jot down 144
to judge 144
judging by 144
judgment 145
jugular 145
juice 145
jump 145
to jump 145
to jump at the opportunity 145
to jump the gun 119
to jump to conclusions 56
just 145
just about 145
just around the corner 145
just as one thought 145
just as well 321
just because 21
just in case 43
just like 145
just now 191
just the opposite 198
justice 146

K

keel 146
keen 146
keep 146
to keep 146
to keep a low profile 216
to keep a record 224
to keep a stiff upper lip 162
to keep a straight face 90
to keep abreast 146
to keep advised 5
to keep an account 2
to keep at 146
to keep books 31
to keep company with 55
to keep cool 58
to keep good time 294
to keep house 138
to keep in check 47
to keep (to bear) in mind 177
to keep in the dark 64
to keep late hours 137
to keep on 146
to keep on one's toes 295
to keep one's chin up 48
to keep one's eyes peeled 88
to keep one's hand in 122
to keep one's head 128
to keep one's mouth shut (keep still) 182
to keep one's options open 198
to keep one's shirt on 246
to keep one's temper 284
to keep one's wits about one 327
to keep one's word 328
to keep out of sight 147
to keep posted 214
to keep score 239
to keep someone company 55
to keep tabs on 278
to keep the ball rolling 17
to keep the peace 206
to keep time 294
to keep . . . to oneself 147
to keep to oneself 147
to keep track 300
to keep up with 308
to keep up with the Joneses 144
to keep (to stand) watch 315
kick 147
to kick 147

to kick (to chip) in 147
to kick out 147
to kick the bucket 38
to kick the habit 119
to kid 147
to kill 147
to kill two birds with one stone 26
killing 148
kind 148
king 148
kingdom 148
kite 148
kitty 148
to knit one's brow 37
to knock 148
to knock at the door 148
to knock down 149
to knock off 149
to knock out 149
to knock someone's block off 29
to knock the bottom out of 32
knot 149
to know 149
to know a thing or two about 287
to know best 24
to know better 25
to know by heart 129
to know by sight 251
to know for a fact 91
to know full well (only too well) 322
to know like a book 31
to know one's place 210
to know one's stuff 273
to know only too well 149
to know the ropes 232
to know the score 239
to know what is what 322
to know where one stands 264
to know which side one's bread is buttered on 33

L

to label 149
lack 150
to lag 150
to lag behind 150
lake 150
lam 150
lame duck 79
land 150
to land a job 143
land of milk and honey 176
language 150
lap 150
large 151
lark 151
last 151
to last a short time 294
last but not least 151
late 151
late in life 151
later on 151
latest 152
the latest gossip 152
to laugh 152
to laugh at 152
to laugh oneself sick 152
to laugh until one cries 152
to laugh up one's sleeve 254
laurel 152
law 152
to lay 153
to lay a finger on 98
to lay an egg 82

to lay aside 153
to lay bare 153
to lay down one's arms 153
to lay down one's life 158
to lay down the law 152
to lay eyes on 88
to lay low 153
to lay off 153
to lay one's hands on 122
lead 153
to lead 153
to lead a dog's life 158
to lead a . . . life 158
to lead astray 13
to lead by the nose 189
to lead one to 153
leader 154
leaf 154
to leak 154
to leak out 154
to lean 154
to lean back 154
leap 154
to learn by heart 130
lease 154
least 154
leave 154
to leave 155
to leave high and dry 132
to leave holding the bag 16
to leave in the lurch 167
to leave no stone unturned 269
to leave (to go) on a trip 302
to leave out 155
to leave out in the cold 52
to leave someone flat 100
to leave to one's fate 94
to leave word 328
lecture 155
left over 200
leg 155
to lend 155
to lend (to give) a hand 123
to lend color 53
to lend itself to 155
length 155
leopard 156
lesson 156
to let 156
let alone 156
let bygones be bygones 40
to let (leave) alone 9
to let down 156
to let go 156
let it go 156
to let on 156
to let one's hair down 120
to let out 156
Let sleeping dogs lie. 73
to let someone in on the secret 241
to let the cat out of the bag 44
to let the chance slip by 45
to let the chips fall where they may 48
to let up 156
Let's face it. 156
letter 157
to the letter 157
level 157
lie 157
to lie 157
to lie by 157
to lie in state 266
to lie in wait 157
life 157
life and limb 157

the life of the party 158
lifetime 159
light 159
to like 160
like a bat out of hell 19
to like better 160
likely 160
the likes of . . . 160
liking 160
lily 160
limb 160
limelight 161
limit 161
line 161
to line 161
the line of least resistance 227
to line up 161
linen 162
the lion's share 246
lip 162
liquor 162
to listen to reason 224
a (little) while ago 323
to live 162
to live and learn 162
to live at 14
to live from hand to mouth 123
to live high off the hog 133
to live in an ivory tower 299
to live it up 162
to live off 195
to live off the fat of the land 94
to live on borrowed time 294
to live on easy street 272
to live out of a suitcase 275
to live over one's head 128
to live up to 162
to live up to one's reputation 226
living 162
lo 162
lo and behold 162
load 163
location 163
to lock 163
to lock horns 136
to lock up (in) 163
lock, stock and barrel 163
log 163
long 163
the long and the short of it is 164
the long arm of the law 12
long live 163
long odds 194
long since 163
a long time 291
a long time before 291
longer 164
look 164
to look 164
to look after 164
to look at 164
to look down on 164
to look for 164
to look for trouble 302
to look forward to 165
to look good (bad) 165
to look high and low 132
to look into 165
to look like 165
to look mad 168
lookout 165
look out 164
to look out 165
to look out for 165

to look out of the corner of one's eye 58
to look out on 165
to look over 165
to look someone up 165
to look the other way 319
to look the part 203
to look up 165
to look up and down 308
to look up to 165
loose 166
lord 166
to lose 166
to lose face 90
to lose one's bearings 20
to lose one's cool 58
to lose one's head 128
to lose one's reason 224
to lose one's shirt 246
to lose one's temper 284
to lose one's touch 298
to lose sight of 251
to lose the thread 289
to lose track of 300
loss 166
Lost and found. 166
lot 166
a lot 166
a lot of 166
loud 167
love 167
to lower one's sights 251
to lower one's voice 311
lump 167
lurch 167

M

mad 168
maiden name 184
maiden voyage 311
mail 168
main 168
to maintain law and order 152
to make 168
to make a beeline for 22
to make a clean breast of it 35
to make a decision 68
to make a detour 70
to make a face 90
to make a false move 182
to make a fast buck 37
to make a fool of someone 102
to make a fool of oneself 102
to make a fuss over 106
to make a go of 115
to make a good (poor) showing 249
to make a great show of 249
to make a hit 132
to make a killing 148
to make a living 162
to make a long story short 271
to make a mess 175
to make a mountain out of a molehill 181
to make a name for oneself 184
to make a night of it 187
to make a note of 190
to make a nuisance of oneself 192
to make a pass at 204
to make a point of 212
to make a scene 239
to make a virtue of necessity 185
to make allowance for 9
to make an impression 140

to make arrangements 12
to make available to someone 14
to make away (off) with 169
to make believe 169
to make (both) ends meet 83
to make clear 169
to make cracks about 60
to make for 169
to make friends with 105
to make fun of 106
to make good 169
to make good 116
to make good money 180
to make good time 294
to make great strides 272
to make hay while the sun shines 127
to make into 169
to make it 169
to make it hard for 124
to make it hot 137
Make it snappy. 256
to make (it) known 169
to make land 150
to make life miserable for 158
to make light of 159
to make look ridiculous 228
to make much of 183
to make no bones about it 30
make no mistake about it 179
to make nothing of it 190
to make off 169
to make one laugh 152
to make one mad 168
to make one sick 250
to make one's day 67
to make one's eyes water 316
to make one's hair stand on end 120
to make one's head swim 129
to make one's point 212
to make one's way through 318
to make oneself conspicuous 56
to make oneself miserable 178
to make oneself scarce 239
to make oneself understood 306
make or break 168
to make out 169
to make out a check 169
to make over 169
to make peace 206
to make sense 243
to make short work of 329
to make someone eat crow 62
to make someone tick 290
to make sure 275
to make the best of 24
to make the fur fly 106
to make the grade 116
to make the most of 181
to make things easy 81
to make up 170
to make up for 170
to make up with 170
Make yourself at home. 168
man 170
Man alive! 170
man and wife 170
man Friday 104
the man in the street 170
man of the cloth 51
Man overboard! 170

Man proposes, God disposes. 170
manner 171
many 171
map 171
marbles 171
march 171
market 171
marriage 171
Marriages are made in heaven. 171
match 172
matter 172
maybe 173
Maybe so (not). 173
meal 173
mean 173
to mean 173
to mean business 39
to mean to 173
to mean well 173
meaning 174
means 174
to measure 174
to measure up to one's expectations 174
media 174
to meet 174
to meet all the requirements 226
to meet one's match 172
to meet the standards 265
meeting 175
to melt in one's mouth 182
memory 175
mend 175
to mend one's fences 96
to mention 175
mercy 175
merit 175
mess 175
method 176
middle 176
mildly 176
milk 176
mill 176
mind 176
to mind 178
to mind one's own business 39
to mind one's p's and q's 201
mind you 176
mint 178
minute 178
miracle 178
miserable 178
miss 178
to miss 178
A miss is as good as a mile. 178
to miss the point 212
mistake 179
to mistake for 179
to mix 179
to mix (up) a cocktail 52
mixed blessing 28
mixed feelings 96
moment 179
momentum 179
money 179
monkey business 39
mood 180
moon 180
moonlight 180
moot point 211
more 180
more and more 180
more often than not 181
the more . . . the more . . . 181

most 181
the most likely is 160
most of the time 293
mother tongue 296
motion 181
mountain 181
mouth 181
move 182
to move 182
to move (right) along 182
to move into 182
to move off 182
to move on 182
to move out (away) 182
to move to tears 283
to move upstream (downstream) 308
much 183
Much ado about nothing. 4
mum 183
Mum's the word! 183
murder 183
music 183
must 183
to muster 183
to muster out 183
My foot! 102

N

naked as a jay bird 26
name 184
to name 184
name-dropper 78
the name of the game 107
nap 185
native (mother) tongue 296
to nearly jump out of one's skin 253
necessity 185
Necessity is the mother of invention. 185
neck 185
needle 186
neither 186
neither am (have) I 186
neither fish nor fowl 99
neither here nor there 131
neither is (does, etc.) 186
neither . . . nor . . . 186
nerve 186
the nerve of it! 186
a nervous breakdown 34
nest 186
a nest egg 82
never 186
Never fear. 186
never in one's life 158
never mind 186
never-never land 186
never to have it so good 115
never to have had it so good 187
news 187
news media 174
the next best thing 286
next door 74
next to 187
next to nothing 190
nick 187
night 187
nine days' wonder 327
to nip in the bud 38
nitty 188
nitty-gritty 188
No buts about it! 40
no doubt 75
no end of 83
no-go 112

No indeed. 141
No kidding! 147
no longer 164
No man is an island. 170
no matter how 172
no matter when 173
no matter where 173
no matter who 173
no-nonsense 188
no object 193
No offense meant. 195
No parking (smoking, etc.) 188
no sooner 259
No sooner said than done. 259
no way 317
no wonder 327
to nod 188
to nod (yes) 188
non-aligned 7
nook 188
noon 188
nose 188
not 189
not a bit 27
not a grain of truth 117
not a living soul 260
not a moment too soon 259
not at all 189
not . . . at all 9
not by a long shot 248
not even 85
not even once 196
not for love nor money 167
not . . . for nothing 190
not for (anything in) the world 330
not on any account 1
not on your life 158
not to agree (to disagree) with someone 6
not to bat an eyelid 89
not to be able to care less 42
not to be able to do anything with 10
not to be able to go on 112
not to be able to help 131
not to be able to make anything out of 10
not to be able to make head or tail (out) of something 128
not to be able to stand the sight of 264
not to be able to stomach 269
not to be able to wait 312
not to be enough 84
not to be long for this world 163
not to be one's cup of tea 63
not to be outdone 200
not to be quoted 220
not to be sneezed at 256
not to get over 108
not to get to first base 18
not to have a leg to stand on 155
not to have all one's marbles 171
not to hold a candle to 41
not to hold water 315
not to know the first thing about 286
not to know where to turn (for help) 304
not to lift a finger 98
not to mince words 328
not to sleep a wink 326

not to take no for an answer 188
not to think much of 183
not to understand a thing 286
not to utter a word 328
not very 310
notch 189
note 190
nothing 190
nothing doing 73
nothing of the kind 148
Nothing ventured, nothing gained. 309
notice 191
notion 191
now 191
now and again (then) 191
now then 191
now you are talking 281
nowhere 192
nuisance 192
null 192
null and void 192
number 192
nut 192
nuts and bolts 192
nutshell 192

O

oar 192
oath 193
oats 193
object 193
objection 193
obligated 193
to oblige 193
occasion 193
to occur 194
to occur to one 194
odd jobs 143
oddly enough 194
odds 194
odds and ends 194
the odds are 194
Of all things! 286
of course 59
of necessity 185
of one's own accord 1
of that time 293
off 194
off and on 194
off-color 53
off season 240
off the beaten track 300
off the peg 206
off the record 224
offense 195
offhand 195
(right) offhand 195
office 195
offing 195
often 195
oil 195
old 196
an old flame 100
old master 172
old wives' tales 281
omelette 196
on a certain 45
on a large scale 238
on account of 2
on all sides 250
on an even keel 146
on behalf of 22
on credit 61
on file 97
on foot 102
on horseback 136

on ice 139
on location 163
on one's back 15
on one's behalf 23
on one's head 128
on one's own 201
on one's own merits 175
on or about 196
on order 199
on other occasions 193
on purpose 218
on sale 237
on second thought 288
on short notice 191
on that score 239
on the average 15
on the contrary 57
on the dot 75
on the double 75
on the face of it 90
on the high seas 240
on the lam 150
on the level 157
on the occasion of 194
on the one hand, ...; on the other, . . . 121
on the other hand 121
on the other side of 250
on the outside 200
on the rocks 231
on the run 234
on the slightest provocation 216
on the sly 255
on the spot 262
on the spur of the moment 263
on the way 317
on the whole 324
on time 293
on top of 297
once 196
once and for all 196
once in a blue moon 18
once upon a time there was 293
one 197
one by one 197
one for the road 230
One good turn deserves another. 304
one-horse town 299
a one-man show 249
One swallow does not make a summer. 276
one way or another 317
a one-way street 197
a one-way ticket 290
one's better half 25
oneself 197
only now 191
the only thing 286
open 197
to open 197
to open fire 98
an open secret 241
to open with 198
opener 198
opera 198
opinion 198
opposite 198
opposition 198
to opt 198
to opt in 198
option 198
...or else 83
...or something? 258
order 199
the other way (a)round 318

An ounce of prevention is worth a pound of cure. 215
out 199
out-and-out 199
out in the open 197
out in the open (air) 6
out loud 167
out of 199
out of consideration for 56
out of courtesy 60
out of date 65
Out of sight, out of mind. 251
out of the blue 29
Out of the frying pan into the fire. 202
out on a limb 160
out there 285
outset 200
outside 200
to outdo 200
to outdo oneself 200
to outstay one's welcome 321
over 200
over and above 200
over and over (again) 200
over one's dead body 30
over the counter 59
over the long haul 125
over there 200
overboard 201
overdue 201
overnight (unexpectedly) 187
own 201
to own 201
to own up to the truth 201

P

pace 201
to pace the floor 101
to pack 202
to pack off 202
to pack suitcases (bags) 202
to paddle one's own canoe 41
pain 202
paint 202
to paint the town red 299
pan 202
pale 202
to paper the house 138
paradise 202
pardon 203
parole 203
part and parcel 203
to part company 55
to part one's hair 120
part-time 293
particular 203
party 203
pass 204
to pass 204
to pass an exam 204
to pass as 204
to pass away 204
to pass by (without stopping) 204
to pass muster 183
to pass out 204
to pass the buck 37
to pass through 204
pasture 204
to pat 204
to pat on the back 204
to patch 205
to patch up a quarrel 205
path 205
to pave the way for 320
pay 205
to pay an arm and a leg 12

to pay attention 14
to pay by installments 141
to pay (spot) cash 44
pay dirt 71
to pay lip service to 243
to pay someone a visit 310
to pay through the nose 189
to pay to the tune of 303
payment 205
peace 206
peace of mind 206
peacock 206
peak 206
pearl 206
peg 206
penchant 207
pencil 207
penniless 207
penny 207
A penny saved is a penny earned. 207
perfect 207
to phase 207
to phase out 207
pick 207
to pick 208
to pick fights (quarrels) 219
to pick and choose 208
to pick holes in 134
the pick of the crop 61
to pick up the tab 278
picnic 208
picture 208
pie in the sky 253
piece 208
pig 208
pill 209
pillow talk 281
pin 209
to pin 209
to pin down 209
to pin one's faith on 91
to pin one's hope on 135
to pin someone down 209
to pinch 209
piper 209
to pitch 209
to pitch in 209
pitchfork 209
pity 210
place 210
plague 210
play 210
to play 210
to play a dirty trick on someone 301
to play a game 107
to play a (practical) joke 144
to play a trick on someone 301
to play ball with 17
to play by ear 80
to play dead (to play possum) 67
to play dumb 211
to play down the merit of 211
to play fast and loose 94
to play for keeps 146
to play hard to get 124
to play havoc with 127
to play hooky 135
to play host 136
to play it safe 236
to play one's role 231
to play right into one's hands 123
to play second fiddle 96
to play (act) the fool 102
to play the lead 153

to play the market 171
to play up to 211
to please 211
plenty 211
plot 211
The plot thickens. 211
to pluck up one's courage 59
poetic justice 146
point 211
point blank 212
point of no return 227
to poke one in the ribs 228
pole 212
policy 213
to polish 213
to polish off 213
to polish the apple 11
poll 213
pooh 213
to pooh-pooh 213
poor 213
Poor me! 213
to pop 213
to pop in 213
to pop the question 220
possible 213
posted 214
pot 214
potato 214
potluck 214
to pour oil on the flames 195
to pour oil on troubled waters 316
to practice law 153
Practice makes perfect. 207
to praise to the skies 253
premium 214
present 214
to present a gloomy picture 208
to present with a gift 110
press 214
to press 215
to press for 215
to press on 215
to press one's luck 167
to press one's point 212
to press the flesh 101
to press through 215
pretty 215
pretty well 321
prevention 215
price 215
to prick up one's ears 80
pride 215
prime 215
print 215
probation 216
problem 216
production 216
to profit 216
to profit from 216
profile 216
promise 216
prophecy 216
proud as a peacock 206
provocation 216
proxy 217
public domain 74
pull 217
to pull 217
to pull a boner 31
to pull a fast one 94
to pull apart 217
to pull down 217
to pull in 217
to pull off 217

to pull on 217
to pull oneself together 217
to pull one's punches 217
to pull out 217
to pull someone's chestnuts out of the fire 48
to pull someone's leg 155
to pull strings 273
to pull the wool over one's eyes 327
to pull through 217
to pull up 217
to pull up stakes 263
punch 217
purpose 218
purse 218
pursuit 218
to push 218
to push one's way through 218
to put 218
to put a stop to 270
to put across 218
to put all one's eggs in one basket 82
to put an end to 84
to put at one's disposal 72
to put away 218
to put down 218
to put heads together 129
to put in a good word for 328
to put in an appearance 11
to put in final shape 245
to put into words 328
to put it mildly 176
to put off 218
to put on 218
to put on airs 6
to put on an act 3
to put on bread and water 34
to put on one's thinking cap 41
to put on probation 216
to put on the dog 73
to put on the map 171
to put on weight 321
to put one beside oneself 218
to put one's best foot forward 103
to put one's cards on the table 42
to put one's foot down 103
to put one's foot in one's mouth 103
to put one's house in order 199
to put one's oar in 192
to put oneself out 218
to put out 218
to put someone on the spot 262
to put someone up 218
to put (lay) the blame on 27
to put the cart before the horse 43
to put the touch on someone 298
to put to a test 284
to put to bed 22
to put to death 68
to put together 219
to put two and two together 306
to put up 219
to put up with 219
to put words in someone's mouth 329

Q

quandary 219
quarrel 219
quarters 219

question 219
quick 220
quite 220
quite a bit 27
quite a few 220
quits 220
to quote 220

R

race 221
to rack one's brains 33
rag 221
rage 221
rain 221
to rain 221
to rain cats and dogs (pitchforks) 44
rain check 46
rain or shine 221
to rain pitchforks 209
to raise a big howl 138
to raise Cain 40
to raise eyebrows 89
to raise objections to 193
to raise one's eyes 88
to raise one's voice 311
to raise the devil 70
to raise the roof 231
to rake 221
to rake in 221
random 222
random shot 248
range 222
to range with 222
rank 222
to rank 222
the rank and file 222
to rank high 222
rap 222
rat 222
rat race 221
rate 222
rather 223
to rave 223
to rave about 223
reach 223
to reach 223
to reach an understanding 223
to reach for 223
to reach its peak 206
to reach safety 236
to reach the end of one's rope 232
to read 223
to read law 153
to read over 223
to read someone the riot act 3
to read up on 223
ready 223
ready-made 223
ready, willing and able 224
real 224
real estate 85
reason 224
to recall 224
receipt 224
record 224
red 225
red-handed 225
red herring 131
red-hot 225
red-light district 72
red tape 282
redeeming feature 95
reed 225
to refuse 225
to refuse to 225
regalia 225

rein 226
to remain silent 252
to remove one's hat 125
repair 226
to report 226
to report for 226
to report for duty 79
to report on 226
reputation 226
request 226
requirement 226
to resign 226
to resign oneself to 226
resistance 227
resort 227
respect 227
to rest 227
to rest assured 227
to rest on one's laurels 152
to retrace one's steps 267
return 227
to return to one's old ways 320
reversed charge 46
to revert 227
to revert to 227
rhyme 227
rib 228
rib-tickling 228
rich 228
riches 228
to rid 228
ride 228
ridiculous 228
right 228
right and left 228
right away (off) 229
right from the start 266
right here 229
right now 229
Right on! 229
right side up 250
right then and there 229
right to one's face 90
right under one's nose 188
rightly 230
rightly or wrongly 230
rightly so 230
ring 230
to ring a bell 23
rise 230
to rise to the occasion 194
to rise up in arms 12
risk 230
river 230
road 230
The road to hell is paved with good intentions. 231
rock 231
rocker 231
role 231
A rolling stone gathers no moss. 269
Rome 231
Rome was not built in a day. 231
roof 231
room 231
room and board 231
roost 232
root 232
the root of all evil 86
rope 232
rough 232
to round a corner 58
round-trip 301
a round-trip ticket 290
row 233
rub 233

to rub 233
to rub against 233
to rub elbows with 82
to rubber-stamp 264
to rub it in 233
to rub one the wrong way 320
rule 233
to rule 233
the rule of law 152
to rule out 233
to rule the roost 232
to rumor 233
run 234
to run 234
to run across 234
to run after 234
to run an errand 85
to run around with 234
to run away 234
to run down 234
to run dry 234
to run for one's life 158
to run into 235
to run low on (short of) 235
run-of-the mill 234
to run out 235
to run out of steam 267
to run over (down) 235
to run smoothly 235
to run the risk 230
to run the show 249
to run up (down) to 235
runner 235
runner-up 235
rush 235
to rush 235
rush hour(s) 137
to rush things 235
to rush through 235

S

sack 236
to sack someone 236
safe 236
safe and sound 236
safety 236
safety first 236
sail 236
saintly 236
sake 237
sale 237
salt 237
to salt 237
to salt away 237
same 237
The same to you. 237
to save face 90
to save for a rainy day 67
say 237
to say 237
to say a mouthful 182
to say good night (good evening) 187
to say nothing of 238
to say the least 238
to say (give) the word 329
saying 238
scale 238
to scale 239
to scale down 239
scapegoat 239
scarce 239
to scare the daylights out of someone 67
scene 239
schedule 239
school of thought 288
score 239
to score a point 212

to scrape 240
to scrape along 240
to scrape together 240
scratch 240
to scream bloody murder 183
screw 240
sea 240
search 240
season 240
seat 241
second 241
second best 24
second-rate 223
secret 241
security 241
to see 241
to see eye to eye 89
to see fit 99
to see how the land lies 150
to see no objection 193
to see off 241
to see one's way to 320
to see red 225
to see someone home 134
to see the last of 151
to see the light 159
to see the point 212
to see the sights 251
to see to it 241
to see to the door 242
See you later. 241
See you tomorrow. 296
seed 242
Seeing is believing. 241
self-contained 57
self-fulfilling prophecy 216
to sell 242
to sell like hot cakes 40
to sell out 242
to sell short 247
to sell someone down the river 230
to sell someone out 242
to send 242
to send for 242
to send on an errand 85
to send one packing 202
to send out 242
to send warm greetings (regards) 314
to send word 329
senior citizen 49
sense 242
to separate the sheep from the goats 246
to serve a term 284
to serve notice 191
to serve one right 229
service 243
set 243
set of teeth 297
a set of teeth 243
to set 243
to set (the sun) 243
to set a price 215
to set about 243
to set an example 87
to set aside 243
to set back 243
to set fire to 98
to set foot in 103
to set forth 243
to set forward (ahead) 243
to set free 104
to set off 244
to set off (out) 244
to set one's teeth on edge 81
to set right 244

to set someone straight 271
to set straight 244
to set the record straight 271
to set the table 278
to set the world on fire 330
to set up 244
to settle 244
to settle a score 240
to settle down 244
to settle for 244
to settle on 244
sex 244
shade of meaning 174
shake 245
to shake hands with 123
to shake off 245
to shake one's head 245
to shake up 245
shame 245
Shame on you! 245
shape 245
the shape of things to come 286
share 246
sharp 246
to sharpen a pencil 207
shave 246
to shed bitter tears 283
to shed crocodile tears 283
to shed (throw) light on 159
sheep 246
to shift 246
to shift for oneself 246
to shirk one's duty 80
shirt 246
shoe 247
to shoot down 247
to shoot from the hip 132
to shoot straight 271
to shoot the breeze 35
shop 247
shore 247
short 247
the short and long of it 247
a short time ago 291
shortly 248
shortly after 248
shortly before (after) 248
shot 248
shotgun marriage 172
shoulder 248
show 249
to show 249
to show around 249
show business 39
to show into 249
to show off 249
to show signs of 251
to show the flag 100
to show to the door 74
to show up 249
showing 249
shrift 249
to shrug one's shoulders 248
to shut 250
to shut down 250
to shut (up) in 250
to shut off 250
to shut out 250
to shut up 250
sick 250
side 250
sight 251
sight unseen 251
sign 251
to sign 251
to sign off 251
to sign up 252

silence 252
Silence is consent. 252
Silence is golden. 252
silent 252
sin 252
to sink into despair 70
to sit 252
to sit back 252
to sit down 252
to sit out 252
to sit pretty 215
to sit tight 291
to sit up 252
to sit up and take notice 191
sitting 252
six 252
to size 253
to size up 253
skeleton in the closet 51
sketch 253
to skim the cream 61
skin 253
sky 253
to slam the door 74
to slam the door in someone's face 74
to slap 254
to slap someone 254
to slap someone on the back 254
slate 254
to sleep 254
to sleep away 254
to sleep it off 254
to sleep like a log 163
to sleep on it 254
sleepy 254
sleeve 254
slender as a reed 225
slip 254
a slip of the tongue 254
slip of the tongue 296
to slip 255
to slip away 255
to slip one over on 255
to slip one's mind 177
to slip through one's fingers 255
to slow 255
to slow down (up) 255
sly 255
small fry 105
small-time 293
to smell a rat 222
smile 255
smoke 256
smoker 256
smoking gun 119
snag 256
snail 256
snappy 256
to sneak 256
to sneak into 256
to sneak off (away, out) 256
to sneeze 256
so 257
so-and-so 257
so as to 257
so be it 257
So do (did, will, etc.) I. 257
so far 257
So far so good. 257
So long. 164
So much for that. 257
so much so 257
So much the better (worse). 257

so often 195
so-so 257
so to say 238
so to speak 260
So what? 322
soap 257
soap opera 198
sob story 271
social call 41
social climber 50
to sock 258
to sock it to somebody 258
soft drink 77
to soft-soap 257
some 258
to some extent 88
some . . . or other 258
something 258
something else 258
something like that 258
something of the sort 260
somewhere along the way 317
song 259
song and dance 259
soon 259
sooner 259
sooner or later 259
sorrow 259
sorry 259
sort 260
sort of 260
soul 260
sour grape 117
to sow one's wild oats 193
to sow the seeds of 242
spade 260
to spare 260
to speak 260
to speak for itself 261
to speak for oneself 261
to speak highly of 261
Speak of the devil. 70
to speak off the cuff 63
to speak one's mind freely 177
to speak one's piece 208
to speak out 261
to speak out of turn 304
to speak to the point 212
to speak up 261
to speak up for 261
speed 261
to spend one's time 294
spic-and-span 261
to spill the beans 20
to spin a yarn 332
spirit 262
spite 262
to split hairs 120
sponge 262
to sponge 262
to sponge off someone 262
spoon 262
spot 262
to spread like wildfire 324
spree 263
spur 263
square 263
a square deal 67
a square meal 173
square peg 206
stab 263
a stab in the back 263
stage 263
stake 263
stamp 264
stand 264
to stand 264
to stand a chance 45

to stand aside 264
to stand at attention 14
to stand back 264
to stand back of 264
to stand for 264
to stand in line 161
to stand on one's own two feet 264
to stand one in good stead 267
to stand one's ground 118
to stand out 265
to stand still 265
to stand up 265
to stand up and be counted 265
to stand . . . up 265
to stand up against 265
to stand up for 265
to stand up to 265
to stand watch 315
standard 265
standing 266
standstill 266
to stare 266
to stare at 266
start 266
to start 266
to start from scratch 240
to start out 266
state 266
state of affairs 5
status symbol 277
to stay 267
to stay in 267
to stay in bed 22
to stay out 267
to stay out all night 188
to stay out of trouble 302
to stay put 267
to stay up 267
stead 267
to steal a march on someone 171
to steal the show 249
steam 267
step 267
to step 268
step by step 267
to step down 268
to step in 268
Step on it (the gas)! 108
to step out 268
to step up 268
to step up production 216
to stew in one's own juice 145
to stick 268
to stick by 268
Stick 'em up! 268
to stick it out (till the end) 268
to stick one's head out 268
to stick one's neck out 186
to stick one's nose in someone else's business 189
to stick to 268
to stick to one's guns 119
still life 158
Still waters run deep. 315
stir 269
to stir 269
to stir up 269
to stir up a hornet's nest 186
stock 269
to stomach 269
stone 269
to stoop 270
to stoop to 270
stop 270
to stop 270
to stop at nothing 270

to stop dead 270
to stop over 270
store 270
storm 270
storm in a teapot 283
story 270
straight 271
straight ahead 271
straight from the shoulder 248
strange bedfellows 22
strategist 271
straw 271
street 272
stretch 272
to stretch a point 212
stride 272
strike 272
to strike 272
to strike a bargain 18
to strike a snag 256
to strike back 272
to strike down 272
to strike home 134
to strike oil (to strike it rich) 273
to strike one funny 106
to strike one's fancy 92
to strike out 273
to strike up 273
to strike up a conversation 57
to strike up a friendship 105
string 273
stroke 273
a stroke of luck 273
a struggle to the death 68
stuff 273
stumbling block 28
style 274
. . . style 274
success 274
successful 274
such a thing 286
to such an extent 88
sudden 274
to sugarcoat the pill 209
suit 274
to suit 274
to suit the action to the word 3
Suit yourself. 274
suitcase 275
to sum 275
to sum up 275
summer 275
sun 275
to sun 275
to sun oneself 275
sure 275
sure enough 275
surprise 276
swallow 276
to swallow hook, line, and sinker 135
to swallow one's pride 215
swan song 259
to swear 276
to swear by 276
to swear off 276
to sweep 276
to sweep off one's feet 103
to sweeten the kitty 148
to swim 276
to swim (across) 276
swing 276
to switch 276
to switch off 276
to switch off the light 159
to switch on 277
to switch on the light 159

symbol 277
to sympathize 277
to sympathize with 277
sympathy 277
system 277

T

t 277
tab 278
table 278
take 278
to be on the take 278
to suit to a T 277
to table 278
to table the motion 278
tack 278
to take 278
to take a back seat 241
to take a break 34
to take a chance 45
to take a crack at 60
to take a dig at 71
to take a dim view of 310
to take a fancy to 93
to take a joke 144
to take a liking to 160
to take a load off one's mind 163
Take a load off your feet. 163
to take a look at 164
to take a new turn 304
to take a nap 185
to take a notion to 191
to take a picture 208
to take a poll 213
to take a seat 241
to take a shot at 248
to take a stand 264
to take a step 268
to take a trip 302
to take a turn for the better (worse) 304
to take a walk 313
to take action against 3
to take advantage of 4
to take after 279
to take amiss 279
to take an interest in 142
to take an oath 193
to take apart 279
to take a joke 144
to take aside 279
to take away 279
to take back 279
to take by storm 270
to take by surprise 276
to take charge 46
to take down 279
to take first place 210
to take five 100
to take for 279
to take for a ride 228
to take for granted 117
to take forty winks 326
Take heart! 129
to take heed 130
to take hold of 133
to take hold of oneself 133
take-home pay 205
to take ill 140
to take in 279
to take in tow 299
to take in one's stride 272
to take into account 2
to take into one's head 129
to take it 279
to take it at face value 309
to take it easy 81

Take it for what it is worth. 331
take it from me 278
to take it lying down 157
to take it out on 280
to take its course 60
to take leave of 154
to take leave of one's senses 155
to take lightly 159
to take long 164
to take note of 190
to take off 280
to take off one's hat to 125
to take offense at 195
to take office 195
to take on 280
to take one wrong 331
to take one's afternoon nap 185
to take one's breath away 35
to take one's own life 158
to take one's pick 207
to take one's time 294
to take out 280
to take pains 202
to take pity on 210
to take place 210
to take potluck 214
to take root 232
to take shape 245
to take sides 251
to take someone at his word 329
to take someone down a notch 189
to take someone down a peg or two 207
to take someone's word for it 329
to take something hard 124
to take stock 269
to take stock in 269
to take stock of 269
to take the bull by the horns 38
to take the cake 40
to take the floor 101
to take the hint 132
to take the law into one's own hands 153
to take the lead 153
to take the rap 222
to take the trouble to 302
to take the wind out of one's sails 325
to take the wrong . . . 332
to take things in one's stride 287
to take time 294
to take time off 294
to take to 280
to take flight 101
to take to heart 130
to take to one's heels 130
to take to task 282
to take to the cleaners 50
to take turns (at) 304
to take under one's wing 326
to take up 280
to take up room 232
to take up someone's time 294
to take up with 281
to take with a grain of salt 237
to take wrong 281
talk 281
to talk 281
to talk at cross purposes 218

to talk back to 281
to talk big 281
to talk into 281
to talk out of 282
to talk over 282
to talk shop 247
to talk through one's hat 125
to talk with one's tongue in one's cheek 297
talker 282
talking-to 282
tape 282
target 282
target date 65
tarred with the same brush 37
task 282
task force 104
taste 282
to taste 283
to taste like (of) 283
tax haven 127
tax holiday 134
to teach someone a lesson 156
to team 283
to team up with 283
teapot 283
tear 283
to tear 283
to tear down 283
to tear up 283
to tell 283
to tell apart 283
to tell it like it is 282
Tell me! 283
to tell . . . off 283
to tell on 284
to tell someone a thing or two 287
to tell someone to get lost 166
to tell (someone) to go jump in the lake 150
to tell time 294
temper 284
tempest 284
term 284
term of office 195
test 284
that 284
that business about 39
That depends. 69
That does it! 73
that is to say 238
that makes two of us 306
that matter of 173
That takes care of that. 42
That takes the cake! 40
that very thing 286
That'll do. 284
That's a horse of another color. 136
That's a tall order. 199
That's beside the question. 220
That's it! 284
That's not the point. 212
That's right. 229
That's that. 285
That's the least of it. 154
That's the limit. 161
That's the trouble. 302
That's the way the ball bounces. 16
That's the way the cookie crumbles. 58
That's your problem. 216
That's water under the bridge now. 315
that's why 324

The bigger they come, the harder they fall. 25
there 285
There are more ways than one to skin a cat. 44
There are no two ways about it. 318
There is a time for all things. 293
There is method in his madness. 176
There is more to it than meets the eye. 88
There is no love lost between them. 167
There is no shortcut to success. 247
there will be the devil to pay 70
There's always room for one more. 232
There's no getting around it. 108
There's no getting away from it. 108
there's no saying 238
There's no use crying over spilt milk. 176
there's nothing to it 190
There's something in the wind. 325
thick 285
to thin 285
to thin out 285
thing 285
Things are humming around here. 286
Things are not what they used to be. 286
to think 287
to think a lot of oneself 287
to think about 287
to think better of it 25
to think highly of 287
to think it over 287
to think twice 287
to think up 287
to think well of 322
thinking 288
thirst 288
this 288
this very day 66
this way 318
Thomas 288
Those were the days! 66
thought 288
thread 289
throat 289
through 289
through and through 289
through channels 46
through the grapevine 117
through thick and thin 285
to throw 289
to throw (to have) a fit 99
to throw a game 107
to throw a party 203
to throw away 289
to throw cold water on 316
to throw good money after bad 180
to throw in one's lot with 166
to throw in the sponge 262
to throw it up to someone 289
to throw out 289
to throw out a hint 132
to throw out one's chest 48
to throw the book at 31

to throw up 289
thumb 289
to thumb 290
a thumb-nail sketch 253
to thumb through 290
to tick 290
ticket 290
tidings 290
tie 290
to tie the knot 149
tight 291
tight money 179
time 291
time and tide 293
time-honored custom 63
Time is a great healer. 293
Time is money. 293
Time is up. 293
tip 295
to tip 295
to tip over 295
to tip someone 295
to tip someone off 295
tiptoe 295
tit 295
to a degree 69
to a fault 94
to a great extent 88
to a man 170
to excess 87
to one's heart's content 130
to one's way of thinking 319
to the bitter end 84
to the core 58
to the last 151
to the last ditch 72
to (on) the right 229
To whom it may concern. 56
toe 295
to toe the line 161
together 296
token 296
Tom 296
tomorrow 296
tone 296
tongue 296
tongue twister 297
tooth 297
top 297
top dog 74
to top 298
to top it off 298
to top someone 298
torch 298
to toss 298
to toss about 298
touch 298
to touch 298
to touch a sore spot 262
to touch down 298
to touch off 299
to touch on 299
to touch up 299
tough luck 167
tow 299
towel 299
tower 299
town 299
to toy 300
to toy with the idea 300
track 300
to track 300
to track down 300
to travel at a speed of 261
to tread 301
to tread on someone's toes 296
to tread softly 301
to tread water 316

to treat equally 85
treatment 301
tree 301
trick 301
to trim one's sails 236
trip 301
trouble 302
true 302
to try 302
try as he might 303
to try hard 302
to try on 302
to try one's luck 167
to try one's patience 302
to try out 303
tune 303
to tune 303
to tune in 303
Turk 303
turkey 303
turn 304
to turn 304
to turn a blind eye 89
to turn a deaf ear 80
to turn a hair 120
to turn around 304
to turn down 304
to turn in 304
to turn in(to) 305
to turn into 305
to turn off 305
to turn (to switch) off the light 159
to turn on 305
to turn (to switch) on the light 159
to turn one's back 15
to turn out 305
to turn over 305
to turn over (upside down) 305
to turn over a new leaf 154
to turn pale 305
to tip the scales 238
to turn the tables 278
to turn to 305
to turn up 306
to turn up one's nose 189
a turning point 211
to twiddle one's thumbs 290
twinkling 306
to twist a person's arm 12
to twist around one's little finger 98
two 306
two can play at that 285

U

unaware 306
under construction 56
under lock and key 163
under no circumstances 49
under one's breath 35
under one's own steam 267
under the circumstances 49
under the counter (table) 59
to understand 306
understanding 307
to undertake the task 282
undertone 307
until hell freezes over 131
up there 308
up to a point 212
up to now 308
up to one's ears 81
the upper crust 62
to upset the apple cart 43
use 308
to use as an excuse 87

to use strong language 150
used 308
usual 309
utmost 309

V

vacation 309
value 309
to vanish into thin air 7
variety 309
Variety is the spice of life. 309
vengeance 309
to venture 309
verge 309
very 310
the very one 310
the very thought of it 288
a vicious circle 49
view 310
virtue 310
vision 310
visit 310
voice 311
to vote 311
to vote in 311
to vouch 311
to vouch for 311
voyage 311

W

to wage war 314
wagon 311
wait 312
to wait 312
wait and see 312
to wait for 312
to wait in the wings 326
to wait on 312
to wait on hand and foot 123
to wait on tables 278
to wait up for 312
wake 312
to wake 312
to wake up 312
walk 312
to walk 313
to walk (to stroll) around 313
to walk around the block 313
to walk back 313
walk of life 158
to walk off with 313
to walk on air 7
to walk on eggs 82
to walk out 313
to walk up (down) 313
to walk up and down 313
wall 313
to wall 314
wall to wall 314
Walls have ears. 314
want 314
war 314
war paint 202
to ward 314
to ward off 314
warm 314
to warm 314
to warm (oneself) up 315
to warm up to 315
warts and all 9
to wash one's dirty linen in public 162
to wash one's hands of 123
waste 315
to waste one's breath 35
to waste time 295
watch 315
to watch 315

Watch it! 315
to watch out for 315
to watch over 315
Watch your step. 268
A watched pot never boils. 214
water 315
to water 316
to water down 316
way 316
way of life 318
way of life 158
the way in 318
way off 320
the way out 318
ways and means 320
wear 320
to wear 320
wear and tear 320
to wear many hats 125
to wear off 320
to wear well 321
weather 321
weather permitting 321
to weather the storm 270
the wee hours of the morning 137
weight 321
welcome 321
Welcome! 321
well 321
Well now! 322
well then 322
wet 322
a wet blanket 28
to wet one's whistle 324
whale 322
what 322
what about 322
What are you up to? 308
What can I do for you? 322
What can't be cured must be endured. 63
What difference does it make? 70
What do you mean? 173
What do you mean you don't know? 173
What do you think of it? 287
What ever do you want? 86
What for? 322
what good is it 116
what has become of 22
what the hell 131
what the traffic will bear 20
What will you have (to drink)? 322
what with 323
whatever 323
whatever it may be 323
What's bugging her? 38
What's eating you? 81
What's gotten into him? 110
What's in a name? 184
What's it all about? 323
what's it to . . .? 323
What's new? 323
what's the good of 116
What's the idea? 140
What's the matter? 173
What's the trouble? 302
what's the use of 308
What's up? 323
what's what 323
wheel 323
when all is said and done 238
When in Rome do as the Romans do. 231

when it comes right down to it 76
when least expected 78
when one is good and ready 116
where one belongs 23
where the action is 4
Where there's a will there's a way. 325
Where there's smoke there's fire. 256
Where will it all end? 84
while 323
a while back 323
white collar 323
white elephant 83
white lie 157
whistle 324
to whiz 324
to whiz by 324
with flying colors 53
with one stroke of the pen 273
with one voice 311
who 324
Who cares? 324
Who would have thought it? 287
whole 324
a whole lot 166
why 324
wide open 197
widow 324
wig 324
wildcat strike 272
wildfire 324
a wild-goose chase 46
will 325
to win 325
to win by a nose 189
to win hands down 123
to win out over 325
wind 325
to wind 325
to wind up 325
to wind up a watch 315
winds of change 46
window 325
wine 325
to wine and dine 325
wing 326
wink 326
to wipe 326
to wipe out 326
to wipe the slate clean 254
wisdom 326
wise 326
to wish 326
to wish it off on someone else 326
wit 327
with 327
with a steady hand 123
with a vengeance 309
with a view to 310
with no strings attached 273
with respect to 227
with the best of them 25
with the understanding that 307
with utmost difficulty 71
within call 41
without a thought 288
without batting an eye 89
without fail 91
without further ado 4
without letting up 157
without question 220
without rhyme or reason 227

wolf 327
wonder 327
woods 327
wool 327
word 327
word for word 329
work 329
to work 329
to work hand in hand 123
to work miracles 178
to work one's way 329
to work one's way through college 329
to work one's way up 3
to work out 330
to work out well 330
world 330
worst 330
worth 331
would-be 20
would rather 223
would that it were so 20
wouldn't be caught dead 68
wouldn't touch it with a ten-foot pole 212
to wrap (twist) . . . around one's little finger 98
wreck 331
writer 331
writing 331
the writing on the wall 313
wrong 331
the wrong side of the tracks 300

Y

yarn 332
year 332
yellow 332
yellow press 214
Yes indeed. 141
You are welcome. 321
You bet! 25
You can say that again. 238
You cannot see the forest for the trees. 104
You can't get a leopard to change his spots. 156
You can't get blood out of a turnip. 29
You can't get something for nothing. 258
You can't have too much of a good thing. 287
You can't make a silk purse out of a sow's ear. 218
You can't make an omelette without breaking eggs. 196
You can't teach an old dog new tricks. 74
You don't say! 238
you'd better believe it 23
You name it and we've got it. 185
young Turk 303
Your guess is as good as mine. 119
your loss 166

Notes

Notes

Notes